TRUE HORSEMANSHIP THROUGH FEEL

BY BILL DORRANCE

WITH LESLIE DESMOND

LYONS PRESS
GUILFORD, CT
AN IMPRINT OF THE GLOBE PEQUOT PRESS

The Lyons Press is an imprint of The Globe Pequot Press.

Originally published in 1999 by Leslie Desmond dba/Diamond Lu Productions

10 9 8 7

Printed in the United States of America

ISBN 978-1-59921-056-8

Library of Congress Cataloging-in-Publication Data is available on file.

TABLE OF CONTENTS

ACKNOWLEDGMENTS

WE ARE GRATEFUL TO THESE PEOPLE FOR THEIR PART IN THE CREATION OF THIS BOOK.

Billy and Sally Askew, Ray Berta, Mindy Bower, Mary and Buck Brannaman, Nick Briano, Rhonda Smith Briano, Barbara Broderick, Kevin and Vicky Byars, Angela Carmassi, Lori Carmassi, Heather Clark, Kellie Conner, Verlaine Crawford, Anne Desmond, Christopher Desmond, Peter Desmond, Paul Dietz, Billy Dorrance, Dave Dorrance, Steve Dorrance, Leslie Dorrance, Polly DuPont, Ken Eckhardt, Dan Evans, Lotte Foley, Deborah Fugate, Jenny Gagner, Gail Gallagher, Diane and Pete Garneau, Max Gawyler, Jason A. Gill, Burch Greene, Joan Glass, Tina Goodwin, Heather Hafleigh, Rich Ikegami, Elizabeth Johanson, Alex Jones, Josh Jones, Emily Kitching, Anna Kerr, Sarah Kerr, Lori Kline, Kaity LaHaye, Aaron Lazanoff, Jan Leitschuh, Richard Field Levine, Sarah Levine, Rachel Marker, William Matthews, Katherine Moewe, Ellen Mosier, Jane and Channing Murdock, Julie Murphy, Kim Murphy, Terry Neill, Ulf Noren, Kathy Peth, Tim Postel, Jesse Rodriguez, Mike Roswell, Iris Salzman, Tory Seavey, Steve Schwindt, Jen Simmons, Lori Smith, Wilson E. Smith, Susan Sonnier, Mary Sorenson, Craig Spencer, Lauren Spencer, Cicci Sunden, Alexis Trotta, Jim and Shelly Turcotte, Carol Wangenheim, Patricia Weedman, Taj Welsh, Will Wyckoff, *The Trail Less Traveled* and Ms. Simmons' Fifth Grade Class, Tularcitos Elementary School, Carmel Valley, CA.

Special thanks to Online Training Solutions, Inc. for their production assistance — Gale Nelson, Steve Lambert, Mary Rasmussen, Ryan Nelson, Leslie Eliel and Robert J. Cadranell.

We are also grateful to the owners of the Hill Ranch in Novato, CA; Holman Ranch, Oak Ridge Ranch and Rana Creek Ranch in Carmel Valley, CA; Summit Ranch and the Douglas Ranch in Paicines, CA; and the Pebble Beach Equestrian Center.

Authors' Notes:

BILL DORRANCE

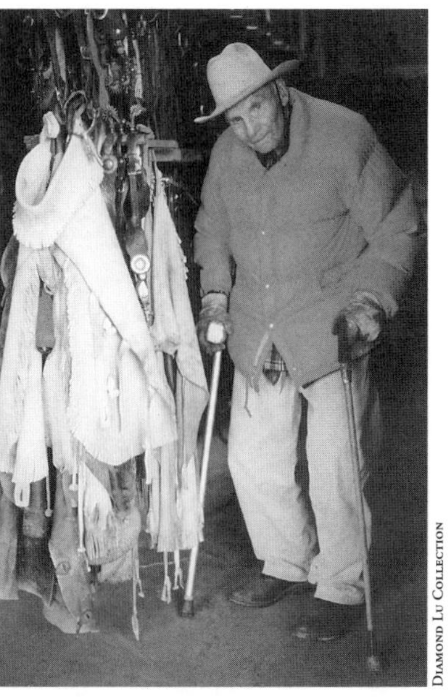

Bill Dorrance in the saddle room at his ranch on Mt. Toro. January, 1999.

Whether we're riding horses or just handling them, I think we're all after the same thing. We all want our horses to be responsive to us. It's just a matter of how we go about getting it done, and I almost didn't live long enough to get this sorted out in a way that was really fitting to the horse. I grew up with horses, of course, and I've been around them all my life, but I realized a long while ago that I was never going to get it all on my own. There isn't enough time. And that's why I like to help people learn how to feel of the horse.

After a person has lived 93 years and worked with animals all of his life, there's a lot of experience that takes place in that time, and that helps a fella to understand what the big lessons are — or it should, I'll say that. The biggest thing that ever happened to me was learning how to work through feel with horses — any horse — right on the start, and to lay that good foundation in there. The important thing is learning how to feel of the horse, and then getting those horses to be responsive to your feel.

I learned other things about handling cattle, and that's all about feel, too. Some people use far less feel than others. But anytime you're working with an animal, all that animal really has to go on is the feel of the person who's around him, or actually handling him.

The problem I see people having with their horses is due to so many of them thinking they can start out quite a ways up the line from where the horse is in his development. Some real important things get passed over when they start way up there. To get the better results, a person needs to start down below where most people want to work with the horse. There's a lot about the horse's instincts and the way he operates that most people never give any thought to, either. This is where they make their big mistake.

I passed over a lot of these important things myself, on the start. You could say that in my younger years, I mainly rode bucking horses. There wasn't anybody back then who talked about what you did, or how you could help a horse. But that's what those horses needed and so did most of the people. But, whenever you can get on to it, it's the right time.

When you're learning how to get with your horse, you're also learning about what there is to see. I sometimes think about when you look over on that hill there, why you may not see anything the first time you look. But, you keep looking and you're liable to pick up something that you didn't see the first time. It's like that with the horse. You're just trying to get with that horse's mental system. This is done through feel, because this is what fits a horse. That's the reason it works. When a person understands this and can get it applied, why that horse can understand what he's expected to do — whatever it is.

There are some other reasons for this book. My main plan is to have this in print for anyone who wants an idea of how the horse operates. The horse needs to have the person feeling real sure about how to present what is expected of him in a way that he can understand. The horse can get sort of lost if he doesn't understand what's expected and he needs to learn what's expected of him way down at the bottom, through feel. What fits me best, in terms of helping someone out, is to help them get the feel of the horse and teach that horse to feel of them. I haven't seen anything written down any place about feel and how you get it applied. Not so far, anyway.

You have to teach the horse, through feel, how to move his feet — and that would be to move forward, backwards, or sideways. You'd move the horse just one step at a time. You'd allow him to stop in between each step. You want to lay in a good foundation to build onto because you'll need to have it there for all the future maneuvers he'll need to make when you have a job for him to do — whatever job it is. And this job could be when you're horseback in the future, when something happens and then, maybe, right on the spur of the moment, there's a need for him to work further up the line in his ability. This is real important to the horse and the person because of how good the results can be when the horse understands you. They can be real disastrous when he doesn't.

One thing's for sure, that trouble spot is where the understanding is missing and when it's missing, then, of course, that horse isn't feeling of the person. To get the better results to show up in the future, that trouble spot will need to be taken care of. That better feel needs to get built in there before going on.

If the same problems come up for people with their horses year after year, well, then, they aren't on to this yet, which is another reason why this is going into print. We aren't writing something for somebody to just read. We're writing about the actual facts that take place while you're riding and handling those horses. We're writing this book for people to *use* because there isn't always the opportunity to have someone near enough to help when you have questions.

You don't have to be a genius to learn this, but you can't be too dumb either. What I'm thinking about is something most anyone can learn, if they want to. There isn't any secret to it. It's just that these messages operate in the horse's mind, and they all come from the horse's brain right down through the rest of his body to his feet. To learn this, a person needs three main things.

The first thing you need is a strong desire to learn it. Second, you need a lot of time. And third, you need to have someone to go to for supervision who's got more experience than you have working with horses through feel. Especially if you have problems with your horse, you need to have someone to visit with who understands this, because that horse will need a lot of support from you. This can work for anyone who is open to getting help.

I asked Leslie Desmond if she would like to do the writing on this book, and she said she would. I'm in hopes that by putting the actual facts down in print, and some meanings to go along with those facts, people will understand the terms we use and the way to get feel applied — and this'd be for those better results people are in hopes of getting with their horses. If there were some photographs to go along with that, we thought that would be a place to start.

We'd be able to do better if we had more time. I'll say another three years work on it would make it quite a lot better, because you can always improve on the way you do something. But there has to be a cut-off someplace. I think there's enough progress been made on it now to give people a little help on the start. I'm in hopes that this is so, anyway.

Not everyone is going to want to do this. And, not everyone who wants to work this way with their horse will understand this book, and maybe they won't for a lot of reasons, but not because it's too difficult. I don't want anyone to think that this is too difficult. If they want to learn this and get along better with their horse, they will.

William Dorrance

Bill Dorrance
November 29, 1998

Authors' Notes:
LESLIE DESMOND

Diamond Lu Collection

Bill Dorrance and I shared a great love of horses, and he invested the last few of his ninety-three years patiently showing me his preferred way to handle and ride them. I often heard it said that Bill, whose rural upbringing only provided for a formal education through the 8th grade, spoke "simply." That is true, and what impressed me most about Bill's use of language was twofold: His carefully selected words always sounded appropriate. And his judicious timing for their use was in perfect keeping with his horse-handling and riding capacities, which were impeccable.

"If a fella's learned how to make the best use of his better feel at the foundation level, then he can help a horse work through one sort of mix-up or another so his intent gets through real clear to that horse. When this happens, it's because he figured out through his experimenting how to present his feel in a way that fits that particular horse. That's what I call *true horsemanship.*"

What also impressed me are the things that Bill did not say. For example, he steadfastly refused to discuss the less-than-perfect possibilities that can occur with horses. He disdained the speculative fascination that many horse enthusiasts have nowadays with endless "what if" scenarios. He preferred to observe horses as situations unfolded. As you will discover in the pages that follow, strict adherence to Bill's lean approach leads to sureness about the skills one needs for competent horse handling.

On July 20, 1999, only five weeks after publication, Bill passed on. His death left an incalculable gap in my life. Such was my grief that, for a time, I could not see the point of much in anything. But now, after nine years of coaching others and working with horses through feel, loss has been eclipsed by an infinite "gain," and it becomes more clear to me with each passing year that through the timeless truth of his message, he lives on.

In the years since we worked around horses together, I have frequently relied on this book to help me stay on the right track. The detailed descriptions of feel are solid building blocks for advanced work. They are also a reminder that good horse handling is as much an acquired skill, an art to master, as it is a blessing for those few among us who can claim it is a birthright.

During my stay at the ranch on Mt. Toro, I watched Bill re-start several horses that trainers had given up on. In these incorrigible outlaws Bill found the best and brought those parts forward, and he did so with the dexterity and fastidiousness one could associate with the nimble fingers of an eighteenth-century lace-maker or a modern-day brain surgeon. Bill would first get a feel of the horse's mental and physical condition up close and then maneuver it one foot at a time at the end of a long, slack rope. If one was scared and fast, worried and sticky, or fearful and resistant, that was of no particular concern. Through what Bill termed his "better feel" each horse soon understood his offer to back up, then to lead up freely and, a short while later, to reach generously to the left or right with a weightless, open shoulder and an eagerness for the smallest job, which, incredibly, might be to move one foot one inch. Where a confounded bystander might dismiss the event as a charade and a ridiculous waste of time, the horse and Bill knew there was great meaning in a slight change of direction. He asked a horse to try just a little bit in the beginning because he was only looking for a little change. There is time for bigger changes, later. With a mental acuity and timing comparable to his feel, he called up in each horse its capacity for renewal and cemented its sureness as he took the horse from the standstill to the gallop, from the gallop to the walk, and later to the stop in one stride without pulling.

As they learned I, too, learned what he intended by the motions of his torso and arms and the slight changes in his line of sight. But most impressive were the subtle changes of the life in himself—the *ki*, or *chi*, the *life-driven* intent. This essential core connection was palpable, and from the chair where he sat, from the post he clung to when the situation called for him to stand, Bill was tireless in his mission to help each horse reveal the most useful aspects of its physical and mental potential in a given moment and use them well. I have seen few sights more graceful than a slaughter-bound misfit exhibiting the elegant feel of Bill's unique presentation.

I moved to Sweden in 2004 and a year later met a young horse trainer, Svante Andersson, from Stockholm. The story that follows is about a racehorse that arrived on his doorstep.

At eighteen months old, the stunning bay gelding was a powerhouse—potential incarnate. Two years later he was on death row and headed for slaughter. It was a typical case of mishandling at the track, a lack of skill and knowledge, but by the time the decision to kill him was made no one cared that avoidable misunderstandings were the cause of his troubles. Early on he let them know that the feel of the handling and training was foreign. The timing wasn't right, either. Again, he warned them. The colt let everyone know that due to his lack of understanding, their expectations were unreasonably high. He had their attention and some changes were made, but more—not less—pressure was brought to bear when his confusion led to resistance. At his wits end, finally, the colt found the relief he sought from various pressures he could not fathom by kicking and striking anyone within reach. He flattened those who would lead him, knocked down the grooms and vets, and bucked off every rider who dared to mount him. He fought restraints, whips, the bit and saddle, and defied every attempt to manage him. Finally, when too many people had been hospitalized, the fine bloodlines and extraordinary price tag that led to his life at the track was written off as a loss by the investors, and plans were made for his disposal. Sadly, this is a common story, but what happened next is not.

The bright bay colt caught the eye of a lifelong horse lover who offered the colt another chance. Andersson's first rides were the typical fast and reckless rides one gets on a scared colt. These were punctuated with sharp turns, spontaneous lateral leaps, bucking, and many other unpleasant aspects.

The horse was turned out in the countryside, and the hand-feeding that contributed to his pushiness was altogether stopped. He rediscovered the joy of a hard run and fast play with other horses in a spacious fields-and-forest setting. He developed his athletic capacity and his judgment about where it was safe to be when and at which speed certain maneuvers were possible. In a few weeks, the habitually pinned ears, grinding teeth, and head-tossing—all evidence of stress and discomfort—had disappeared. The colt no longer chewed frantically on the steel bars that confined him. Pacing back and forth at the paddock gates became a thing of the past. At last the grass he longed for was under foot in summer, and in winter the freedom to be a normal horse with a thick, natural coat replaced the heat lamps and blankets used in former times.

In a few weeks he could be led without trampling the person on the other end of the rope. Instead, he looked with interest at the people, horses, and other things around him. With gratitude in his attitude, he stood with slack in the lead and offered a flexible, graceful arc in his neck. He was on a quest now for the answers to questions his expression clearly held: "Hello, who are you?" and "What do you want?"

He started to enjoy the feel of a brush and the stroke from someone's hand. When a halter or bridle or a soft brush for the face was offered from a spot behind either elbow, he learned not to push on anyone who was not really in the way. When he was approached like this, his neck lost its ironclad tension because he could still get a good look at things coming toward him from either side or behind. The position of his shoulders and hips could be adjusted easily to accommodate the daily chores when he was loose at pasture or in the confines of an aisle way, wash rack, stall, or trailer.

The sense of belonging to someone who wanted him to succeed replaced anxiety-ridden regimens and the setups for failure. The colt was coached slowly past his reputation, and for those who knew and liked him, these rumored changes led to the obvious conclusion: *a horse behaves better when he feels better.* Soon he could distinguish between the different feel in subtle requests: *prepare* to start, *prepare* to slow down, stop; and, *are you ready*? to step forward or back, left or right. In several more slow sessions, he learned how to elevate the withers, flex any which way at the poll, reach with the neck, and to move the shoulders, ribs, and hips for reasons that he finally understood. After a few more months, Andersson led guided rides through the wilderness on him.

"I used the exercises that Bill recommended, and it put an end to his confusion about people. This was a big relief to us both," the trainer told me. "If I understand his message, I think Bill agreed with the earliest impressions that I formed about horses—there is never a reason to punish a horse when his behavior is regarded from his own point of view."

I cherish this example of respect for a troubled horse and the time it takes to re-train one correctly. I hope one day it will become the norm to start all horses using Bill Dorrance's approach to feel. Until then, it remains my solid plan because it works. Horses understand it immediately. Bill said, "If a fella works at this a little, why it won't be too long before he's just going to release his horse to the maneuvers he has in mind, and that pressure part isn't going to show up in there at all."

Before closing, I want to tell you a bit more about Bill Dorrance. It was June 6, 1999, and *True Horsemanship Through Feel* was hot off the press. Since June 2, sixteen of us tackled nineteen pallets. With the unpacking and signing done, the books were put in addressed mailers. Postage was slapped on and three carloads of books had already shipped from the post office in Novato, California. An 18-foot freight truck stuffed to the max with parcels destined for Europe and Canada was also en route. Nearly done. We were taking a short break when the phone rang. It was Bill.

LD: Hello!

BD: Hello, yeah, Dorrance here. How are you all getting along up there . . . I believe it's Novato you're in now, is that right?

LD: Well, we are still at it Bill. There is a lot to do here now, and we have just about got the last of the pre-publication orders packed into envelopes—they are ready to close up and send. A truckload has already been taken to the post office earlier today, and by noon tomorrow we should be done with the first shipments!

BD: OK, that is good. Well, I was just thinking maybe I had ought to write just a little more on our book, yeah, that's it . . . if a fella thought there was still time for it.

[LD: Said nothing.]

BD: . . . Hello?

LD: Hi Bill. I'm just thinking about this . . . that's all . . .

BD: Oh yeah, OK then, well, yeah, that's right, there was just that little piece of it in there that didn't make it into our book yet is all, and I was thinking . . .

LD: Bill, I'm sorry to cut in here, but the book is already here. It is back from the printer now, back from China, and we are shipping it out this weekend.

BD: I know but where there is that part in there that we didn't get into our book, I was just thinking how it could be pretty important for the horse, that we get that in there.

LD: What did we forget, Bill? We can't unpublish this book but we can re-publish it. We can certainly re-publish it with your additions in there . . . would that be all right?

BD: Well, I'd rather we got it in this time. Yeah, that's right. If we can. Yeah.

LD: [Stunned. Said nothing. Then, finally . . . .] Bill, what is it that we need to put in our book? Is this important enough for us to open these packages that are still here?

BD: Yeah, I think so. It can really help a horse alright, if a fella had this to think about sometime.

LD: Then, are you thinking that I should write something down to add to these books before they leave Novato in the morning?

BD: Yeah, that's right.

LD: You mean add something on a piece of paper inside the book cover, just stick it in there . . . just like that?

BD: I think so, yeah, that's it.

LD: Have you got the wording of what you want to say all ready to go? You have it ready now? Or is this something I need to come down to the ranch and visit with you about?

BD: No, I've got it alright. What a fella needs to be aware of is that horsemanship through feel is handed down from one friend to another. It isn't for sale, no, it isn't for sale. And I'd rather think that a fella, before he gets too far along on the training end of things where horses are concerned, should know about this on the start.

As Bill wished, around 5,000 little pieces of paper bearing his message—"Horsemanship through feel is handed down from one friend to another"—were Xeroxed at the copy place that day and stamped with his signature. If you were fortunate enough to purchase the first edition (printed in China, 1998–1999) or the second edition (printed in Canada, November 1999), maybe you found that little message Bill wanted us to stick in there at the last minute, for you.

Leslie Desmond

Norrland, Sweden

July 17, 2008

INTRODUCTION

Bill Dorrance and Buck Brannaman visiting at the Dorrance Ranch on Mt. Toro, Salinas, California, in 1997.

I'd heard of Bill Dorrance from a friend of mine who'd bragged for years about his horsemanship, and Bill's skill with a bridle horse and the way he handled a rope were legendary.

I was about as desperate as I could possibly be. I'd been working with a real nice roan horse and I had him turning around pretty good, or that's what I thought anyway. But it seemed that if I asked him to put any effort into it, maybe enough effort to turn a cow in a hurry or do a job, he seemed to be going as fast as he could possibly go. And it wasn't very fast. I got so frustrated trying to train this horse I was just to the point of tears. I couldn't seem to make any headway. Nothing meant more to me than being a good horseman. "Well," I thought, "it's worth a shot. I'll call Bill Dorrance."

I knew Bill lived around Salinas and with a little bit of investigation I found his number and called him up. I said, "Bill, you don't know who I am, but I need some help with my horse. A friend of mine told me what a great horseman you are and I've admired the things that you've shown him. My horse turns pretty good, but I can't seem to get him to put any effort into it."

And at that point, I was so frustrated that I guess I was hoping that Bill would just tell me to take the tail end of my mecate and whack him across the shoulder, or maybe turn my toe out and use my spur to get him to put some effort into it. Of course I didn't want to hurt the horse — I've always liked horses, and I really liked this horse. But Bill acted like he'd never heard a word I said.

He started talking about the hindquarters of the horse. He said, "You know Buck, if you can move the hindquarters right or left on a horse you can get him arranged to where he can do some things that you didn't think he could do." And I thought, "Well, how sad. Poor old Bill has gotten so much age on him that he didn't hear what I asked him."

So I asked him again, in a different way, how I could get my horse to turn around a little sharper so I could get him to work a cow a little better. Again he said, "You know, a fella can get a horse reaching backwards a little bit, that will help you, but really it's amazing how much the hindquarters have to do with all of these things a fella does with a horse." And I thought, "There he goes again, talking about the hindquarters of a horse. It's just like he doesn't hear a word I ask."

One more time I asked him what I should do about my problem with the frontquarters — of course, that's where I thought the problem was — and again we ended up talking about the hindquarters. I decided that no matter how I asked Bill about this problem I was having, he was not going to understand me.

I gave up on it for that day. I just thought we'd had a nice conversation. At least I got a chance to talk to the legendary Bill Dorrance on the phone and that really meant a lot to me. So I left it alone.

I realized later that Bill had understood me just fine. I realized then what had been so obvious to Bill. But the next day, when I went out to see the horse I felt sorry for him. I was down on myself about the way I'd been with him — I'd been really riding him hard for a few days, just trying to get this. So I made myself a promise that I would just take a ride on the horse and that day we would just enjoy each other. We'd just take a ride out through the hills and I wouldn't ask him to do anything difficult or anything that I didn't think we could do. I was really down on myself. I even got to thinking that maybe I'd rekindle my trick roping career because I'd been pretty successful at that. I was starting to think that maybe this horse thing was something I wasn't going to be able to do very well.

All through the ride I just tried to leave the horse alone. On the way back to the barn I thought, you know, maybe I just ought to see if I can stop him with one rein and untrack his hindquarters a little bit. Maybe I'll just see if I can get him to step over behind. I thought I ought to do a little something positive before I put him up for the day. I tried to do that and, of course, I felt like my rein was tied off to a big rock or to the back of somebody's truck. I couldn't get anything accomplished. He hardly had any bend in him at all. I couldn't get him to step over behind — that almost goes without saying — and that kind of surprised me.

So, I worked on that for a few minutes because I figured — as down on myself as I was that day — at least I could accomplish that. After a while I could get him to untrack his hindquarters a little bit, step over behind, and bend a little bit more through his loin and ribcage. He had a little more feel on the end of the rein then. And after having shaped that up a little bit I tried to keep my promise to the horse that I wouldn't bother him, or pick on him, and I started back toward the barn.

As I got close to the barn it started getting to me — I really wanted to get this sorted out. So I stopped him and asked him to turn around, just as if there were an imaginary cow in front of us. Well, he turned so fast that my hat just about flew off my head and he damn near turned out from under me. I'd never felt him turn that fast before.

I thought, "Gee, now you better leave that alone because it's not going to get any better than that, that's for sure, and the way you've been riding the last few days you'll probably wreck it in the next few minutes." I walked a brisk walk back to the barn and unsaddled him before I destroyed what I'd been trying to get.

While unsaddling the horse and putting my gear up for the day, I realized that somewhere along the line I'd lost the hindquarters. I had control of them at one point, but I got so busy trying to be this "horse trainer" — and I say that with much chagrin — that I'd lost the basics that got my horse ready to go on in the first place. Having lost the feel in the horse, I'd also lost the basics and the preparation. There was no way I was going to get him to turn around any faster.

Given everything he had to go on, and based on the way his body and his mind were arranged, there wasn't a lot more he could offer me. He was turning as fast as he possibly could. But once I got the hindquarters freed up — stumbled on to it by stopping with one rein — I thought, "I'll be damned... Bill tried to talk about the end of the horse that needed work and I didn't want to talk about that."

To make a long story short, a few days later I talked to Bill on the phone again because I really wanted to tell him about this horse. We didn't talk but just a few minutes and he said, "How did things work out on that roan horse that you were telling me about?"

I said, "Well, Bill, I found that those hindquarters were not shaped up very well. His hip was in the way, it wasn't up underneath him, and considering the way he was prepared, he was turning about as fast as he could possibly turn. I got that shaped up now and he's happy to turn for me. We're getting along good again."

I've often said that if you took away the fact that Bill Dorrance is a great hand with a reata and a gifted horseman, what you have left is just a really fine human being. Bill is a good man. Considering I wasn't really listening to him, he could have said any number of things to me. He could have said, ""Well, I told you so," or, "If you had listened to me in the first place." But he didn't say those things. He just said, "Well, that's real good that worked out for you, Buck. I'm glad that things are starting to shape up between you and that horse."

He didn't rub in the fact that he was right. It wasn't about being right or wrong. He was a true gentleman about it. The sort of consideration Bill showed for me is the same consideration that he has shown other people and horses his whole life.

From that point on, it's been obvious to me what a special gift Bill Dorrance is to all of us, and in his book Bill is going to give you another gift. I hope you treasure that the way I treasure the friendship Bill has given to me over the years. Enjoy this book. I know I will.

Happy Trails. And thanks Bill.

Buck Brannaman

BUCK BRANNAMAN

Chapter 1:

BILL TALKS ABOUT HOW IMPORTANT FEEL IS TO THE HORSE

Horses are intelligent and they can make decisions. This is the reason that they can sense what a person wants them to do and will try to understand a person's intent. Through his natural instinct of self-preservation, a horse will respond to two kinds of feel that a person can present. He will respond to a person's *indirect feel,* which means that he will either react to or ignore a person's presence — *and how a horse responds depends entirely on the person.* This indirect feel is what you have out in the pasture or corral, when you don't have any physical contact with the horse, like a halter or snaffle bit. A horse will also respond to *direct feel,* which is when you have a physical connection with the horse through some part of your body, the halter or the snaffle, or a rope any place on his body, even if it's connected to the saddle horn.

When it's effectively applied, either direct or indirect feel from a person can influence the horse's mind and body to match up with the person's plan of how they want that horse to be doing things for them. Using feel, a person can shape the horse's desire to stay with them, and they can determine the horse's direction and speed and frame of mind when they want him to move. Through feel, a person can get the horse to think about and do many little things that are very important to the horse and to the safety of the person. These little things can be felt by the person and the horse too, of course, but they aren't visible to everyone's eyes. That's because these observations take a lot of time and not many people want to spend their time this way.

A Horse's Basic Nature and Sensitivity

To help the horse learn to understand what you want, you can make use of his nature. He is naturally curious and is apt to investigate things he hasn't seen or been around before. He is also liable to run away from those same things. There's a spot somewhere in between (those tendencies) where an observing person can develop some skill at blending in their plan for how they want the horse to maneuver with the horse's willingness to do these things for a person. We can work with a horse this way because it's part of the horse's basic nature to want to get along.

Diamond Lu Collection series

These horses are galloping in response to the indirect feel of a person on another horse who's driving them. They are all feeling of that together and they are moving together. When they do this, each of those horses is influenced by the indirect feel of all those other horses galloping along.

A young fella is helping a younger person learn about indirect feel. They are using a flag to bring up the life in those horses and move them.

The horse in this picture is responding to the direct feel of that lead rope.

Gale Nelson

This horse is responding to the direct feel of the rider's whole body and her reins.

But the actual fact, as far as the horse is concerned, is that interaction with human beings is not natural. For a person to sit up there on his back is even less so. This is the reason we need to observe the horse and learn to feel of him and help him feel of us. To get the idea of feel, the horse handler needs to understand how the horse exists and survives in the world, which is through his senses. When it comes to cooperating with the human, we're talking about the feeling the horse has in every square inch of his hide and all through his mind, as it relates to a human touching him directly *or* indirectly.

This is because feel is all the horse has to go on, on the start, and he learns this from his mother. That's as far back down toward the bottom as a person might think he could go, or be able to go at all. The mare knows how to get things working for her. And that's all she uses to get an understanding going — just the feel that she presents. Sometimes just her whiskers mean a lot to a colt. I mean, they can be enough to really get an important message across to him without too much motion in either one of them showing up. But even just the feel of those whiskers can reassure a colt and he'll stay in that lying down position and be sort of sleeping there. Or he can get up from the littlest touch of those same whiskers and get so he's moving right along. That's because the feel of her intention in those situations is different, and the colt knows that. To a person watching this, there's a good chance the mare's actual body motion that caused the colt to stay or leave would appear to be the same. But there's a big difference in her feel, as far as that colt's concerned. It works as good as it does because that's the way a horse is set up for things about life, right at the beginning.

Diamond Lu Collection

Lightness and Life

Lightness and some other things about a horse's natural way to be, like collection, are things a person wants to be able to rely on. In order for the horse's lightness to carry over when a person sits up there, lightness between the horse and the person has to be built in on the ground and experienced there before they ride him. This is done by using feel, on the start. The person should be focused on getting the best possible connection with the horse on the ground, through feel, if they want to have those parts of the horse (the capacity for lightness and collection) available to them when they ride. This way the horse can do what is expected of him without resisting the rider. It's up to the rider to gain an understanding of how each horse needs to have information presented, and there's a great deal of variation in that. *When the horse understands what you want, he will do what that is, right up to the limit of his physical capacity and sometimes well beyond it.*

It seems that it's the life in the horse that causes lightness to be in him. It's that, added to his self-preservation instincts, that are the real cause of lightness all right. The way he uses his strength and collects himself up for some quick moves, why all this seems to come from the same place too, and I'd say that it comes from his life. Even a horse that isn't much for looks can maintain an attractive appearance when

Diamond Lu Collection

Life itself, along with the desire and ability to move, is the source of lightness.

he's thinking about going someplace. His energy and those instincts just spoken about, and the ideas that he has inside of him, and the way all of that gets to working together in there, why that's what makes that horse appear the way he does when he's light. It's those same things that make him look the way he does when he isn't light, too.

If your horse is not well prepared to understand what you expect of him on the ground, then lightness might not show up the way you'd want it to when you ride. Or, it might not show up at all, it just depends on so many things. The best thing, of course, is not to take the lightness out of him in the first place. Unless a person had some help on this, they'd need quite a lot of knowing about horses. But it can be done.

To accomplish this, you'd develop that horse's responsiveness to your feel. It's only through feel that a rider can make use of the lightness in the horse without creating resistance. When you build that foundation through feel, it becomes possible to direct the horse in any maneuver — at just about any speed, anytime you need to — and have it weigh almost nothing in your hands. *When you can direct a horse's movements through feel, then there's understanding taking place between the person and the horse. That is the sign of true horsemanship.*

Preparation

Most people don't realize how important it is to start right down at the foundation level, and work with that horse where he can understand their feel. No, they come into horses with other ideas about what's important to accomplish through their involvement with them. People, I'll say most of them anyway, aren't comfortable around a horse unless they are trying to operate him through some equipment they put on him. They think this is all the preparation they might need. The horse finds this out about the person when he doesn't understand what they are expecting him to do, and this gets real confusing to him. He doesn't think this way. When things really aren't clear to the horse, it's usually just about the time that a person starts to come in there with a lot of extra pressure on him, and of course this causes the horse to prove that he doesn't have any idea what he's supposed to do. That's what overexposes the horse, and you'll try to avoid doing this. (Bill talks more about overexposing the horse later in this chapter.)

When people work on up the line without that foundation laid in there real good, they don't have much to build on. Without the preparation he needs to have built in, why that horse is lost. He has no other way to be sure what he's supposed to do.

Time is the Best Investment

Some people have a tendency to pay a good deal of money to get things done for them with their horses, but the investment they don't seem to make is in terms of time, and putting that time in with their horse. This is so important to the horse. It's going to take most people quite a lot of time to learn how to apply feel once they do understand it, because there's so many little things that you do with a horse to get the right thing happening. You pretty well have to be on the horse to feel all those little things. You might have a book a foot thick before you got done writing down about all the little particles that go into making up feel, and we can't do that, but we will try to talk about a lot of them.

People are going to be in a better position to handle a horse if they spend whatever time it takes to get some real useful knowledge. That's what they're going to need to get in order to present their feel to the horse clear enough so he can understand what they expect him to do. So many times, what's clear to that horse is almost nothing.

The Importance of Being Relaxed (for the Horse and the Person)

I'm in hopes that in the future people will not be starting their horses at a place that is at all beyond their capabilities, or even past their understanding. If people knew how important the groundwork was, that's where they'd want to start with every horse, every time. It's when the people aren't relaxed that those horses get so tight and don't have a good feel to offer back to the person. Sometimes those horses are tight anyway, for reasons of their own, and being around a person who's not relaxed just gets it a whole lot worse, I'll put it that way. The horses can get real bothered about what's taking place when they don't understand it. So we need to spend quite a bit of time with these horses and help them get relaxed.

It's important to have a horse with a nice mellow feel. This is really more about the way his mood and his mind are, but there's a place in there where his body takes part in the understanding of this mellow feel. *Without that person around, the horse is that nice mellow way in most cases.* So, if he's not that way when that person is around him, then it's up to them to bring this out in the horse. Even if you didn't have a lot of experience, you'd know he's got that mellow feel to him because he won't be moving all around and pushing up against you. His head won't be coming up either, because it takes a normal position when he's this way. It's a real mellow feel we're talking about now, and it's sure a desirable thing to have built into your way of doing things with horses.

Each Horse Presents a Different Feel

Each horse is an individual and, because of this, the feel that each horse presents back to you in response to what you do is going to be real different. It's not only different with every horse, but it's going to feel different and be different every day with the same horse until you can get on the right track with that horse. And even when you get real well acquainted with that horse, why there's going to be things that come up that won't fit the horse. Something will happen and you'll need to do a little experimenting to get back on the right track. No, it could be real easy for a fella to get discouraged and think he was way off, or doing things entirely wrong, if he wasn't clear about this fact ahead of time. I wanted to mention this because it could get real confusing to a person about just what they should be doing to help that horse. The main thing is that there's no one answer and no one formula on this, but that's what a lot of people would like to think, and some do think that anyway. But if a person has a real desire, they can learn to apply feel in a way that's fitting to almost any horse they happen to be around, that's for sure. It's just going to take some time.

Some people want to know if working with horses through feel will work for every horse. It all depends on the person involved and how they understand and apply feel. Whether the person understands it or not, feel is all the horse has to go on. There's such a variation in there when you're working with a live animal, and there's as much variation in the people, too. On some horses it's kind of easy to pick up that feel, and with others it's rather slow. On the same horse, you'll experiment applying feel in several different ways to see how much firmness or softness you'll use in different situations, according to what seems to fit that horse the best.

Variety is Real Important to the Horse

To bring out the best in the horse, which is what we want to do, nothing is presented in one fixed way. The adjustability those horses need from a person is difficult for many people to understand. If a person comes at that horse just one way, why the feel of that horse is going to be lost. When you've lost the feel of him, his interest in feeling of you just disappears and straight away he's liable to start working on his own ideas about what he thinks he ought to be doing instead. If that feel is missing between you, then he has no idea what you might want, so you'd start to do some experimenting to get that feel back and working for you again.

There's an idea in circulation now that since the horse is just an animal, he ought to be the one doing all the adjusting and figuring out of things that a person wants him to do *for them*. It's been this way a long time and maybe it's even been this way most of the time in most places. But the way I see it, that isn't how it works.

Surprising things can happen when people think this. And this is too bad for the horse. In some cases, it turns out to be really too bad for those people, too. As long as you're planning to be around horses, it's a good idea to be speculating all the time as to what little changes you can make, or what new little things you could do so that things go smoother between you and that horse. That's what we mean when we speak about it being "up to the person to make the change." It's not liable to be the other way around because it probably wasn't the horse's idea to be around there in the first place, and if it were left up to him he'd probably rather be some place else.

Consistency is an Important Part of a Good Foundation

There are many different ways to present feel to a horse so you're continually going to be searching and adjusting. By that, I mean just changing what you present to him as the circumstances change, and as that horse's movements and (facial) expressions change. You'd be doing this *all the time* that you're working with him, and *be all the time real aware.* This calls for the person to be in the frame of mind where they're ready, on the spur of the moment, to try and fit that horse better by making a change in what they're doing. But, by putting in that last part there about *all the time* being ready to change what you do, we're not saying that being consistent with that horse isn't real important too. *It is real important to that horse's foundation that a person be consistent.*

It seems like a contradiction to say "variety is important" and then to say "consistency is important." This just shows how putting this into print can be kind of confusing. Sometimes we just have to switch around those words to explain certain things. At the same time it's apt to be confusing, it can be the truth. It's just that feel takes in so much for the horse and for the person, too. It's real easy to see how a person could get confused if they think we're saying something that seems like the opposite way in meaning of what was spoken about just before. In this book there might be a lot of things that seem, maybe, like they go against something that was said before. The reason for this is that there's so many different things that can work, and so many different ways that one same thing can work, it just all depends on everything involved *right then* as to what a person and a horse can get together on.

I'm in hopes that things can work out and feel right to the horse and the person, at the same time, regardless of what's needing to be done or taking place around there. If they're relying on feel that goes two ways, then it will work out and it will feel right, that's for sure.

The Horse Tells You How He Feels, The Best Way He Knows How

A person with experience around horses can point out to you the little ways that a horse shows his concern about something that he isn't understanding. If the person handling the horse knows what to look for, the expression on the horse's face and his body movements give a real clear indication that something hurts or frightens him *before he becomes unmanageable.* Experienced horse people can tell between something that will cause the horse to become unmanageable and other distractions that just aggravate the horse a little. Some things can be quite upsetting but still are tolerable to the horse. In time, your better judgment will help you on this.

Understanding a horse is something of an art. That's one word we could use for it, I'd say. It's more than knowledge. It's a sense about the horse's frame of mind and his thoughts about things. This part can't be learned from a book or videos. This ability can come only from experience. It reflects a deeper understanding of the horse than most people have, and it has a foundation that is based on many hours of observation and on feel that goes two ways. It takes exposure to many horses before a person can pick up on the important small things they need to learn, but these are things that will prepare the person to head off trouble or, if that is not possible, to offer that horse the kind of direction and support that he needs to make it through whatever is bothering him.

Anyone with a sincere desire to achieve this connection with a horse could develop this ability. They need to have the time to devote to it and someone to help them once in a while. The main source of information they'll rely on comes straight from the horse. And if horses haven't been part of daily life from an early age, this is not as easy as it would be for someone raised around them. But a person could still get pretty accomplished at this anyway.

When the Horse is Overexposed

It doesn't really matter how much experience a person has had with horses, sooner or later something will be done, or not done, that will cause a horse to become what's called "overexposed." This refers to anything that the horse can't adjust to, can't handle, or that doesn't fit into the way he understands things. He gets far away from the place where he's comfortable, and he gets way off in his connections. This lack of understanding about things can put the horse in a real bothered mental state that shows up right away in his physical system.

When a horse is overexposed on the mild side, that horse might show signs of some agitation or nervousness (like sweating, grinding the teeth, holding the breath, panting, or prancing in place). On the other end of the spectrum, which is what we're trying to stay far away from, it can become a full-blown disaster. This does not need to be described because it's real obvious when this occurs. Great care should be taken to avoid putting a horse in this situation.

The causes for this run the gamut, but we're in favor of listing some examples right here. These are some things that people might do directly to the horse, unintentionally we'll assume, that could cause him to become overexposed.

You'd be sure to avoid trying these things:

- Tying him for the first time without the horse knowing that it meant he was supposed to stand still.
- Hobbling the horse without teaching the horse how to yield to pressure on his legs.
- Giving that horse a good poke from a spur he didn't know was there.
- Falling off a green colt the first time that colt takes a little jump when he starts off at the trot or lope.
- Banging him in the teeth with the bit.
- Letting him step on his reins.
- Spraying him with anything while he's tied before he's been well prepared to accept this.
- Forcing him into a trailer and then closing the doors and taking off.
- Allowing a saddle to turn under his belly from your cinch being too loose.

That should give people some ideas about things they'd hope to not ever do.

One thing more on overexposing the horse. *It's not a matter of if this will happen, because it will. Sometime.* And when it does, it ought to be looked on as an opportunity to learn how to do things a little different the next time. People need to know that this is not to be thought of as a failure of any kind, but of course we're in hopes of avoiding these things that can overexpose the horse. No one can predict exactly how a horse will react in any situation — the fact is, if your horse isn't well enough prepared to handle something he encounters, this can even happen when you're nowhere around. All you can hope to do is be more observant when you are around horses and become better prepared to help the horse keep his mental system on the right track.

When Feel is Lost

Feel is anything you do with an animal, because that's all an animal has to go on when interacting with a human. It could be a good feel, or one that is not so good. We wouldn't call it a bad feel, because that takes in so much that I'd rather not speak about that. Let's just say, if it isn't the best feel a person is using with that horse, then it's a feel he misunderstands. And if it's this way for that horse, he could anticipate what you want and just take over — which happens when the feel is lost. Or, he could respond to what you do in a way that agrees with what you had in mind. That's two things that can happen and they're real different. There's two other things that are liable to happen when the feel that horse gets isn't the best. One is, he might not get in a hurry and take over, but he still might have some calmer ideas of his own operating in there that don't quite fit that person's plan. The other thing he's liable to do is to show no response at all. Or, I'll say, it's not one that's obvious to most people. Whether a person can see it or they can't, there's so much feel taking place in every situation, and a fella needs to be aware of this.

Making Assumptions About a Horse

So many problems come up for the horse because there's an assumption made by the person that the horse just automatically knows somehow what he is supposed to do, and that's if something goes wrong, or it doesn't. These things just spoken about (above, in "When the Horse is Overexposed") aren't understandable to the horse on the start because they aren't natural. It'd be real strange for those horses to know about any of these things a person is liable to do before it was done to them, but people forget this part. Most of them just go ahead with their ideas without the preparation part laid in there for that horse to fall back on. When you consider that if it were up to the horse he'd be out grazing on the hillside with other horses, or hunting up a shade tree some place, why that horse couldn't possibly understand what a human being planned for him to be doing.

Taking Responsibility for the Horse's Problems

When it comes to discussions about handling and riding difficult horses, I've noticed that people have a tendency to avoid taking responsibility for the horse's problems. The idea people have, generally speaking, is that when a horse is difficult for someone to handle, this is mainly due to external factors. But the need to present an understandable human feel to the horse is one factor that is never mentioned, and it should be.

It's too bad that people are so ready to blame their horse's poor response to them on a deficiency in his makeup, or on a previous owner, or trainer or farrier or vet. This is what's said and done so often. They wouldn't need to spend time blaming the horse or other people for the situation if they had an idea of what changes they needed to make in themselves. That's where the problem is, them not being able to figure out what they should do.

When people aren't willing to consider that there's a possibility of their own role in creating a problem for the horse, or keeping one going that already exists, well, then those problems aren't likely to disappear until the horse does.

Regardless of the reason a horse is the way he is, if the person can't control him without the use of force or fear, one thing is certain — the person involved isn't yet able to offer the horse a feel that he can understand. If an understandable feel had been presented to the horse in the moments before, *and for sure during* the period that he wasn't in that person's control, he would have been feeling of that person, and he soon would have been under their control. When you have feel that goes both ways, you have that horse's respect and cooperation. Really, it's just about that simple.

If people can't take an honest look at their own problem — and that could be the inability to present a feel that the horse can understand — that's when the horse's problem starts. And that's an actual fact. When a person figures out how to present an understandable feel to a horse, then, I'll say for the most part, that horse's problems will be eliminated.

Since feel is the horse's language, our safety — and his, too — just really depends on us learning how to present what we want him to do, *through feel.*

Learning to Observe and Experimenting with Your Own Presentation

We're striving to get people to understand, through feel, just how the horse accepts this thing called feel so that he will have a better way of operating. Further up in this book, we have some pictures that show how to get this other way to start working for you. We're striving to explain the easiest way for the human to present something he wants from the horse without using force or fear to motivate him. The use of fear and force have been around for a long time, but nowadays a lot more people are demanding that the horse respond through force, instead of *helping* the horse to understand what they want another way.

"Asking" — this is what people say sometimes, but what we mean is *helping the horse*, or *presenting something to him.* What we're interested in is the person's frame of mind when they want the horse to do a certain thing. That word "ask" is really a lot more in the area of communication that's between people, so we wouldn't say "ask." What we'll say is that *before you can learn how to present something to the horse through feel that he's going to understand, you have to learn how to observe and make sense of the way he operates his body and how new information is processed in his mind.*

And you'll remember that each horse is different and has a different capacity to understand your feel, and the way he understands it determines how he will respond physically to what's presented. His mental system plays a real important part in this.

The biggest problem is getting people to understand that *there is* a way to communicate clearly with the horse through feel — and that'd be with any horse. People need to see that it can work. That's the main thing. Getting a clear understanding of this from print is not quite the same as feeling of the horse when you're right there next to him, and having what you present to that horse make sense. But it's a start. For a lot of people, maybe reading this book and having these pictures to look over and compare is what it will take to get them interested enough to go someplace and see how feel actually works. *Those horses need people to understand that there's hope for some improvement if people can just figure out how to present things to them through feel.* People can understand this if they want to. I'll say in most cases they can. This is a proven fact, so there's hope all right.

In order to prepare yourself better for the future, you need to have an honest understanding of the feel that you are able to present to the horse today. If there are going to be some improvements later on, then the picture in your mind about what the horse needs you to do in any situation has to be clear. Of course, this will take some time to develop. (Bill speaks more about developing a clear picture of what you want in Chapters 2 and 4.)

Observing Other People Work with Horses

I like to watch anybody on a horse and to notice what they're doing. I like to see what they have to offer the horse and to see what the horse comes back with to offer them. I think there's really such a big difference in what people do, and how they apply feel. Some are more skilled at this than others and they're the ones that I really enjoy watching, because they hit on the best way to present feel to whatever horse they're working with at the time. Those are the people who've spent quite a lot of time at this and haven't overexposed the horse to something that he's not capable of understanding. Of course they know where the limits are on that, and they respect those limits. These limits vary from one horse to another, and a person with skill knows that.

Working Through a Gate

One thing I always enjoy is watching someone on a young horse that hasn't had too many rides. I like to see them work their way through a swinging gate. Not a hazardous one either, but a good, solid, balanced gate. When a horse hasn't had the experience of going through a gate, but has been prepared ahead of time, then right from the start he'll be prepared to get through the gate real smooth because he already knows how to step over and be responsive to your feel. When the rider's presenting a feel to the horse so that the horse knows what to do, and he knows how to maneuver and work his way through that gate — why to see that is real pleasing to me.

The gate. We could sure talk about that some more. It depends so much on that individual horse, as to what you present him with so he can understand how to work himself through there. Some horses on the start just need to get used to seeing you put your hand on the fence when you're on his back. Some horses will just want to move right away from there. But, you'll get them used to it, so they find out it's fine. Some horses will need to be brought back alongside the fence. We'll say, maybe, the horse is skeptical about the gate just because it's something different. I usually don't go right up to it, I'll go up behind it. I'm liable to ride a horse farther back than that gate, right up along the fence. Then I'd work my way up to the front of the gate, so the horse is standing there, and he's comfortable enough. So many people go right up to it and then try to make him get headed in there sideways, just like that, without giving any real thought to what that horse might be thinking. And way before he's got any understanding about what they want, they go right to kicking him, sometimes just as hard as they can.

So much of the time it's kind of like this at those gates, and some horses don't seem to mind too much. Others get real bothered about this style of getting up to the gate. Because they haven't got any idea what's expected of them right there and then, when that pressure comes in there, well I'll put it this way — some things can happen that would surprise you. The person left out the preparation part for the horse, and when they left that out, they left out the feel in their connection to the horse, too. So, after you're sitting up there, the better way to do things is to build onto what you already got started through feel with the horse on the ground. *It's the control of the feet through the mind that a person's after. If you've missed that on the ground, on the start, why you've missed the part that means the most to the horse.* After that, no matter what it is that the person wants him to do — and that'd be within reason of course — it's really just left up to that horse's guesswork and self-preservation. But the actual fact is that he's just lost, and the person is too.

Supervision

If a person wants to expand their knowledge of the horse, they should get started from way down at the bottom with supervision. Then they can carry it on up the line to a higher point on their own. If people aren't getting feel applied so that they can accomplish something on their own, then they're likely to stop advancing in their knowledge of the horse. A lot of people would try to handle their horses with feel if they only knew how to go about it. Since life's too short to get it all on your own, it's real good to see how other people do things. And if a person has something to read, it might help them to advance in getting feel applied.

I'm in hopes that by putting some things down in print, it could be a big help for some people when supervision isn't available. Of course we can't get everything into print, but what we're hoping to do here is to get the idea across of how important it is to the horse that a person learns how to use feel. Once they're convinced of this, they'd just need to learn how to apply it in a way the horse can understand what they expect of him. This way, they can advance on their own with the horse from a better foundation. This foundation we're going to call *feel.*

It Takes A Lot Of Time

Like I spoke about before, it's real important to invest time in those horses. Give yourself and your horse the time it takes to get right. By this I mean: Prepare yourself and your horse to understand each other through feel. Horses know all about feel. But they haven't got any idea about our concept of time, and I question if some people really understand what it's for either, especially where it concerns a horse.

Chapter 2:

LEARNING HOW TO FEEL, AND RELEARNING TO LEARN

To learn anything that's going to be useful to you in the future, you really need to start at the beginning. Where it concerns horses, you need to learn how to get with their movements. It seems that most people think they need to oppose the horse's movements. When they do, it teaches that horse to oppose theirs. If you don't have a feel of where the horse's feet are, then you won't be able to control those feet. This is an actual fact. You have to learn to travel right along with the feel of that horse whether you're on him or not. The best place to start learning how to do this is on the ground, and the exercises in Chapter 4 will help you get started with this. You can learn this fast or you can learn this slow, but whichever it is, you are going to have to get with the feel of that horse. This has to happen before you can teach the horse to feel of you. If you miss this part, then no matter what might be said, he has not learned to respond to your feel and a lot of things just aren't going to work out.

Having an Idea in Mind and Presenting it to the Horse

In this book we're trying to prepare people to develop a workable mental picture that will be useful to them in the future when they're working with their horse. They need this preparation in place so they can help that horse understand what he's supposed to do.

On the start, people can't help presenting things wrong to the horse, because the picture they have in their mind about so many things concerning a horse is either incomplete or way off. We're in hopes that this book will be helpful to people who want to get a clear picture and present it to their horse in a way that fits him better than what they might have to offer him today. *What a person has in his mind to present to the horse needs to be something that's possible for a horse to actually do. Then the person has to be able to understand it themselves, through feel, and apply it in a way that the horse can understand.* This is difficult because no two horses are the same, and there's plenty of adjusting a person needs to figure on for this. Even if the picture they have is okay, when they handle a horse with more firmness than he needs, they'll get a wrong response nearly every time and think the horse is at fault. When that's their thinking, they're liable to just apply a lot more pressure on the horse — *which really mixes him up.* And from the horse's response, the person can get the idea that he doesn't want to do what they'd like him to do. This is correct in a way, but it's really just because the horse can't figure out what they want him to do, because he doesn't understand that pressure-feel they put on him in the first place. What makes this so bad is that those horses — I'll say most horses — would cooperate if they could only understand.

Helping the Horse Understand

It's understandable that so many people feel uncomfortable about the strength and size of a horse, because that horse is bigger and stronger than they are. And it's not surprising that people think that *instead of helping the horse understand, they have to make him do things.* It's the "making" part that causes people to use a lot of unnecessary firmness, which is exactly what those horses can't understand. But people just don't know. And when they're using that real poor feel that so many of them have on the start, well, the way they set it up really makes it difficult for the horse. I'm speaking about any horse, but some horses can fill in for a person who lacks experience.

As soon as he learns to get with your better feel, he'll be under your control. If you haven't had an opportunity to learn this, then you'd continue to think you have to *make* the horse do something, instead of *helping* him to do it. Before that can come through, he has to be reassured that he can find what you want without being forced.

No, that unnecessary firmness that's presented by some of the beginning people, or any people, just isn't fitting to the horse. And with those younger horses and troubled horses, especially with them, their mental systems are liable to get much worse in the hands of someone who lacks experience using feel.

I'm always pleased when I see an older, gentle sort of horse next to someone just starting out, and it's real pleasing to me when I see more experienced people handling those young or troubled horses. They're liable to be the ones who can offer those horses an opportunity to pick up a better feel. Generally speaking, those horses will have a lot less mix-up when they aren't handled by people who haven't done much with horses. But you'll see all sorts of combinations out there anyway, and room for improvement in most cases.

Preparing people for this can be quite a problem because it takes in such a variety of things. The student has to have a real strong desire to learn this and they have to be willing to take whatever time it takes. It takes far more time for the person to learn what to do than it does for the horse to learn. This is because the person has so many more little things to contend with. Mainly, it's their thinking that needs to get switched over, especially people who are kind of stuck in their way of thinking. I'd rather think that these people just haven't had the opportunity to learn something different. Or, maybe they didn't think it would fit them too well, but either way, they just haven't met the right people so they can get that feel built in there and get it to operate for them and their horse.

Nobody can help anybody until a person wants something different. People try to get along the best way they know how. And those people, why they're probably going to be all right anyway. They're learning just the same as any of us, one day at a time, one ride at a time, until the pieces of the puzzle start to fall into place. Or they don't. We're in hopes that they will, of course, because that's what's going to be best for the horse, and for the person.

Working with Feel

Regardless of what we're doing with our horses, we're working with feel, and that's true in just about any part of what you're doing with any animal. Whether it's a good feel or a bad feel that's presented to the horse — that feel is what causes him to do what he does because he learns through feel. This is an actual fact and no matter where you start, learning this little particle is real important. One thing's for sure, that horse is uncomfortable when it's a bad feel.

No, if people have the desire to learn this and have a lot of time to practice, there isn't any question that they'll get that better feel sorted out and get it to work for them. Once they've got a start on it, they can get to where they're able to feel of their horse, and get their horse feeling of them pretty good, too. When it's at that point, we can say that we've helped the horse, but our real goal here is to help the people learn what they need to know. I've always felt that what we're speaking about here is just a little different than what others are doing.

Two Kinds of Feel

I spoke a little about this in Chapter 1, but it's important enough that I'm going to speak about it again here. In fact, I'm going to speak about these two types of feel throughout this book. I want to keep reminding people about this because feel is all the horse has to go on *in anything he does.* I think it's good to see something important described in different ways, especially when it's this important to the horse. As far as that horse is concerned, if people forget about this, or don't understand it, then they've missed the most important part. Without feel figuring pretty heavy in there, why that horse, he just gets lost. So, even if it's spoken about in one place in this book, it's liable to be spoken about again in some other part of this book, just in a little different way is all.

In this picture, the girl on the ground is using a combination of direct and indirect feel to send the forehand of this horse out away from her a little more, so the rider can practice counting the footsteps on a bigger circle.

There are two kinds of feel and it is important to understand the difference in them. *Direct feel* is when you have a physical connection between you and the horse and *indirect feel* is when nothing (no physical contact) is between you and the horse. With direct feel, he learns to feel of you from that physical connection between you. With indirect feel, he learns to feel of you and understand what he's supposed to do from the way you maneuver around him. This ties right in with how you present what you intend for him to do. Most people miss out on this, because they really haven't got any idea that the way they're feeling and moving around that horse even matters to him. But that's exactly the thing that matters the most to him.

There's No Magic To This

When an instructor says that they got through to a horse on something because the "horse told him," well, some people think that there's something magic happening, but there isn't any magic in that. None whatsoever. The horse's message got through to that person through indirect feel.

A person who understands (how to interpret) the horse's expressions and movements (or lack of movement) knows that feel goes two ways, not just from the person to the horse, but from that horse to the person, too. Whether or not they can recognize it — or have the time and ability to make a fitting adjustment — it's there for the person to respond to. It's there because that's one of the main ways that a horse gets his message across. The other way he does it is through direct feel, and this sometimes doesn't work out the best where a person is concerned.

Instruction

A person needs to find a good instructor who has more experience at using feel than they do. Or, they could get some supervision. If they have luck in that, a person can get on the right track. But without that happening, well, they just skip right over too much.

The Real Masters Understood Feel

The real masters could follow the feel of a horse regardless of the horse's level of preparation and development. Their judgment was real good because they had studied and experimented with a lot of horses. There were so many different little things they did to see which ones the horse would understand the best. We'll call that different little particles of feel. Some of them *really* understood how to feel of those horses, and they knew how important it was *to go with them*. They understood how to pick up the feel of a horse and blend in with him. Of course, that gave the horse the opportunity to feel of them in return, so they could direct the horse wherever they wanted him go. Those fellas knew how important it was to spend time with those horses on the ground before they rode them.

For example, De Kerbrech, (Faverot De Kerbrech {1837 – 1905}, a French officer in the cavalry of Napoleon III) really understood horses. He had it fixed up so the horse could succeed. There is a way to do this and speaking of it reminds me of something.

One day, a young friend of mine started to ride a young horse up to the saddle room. It wasn't this horse's idea to go up there, not by any means. No, that horse was real concerned about being up at the saddle room, so the boy took another route. He didn't make that horse go there because he knew that horse needed some direction and support while he was that concerned. The concern that horse had about things at the saddle room, why it caused him to have a little extra life available. So, he first got the horse to feeling of him better and they went someplace else together with that excess of energy the horse had built up. It suited that horse real well to get that taken care of. Because of how that boy could feel of a horse, there wasn't any part of the horse getting upset that came in there. Of course, that extra life coming to the surface is always useful when you're helping a horse to understand what you want him to do. Well, it's helpful if you have an idea about how to feel of a horse and get feel applied, I'll put it that way. But this boy could offer a better feel to the horse since he grew up around this way to be with horses and, of course, that's what got them together. After that, the horse was ready to go just about any place for him, and they went right up to the saddle room. All that horse needed was enough time to get with him on the idea through feel.

The first time I read Beudant's book,[1] was in the 1950's. The way he explained things, there was no doubt in his mind about what a person needed to do to get these little things working for them and their horse. Of course, being an officer in the military, he had an opportunity to work with a whole lot of horses and men. He understood real well that those horses needed his students to be real adjustable about how they did things. There probably weren't too many of those fellas he had under him that were raised around horses, so what he was teaching needed to be taught in

---

[1] The book Bill refers to is by Capt. Etienne Beudant ("Horse Training: Out Door and High School," Charles Scribner's & Sons, New York, 1931). Capt. Beudant was an officer in the French cavalry, and served his tour of duty with the French Remount service in Morocco. His book was first published as "Extérieur et Haute École" and was translated into English by Lt. Col. John A. Barry, U. S. Cavalry.

a way that those horses could learn to get along, especially with those fellas who lacked experience. I'd say there isn't any question that Beudant understood the importance of feel.

A Good Instructor Understands People

For someone who's interested in learning about working with horses through feel, it's real important to have an instructor who thinks there's value to every question that is asked. Regardless of how it's asked, there's two ways to answer any question — one way leaves the person with a greater understanding, and the other leaves the person more confused than before. We're in hopes that any answers given will have some meaning that can carry for these people, because they need to become independent of an instructor. For it to have this kind of meaning, those better instructors will always explain things to people in terms of feel. Their demonstrations are going to give people support for those same ideas that are spoken about. People will fall back on what they heard, and the memories of the demonstrations they actually saw.

A Good Student Learns to Observe with an Open Mind

It's also up to all those people who are learning how to handle horses to have an open mind, and be willing to listen, and try to understand what they hear. Then they can make their own judgment about how what they've learned might work for them. Sometimes it can be real useful just to watch and listen to another fella, even if you only come away with an understanding of what you *don't* want to do. But to even get that done, you need a really open mind — *and you need to invest that time.*

I'm in hopes that people can get some extra confidence if they realize that it isn't completely up to them to get this figured out on their own. Life is too short for someone to get all this without some help. People who are a little further up the line working with horses using feel might be willing to help out. This is what we're counting on anyway. A person needs to find a good instructor who understands feel and has it built into their own foundation. People who don't know about feel can learn so much from watching demonstrations of things the horse and person can do together through feel.

The Importance of Gaining Independence From the Instructor

I don't think there's an end to learning if you're going about things in the right frame of mind. I want the people getting started on this to understand things in a way that they can become independent of the instructor, and I think that the better instructors understand my ideas on this. There probably isn't always going to be somebody around to help beginners carry on all the time. Getting independent in your learning process and moving on up the line a little at a time with your horse is real important, because so much of the time those horses are looking to the people for support. This doesn't mean that a person wouldn't go to an instructor for help some time in the future. In fact, it's ideal if a person can check back in with a good instructor every three or four days. But since that's not always possible, I'm in hopes that people will get to a point where they can advance on their own quite a bit.

I think it's great when the student gets to the point where he can pick up more things and do things in a better way than the instructor. That should be real rewarding to the instructor. To see someone that they've worked with pass them up with some new things that they can notice and do with a horse, and maybe even with other people they're helping, why I'd rather think that should make the instructor feel pretty good. It means that other fella's able to help those horses figure out what they're expected to do, which is the main point of any instruction anyway.

Sometimes, it might seem like an instructor is presenting information that is not even possible to apply, and the way some instructors try to show things, it may not be. It doesn't mean that instructor isn't trying to help, and it doesn't mean he doesn't understand feel. He could all right, and he might even be one of the few real good horsemen. When people think they understand what an instructor says, but two months or one year later they're back where they were when they came for help the first time, well, to me, that is a sure sign the instructor missed something when he was working with those people. *It proves that those students didn't understand what the horse needs in terms of feel well enough to move ahead on their own.* I want to try and close up that gap with this book.

Learning From the Horse

A person can learn a lot about feel from a horse, if they're that kind of person. For most people, getting help from someone who has more knowledge is real beneficial. I've seen different types of good horsemen and one is apt to do things a little different than another. No two people are the same. Those people may not all be working at it exactly the same way, but these better horsemen are working at this in a way that helps the horse understand. There's plenty of horse trainers, but not too many are good horsemen.

In my way of thinking, the good horsemen are far above a good many of the people who have themselves listed as trainers. There's quite a difference between the two, I'll say that. The main difference is that most trainers haven't had the opportunity to learn about the feel necessary to become good horsemen. A good horseman knows how to learn from each horse he works with. He knows how to present an understandable feel and he'll adjust to the individual horse whenever it's necessary, so the horse can stay with him mentally. You have to be real careful not to overexpose your horse, which was spoken about in Chapter 1. A true horseman isn't liable to do this very often.

Having Empathy for the Horse

Empathy for the horse is the capacity of a person to be able to feel what the horse feels, to read a situation the same way, and to have an understanding of what the horse is going to do in response to that situation. That's empathy, or feeling with the horse, and it's a real effective way of learning from the horse. Even before the horse does whatever he's about to do, a person who's this way (empathetic) is going to understand the reason a horse does something. It takes time to get that deep knowledge of horses.

Giving Yourself and the Horse the Time it Takes

If you don't have much time, it's best to not start working with a horse. It's going to take time to build feel in a horse. You send a kid to kindergarten just to get him used to things. People can understand that, but then they take an animal that isn't near as intelligent as a human and they expect him to get it all figured out, and start performing things right from the start — *without preparation* — when he's only two or three years old. The way some things are put across to those horses, it's really quite amazing how they can figure out as much as they do. It's not surprising that so many of them get real mixed up, and there really isn't a lot that most people can do with them after an education like that. No, when those younger horses get pushed so far beyond what they can understand on the start, and where their physical systems aren't developed enough to handle it — why it's just a great waste of something that could have turned out a whole lot different, and a whole lot better. That's the sad part.

But, if people feel like they don't have time, they don't have to stop riding, or do anything different than what they want to. It wouldn't be for me to say they shouldn't go ahead. Depending on the circumstances — that horse being the main one — they might get quite a bit accomplished anyway. But if they don't have time, that eliminates quite a variety of things they can do with a horse when a situation isn't working out for the best.

If you're content to just go along there — the horse might be wanting to throw his head around, or poke his nose up, or out, or down, or maybe he'd be liable to go too fast. If you don't have time to learn what to do to avoid that happening, you'll just go along and put up with the situation — whatever it is. If it's okay enough to get the job done, well, I've seen a lot of fellas just go along with it, even though it wasn't the best.

The best way I know of to get most horses to feel of you on the start is to teach them how to lower their heads and to lead up real free. No, I'll say you'd teach this part first *to most horses,* because with some you'd maybe need to do something else before you taught them that. And you'd teach the horse how to back off the slightest amount of pressure, and to stand real still and wait for you. That real still spot is just right in between the two (leading up and backing up) and you'd have no pressure on him *whatsoever*. There's quite a little written about this further up in the book.

Most instructors don't have time to teach it this way, so it doesn't get talked about. This is understandable. A person ought to spend that time anyway, because this is so important to the horse. Now, just reading this doesn't mean that people are going to be able to go out there and have it work for them, just like that. It takes time and a real strong desire to learn this — to the point of getting good at it. A person has to have someone with more experience to show them how to do these things, and then there has to be time enough for things to soak in.

Well, let's think about something else now. We send a kid to kindergarten for eight or nine months just to get him used to school. It's not really about what he learned exactly on one day — it's getting him used to how things are done in a way that they aren't done at home. It's where a kid can learn to adjust to each situation. Learning about feel is like that and the horse needs time for adjusting, too.

"Getting By"

Sometimes things that seem to work out really don't feel right to the horse. And maybe the person gets the same idea that things could have been done in a way that had a better feel to them, too. We call that part "getting by." We'd rather that people didn't have that experience. But sometimes you need to go through that to get to what we're talking about in this book. It's part of the process of figuring things out, and of course there's a lot of value in comparing how things feel, and are, when it comes to handling horses.

If you're working through feel, why it's an entirely different way of going about things than just getting by. Some people like just getting by because they don't like a lot of challenge, and most things can be handled using the methods they're used to. Unfortunately, those are exactly the methods we're trying to stay away from, and that'd be any use of fear and force to make the horse cooperate. This really doesn't fit a horse at all. It doesn't bring out the best appearance in the person either. But not everyone who works with horses likes them, and that's an actual fact. Another fact is that so many of those people who don't like horses really aren't honest with themselves about how they feel towards those horses — and maybe about some other things too. Unfortunately, these people are not concerned about bringing out the best in the horse or themselves. When it's this way there's room for improvement, I'll put it that way. And I'd like to think there is also a place for some hope.

Getting by is what so many people end up thinking is all right because they haven't had the opportunity to see how good it can be when a horse is operating through feel. Another thing that a lot of people have is some luck. Until something happens and they find out how fast a situation can deteriorate, well, it's just luck they've got to go along with the getting by method. But once a person is onto the actual facts about what the horse needs them to understand, then getting by won't fit most people anymore and the luck part doesn't need to figure in there so heavy. We're interested in true horsemanship anyway, which is the most useful kind I know about because it's what the horse can understand.

It's just a great waste of time to do things that the horse can't make sense of, and I'll put it that way because I've had some experience doing this. I was real fortunate to get some help *in time*. I almost didn't get to learn how to get these things applied through feel. These are the things that a horse needs a person to understand, and it's the main reason I'm finally getting it down in print.

Making a Change in Yourself

So many people are just in it (involved with horses) for reasons that don't need to be mentioned. But, I'd rather think that if they had the opportunity to see how beneficial another approach can be — to all of the individuals partaking in it — they might have an interest in making a change in themselves. They ought not to think that investing in any gimmicks to get the job done, whatever that job is, would have lasting value to the horse when it's really the change they need to make inside themselves that would achieve that. Or it could be people who understand what we're talking about just weren't circulating close enough to where other people were when they had some extra time to think about this. And thinking this way is going to take some extra time. It's really a question of how a person wants to spend the extra time they have.

Unlearning

A lot of people are going to start way up the line and miss what needs to take place on the start. They might realize this someday, or maybe they won't. I'd say that the people who've got the hardest learning job ahead of them are the ones who learned a way that wasn't the best way, on the start. It's harder for them because there's usually quite a lot of unlearning that's got to take place at the same time they're trying to sort out this better way. This could be true of learning on any subject, but where you're working with an animal, there's so much variation that takes place in there. We're in hopes that in the future people will want to learn how to handle their horses through feel, right at the start. And, if they have that real strong desire to learn about this way *now*, why they can all right. Even though they might have a lot of unlearning to do, I'm in hopes that the pictures and exercises in this book will be useful in their progress.

Habits Our Horses Don't Need Us to Have

There's some habits that a person can get into that are the start of some trouble spots in the horse, and these are apt to show up later and be spoken about as big problems *coming from the horse*. These are the kinds of habits that people are going to need to unlearn.

One real common habit is the way so many people stand right in front of their horse. They're liable to crowd right in on him at the front, and feed him out of their hand. Horses that have a tendency to nip at a person and crowd up close to them are liable to be the ones that expect to be in line for those handouts. It's sure not the best idea to teach your horse about this, and it could be among the worst.

There's an important line that needs to be in there between a person and the horse. Feeding a horse this way leads to so many other problems that are caused by the disrespect he learns from people who teach him to cross that important line so he can get those handouts. *The actual fact is that when people cross that important line, they are teaching that horse to be disrespectful.* But most people don't realize this.

If you have good feelings for the horse, why there's a lot better ways to show him this than feeding him from your hand. The way I like to teach people to show this to the horse is by teaching them how to feel of the horse. Then the horse can learn to feel of them and the two of them can move up the line together. Things are liable to work out for them real smooth when it's this way.

(It's not the treats that are a problem, it's the encouragement the horse gets to disrespect you and your space in the course of receiving treats that becomes a problem. When your presentation changes, his response to you will change. If he has to reach down to the ground to eat his treats or find them in a bucket, a horse will appreciate them just as much.)

Little Problems People Ignore Lead to Bigger Problems They Can't Ignore

Diamond Lu Collection

This horse is ignoring the feel of the left rein. The young rider is being supervised and the first thing they'll need to do is get that horse's attention. It is real easy for people to miss the importance of this on the start.

People might know about some other little problems, but maybe they've decided that those are problems they can live with. For example, some horses just walk up to you or try to pass you real close and then bump into you. Or there's the horse that just starts walking off while you're still trying to get on, because he hasn't got any idea he's not supposed to do that.

The actual fact is it's those little things that are overlooked by the person that lead up to the horse taking over. Most people don't realize that it's a lot easier to take care of those little things than it is to take care of the bigger things that can happen afterwards.

The information about those little things is right there on the surface for people to notice, if they know what to look for. Most people aren't thinking about them because they think those things are so small they don't matter. They don't realize the horse is letting them know, in so many little ways, that he's confused about what he's supposed to do. There's only so long the horse can go before he decides he's had enough of that confusion.

Kathy Peth

This mare is going through the motions of following the rider's feel, by turning her head and neck to the right. Someone without much experience wouldn't know there's still a spot that needs to be taken care of. From the expression on her face it's clear her thoughts are someplace else.

Some people are going to be aware that even some of these little actions have a disrespectful feel to them, but they haven't got any idea about what to do. And most of them don't have enough experience to know what other sorts of things are liable to develop because these smaller things haven't been taken care of, *first.* It can be real helpful to have an instructor who can point out some of these things, and of course it is a good idea if this person who's supervising has a greater understanding about feel, and learning how to apply it, than the person they're helping.

One thing's for sure: If these smaller things which most people don't think are problems get taken care of, that will head off a lot of the undesirable things that might happen later on. There's another way I'll say this. If people knew how important it was to get these smaller things taken care of down below — before the bigger problems showed up — *those bigger problems wouldn't show up.*

I'm in hopes that people will start thinking about these things, because that's exactly what those horses need them to be thinking about. Even in the small, unwanted actions like the ones just mentioned, there is so much information the horse is giving the person about what he's not getting from them in the way of an understandable feel. That horse needs to get real well acquainted with the better feel a person can offer to him, so that if something happens that confuses him or scares him in the future, he's going to have an understanding of what's expected of him, *through feel.*

There isn't any question that the horse needs support from the person. But, most people don't see how this support part fits for the horse — *in terms of feel* — or for themselves in connection with that horse. For example, people are inclined to overlook the connection between a horse leaving when you start to get on and not understanding the feel you present when you want him to stop, or turn. Most people just don't know about this, and some others don't think they need to know. But they really need to understand this.

It takes an observing person to realize that quite a lot of information is available in those disrespectful parts of that horse that can affect a person's safety. This disrespect is tied to a lack of feel in his foundation. It tells a person what is liable to take place later on that isn't the best, especially when they're sitting up there. It's really quite amazing what a horse will do for you, if he only understands what you want. And it's also quite amazing what he'll do to you if he doesn't.

Diamond Lu Collection series

Experience and Judgment

A horse's actions and the expressions on his face show an observing person quite a lot about what he's understanding *at any point*. What works is going to depend on what's taking place right then, and on what his experiences before that time have been. It will depend on your experience, too. That's where your judgment comes in. But whatever you present to him, you'll be using feel to get your point across and you'd be all the time thinking and understanding that there's some real delicate spots in that feel you're applying that can affect the horse in an undesirable way. Of course you'll try to avoid those spots. These are not the same on every horse by any means, and they aren't even there on every horse, but they could be, and that's what people need to be aware of.

When it comes to talking about this part, a person is liable to have some questions. A good instructor can demonstrate some things with an inexperienced horse and also answer questions. And this can be real valuable to the people who are watching. But if you're on your own, and you haven't had the experience to know what to do to help that horse if you happen to stumble onto a delicate spot, you'd just want to be real careful is all. Here are some things you'd hope to keep in mind as you work with your horse: You'd be sure not to have the lead rope looped around an arm or an ankle. Your body, especially each arm, should be in position to serve its best function to help the horse as the situation changes. You'd hope to not block the horse from doing what you'd just caused him to do. You'd be thinking ahead at least a move or two and always have in mind a place to allow the horse to move. That's because the circumstances can change in a way that really threatens your momentary position of control.

A person who's instructing another fella wants to mention this all right, but at the same time, there are just some things about working with a horse that a person has to discover on his own. And this could be a wreck or something far less concerning, but either way, a person doesn't want to get hurt or position his horse to get hurt. So he'll do whatever he can to avoid that happening, and he'll do this in the best way he knows how.

When Someone Doesn't Have Much Knowledge

When someone doesn't have much knowledge it's all right. Just by being aware of this, you're in a position to gain more knowledge and to get your horse to feel of you. Because when you know where you want to go, and you know what your horse is capable of doing — and by that I mean doing things for you the way you know how to present them to him today — then you'll stay within that range of understanding. You and your horse will learn to go up the line together from that point, and when it's working this way he knows what he can expect from you.

There's an understanding on the horse's part about being with a person, and the feeling of being together with that person is something he depends on. This is so important to the horse, and most people don't realize how lost he gets without this connection. He needs to know what he can expect from you through feel, because that's what feels right to the horse. Even if it isn't much, the horse needs to be sure about it. This can carry him quite a ways, because what a person and a horse have between them is right, if it feels right. When it's this right-feeling-kind-of-way, that is enough to move ahead with, even if that progress seems too small to mention.

One thing's for sure, that horse is aware of the very small things that take place because his survival is tied right to him knowing about even the littlest particles of activity around him. He's going to notice all sorts of feel (direct or indirect) that a person would be liable to miss. The beneficial part to this is that even if it's just some real small thing that's working right, it's enough to continue building on, through feel — so long as the other things you need to complete the job show up.

A Horse's Sureness

For someone who doesn't have much experience with horses, a horse's sureness is what makes him safe to be around. But there's another side to this. No matter how many years of experience or how many horses a person has ridden or trained, if that person doesn't have feel working for them with the horse that's on the end of their lead rope, surprising things could happen. That'd even be the case with a horse that has some sureness.

Experimenting

Like we spoke about before, you need to be experimenting all the time. The way you make small changes in how you set up little projects for that horse can make things a lot easier for the horse to understand. A project could be as simple as seeing if you can get his attention without touching his body. Or you might stand next to him and try to see how little it takes to get him to shift his weight off one foot, without actually moving that foot — just little things like that. (Exercises like this are described in more detail in Chapter 4.) All the time you'll need to be experimenting and adjusting to see what's going to work out the best. This means it should work best for the horse and fit the way that horse is operating and is feeling about things at that time. Of course this takes in quite a lot, but in your experimenting, you'll hit on the things that work best for each of the different horses you're working with. It's not too difficult to find out whether that horse understands what you expect him to do. If he doesn't, well, that's something that shows up pretty quick. It can turn into a real problem. When that happens, you just change what you're doing on the spur of the moment to try and fit him in a better way, through feel.

Setting Things Up to Succeed

To see how someone who's experienced at this gets it to work for them and the horse, why that can motivate a person to try it all right. But it's very difficult for a person to just watch this happen between another person and a horse and then go and get it applied that way themselves. It doesn't happen that way. People who haven't understood the idea of preparation through feel to begin with, are liable to see something done this way and go home and try it once. When they find that the horse didn't understand what they expected of him, they're liable to blame that horse and give up on all this and revert back to what they did before. I know this happens. That's why I'm in hopes that people will *use* this book, so they can continue to improve with their horse. I'm really in hopes that they will want to improve on their try. Because if a person's try doesn't figure in there pretty heavy, why they're going to be lost in this, and that horse will be left to figure things out on his own through guesswork and his instincts of self-preservation.

We're setting this book up for people to succeed. And when they do, that's how those horses are going to be able to come through for them. And, from time to time, those small achievements are going to show up and people could sure call them a kind of success. No, to get this success, there's no question that they'll be starting way down below where most people want to be working their horse. But that person will have it in their future plans to build onto those good spots they get established in that horse's foundation. What a person could call success later on might be something a lot different from what was successful for them on the start, but that's due to things *all the time changing*. Most things that concern a horse change anyway. And that includes your progress.

The Fear of Making Mistakes

So many people worry about making mistakes with their horses. These people seem to hold themselves back by not trying something new, because when they get in that spot, they don't know what to do to make things feel better. If a person doesn't allow for the freedom to risk making a mistake by experimenting, two things are nearly always assured: First, that person's learning process has stopped, and second, their intolerance of their own mistakes nearly always carries over to intolerance of the horse's so-called mistakes. This usually leads to punishment of one sort or another that is rarely understood by the horse. If the horse really understood about the punishments a person has for him, that method would produce lasting positive results. And it doesn't.

From the horse's point of view, when there's a lack of understandable human feel combined with an intolerance of mistakes that he has no idea about in the first place, and where there's punishments added onto that, well, I'd say it just reduces the chances for a meaningful connection between a horse and a human *right down to zero.*

Mistakes are an Important Part of Learning

It's best if a person doesn't get discouraged by the idea of making mistakes or needing to have to start at the bottom, because that's where the horse learns to understand your feel. You build right onto that and you proceed up the line together from there. A person who has spent some extra time thinking about these things ahead of time, before actually getting with that horse they're going to work with, why they aren't liable to stay for too long in one place. They'll be progressing on up the line.

Some Ideas to Go Along with Relearning

The rest of this chapter was written by Leslie Desmond and published in *The Trail Less Traveled* in 1998. I thought we should have it printed here.

Rather than define "relearning" or interpret it's use, I based this article on conversations about learning that I had with several people. They all own horses and have a strong desire to improve their horsemanship.

Four years ago, two riding pals asked me to write an article about learning. I did not consider them students, although one asked for a little help occasionally and my other friend wanted "pointers" a couple of times a year, for which she insisted on paying. I protested her payments until she finally explained that paying for the information meant that she would learn. It was my first exposure to this sort of thinking. Although I really didn't understand it, I wanted to.

They were both good riders who'd learned "the old way." They wanted to make some changes in the way they did things, and to improve the way they handled horses overall. They pressed me to share with them anything that I knew about learning how to *relearn* to ride. I had also learned from someone in the "old school," and the switch to working through feel had not been easy for me. I said I had questions about learning and relearning, too. In fact, I had a lot more questions than answers. This struck me as a good opportunity to ferret out some answers, so I started researching this article right then. It began with one question, and a few days later I asked three other people we knew the same thing: "Do you like learning?"

I was surprised that all of them answered my question the same way — with a question: "What do you mean?" What did they *mean* what did I mean? Apparently, not one person understood the question — not even the friends who wanted me to write the article. It was as if they hadn't heard what I said. So, I rephrased it: "I mean, do you enjoy the process of learning?"

Some wanted still further clarification of the question, and a couple asked me to set parameters so they could give me, I presumed, a sort of qualified answer. But I didn't have any answer in mind. At that point I was simply starting to think about the learning and relearning problems that people have — I include myself in this — and I was doing a little research to get some ideas for a story about it. After more discussion, the answer eventually came out. It was unanimous. They all said, "No," they didn't really like the learning process all that much.

That put my interest in this "assignment" on the upswing, so I asked them, "Why not? What is it you don't like about learning?"

Their answers varied and generated a few more questions from my side. They gave me written recaps of their positions to go over. These really got me thinking. Two of these people were parents, one was a school teacher and two had jobs that involved supervising the work habits and production efficiency of other people. And not one of them said that they enjoyed learning. I knew two of them quite well, and the other three were casual acquaintances. It seemed that at one time or another I had seen all of them feeling good about new discoveries they'd had with their horses, but I could have been mistaken about that. Anyway, they seemed confident in their answers and I didn't doubt them, but it left me feeling confused.

I'll summarize the four reasons they gave for their collective "No" response. At the top of each person's list was the fear of making a mistake. I thought that said a lot more about their teachers than it did about them, and I said so. It seemed to me that this fear could perhaps have come from experiences with other teachers, in addition to their riding teachers. Only one woman was up for discussion on that line of thought, but it didn't go far. I realized then that some people reserve an almost sacred spot for teachers, *even when they are not effective at their jobs.* That's the part that bothered me. Teachers, they all said, are authority figures. I concluded then that trying to learn in a state of fear was more common than I thought. Up to that point, I only knew it had not worked for me.

The second reason they said they didn't enjoy learning was the fear of "being" or "appearing to be" stupid. Those are very different things — "being" and "appearing to be" — but nonetheless, that's what they said. However, these people are not stupid, nor, to my knowledge, do they appear that way. They all are very bright. If anything, they are overachievers.

The third reason, they said, was fear that the learning process might expose them, ultimately, as being *unteachable*. Three of them supplied "evidence" to validate their shared concern. "I don't test well." "Well, I'll never learn it all." "I don't have to be *that* good at it." At that point I have to say that the baffled feeling I had about my little research project was replaced by one simple thought: If the mind is well-stocked with fear-based beliefs and a plan to substantiate them with failure, it pretty much guarantees that learning will be a futile, unpleasant experience. If the hoped-for results are not even imaginable, then what is the point of trying? And then I wondered — Whose responsibility is it to make learning fun, anyway? I still don't know the answer to that.

The fourth reason really knocked it out of the park for me. Two people said that, in addition to one or more of the above reasons, they were also afraid they might become better than their teachers. They said they absolutely didn't want that to happen. Neither one could say why. Bill Dorrance's response to this was, "That's the last thing they should be worrying about. But if they were going to pass up their teacher on some things, why I'm in hopes they'd have an instructor who could be real proud of them for whatever they'd figured out on their own with their horse. That means the instructor had gotten through to them on some real important things, mainly becoming good at understanding about the learning part of things, so they could get independent of that teacher and figure some things out when he wasn't anyplace around there. And another thing that instructor should feel real proud about is that it was *their* student, and not somebody else's, that passed them up because, really, it was that instructor who laid such a good foundation into that student who wanted to get that new knowledge. Or, I'll put it this way: They sure helped that person get some good ways of going about things built in there, solid, on the start."

These informal interviews brought me new insight about the learning process, and a couple of questions. Isn't the twist of self-defeat built into an approach that combines 1) the fear of failure or success, 2) the confidence to pronounce mental and/or physical inadequacy, and 3) the "proven" capacity to fail? How do all those ideas help anyone learn? The messages aren't easy to interpret or reconcile because they don't add up. But I think they are more common than I thought before. How can the horse get a clear message from a rider who has all that going on inside? Even if the horse could fill in well enough to get a clear, positive feel back to the person, that message from the horse would be evaluated according to what that person believed about themselves as a student, anyway. At least it seems so.

Born to Learn

I always thought we were born with a learning frame of mind. The infants and toddlers I've known always appeared to have one, and baby animals certainly do. If left alone, this instinctive capacity to learn becomes a way of being that is fueled by a joyful spirit and strength of purpose. If you look around, you can find examples of it out there. But usually something happens to change it. Sadly, and in very short order, the learning frame of mind we start with seems to diminish or altogether disappear. As we are instructed in the performance of simple tasks and guided towards the fulfillment of even the smallest goals, what some of us learn early on about learning seems to destroy the instinctive capacity to learn efficiently and joyfully. In fact, it appears that even when the learning capacity is still there, some people feel it's safer to avoid student-teacher situations altogether. That certainly puts a cap on learning. After these discussions and a lot of thinking, I can't see how anyone who invests in self-sabotaging ideas like the ones mentioned earlier could derive much benefit from learning situations that involve horses. This is nothing short of a travesty, because there's nothing quite like the time you spend with a horse.

Where "failure" to learn something is the result of one's best effort to learn it, perhaps a few things are missing: A burning desire to learn, qualified help, and enough time to practice.

Bill claims that successful learning requires all three. "Even under the best circumstances, with any one of these elements missing, the process of learning whatever it is that you're trying to learn is apt to be disappointing."

Born to Balance

Consider some of our earliest learning projects. Crying and reaching, for example. What inspires this? Hunger, the need for warmth and physical contact, basic curiosity about the nearest moving object — and there must be other reasons, too. Shortly after we reap the harvest of well-timed crying and reaching, we learn other things that are connected to our survival. On the way up, we learn to crawl, sit up, stand and then we learn to climb. On the trip back down, we learn how to fall, then to fall without hitting our heads, to stumble without falling, sit down, bend over and so on. In short, we learn to focus our attention and to mobilize and direct our energy. *We learn how to balance.*

Most people spend two or three years learning these things. As we developed these abilities, a burning desire to learn them may not have been in the forefront of our awareness. But it wasn't entirely lacking either. Time to practice was essential, and someone to imitate was important, too. It's no different for a colt. By comparison, the equivalent of these basic human maneuvers — and a lot of other great moves — takes a healthy colt that has enough room to move just a couple of days to sort out. And in a couple of months? The moves are mastered.

After these earliest lessons, most of us went on to hold a bottle and then a spoon. Then we started taking off our clothes. No sooner did we get the hang of that than we were taught to put them on again until, somehow, we either survived or thrived in elementary school and social situations throughout childhood. Onwards from there, we learned to look after ourselves, raise families and hold jobs.

Some people went on to become instructors, showing others how to do what they were taught. Understandably, most people teach the same way that they were taught, and the lessons come full circle. I suppose that those who begin teaching without probing into the foibles of their own learning process may pass on to their students whatever they learned about learning — for better or for worse.

Maybe if people are used to feeling awful while they are trying to learn something new, it is worthwhile to leave out that part of future learning episodes. Because open scrutiny of instructors and their teaching methods is rarely encouraged, it seems that we learn to overlook the environment in which we are taught.

Bill suggests that "Maybe we oughtn't do that. A good instructor needs to be able to answer any question that's asked in such a way so that the student can understand the answer. That takes an unlimited amount of knowledge[2]. You need to understand horses and people to be able to do this in a way that's fitting to the public." He continues, "There's an unlimited amount of things with horses that need to be understood. And the instructor — we'll say a good instructor because we really aren't talking about the other kind — why he really wants to help a person so that when they get home they'll have some idea of how to get these things that we're talking about applied, through feel, of course. But this takes time and the process should not be rushed."

Patricia Weedman

Bill on Beaut. He's speaking with a student about how he holds the reins.

The best horsemen say the horse is the best teacher.

Horses learn fast and they learn well. They forgive readily but they rarely, if ever, forget. Perhaps the best horsemen became that way because they valued these qualities in the horse, and could accept important lessons from him. Maybe the best horsemen are simply good students. If they gained knowledge as the horse's student, then it was probably through many hours of observation and from their efforts to instruct him that they did so. I do feel certain of one thing, and it is that the idea of "best" is at best, subjective. It is an abstraction and it is irrelevant to the horse. Over the years, I've known many horse people with a fervent desire to *be the best* who not only lacked the inspiration, but altogether missed the lessons from the horse that are necessary to achieve the oneness with him that would qualify them to be among the best.

Whenever I hear someone say "the best," I think, "The best? According to whom?" A person can only do their best from right where they are, that day, that moment, with the horse they have right then, in whatever circumstances they find themselves. If we are going to accept the verdicts of those who would judge our horsemanship, then who is more qualified for that job than the horse?

Putting notions of "good," "better" and "best" horsemanship aside, you can always find a good horse to buy. Well-trained horses are a little harder to afford, but good horsemanship is not for sale. For some people, good horsemanship might involve a decision about their own frame of mind. For others, the definition of good horsemanship could be the process of learning to live in the moment and to learn the lesson of the moment, like a horse does. Good horsemanship has its unpleasant

---

2 Bill means the potential for never-ending expansion of knowledge "due to the person having a wide open mind."

moments and there are certainly times when one's best efforts yield less than the "best" results. I think of good horsemanship as an approach to learning that combines the flexibility of thought and actions with a willingness to experiment and to indefinitely postpone negative judgment. Judgment of the horse, of oneself, the previous owner, the last trainer — all of them.

Perhaps, in the process of experimenting, we could try to replace the fear of making a mistake with a relaxed, upbeat approach to trial and error. If we follow the path that far, we might decide to take another lesson from the horse, who never seems to learn much when he is afraid, except to be more afraid. And then, too, there's what Bill said about the three essential elements that are needed: *A burning desire to learn more about the thing you love, whatever it is; a good teacher; and plenty of time to practice.* "Those things *really* need to figure in there, especially where it concerns things that a person learned to do on the start that just aren't the best."

Chapter 3:

HOW I GOT FEEL WORKING FOR ME AND MY HORSES

Patricia Weedman

I FIGURED THINGS OUT THE WAY A GOOD MANY OTHER PEOPLE DID. I wasn't a genius, so I had to learn it. The time when it would have been the most valuable to me was when I was younger. There wasn't anybody around back then who talked about how you started a colt, or rode a horse or roped one either. My horses didn't understand what I wanted a lot of the time, but I always knew they could do better for me than they did.

Oh, there were some real knowledgeable people out there all right, and some of them were doing a far better job than others. But no one said much about what you did — and that's if you were on the right track, or you weren't. You just went out there on your own and did the best you could. I liked our horses, so I had a real good feeling towards them, regardless of what they did. I felt that if they only understood what I needed them to do, why they'd do even better.

So, back then, it was up to the person to figure out how to apply this feel. At one time I didn't even think about the word "feel." I was just kind of pulling on those horses. Things were way off in the timing and just about everything I did wasn't done very well. But just because the horse was doing different than what I expected him to do, that didn't mean I was going to punish that horse, because I kind of liked our horses. And it seemed to me like they really were trying. As I look back now, why there isn't any doubt that those horses were trying. It was the way that I was presenting my feel to them that made it difficult for them to understand what I wanted.

I Missed the Little Things, On the Start

I used to think that I better get my horse going in the direction I wanted him to go, right on the start. When it didn't work out like I wanted, why I thought that horse had just figured out how to get by me. Maybe some other people have ideas like this, and I rather think that they do. Well, there is a lot of truth in that, because if my horse didn't go where I wanted, and I didn't help him go someplace else, he'd sure take over and go where he was planning to go. He sure did that. And that is always bad for the horse because he learns that taking over is all right, and the disrespect that goes along with that gets built into even the littlest things that you do with the horse. This can lead to a situation that might surprise a person.

After working at these things for some time, I got to thinking it's really just a lot of those little things that are getting by the person, and that sure is the lead-up to the horse getting by them. Most people don't have any idea about this, or know that it's a lot easier to take care of those little things than it is to take care of those bigger things that can happen afterwards. I didn't used to know about this either, and I almost didn't live long enough to figure it out.

See, on the start, what I missed was all those little things that were there to let me know that horse was about to get by me in the first place. That information was right there on the surface, but I didn't always know what to look for. I used to think that some of those things were so small they didn't matter. What I didn't realize was that the horse was trying to let me know, in so many little ways, that he was just confused about what I wanted him to do.

There Wasn't Much Teaching Going on in the West in Those Days

In those days, there wasn't anybody teaching about the Western part of riding. English riding appeared to be way ahead of Western riding where formal instruction was concerned. They had instructors for that English style, but it seemed to me like their horses had far less to do than ours. Most of those horses were going straight ahead in their jobs. The Western horse had to stop and start going on the spur of the moment for the jobs he had to do, and these horses didn't have much time at all to learn how to maneuver and turn in every direction like they needed to. And when you're sitting up there, why that word "every" takes in quite a lot.

I Watched How Other Fellas Did Things

When I left Oregon and came to California in November of 1931, there was a lot of knowledge I didn't have, that's for sure. I worked at a few different ranches over the years, just starting colts and working with cattle. And I spent time visiting some ranches in Nevada where my older brother worked. I was offered work, but it was just as cold there as it was in Oregon. So much of the appeal I felt California had to offer was that you could ride a horse all year. A fella could work outside without the problems you'd run into so often in that colder country. Besides, my younger brother, Fred[1] was down here. He and another fella had some horses that they could

---

1 Bill's younger brother, Fred, passed away in 1940.

get to maneuver real good for them. And from them I found out some better ways to handle a horse.

One bachelor fella I knew had a little camp over in San Juan. He'd started some colts, and he did day work at different places around there and he braided quite a bit. I went out to visit with him sometimes, and I'd stay there with him when I was between jobs. He never asked his horse for anything beyond what that horse was capable of doing for him. There was quite a bit that he didn't have knowledge about, and of course he didn't speak about that. But he didn't say much about what a fella would do to get things working like he had going with his horse either. That's the way it was back then. It wasn't that it was a secret, it's just that if you'd been asking quite a few questions about anything, they'd think you were a little on the dumb side, and for sure no one wanted to be in that class.

It was amazing just how much that fella did have going for him. The main thing he had was a good feel to offer his horse. We didn't have a word for that back then, it's just the way he could operate. That looked real good to me.

There were a couple of other fellas in San Juan. One was partly Mexican and the other was mostly Mexican. They were in their 50's when I was about 25. They could really handle horses. That's because they both really understood a horse. One didn't sit a horse too good *at all.* No, he didn't look too ordinary sitting up there. And I could almost not get past that in my thinking, but those horses told me quite a bit about how effective he was, so I learned what I could just from watching those two.

Then I saw quite a few useful things happen with another fellow and his horses. He managed a ranch over in Hollister (California) and I worked for him. I'd give his name, but he's got family here and no one would even think he'd been much of a horseman anyway. He didn't have boots, and he didn't wear anything a cowboy wears — not one thing. I don't think he owned any of that stuff. But he was an artist with a rope. He was plumb good at that. *And he had such a good feel of a horse.* His dad owned a real nice buggy team and he was the only boy out of the three or four boys in the family who was allowed to drive that team. I never saw him in action on that, but we put up a little hay with a team in Hollister and he never *made* that team do anything. They were real happy to work for him. Everything he did with those horses went real smooth, and that made a big impression on me.

I remember watching him one day on a real upset kind of horse. I was riding up the road and just prepared to do a little visiting with him or anyone who might be up that way when I saw him on this horse. They were not going along so good by this place just on the side of the road. It was where they'd grease up the machinery and work on mechanical things for the haying operation. There was mechanical things stacked up all over and that horse had no plans to walk by there. I watched this fella and never saw him force that horse one time. It was all done through feel — real slow and gentle — and the main thing was, I could see how really effective it was to handle a horse that way. He was a good horseman. In not much time, without any fuss, that real scared horse just got over being scared. Then they walked on up the road.

I Went to the Shows and Rodeos, and I Read Some Books

When I used to go up to the rodeo or to a horse show someplace, I'd always watch what some others did with their horses. If I got home in time, I would go out and get a horse and saddle it up so I could practice the things I saw that day, and try to get my horse to learn to be better. It felt good to do that. By then I had read Beudant's book, and of course because he was more experienced, I wasn't to the point where he was. But I think we are all headed towards the same direction with our horses, trying to get them to be more accurate and responsive to us.

I read about some techniques other people had tried, but they were far from what I needed. When I got that information, why I didn't have much to go along with it except the desire to work with the horse. I didn't have much knowledge then. I tried to use what I knew and get it applied in there, but that new method made quite a little use of force. It didn't fit me or those horses real well, and those war bridles were supposed to be the answer for so many problems that people had with their horses. They had some instructions for that. To my way of thinking, if you were going to train a horse in one of those rigs, why you'd need to have enough understanding about how to use one of those gimmicks so as to not need it in the first place. I did some testing and experimenting to modify that approach quite a lot and that's how it got to be better than nothing, which was about all I had to go on before. One modification I made to that, for example, was a lass rope halter instead of a war bridle. (See Chapter 4, Part 2.)

Patricia Weedman

Bill is using a lass rope halter to teach this 5-year-old gelding to lead up at the clinic in Pebble Beach, California in 1997.

There's no place for war when it comes to a horse and there shouldn't be any mention of it. But for a lot of people who start to work with a horse, that's just exactly what it becomes — the war with the horse is on all right. When that happens, that's the last straw.

My Two Biggest Lessons

There were two things that happened that I can say were the most important things that helped me to improve my horsemanship — that being the proper way to sit on a horse, and learning to feel of those feet. I'd never have understood it as well without these things, and in some ways I guess you could say that until I learned them, I was really just getting by the best way I could.

How I Learned About Better Posture on a Horse

Let's just say there wasn't any time in my life that I was content with just getting by. I always felt there was room for improvement, and I wanted to help my horse but I didn't understand how to prepare myself to help him. I certainly didn't get it all at one time and I was fortunate that it came kind of gradual, anyway. Now and then, some little things just showed up. Like a girl I rode with one time in the Carmel Valley.

She never rode Western on a ranch before. She came from the city and rode English where she'd worked at a stable outfit. I was about 35 years old and I'd been riding horses all my life. I was riding a young horse that day and he was really on the buck. I hadn't understood the preparation that this horse needed and he was real unsure about things. He was especially unsure about me. I knew he could get lost pretty easy and just go to bucking at any time. I claim every horse knows how to buck, it's just that some will do a better job of it than others. This horse was accomplished, I'll put it that way.

Well, this lady said she'd been to riding school. I didn't know much of what else to talk about except horses, and she was a real friendly sort of person. I remember sitting on that horse while we went along there, and I had a brace in my legs and my butt was back against the cantle and my shoulders were really pitched forward, because that was the best way I knew to be ready in case that horse went to bucking — which could have been anytime. When I asked her what were some of the first things she taught those fairly young kids, why she said it was posture on the horse. I'd never given that any thought. I asked her, "What is the better posture on the horse?" Because right then, why I was pretty sure I didn't have it. Well, this nice lady wasn't about to offend anybody, so she talked about something else.

We went along there a little bit, just checking the stock in the field. It was a pretty big field. I decided maybe she hadn't understood me, so I asked her again. I spoke right clear to her, I mean I was real direct and everything. I asked her, "What is the better posture on a horse?" And she kind of smiled and talked about something else. I knew for sure she'd heard me that time and for some reason I kind of felt like she didn't want to talk about it. So I said, "I seem to be having quite a little difficulty finding out from you about having better posture on a horse." She really smiled then.

She said, "It's just like it is when you're standing on the ground. Your shoulders are balanced above your hips, and you have a little curve forward in your back. You're

Diamond Lu Collection

This young fella is helping a less experienced rider learn how to sit deeper in the saddle. This kind of supervision can be reassuring to someone starting out, even if the person helping is in the same range of age. Where horses are concerned, the age of a person doesn't matter too much, as long as the message gets through.

standing balanced and your feet are in under you where they should be in order to get your hips balanced right over them. When you're walking along in good form, your body is fairly balanced on the horse, and it's sort of like it is when you're standing on the ground."

I wasn't brave enough to try it right there in front of her. Of course it would have been a great opportunity to talk and learn more about it, and I wish I hadn't missed that chance. But I wanted to try it and right up ahead where the road split around a big hill, I knew there'd be about a 20-minute ride around the loop before I saw her again. I told her to go around there one way and just check on things while she was riding along, you know. Then I went around the other way and as soon as she got out of sight, why I pulled myself up and rode the way she said and it felt quite good to me. And after that day, whenever I thought about it, I did that. And it felt good when I did. When I sat up straight the brace came out of my legs. Of course my horse felt that and he just started to feel real good to me. Before that, there were times when I got caught off guard a little bit and I'd rub my tail bone raw on the cant board (cantle), and I thought maybe there was something wrong with that saddle. A fella's backside can get so it's just real sore when he's not sitting in that saddle right and his horse gets on the buck, but of course, we aren't born knowing the right way to go about that.

Mindy Bower

The posture on this fella looks real nice because he's balanced just right and he's not interfering with his horse. His shoulders and hips and heels are lined up just the way you'd want to be when you're riding. You can see where there's a float in the reins, and it's always desirable to leave that in there when you can.

Time went along and it felt better to me to sit that way and most of the time I did. The ride I had that day changed the way I rode from then on. The real sad part about it was that I never saw that girl again to tell her what a great thing she'd done for me. If that nice lady happens to read this book, I want to thank her right here for what she did for me. It's on account of her that I've been able to help a lot of other people. And that really means a lot to me.

How I Learned About the Timing of the Feet

Right after World War II, I rode with a young fellow and he was on a big, heavy horse with a heavy stride. There was not much life in the horse at all. Those big feet

WHEN A PERSON HAS HIS BODY BALANCED AND LINED UP RIGHT, AN EXCESS OF PRESSURE DOESN'T COME INTO THOSE REINS WHEN THE HORSE IS TROTTING, OR ANYTIME.

SOMETIMES A RIDER MIGHT HAVE TROUBLE GETTING THE STIRRUPS LONG ENOUGH SO HE CAN GET HIS LEG TO HANG JUST RIGHT AND STAY UNDERNEATH HIM.

just thumped down hard on the ground and seemed like every step just might be the last step he took. The one I was riding that day was one of the nicer horses I ever rode — just as smooth and as soft as could be. She was real willing to pick up your feel. The fella I was with knew that I could improve my riding, but he also knew by the looks of me that I wasn't really with the horse as much as I could be. But he didn't know how to explain this so that I could understand it.

He said the horse I was riding was a nicer kind of horse with a nicer feel, and I agreed with him. I knew it. He was talking about really getting with that horse and riding the feet with a feel. So much of the time before that, why I'd been just sitting there. We separated to check different parts of the field and I started counting off the steps after that. A little while later we traded horses and then I was on the old slow poke. I kind of discovered that I wasn't traveling with those horses in the best way I could. So, I started counting with the horse's steps. I counted 1-2-3-4 when I thought they came off the ground. I found I was late on the start and was counting when they hit the ground.

There were no distractions if I shut my eyes, and when I'd pay attention to just one foot, then I could get it. I got my body shaped up to direct that foot as it was coming off the ground. Say if I wanted to turn the horse one direction or another, I started to get in time with that foot as it lifted up, instead of when it was going down. Because of the way I was doing it at first, why that old slow horse had all his weight right down on that foot and couldn't lift it up for me anyway — not until the other feet got arranged so that he could. See, I was late in the timing when I tried to direct that foot someplace and it was going back to the ground. So of course that horse had no idea what I expected of him when that rein would come tight and his foot was just heading back down to the ground. It was pretty important when I learned to put that foot someplace as it was coming up, because that's when it hardly weighed anything. I could move it one way or the other and the horse didn't offer to resist at all. He needed a place to put that foot down anyway.

After that I realized the importance of following the feel in the motion of that horse, and I did a lot of experimenting. I tried moving my arms in time with his shoulders, and of course his back leg motion got my whole body moving. There's a different feel back there in those hind feet, because the seat of your saddle will raise right up and forward, and tip just a little to one side or the other with every step. Another thing I tried to do was pay attention to see which one of my hips was getting pushed up when he moved a back leg forward. I realized it was that motion of him picking up that back leg and bringing it forward, up underneath himself, that really moved me around. I kept track of that in my mind until my body just understood the feel of those back leg motions when they came up, or down, or anyplace in between. After some time, it got to be natural for me to operate right along with that horse. I was able to just go with his movements and then there wasn't a lot of extra thinking to do. Before that, I was just sitting up there and missing a lot of opportunities the horse had for me.

When I'm helping someone, I ask them to try counting out those steps like I learned how to do. I found out that if I just started with a front foot, let's say the right front foot and then, I'd say to myself, "one" as the foot came up. To get in time with that front foot, it sometimes helps to look down and see that motion in that shoulder. Before I got this figured out, I didn't realize how much motion there is in those shoulders. After you see how that goes, you'll feel it better with your eyes closed. A fella has to be sure not to ride under one of those low oak trees at that time. Maybe some people would like to have another person lead the horse while they try this, so they can feel more relaxed. And anyone who's liable to grab those reins and jerk on the mouth when their eyes are closed ought to be led, regardless, because it's real important to keep that horse from getting confused. But however you do it, when you get with that one front foot, then you'd go to the other, and then progress the rest of the way around the horse to the back feet until you can feel all four feet coming up, and going back down. This way you learn to feel of his whole body.

Learning anything, especially where a horse is concerned, is really quite a lot of work. But I really wanted to understand more about those feet, and understanding how those back feet operate was harder for me than getting onto the timing of the front feet. So, to get better at understanding about the hind feet, I'd just listen to them real close. Maybe I'd walk that horse over a bridge, or walk him on a tar road. When you do this, your ears start to work better. That sound is so important, because on the start not many people know if those back feet are in the air or not, and

Diamond Lu Collection

When you are first learning how to count the feet, it helps to have someone lead the horse so you can concentrate. This older horse is a good teacher for these young children, who understand the basic ideas, but don't have a lot of experience getting feel applied yet. It appears that they are off to a pretty good start because they are all relaxed and seem to be focused on their jobs.

Diamond Lu Collection

If you weren't raised around horses, it's helpful if you can learn to post or sit the trot while someone leads your horse at first. This way you can learn to keep your balance up there without hanging on the reins and the mouth to stay on. Surprising things can happen sometimes if that's how you go about riding a horse, so it's best not to do that.

what you observe through sound will help you in your speculations about the placement and timing of those feet.

Diamond Lu Collection

This young boy is learning how to shift the weight back and step the front leg out to the side as it comes off the ground.

I found that the more accurate feel I had to offer the horse, the less "trouble" he offered me, and it wasn't because he did something different. And that idea of a horse being a problem for a person is really not the best way to think of the horse anyway, but still that's what some people do. No, that horse was able to improve because I was understanding his movements. I was working from a better place in my understanding of the actual facts about the horse, and was able to help him when he needed some support. That felt real good to me, and of course there's no trouble when there's understanding. I could say that I learned to time my request for his feet to move with that individual horse's ability to do that, so he could follow the feel of the directing I was doing there. When those horses started to understand my feel and timing, they did whatever I needed them to do, just like I wanted. Things started to work out for me and my horses when I could move those feet where I needed them to go, but I had to get with them on the start.

How I Learned When to Ease Off

There was a fella who was having a problem with his horse. He was trying to get that horse to settle down and go slower. And I could sure understand why he wanted that, because that horse was really hepped up and he couldn't get much done in his job with his horse going that way. But I knew the horse, and the firmness that fella was using really bothered him. I told him that this was going to be a long, drawn-out job if it was taken care of that way, using that much firmness.

It isn't so easy to describe in writing just how much firmness to use and when to use it. I experienced a time when I used too much firmness myself. The way I'd been getting it applied just caused this horse to think about that firmness, and not about the slowing down part that I had in mind. Our minds were really far apart on the plan I had for slowing him down, so I had to experiment a little to see what would get that horse to switch his ideas around. I rode him as light as I could. I found that he wasn't bothered as much when I got closer to him in feel, and by that I mean the way our bodies were moving together in time when he was galloping around there. I went with him on it. And when I was pulling on him and he tried to push up against that bit, I let him.

It wasn't a feel that I would hope for and there's some people, if they'd seen this, might have said I let the horse run away, but what a person called it wouldn't matter. The actual fact is that's what I needed to do — because I had to adjust to fit the horse. I needed to get with him right where he was, right then. All the extra firmness that I was using before was so bothering to that horse's mental system. In that frame of mind, he couldn't possibly understand what I wanted him to do for me. It was way too much for him.

Looking back on it now, why I see that I was just getting him riled up. It was just so bothering to him, to the point where it was real difficult for him to try to do anything except resist my feel. If I'd only known this better way, I'd have understood that he was really trying to get with my feel on the start. That horse really wanted to get with me, only I didn't know about that part of the horse's capacity, even in thought. *That's what I'd missed.*

With as little as I had to offer the horse then, why he couldn't do much thinking. What I needed him to think about was settling down, and I was in hopes that he would. But that idea was no place near his thoughts then, and it takes thought for a horse to settle when he's so bothered on the start, or anytime.

As we went along there we were going quite a lot faster than I had in mind, and I started using less and less firmness as we went along, and he started to settle down. The reason being, I was getting with that horse, and by that I mean moving in time with those feet and his whole body. And because I got with him, he started looking for a better way to get along and I was in a good position right there to help him find it. The important thing is, that change had to come in myself so I could be there to help him *when he got ready*. Those are the main things people need to understand. Right now, there's a need to mention that it takes a lot of knowledge from actual riding experience to be able to do this from the horse's back. Someone without this experience can get the same changes working for them on the ground, and that will carry over to their mounted work if they can get some good help. Without a lot of riding experience and some good help, things might develop in a way they wished they hadn't, I'll put it that way.

At one time, there wasn't any way I could have done this because I didn't know about it. Even after I did understand it, the actual facts of how to get it done came gradual. A fella's really pleased when an opportunity comes up so he can test out what he thinks he understands. Then, there's another way to think of this too, and that's the importance of being able to adjust to fit each horse. That's what it takes, an adjustment. And that part comes from a person having an adjustable frame of mind. Some people are going to be better at this than others. See, that firmness a person comes in with might have been just what was needed for the horse you were working before this one. I learned that firmness is what some horses need, and it's what some never need.

That day, I had a snaffle bit on the horse that was going way too fast, but it could have been anything and it wouldn't have mattered.

It Can Work Another Way

Another time, I had a real good little horse. He was in the bridle. You could say that for me he was well settled. He had a lot of fire in him, but he was a horse that could really stick close to a person, and with me, he did. One day I'd got a late start behind eight or ten other fellas, and some of them turned off and headed over to another place. When I started out, this horse really wanted to catch up with those others. He didn't want to feel of me, he wanted to go.

So I got him to going and kind of circled around a little. I'd bring him out in a circle one way and then the other. We came to a spot there where the cattle had passed through when it was muddy. It was still muddy in those foot tracks but the rest of it was hard as rock. He was coming around in there and he stubbed his toe and fell flat down. I got off him and out of his way and he got up. When I got back on him, he acted like nothing had ever happened at all. He was just as quiet and calm as he could be. I just had a float in those reins and he just walked on to where we were going in the first place, and never acted like he'd ever been stirred up or anything. The horse didn't get hurt and I didn't either, so it was real amusing. I thought he would still want to go a little too fast, but he'd changed his mind.

That was an unusual thing to talk about. We need to talk about feel some more.

The Connection Between Posture and Going Too Fast

I tried slowing a horse down one time by galloping him and letting him find a slower pace. It was in the winter and the ground was soft because we'd had a lot of rain. I galloped him around this knob on a hill and I was sitting on him in the easiest place for me to sit — and that was forward. I was actually encouraging the horse to go forward and I never thought about that at the time. There were times when he was looking for a way to slow down but my position on his back wouldn't support his inclination, which is really too bad because he wanted to get with my idea, and I realize that now. I found out I needed to sit in a way that would discourage him from going too fast, and if I'd only known about that then I could have helped that horse a lot, because he wanted to slow down.

Another fella rode that horse too, and he rode him enough to know that he was a difficult horse to get slowed down. He never got the slowness instilled in that horse, and I didn't either. But the way I was trying to work with that horse was way beyond what I was capable of understanding then anyway. If I had understood more about feel then, that horse would have slowed down. But eventually I was able to apply it. I finally got it figured out on my own, but I didn't learn it from that horse. I learned it from another horse that had the same problem, only it was easier for him to make the mental changes that needed to come through in order for those feet to slow down. I built onto that knowledge with the faster horses I rode after that. I learned the importance of how and where to sit, depending on what you want the horse to do.

I Rode a Lot of Horses That Went Too Fast

One time I took some advice from a fella about a certain horse that was wanting to go too fast. That fella told me to just take him around in a circle. Well, I was taking that horse around in a circle all right, and instead of following that horse real close there and staying with him on the start, why I was really just asking that horse to go fast — too fast. And instead of learning how to feel of me, which he couldn't do because I had no idea then how to feel of him, why he just got real good at running fast in a circle. I didn't get much accomplished that way and the horse learned not one thing about slowing down from that. Later, I figured out this fella was just talking about grinding the horse down. That way he'd get plumb tired and he'd want to slow down because he was wore out. There's not much horsemanship in that approach, but a fella will do this sometimes, if that's what he knows how to do. One thing's for sure, it gets a horse real strong and builds his wind up so he can go further the next time. That's one thing I found to object to in that way of slowing a horse down. But the main reason I was continuing to look for a better way, was because that horse didn't have *any idea* that I wanted him to slow down using that running around in circles method in the first place. That's the part that was bothering me.

If it was up to him and he was out there in the pasture galloping on his own, why I knew he could just stop any place he wanted to, just by doing it. I knew that. And I knew that he could do better for me, if he only understood what I needed him to do. If I'd been able to get my idea across to him, why he could just slow those feet down one at a time, or all of a sudden too, and when one of them finally didn't come up, then none of them would, and you'd call that a stop. A horse can do that right when you want him to if you know how to get him prepared to understand you. It doesn't have to weigh anything in your hands, not more than what those reins weigh, and he can look as natural as if he'd just stopped on his own, without you sitting up there on his back. The time between when you decide you want those feet to stop, and when they actually do stop, can be just the time it takes to have that thought — when you've got feel working for you.

What I needed to have been told was to take that horse and step him around just as slow as that horse would step. Thinking back on it, I know I was wrong to let that horse go that fast because I got him so mentally stirred up, he didn't know where he was with his feet. When he went fast he was getting ahead of me, and no more than I knew about feel then, why I was just pushing him way out there ahead of me and neither one of us were in the best place. But, it wasn't often that I had anybody around who was more experienced than I was, so it was a slow process.

It All Started to Get Clear for Me — And My Horses Started to Improve

After I got onto better posture and the timing of the feet, I found it was important to get a horse to mellow up. I already spoke about this earlier in this book, but it's real important, so I'm going to speak of this again. That mellow feel is really more about the way his mood and his mind are, but there's a place in there where his body takes part in his understanding of this mellow feel. It's when he isn't pushing on you at all. His head doesn't come up and it takes a normal position.

Right around this same time, I learned the value of building in that cornering effect. On the start, it's better to teach him how to corner (bend left and right at the poll) at the standstill when you're on the ground. I'd bring the nose around one way or the other just a little. When that got good, it was the better foundation for doubling a horse. I learned how to get those horses flexible and responsive, so I'd always have that in place to rely on, in case I needed it. That cornering feel carried right on up the line, for whatever I happened to be doing and, when I needed it, I had a lot more control of those horses at the walk, the trot and the gallop. It was real helpful for me in the jobs I had to get done on horseback.

When all those things got to be sort of natural for me, why I started really watching other people when they were riding. Some of them looked far better than others.

I'll Never Forget the Way That Boy Rode

It was pretty soon after I got these things figured out that we were moving some cattle. A man and his 14-year-old son were working in the hay field. The boy really loved to ride and he talked his dad into letting him go with us to move those cattle. Getting to go with us that day was so important to that boy — just to be a part of it, and to be driving those cattle. That boy probably had as good a way of moving around afoot as anybody I've ever been around. It was just natural for him, and it carried right over to his riding. That day he sure wasn't riding the best horse, but he was right with that horse all the time. That boy never went beyond that horse's limitations. He helped that horse to step up and turn cattle, and to slow down. He was using his legs to get that horse to maneuver, and he never got the horse off balance with the reins. I'd watch everybody that was on a horse and that helped me. I was the manager for the ranch so I had a lot of other things to do, but I could never forget the way that young boy rode. I never knew his name and I never did see him again.

Winning at the Salinas Rodeo and Learning at the Cow Palace

I used to have a horse that I wanted to use as a stock horse for the show, but then I realized there was a problem because I didn't know how to stop him. That was before I learned how to get those horses prepared. As I've spoken about, this took some time. After that, I did some showing and I was up against the pros. I had a horse that was good, but I didn't have the time to work my horse like the rest of those guys did. It takes time to get a horse in good condition. Those guys had the time to ride a lot and practice on good horses in a good arena. Some had time to work those patterns. I didn't have the time to do that, or to get my horses in tip-top shape either. I had a one-man ranch is why. But I kept them light and in the bridle, and I wasn't forcing them into anything, like the turns or the stop. I had to have a better horse than a lot of those guys, so he could fill in for me. My horse had to outwork the other guy's horse. We did that.

(In 1948, Bill won the Hackamore Class at the Salinas Rodeo on Sparkey, a 4-year-old gelding. In 1957, he won the Bridle Class on Patrick, a 6-year-old gelding that Bill says was "the best riding horse I ever had." G. S. Garcia saddles were awarded to him in both events.)

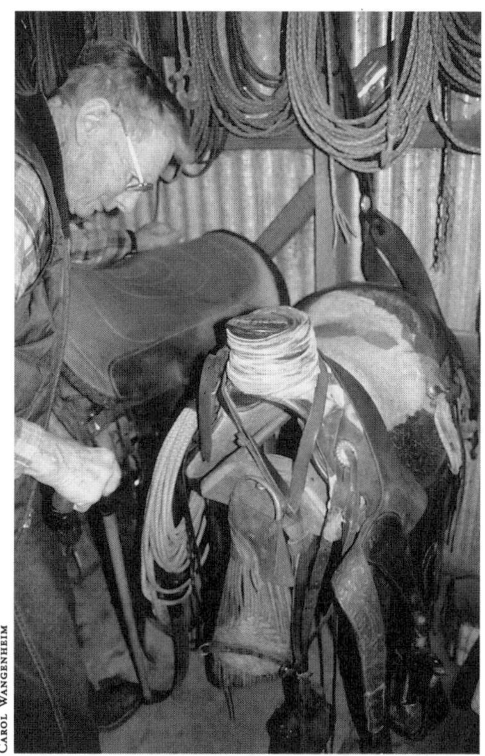

Carol Wangenheim

Due to my left hip getting replaced, I had to stack some extra padding on the seat of my saddle. The sheepskin's about rubbed off there now, but that saddle has really held up good for me. I won it in the Hackamore Class at the Salinas Rodeo back in 1948. It was made by G. S. Garcia.

Diamond Lu Collection

When you have the mane cut this way, a fella'd know a horse was already going in the bridle, so he could ride her that way if he wanted. If it was trimmed clear off in front of the saddle, there'd be a good chance that horse could go in either the snaffle bit or a hackamore, but nowadays there aren't as many people riding in the hackamore as there used to be. The other reason it's nice to trim your horse up is so there won't be any doubt that the horse belongs to someone.

I went up to the Cow Palace in San Francisco a couple of times. I took Patrick. We never came in first up there, but we were never out of the money either. One of the main things I did learn from going there was that those judges were missing something, and they're still missing it today. They all cared so much about speed. I tell you, it's hard to find a judge who knows how to handle a horse. Even back then a fella could see that there were so many mistakes being made with the horse, and especially in those shows.

In the 1960's, Some Fellas Really Understood the Importance of Feel

I judged a little, and I could have gotten my card and all that, but that was over 30 years ago. I wanted to get all those young guys started on working their horses slow and accurate. Back in the early 1960's, me and another fella got going on this idea pretty heavy. We called our new group the California Western Cow Horse Association (not to be confused with any organization that exists today). We had 25-30 people those few times, it was maybe about a year we kept getting this group together. We tried to meet twice a month when that could work out, but not everybody could devote the time to it that they wanted. These guys were onto it though, I mean they really understood the importance of the slow work. A lot of them were working stockmen is why, and they liked the idea of getting together to work the horses real slow, just for accuracy and feel, and not for speed.

We got a camera and we made some home movies of the rides, so we could look at these rides later and talk things over. I don't have any idea where those movies are now, but I wish I knew. Me and this other fella were going to judge it, and then teach those others how to judge this other way that we're speaking about here in this book.

The Pace Picked Up Again

People tried out this slower way, and talked a lot about it. For a while it lasted, and we were looking for someone to carry the torch for the Association. For a year we tried to find the right person, but I didn't know who to get and then it all died down. I was real disappointed. Me and this fella were going to help anyone who could have done that. It was a good idea, and it would have been so good for the horses if we'd found someone. But we couldn't find anyone with the time to devote to it. If you looked around now, you could probably find someone who could carry it on. There really needed to be someone to organize it. Anyway, after that, it seemed like the pace picked up a little every year until those horses got to being fast again.

Nowadays, it's too fast for those young horses. People are making them go much too fast, especially on the stop and in those turns. Their mental and physical systems just don't hold up long that way.

There's Room for Improvement at the Futurities

When the Snaffle Bit Futurity first started here in California, so much of it really came from the guys in Nevada. Fellas from here would travel up for the Open Stock Horse Class. They started taking their better bridle horses there, and then they got the idea of the snaffle bit, but they worked those horses too fast in those. I told them, "I hope that whatever you do, just don't go in for speed." I told them I hoped that they'd go in for the nice way these young horses can handle instead. For a while it worked. Those fellas, some of them, why they really knew about the value in this, because they could feel it in their horses. A lot of these guys had real jobs for their horses, too, so they knew it was beneficial for every day. But every year it got faster and faster. And today, of course, why a lot of what goes on in those shows doesn't fit those young horses at all. That's why I say that there's still room for some improvement.

If they had 150 points to use in the Snaffle Bit Futurity, they shouldn't judge for speed unless you had everything else. Speed could be marked as an added bonus if you already had 100 points for the rider, and 50 points for the horse. The horse would be judged on how he watched and worked the cow. I'm really in hopes that the people who train horses for these shows, and the people who judge them too, can see the value to this. But I don't know that I'll live long enough to see that change.

Getting Together with Beauty

At the time Beauty was brought here in 1994 — and I usually just call her "Beaut" — I think she was eight and I was 88. A fella I knew had taken her from some people who said they had no use for her, because she kicked other horses. They were going to put her down. She'd been raced and then they went to playing polo on her. The way they jam those other horses into your horse to ride you off the ball, why if any horse got anywhere near her she'd just kick him straight away. That put a stop to the polo all right, and I assume on the race track she wasn't fast enough. Well, this fella I knew decided she was far too good an animal to have that happen, so he took her. But he didn't need her at all, so he gave her to me.

Diamond Lu Collection

Beauty in the bridle.

No better shape than I was in, why she wanted to go way too fast for me. Well, considering the jobs she had in the past, there isn't any doubt that she'd gotten plenty of encouragement to gallop just about any place they needed her to go, and it took me several months to get her slowed down. It was a slow job, to get her to feel of me horseback, but I had to get things taken care of that way, on account of I wasn't getting around afoot the way I used to.

Diamond Lu Collection

Bill and Beaut (far right) holding a calf at the Dorrance Ranch Spring branding, 1996.

She was scared of the cattle here at the ranch, because she'd never been around them. And if they got up too close to her, why she'd haul off and kick them too, so I had to get her over that. It got so after about a year I could do anything with her and she got so she wasn't afraid of anything, because she learned she didn't have to be afraid. There wasn't a need for it.

She got so I could rope off her and part out cattle, and we took her over to some clinics where I worked some other horses off her that had trouble leading up and one thing or another. No, in the end she turned out all right, Beaut did.

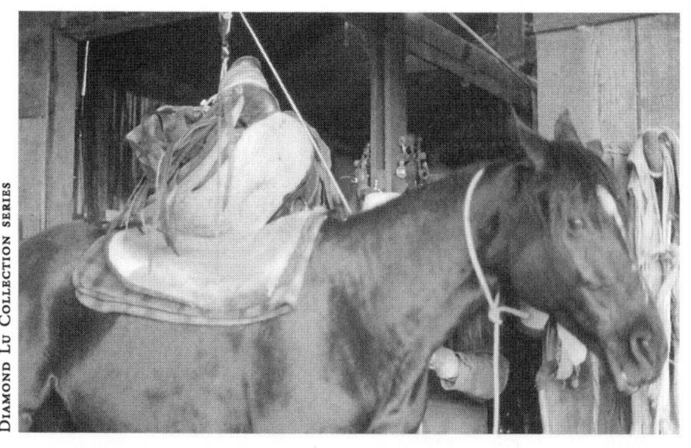

Due to my age, I had to experiment to see what was going to be the best way to get my horse ready.

But, before I even got her saddled the first time, when I was offering her something to feel of, why she'd get so hepped up she didn't have any idea what my feel was going to be like, and really, she was just plumb scared. It seemed like she thought she just had to make a lot of those real quick moves about every little thing. The way they'd run that horse and been turning her every which way, she didn't have any idea that I had a purpose in mind for anything I did. She was about as mixed up as any horse I'd seen in a long while.

That spot I needed to take care of on her, well, I'll say it was just set in as solid as it was on her because she never had any security from the rider. Her riders before didn't know how to offer her security. Well, the more these horses get so they feel of you, why the security they need comes from you, and that gives you more control. The horse will really take something good from a rider who's able to reassure them. It's a real sensitive thing to talk about because it's such a fine line you're working on, especially with a troubled horse.

It Took All the Knowledge I'd Accumulated to Get Beaut Switched Around in Her Thinking

It's always nice when a fella gets to be my age if there's some steps up to a ramp, so he can get on his horse from a better position.

Another thing that made it difficult for Beaut was that she really didn't have any purpose in mind of her own and, at that time, she couldn't because I was having to stay too close to her physically to give her the chance to learn to feel of me, and this really bothered her mind. She didn't know how to pick up my feel and go with that, because no better than she'd been handled before, she didn't know she could. I'll admit that I used every bit of knowledge I had to get her straightened around. I was the last stop for her, so I wanted to get things working out for her the best way I could. The main reason being, I wasn't so young anymore and I wasn't going to live forever.

Some of the time — and this is before we got together on things — why I was letting her go in circles, and letting a horse go in circles can be a lot more than just sitting up there while you're going in circles. Not everyone is going to know what I'm talking about here, but some will. There's a way to do things, but someone watching isn't always going to know the difference between watching someone who's just sitting up there riding around in circles, and someone sitting up there riding in circles *and getting something done.*

There's so much taking place when that happens that it's important to include here, even if some people aren't going to understand it the first time they read it. If they can find some meaning in the other things in this book, then I'm in hopes that their powers of observation will start to improve when they see a horse and a person operating in circles, or doing anything. That's the improvement they're going to have to make anyway, if they want to build feel into the way they handle and ride their horses.

You could say that this closeness I had to keep there with Beaut, which was so bothering to her — well, I did it this way so I could get with her as she slowed down. I didn't want to be out of position and miss any chance she gave me to know that she was ready to feel back to me. Based on how I'd been prepared, I didn't know if there was another way to go about this. I was real pleased when she could eventually give some thought to getting with me. She started to do this when she was turning away from the direction she wanted to go, which was home. When she got ready to be slower and she felt my slowness, then we were together for just that little time, and you almost couldn't measure it. At first it was only part of one second before she thought she had to be going again.

It didn't take a lot for her to get hepped up. It only took just the littlest turn in the direction of home and she'd get built way up with that excess of energy. So when she turned towards the direction I wanted her to go (away from home), that's when I lightened up on her. I offered her that lighter feel before she started to think about the turn that'd face her towards home, because I sure didn't need her to get built up about that idea of home anymore than she was. If I had lightened up on her after we were headed home, why there's a good chance that she'd have tried to run on back there because she and I weren't together. Before we actually did get together, we'll say that I offered my feel to her the way it should have been offered. When she'd get her body straightened out, why she was just going to take off for home, regardless. So I stayed with her pretty close, and before I'd feel her wanting to take off, why I might have turned her back this other way. It wasn't the easiest job at my age, but when my timing got right, and was added to the feel I'd presented, why that was what finally got her to make the little change I needed to get a good foundation started. With that better timing and good feel, I could head off that excess of energy she always had on hand when she'd make the turn towards home.

Well, one thing's for sure, I made sure that it was kind of difficult for Beaut to make that real fast circle she was wanting to make, because when I came around to where there was a bank, I just left it up to her to go into the bank and galloping didn't fit her so well right there. Whenever I came to the edge of that bank, she got so she didn't want to go over that edge at the gallop, so I'd have her headed right there. I wouldn't want anyone to get the idea it wasn't safe judgment. I did more of that fixing on her than any horse I'd ever rode. But all the other horses I'd rode, why I was younger then, and they weren't as mixed up as Beaut.

Diamond Lu Collection series

Bill on Beaut at Joe Wolter's spring branding, 1996.

If I'd been able to ride faster and gone out in the hills, and just gave her a place to go climbing up and down, I could have seen some bigger changes in Beaut before I did. I was at quite a disadvantage in that smaller area. I think when you're trying to get with a horse that's been through quite a few different places where people gave up and sent her on down the road for good, why it's always just a little different than starting a colt. But it's really the same, too, because no matter where that horse is mentally, through feel is going to be the better way to get your ideas across to them. It's just how you're going to present that to them, is all.

But with Beaut and the way she was on the start, see, she just kind of proves that if you take your time and experiment quite a little with your feel and timing, why even a really mixed-up horse can start to get switched around in their thinking.

Joe Wolter and I are just talking a few things over before we separate to gather up the cattle from different parts of the pasture for the branding he was having that day.

That mother cow is a little concerned, but the nice slow way these fellas handle their cattle, why there weren't any problems that came up at the branding that day. Where you see those cattle standing there, that's like it was done way back. Holding rodear is what you call that and it's a real important job. The fellas who mess up on that are liable not to be too popular around there if what they did to scatter those cattle was avoidable in the first place. Nowadays they have a lot of fences and corrals at most ranches. There's always a place for a good hand at any outfit.

Chapter 4: HOW TO GET FEEL WORKING FOR YOU

One thing about this chapter, there's a lot in here. I'm in hopes this first part is going to set a person up to be able to understand more about applying feel in a way that really fits a horse. They need to know about getting themselves mentally ready to be with the horse, and getting the horse mentally prepared so he'll want to be with them. The horse also needs to get physically shaped up for these exercises, and where it concerns the equipment you're going to use, we've put some examples of how to put on a halter and a snaffle bit without causing the horse to want to go someplace else. The exercises in here are demonstrated for you the best way we could show it with the pictures we had available. If we were writing this book again, I'd say for sure we'd need more time and some different pictures, in some cases. This is just our first book so we want to let people know that we have improvements in mind that can be made in the future.

Getting Ready For the Future

The best way I know to put this into words is to say that until the horse is ready to look to you for the direction and support he needs so he can stay relaxed and follow your feel — you need to follow *his* feel. *By that I mean to be ready all the time to get with him, and all the time be aware of when things start to change in that horse's mental system.* This is so important to think about and put into practice, because this way it's possible to get better results whether a horse is young, or old, or troubled or not.

If a horse understands that a person is in favor of him, and that their mental focus and physical abilities are available to him, then he can pick up some reassurance. As long as what a person does to help a horse doesn't bring out the horse's self-preservation instincts or disrespect, a time will come when that horse realizes a fella's there for him in a way that maybe he hadn't thought about or understood was possible. And before that happens, most horses will do some experimenting and speculating of their own. In most cases, a horse wants to find out what your purpose might be in getting near him, and that's whether you're holding on to him or just being around there.

If he's not bothered about you being nearby, or about any other thing, then it's just going to be a matter of time before his curiosity and his intelligence get to working on the idea that you might be there for a useful purpose that he has in mind. Because that horse, why *he's always got things in mind.* At a certain point, a shift will come into that horse's thinking and an observing person who's spent time at this will see it. The horse takes on a slightly different appearance — his expression changes — when he starts thinking about how you could be a help to him. It's your job to know when his ideas are starting to get over in the neighborhood of thoughts like this.

When that change shows up, the horse is ready for some little adjustments that could put him and the person onto a better way together. He is feeling of a person then, and that's an opportunity for that person to have a plan in mind of how to help the horse — through the best feel that he has to offer. *But one thing's for sure, when the horse is ready, he's ready right then.* This needs to be at the very top of your thinking.

A person who wants to learn about feel is interested in these things, and hopes not to miss these opportunities. *The time to get with the horse is right when he's ready to feel back to you.* So you are going to try to be ready — and when it's right, you are. So many people ask if they'll know what it's going to feel like when it's that better way. Well, there isn't any doubt that you and the horse will know, because when you get together through feel, it's not like any other feeling and you'll know all right.

You Might Miss Some Chances

With certain horses, it might be that you don't get a chance like this too often. And when it does finally show up — and you miss it — well, maybe it won't show up again for a long time. Or it could be there just real quick, and then get missed again before your body motions and position adjust in time to let the horse know he did what you had in mind. On the start, it isn't easy to see when the chance to get with the horse is there for only one second, or even less. Sometimes that's really all you have. That's why you need to have a plan ahead of time. Those better plans, why they have adjustability built right into them.

There's some horses that will let you have all the chances you could want. That kind of horse is just waiting for you to get things sorted out, and it's real helpful to be around a horse like this when you haven't got much experience. A fella's guesswork isn't a threat to a horse like this. And a horse like we're speaking about now isn't apt to bring your own feelings of self-preservation to the surface. I'll say he's not liable to, anyway. The difference in horses is just like it is with people — each one is an individual. No two people are alike and no two horses are alike. That's the beauty of it.

The thing to remember is that there's all kinds of exceptions to anything that a person could say or show you about this. There's no formula to it that's going to fit every horse or make sense to every person. That's where this idea of presenting an understandable feel to a horse can stump someone who isn't willing to experiment and really apply themselves to learning this with a wide open mind. A person with an attitude like that isn't going to learn much about horses. But people like this don't seem to mind and this approach isn't for everyone anyway. My main plan is to get these ideas across to those people who are interested in connecting with their horses in a way that's sure to fit the horse.

The Best Place to Start is On the Ground

It seems like the best place to start is on the ground with the horse in a halter or snaffle bit — whatever fits the situation. Generally speaking, you'd want to practice these exercises (Parts 1-7) in the order listed here, but which exercise you'd actually do first just all depends on the individual horse's mental system and the amount of experience you have. It might be you'd have to switch the order of the first three exercises a little, depending on how he is. How the horse responds to the things you present to him on the start will help you decide if you should change the order or not, but for the general run of people and horses, this order works best. Just do this the best way you know how. Taken together, these exercises will help to develop lightness on the ground that will carry over to your mounted work. For many people, the hardest part in all this is seeing that connection.

If he's a skeptical horse you'd have to get him over that first, but if he's a gentle kind of horse, why you'd first teach him to lower his head. Generally speaking, positioning that head and neck and getting the feet freed up ought to be a person's first choice of how to invest their time in a horse. I'm in hopes that before you'd sit up there you'd get real familiar with how these exercises are done, and get that horse operating real smooth and slow for you. Before you'd act on any plans to ride a horse, you'd want to work on the ground to teach the horse to move his feet in any direction you wanted — and any direction there's a need for him to move.

Before we get started on the smaller particles of feel in these maneuvers, it's a good idea to have some real clear thoughts in mind. One main thought I like people to be on the lookout for is that spot where a person's thought becomes the horse's idea. There is complete control over the horse when this occurs, and this control is no part of any contest whatsoever. I don't mind saying again that *there's no place at all for ideas about dominating a horse in the connection we are building here*. That would be way out of line.

When you are trying to learn how to use feel in the best way, you need to always keep in mind that less force on the horse can help him to become lighter and more willing. Your groundwork and your rides will have an effortless feel and appearance once you understand how to build that soft feel in there, and have him operating for you without resistance of any kind. Then your horse won't weigh anything in your hands — just the weight of the lead rope or the reins is all.

For general handling purposes, a fella wouldn't need to hold a rope any tighter than what's shown in this first picture here (Figure 1). If there was a need to then he would, of course, but we're in hopes that the feel he's built into that horse's foundation gives him enough control over the horse to where it's not necessary to use firmness as a general way of going about things. Before practicing the exercises mentioned later, and the maneuvers shown below (Figures 2-5), it might be helpful to look over the haltering and bridling information that's written about here.

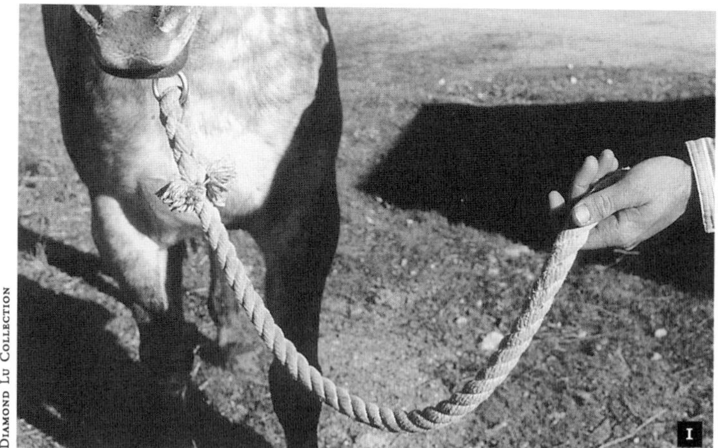

Diamond Lu Collection

Patricia Weedman

This is what it looks like when your horse doesn't weigh any more in your hand than the weight of the halter rope.

Patricia Weedman

This horse weighs more than he needs to. That feel sure isn't the best. It's not going to feel much different than this on the reins until he gets to operating through feel. This is where your experimenting can help you help the horse.

Patricia Weedman

This lady switched sides to build in some feel where she could. Not many people had worked the horse from that side, and she got good results by working up close on the start.

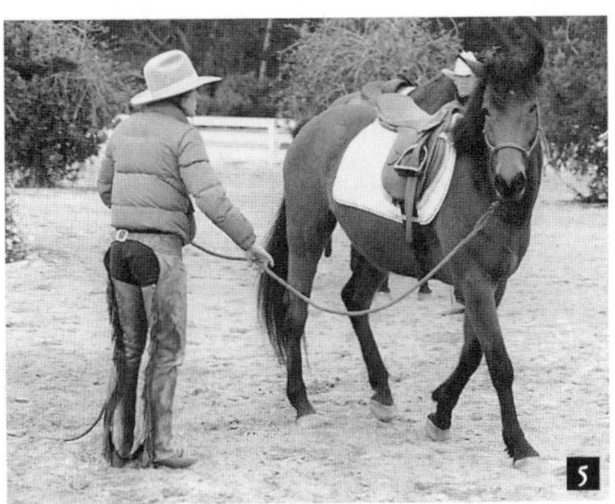

Patricia Weedman

After that, she did a few experiments to see if the feel she was building in would carry over to work on a longer line and still maintain a float.

Preparing to Halter or Bridle Your Horse

Almost everyone has trouble bridling a horse in the beginning. We're going to assume that anyone working with a horse has the time it takes to get the job done right. This all takes quite a bit of time. That's a very delicate part, getting the horse to feel of you through the bit. It's a very important part of getting your horse started off with the best feel possible.

Most of the problems result from a lack of preparation. This should be a smooth experience for both of you and if it becomes a wrestling match, stop right there. In a case like this, maybe the horse is unclear about what you want because the presentation isn't clear, or he might resist because what you're doing is aggravating to him. That means some important things have been missed in your understanding of the equipment or the way you've prepared the horse to understand what you want. If things aren't calm as you bridle a horse, then your safety is going to be in question and you'd better go back down the line a little.

To prepare for haltering or bridling, the horse must first be willing to lower his neck and turn his head towards you. We'll assume the horse can do this with no trouble, but if trouble comes in there at any time and he'd rather do something else, why that's your real clear signal from the horse that he's missing your feel and you better do something else.

Putting On a Rope Halter

These pictures show how you'd want to stand and how you'd want your horse to look while you're tying on a rope halter (Figures 6-7).

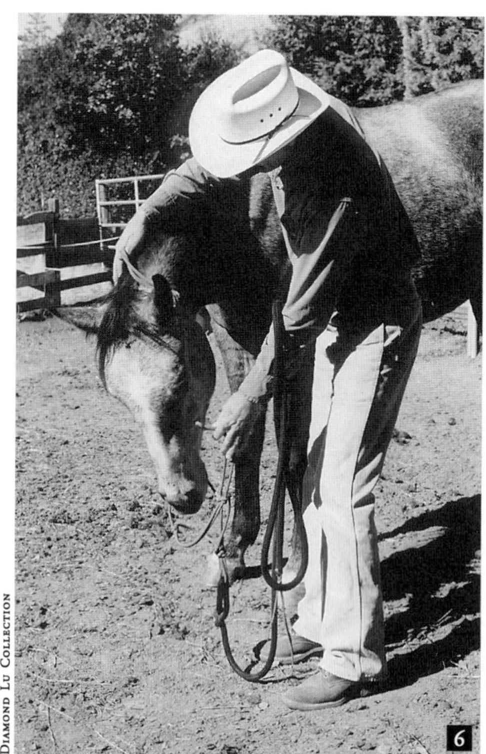

6

Diamond Lu Collection

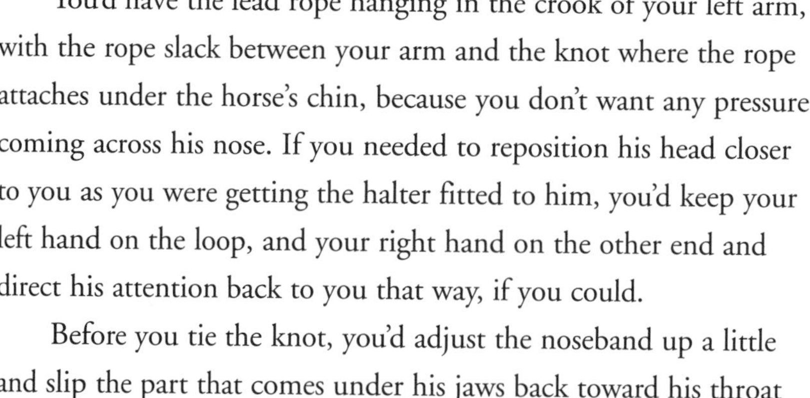

You'd have the lead rope hanging in the crook of your left arm, with the rope slack between your arm and the knot where the rope attaches under the horse's chin, because you don't want any pressure coming across his nose. If you needed to reposition his head closer to you as you were getting the halter fitted to him, you'd keep your left hand on the loop, and your right hand on the other end and direct his attention back to you that way, if you could.

Before you tie the knot, you'd adjust the noseband up a little and slip the part that comes under his jaws back toward his throat area the best you can, so the rope doesn't tighten up across the side of the jawbone. It's not good when that happens. Not all rope halters are made of the same material, and not all halters fit a horse just right, no matter what they're made of. This one shown here would fit better if the cheek pieces were a little shorter. You do the best you can with what you have.

7

Diamond Lu Collection

With the end of your lead rope still over your left arm, build your knot as shown in these next pictures (Figures 8-14). Keep three things in mind for this. The first is not to reach the fingers on your right hand back too far through the loop you're making. Second, when you go to snug up the knot, don't pull the tail end of that rope unless you're pulling against the loop and knot you've just made as it's held in your left hand. It can easily confuse a young or troubled horse if you just yank on that rope to tighten up the knot, and it won't tighten up good using that approach anyway. If you tug on that end part, it's going to jerk his head and that's something he won't understand. The third thing to watch out for is real important: Any time you're haltering or bridling your horse, or lowering his head — even in your practice — *do not lean over his head with your head or your face*. If he gets startled or distracted by anything and suddenly pops his head up to look around, you sure could regret that your face or your chin got in his way.

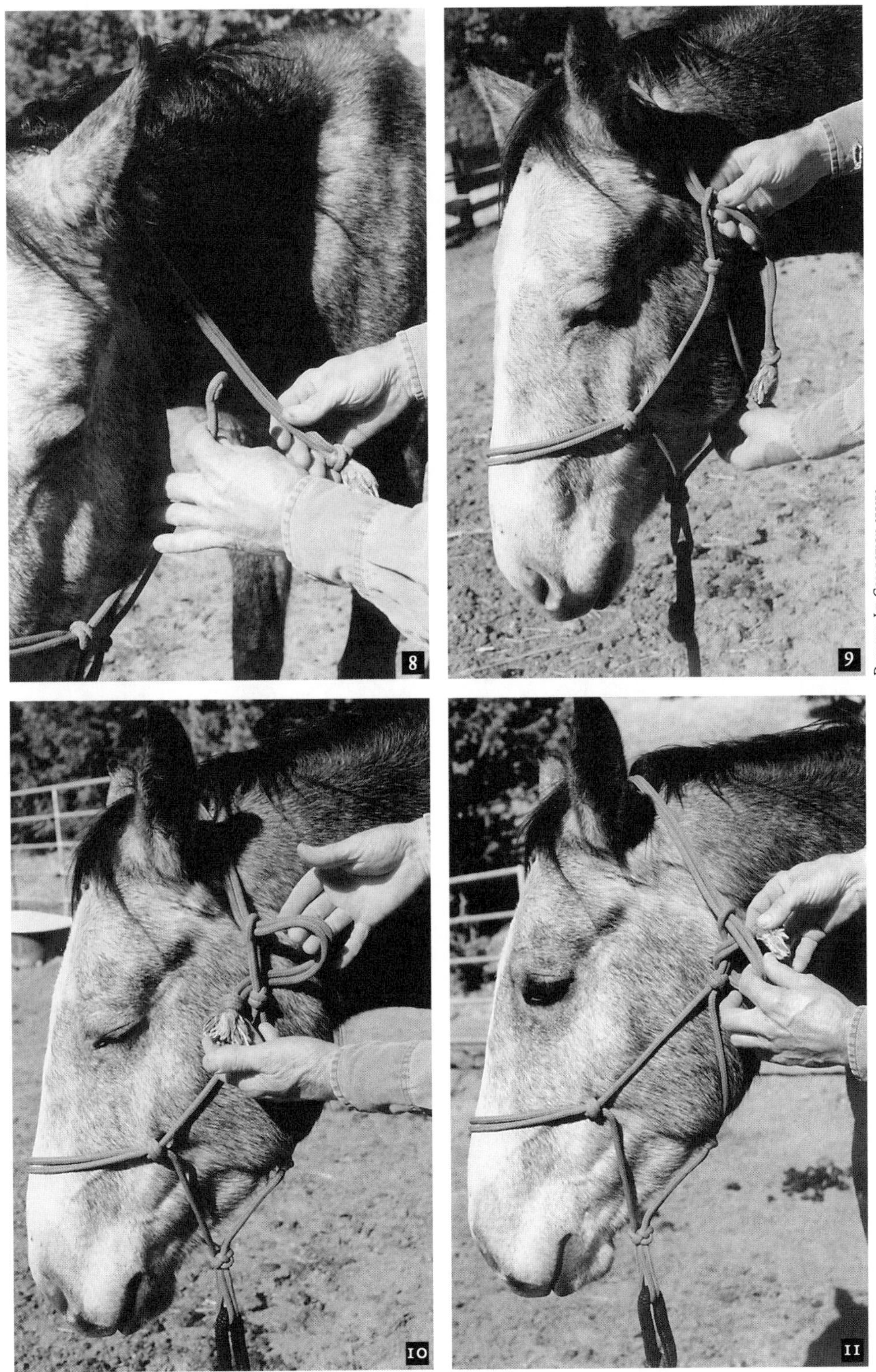

Diamond Lu Collection series

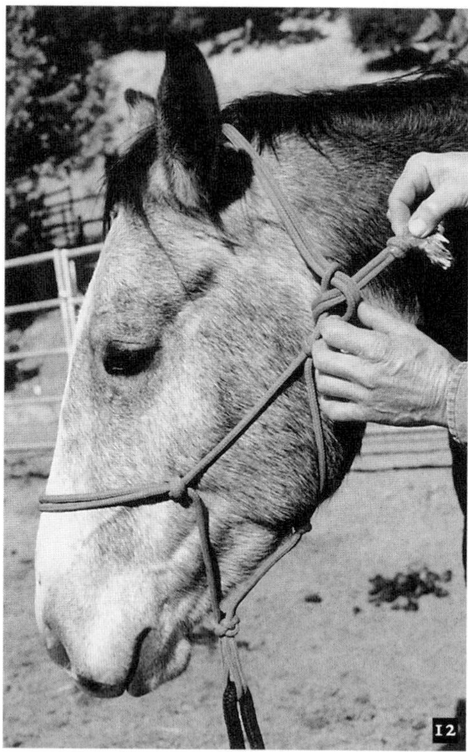

12

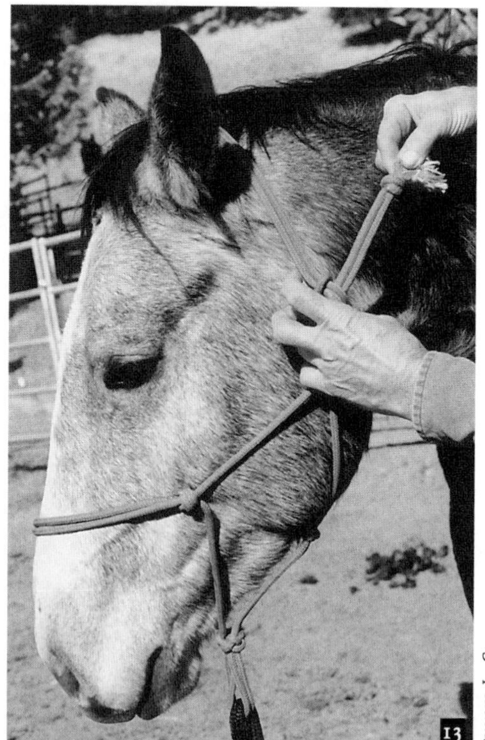

13

Diamond Lu Collection series

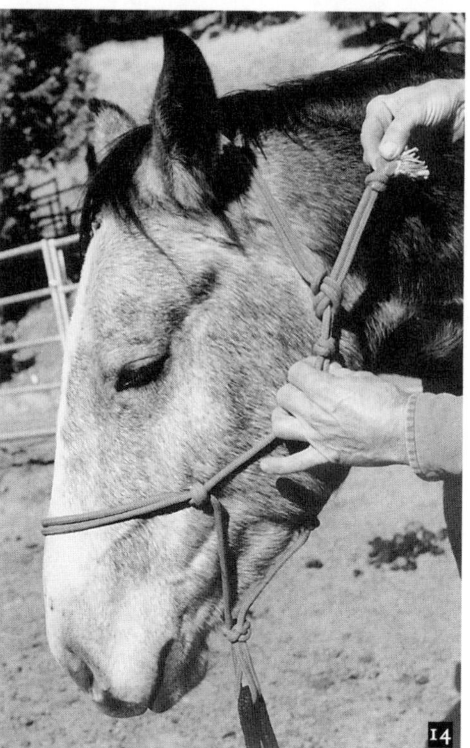

14

Anytime you happen to be standing next to your horse between his head and the shoulder, you can practice tipping the horse's nose towards you. If you put his halter on and take it off with his head and neck

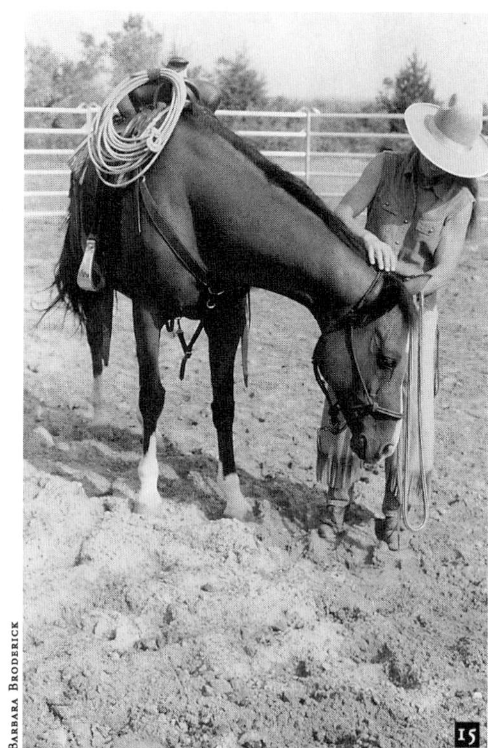

15

Barbara Broderick

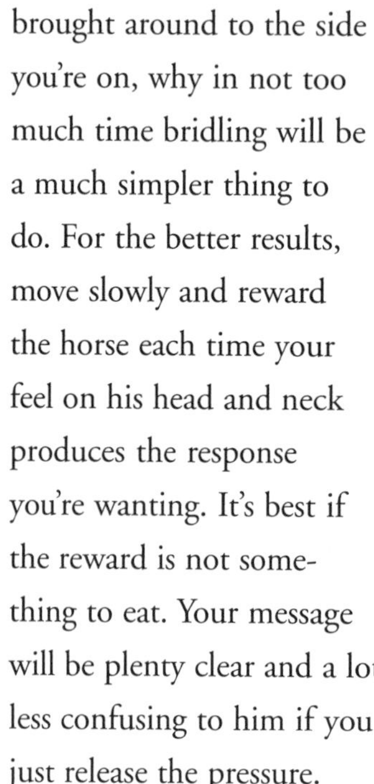

brought around to the side you're on, why in not too much time bridling will be a much simpler thing to do. For the better results, move slowly and reward the horse each time your feel on his head and neck produces the response you're wanting. It's best if the reward is not something to eat. Your message will be plenty clear and a lot less confusing to him if you just release the pressure.

Some Things to Consider When You Adjust the Snaffle Bit

A fella won't assume his snaffle bit (headstall) is going to fit every horse, so he'll want to let those holes out some before putting it on any horse. This is sometimes beneficial even for the horse that usually wears it, especially if the leather is new or stiff for any reason. You'd let the bit down a couple of holes before you put the bridle on for the same reason a fella generally unbuttons his shirt and unlaces his boots before he puts them on, if he owns those things.

In the majority of cases, it's possible to adjust a bit low enough to keep pressure off the corners of the mouth without having it resting against any teeth. If it's not bumping his teeth and not drawn up too high in his mouth, the horse will work his mouth and gather up the bit to a place where he can kind of hold onto it. At first he may chew on it or toss his head, but in a short time, he'll know where it feels the best to him and he'll carry it there. You'll rarely see a horse impose wrinkles on his mouth with this approach.

Most horses will close their mouths naturally when the bit is adjusted low enough to allow for that. With a calm mouth like the kind I'm thinking of, why I doubt there'd be any need to buckle his mouth shut. To close off his natural jaw movements produces tightness all through the horse anyway, and as far as a horse is concerned, there's not anything natural about that. What he feels in his mouth directs his mind to position the bridge of his nose, or shifts the angle of his head and neck where we need him to go, so you'd want to be as accurate as you could about the message you give the horse in his whole mouth area in the first place. I'd say that's one of the most sensitive places on a horse.

For sure you'd want him to be clear about your intentions after you're sitting up there, and with the bit adjustments we're speaking about now, why you'd be helping the horse be able to offer back more accurate responses to your feel — and that'd be anyplace that your feel is applied to him. The reason being, when he's not distracted by discomfort from poor fitting equipment, more of that horse's attention is liable to be available to a person if they know how to get it working in their favor. There is a fine line there.

When it comes to pressure on those reins, why we'd like the horse to respond *before* the slack is taken out. This desirable response is easier to achieve when the weight of the bit and reins is carried across the back of his head and not all the time pressing into his jaw or the corners of his mouth. Then he can feel the movement in your fingers, or hands or arms without any lapse in time from when that movement took place. When this happens, it's real beneficial to his mental and physical systems. On a horse that's mostly had experience with real firm adjustments, or rough handling on the reins or halter rope, it might take a little time for him to adapt to the new feel of it. After some practice with a looser bit adjustment, the horse is apt to respond more quickly and accurately to less pressure from the rider's legs and arm movements.

There's liable to be a calmer expression on the face of a horse that's just had that excess of pressure taken off him. After that relief comes in, those horses aren't liable to chomp on the bit, or push against it near as much when they're asked to do something. They're also not so inclined to wring their tail. I've noticed a good many horses do this when that pressure adds up for them. It's real unattractive when a horse does this. Of course, that's only one way that a horse can let a person know that he's not comfortable about something. Changing the bit adjustment is not a cure-all and there's no magic that is produced when you do loosen things up for him. But, as far as that horse is concerned, he's a lot more comfortable if he can work his mouth and keep it relaxed, and I'd rather think he can free up the part of his mental system that is set up to focus on things when that (too tight) equipment isn't figuring so heavy on his mind. When his jaws are free and loose, and his head and neck stay nice and flexible and soft, well, this is really pleasing to the rider. It would be to most riders, I'll put it that way.

One more thing I think is important for people to think about — and observe when they can — is to see how those horses that are allowed to travel with their mouths real relaxed don't tend to get tight all through their bodies. They're not so liable to get going in a constant jig. Having that bit pulled up high makes some of them just plunge their head down towards the ground and then flip it forward to try and get some relief. It's just a natural thing for a horse who's ridden this way to want to root his nose out, and no pulling on that head is going to relieve the horse from his real concern, which is that poorly fitting equipment.

Richard Field Levine

Richard Field Levine

Generally when a horse gets to fighting the adjustments on the head gear, and that'd include those chains they use over the nose, why then someone's liable to recommend some other tighten-up rig to put on him to fix the problem. Well, they're bound to end up with a response from the horse that's even less desirable than it was before. We've got things written about this somewhere else in the book (Chapter 9).

No, all the problems there are for horses sure can't get blamed on the equipment. I'm not suggesting there's anything wrong with what people are using as far as bits go. That's not realistic, and if a person has some education on feel and quite a little experience, why any sort of bit will do. No, they can figure out how to get by with almost any bit that's around.

18

Diamond Lu Collection

19

Diamond Lu Collection

When someone has a horse that carries his head up, or has his nose poked out, they are liable to be in search of some guidance. They also want help for the horses that have those real stiff and unbendable sort of necks when they're being handled or ridden. What they're going to find out quick if they get good supervision is that the problem isn't the horse. They'll find out that whatever feel is presented to that horse is the way that horse is going to go for them, and for the next person after that, too. These problems come straight from the rider who operates those reins with a feel that maybe isn't the best (Figures 18-19). And there's some people who really do know this. When this way of handling the horse is allowed to continue for too long, the horse's dissatisfaction with the way a person is going about things is bound to show up. In some, the evidence of trouble will be there right off and in others that have a different temperament and background, it will show up later. When a person ignores the little things the horse does to try and let them know how objectionable their feel is — well, that's going to get him going on some habits like head slinging or rearing. And it's even worse than that in some cases. When it gets like this, a person can think things about that horse that they shouldn't.

Those irritated horses have run out of other ideas. They have no way to get along with that feel, and they're liable to operate with a real dull response to that rider's leg feel, too. Most people are not able to see the direct connection there is in that. But we're in hopes that they will, someday, because all these things just spoken about can be avoided. A fella just has to try to eliminate his dependence on any habits he has that don't fit a horse.

Putting on the Snaffle Bit

When it comes to putting on the bridle, there's a number of things to keep in mind. These have equal importance to the horse and shouldn't be skipped over if you're after the better results. A horse that's bad to bridle tends to be suspicious of other things people are apt to do to him, and the real firm brace he can get resisting this procedure will carry over to many other things you'd do with that horse. Of course, it goes almost without saying that *you'll take your time in preparing a horse to know what's expected of him.*

A fella needs to get the horse comfortable with his fingers in the horse's mouth and around his muzzle. Your moves there should be slow and gentle, and no thought of having food in your hand should come into this. There's people who use honey and syrups for this, and other food to inspire him to open his mouth up, but we're not using things like that because we're using feel, which is what the horse's mental system can understand. It's important to use the flat of your hand near his lips and not just go poking right into his mouth without some preparation, or he's going to fall back on some instincts to protect himself. Pulling away from a person on this part is the best way a horse can let that person know he ought to make some little adjustments to his presentation, because to that horse it's obviously not the best.

This will take time for some people to get used to, and any fear someone has about this is understandable on the start. That's a good reason to get supervision in your beginning attempts to bridle a horse. If you have this sort of concern — maybe about a horse biting you or something like that — well, the horse you learn on sure ought to be one that's real gentle and on the older side, if possible. I'd rather not ever see a person who lacks confidence in this area be the one to introduce a snaffle bit to any horse that wasn't real experienced at having one put on. When this happens, the horse can really lose out on a valuable opportunity to get comfortable with a person's better feel.

The next set of pictures show how you can help a horse get used to you handling his head and his mouth. You'd want him to be good about having your hands on his face and ears, too, and you'd remember to get him good from either side like these pictures show. You'd stand by his shoulder, with his neck bent towards you, leaving enough room to bring his head around without crowding you. Start on the side of his mouth that's away from where you're standing, and when he's good on that side and relaxed about things, then you'd get him good on the side near you. You want him to know it's your hand that's there, and not something irritating him on those whiskers, so put your hand all around there real gentle and smooth.

At any time you're working with him, he might want to lift his head up or move it away from you, like when he feels your hand on his chin (Figure 20). Some horses will just pop their heads up when they feel that, so if he does, you'd just go with him and when he settles, right then is when you'd take your hand off. Then you'd take a fresh start. With your hand alongside his mouth (Figure 21), work your fingers a little at the corner of his mouth. Just the tips of your fingers go in his mouth at first (Figure 22). He may want to work his mouth, and that's normal. If your timing's good, he'll find a place where he can relax with the ends of your fingers in there (Figure 23). You'd do the same from the side you were on after that. Put your fingers in just enough so he opens his mouth (Figures 24-26). You'd want to be sure to do this from both sides of the horse, even if you plan to only bridle him from one side all the time (Figure 27). With this preparation built in at the foundation level, why bridling a horse shouldn't be a problem for any person who could handle his mouth this gentle way — by using feel the horse could understand.

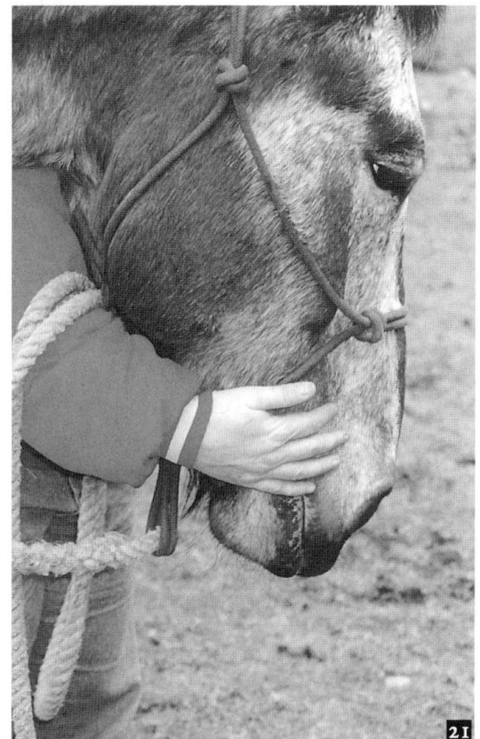

Gale Nelson series

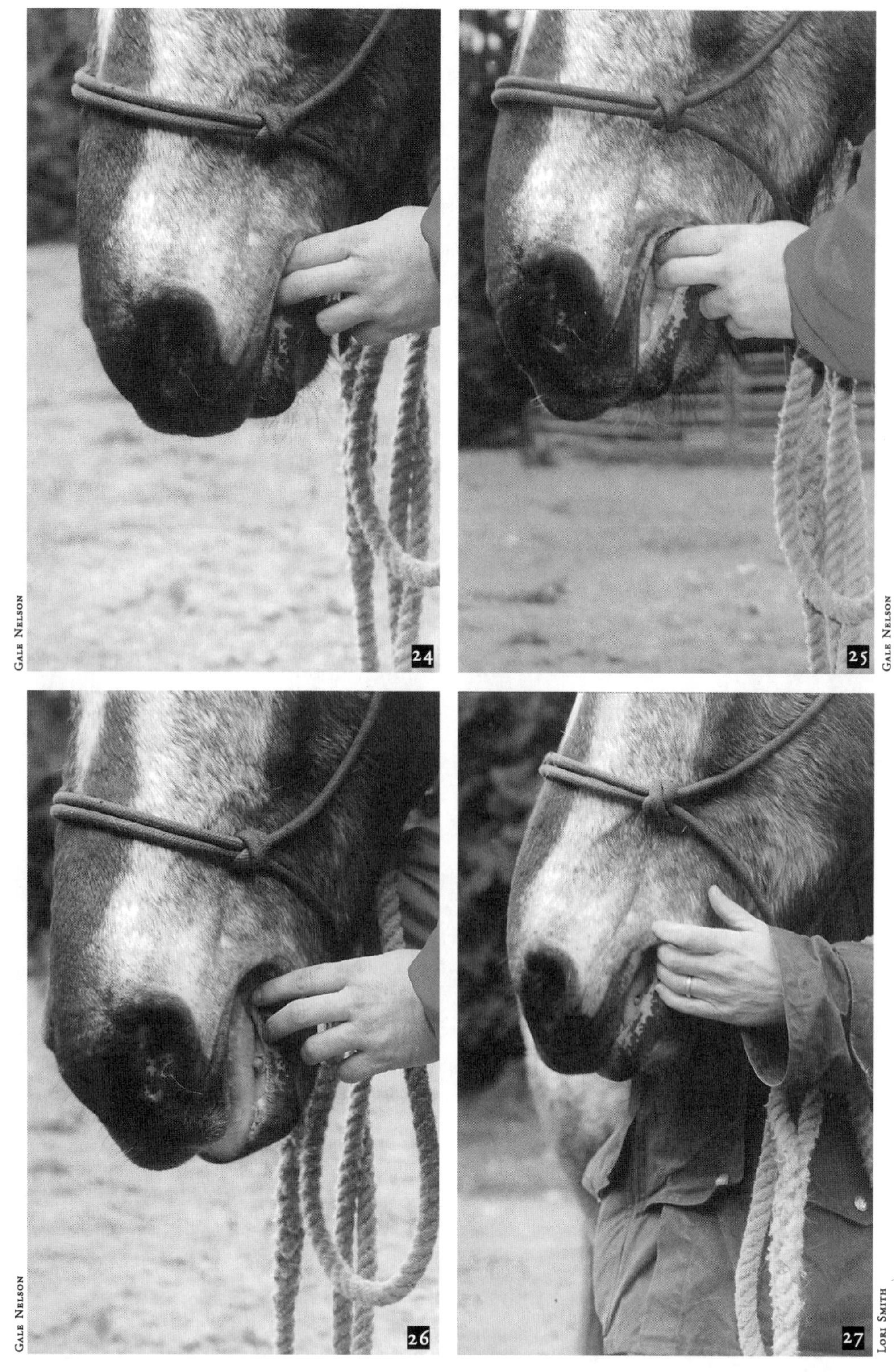

So many people who have difficulty bridling a horse are just lacking knowledge about feel. With enough desire and time for practicing, a person will gain confidence about their moves when they realize a horse is going to respond to their better feel when they offer it to him. What's bothering to me is the way some people find it convenient to think the horse did them wrong when they have trouble bridling. This causes them to say things that don't favor the horse. I'm in hopes we can cut down on some of these reports because, really, the horse has no idea what he's supposed to do until it's presented to him by someone who's had experience handling his mouth, using feel. If those more experienced people are inclined to help others learn this, it's of great benefit to the horse.

Three things are especially important to keep all the time in mind when you're trying to bridle any horse. You're going to be sure not to poke him in the eye when you bring up the headpiece to stick his ears through, and you'd not want to bump his teeth with the bit. The third thing a person oughtn't do is crumple up his ears or fold them over in any way. Some people sure know about these things already, but we're in hopes that what we're going to show you and speak about now will be helpful to people who haven't had much experience doing this.

Figure 28 shows the standard set-up in the horse's mouth. That space in there is where the bit rests, and care should be taken that the bit isn't adjusted too high in his mouth. A lot of people are inclined to start right in with an excess amount of pressure on the horse by adjusting the bit way up, as shown before. When it's comfortable for the horse, there's enough play in that adjustment so he can work his mouth some and pick that bit up and hold it with his tongue and those other muscles in his mouth. It feels good to him to hold onto it when it's his idea, and the adjustment just mentioned is what helps the horse to have that idea.

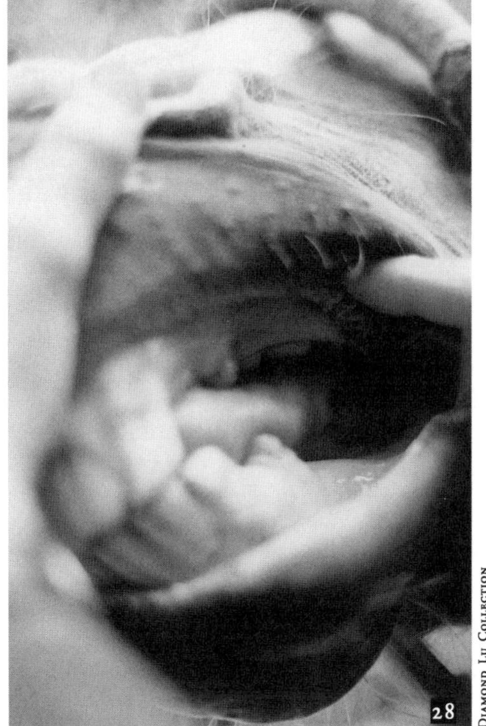
28

Diamond Lu Collection

We'll assume that your horse is comfortable lowering his neck and tipping his head towards you. Present the headpiece of your bridle in a way that allows him to stay with you. Poking him in the eye with the buckles or banging him in the teeth with the bit will encourage him to leave or sling his head. Cradle the bit in your fingers so the bit is well-supported with your thumb pointing up, over the top of the mouthpiece.

Slide your thumb into the corner of the horse's mouth. There's no reason to rush when he opens his mouth, but that's exactly what most people do on the start. They just get in a big hurry and force that bit in there. Generally speaking, it's that poor feel and some faster actions in a person's bridling habits that have soured many a good horse about having the bridle put on.

There's a lot of variation in the actual technique a person has for holding a bit to bridle a horse. The habits a person has are their own and I wouldn't change anything about what a person had in mind, if the feel that went along with it was good enough

Diamond Lu Collection

for that horse. The person in this picture likes to hold the snaffle bit this way (Figure 29). Other people will support the bit a little more by putting their thumb under the mouthpiece like the first finger is doing. Some people use the first two fingers and the thumb under the mouthpiece and some others put their thumb just under the top of that ring on the side there.

The whole point of this is to just cradle that bit in your hand so it's got the general shape shown here, and is ready for the horse to accept when he's ready. There'd be no cramming the bit into place when he starts to open his mouth. It's the function of the right arm to lift the bit up as the left hand guides the bit between the horse's teeth. There'd be no force needed at all in this process. Instead, raise the bit into position by lifting the bridle up with your right hand, and then guide the bit into position with your left hand. If he starts to sling his head around or move his feet, your better judgment will tell you whether to see the job through or start over.

Be real gentle and patient as you teach your horse to understand that he's safe when he's with you. You'd keep the horse well away from any surprises when you're working on this and by no means would you want to do any yanking or jerking on the reins. The main thing is to take your time. *Take all the time it takes to get the bridle on without upsetting the horse.*

Because it's easy to mishandle the ears, care should be taken to see what sort of contact is all right with the horse on his ears, and all over his face and neck. As you lift the headstall up, be careful not to rub the buckles across his eyes in the process. Figure 30 shows how you can hold onto that headpiece in a way that doesn't poke the horse in his eye, and this fella's got it in good position to slip the horse's right ear under it first. The ear that's closest to you is the one you put under the headpiece last — after you've cleared the eye and tipped the ear under the headpiece on the other side of the horse.

Diamond Lu Collection

If there's any adjustments needed in your headpiece, why it's loose on your side and you can make those adjustments without getting anything too tight on him. One thing you'd sure not want to do is fold those ears over. Cup your hand behind them and tip them forward. This approach will fit the majority of horses best.

There's a lot more to doing this correctly than most people imagine. If you can practice on a horse that's used to people making a few mistakes on this, why you'll catch on to it a lot easier. But a touchy horse will teach you even faster about certain things, so it's just up to the individual how he wants to learn it.

Sometimes an inexperienced horse will get a little concerned about the leather lip strap rubbing up against his bottom lip. It can tickle him and make him think he ought to get that in his mouth, or he might lift his head up to see if he can get entirely away from it. A person will experiment to see how a horse responds to having the snaffle bit put on, and do whatever's necessary to keep the bit and the lip strap separated. The fingers on the left hand don't have any business pushing the bit against the teeth. When people forget this, undesirable results will show up right away. You'd not fight the horse about this. It's an adjustment the person needs to make. You can see from these pictures how to guide the bit into place. Be *all the time* real gentle, and keep that leather chin strap out of the way (Figures 31-33).

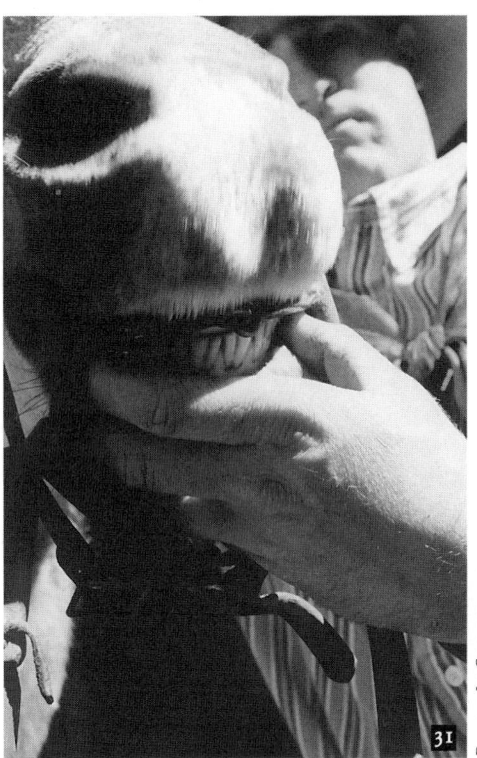

31

DIAMOND LU COLLECTION SERIES

The actual fitting of the headpiece after the bit is in place includes straightening the brow band across his forehead and then buckling the throat latch. There's a few thoughts about how tight or loose it needs to be, but its function is to hold the bridle on his head if the leather straps on one side of the bit break. You'd adjust it with this in mind. It should not flop down below the jaw bone, or be so tight you can't get a few fingers in there under his windpipe. He's liable to expand his throat in any running jobs you've got for him, so you'd be careful it wasn't too tight on him.

32

33

Shortening the Mecate to Work Your Horse on the Ground in the Snaffle

In certain situations, it can be handy to know how to shorten your reins and lengthen the lead on your mecate. If you need to pony your horse someplace without a halter and rope, or if you want to work with your horse from the fence, or on the ground in the snaffle, this simple adjustment can make a big difference in how effective you'd be.

There's something I want to remind people about right here, before you go to shorten up this rein. If you're just standing around there visiting and what-not, you'd remember not to tie your horse with the tail end of your mecate when your reins are looped over the saddle horn, or buckled through your throat latch. This can damage your horse and tear up your gear. I'll speak about how to tie your horse with the tail end of your mecate later, in Chapter 7.

34

Richard Field Levine

Bridle your horse, and leave the throat latch undone (Figure 34). Start with your reins as far over towards the left side of your horse's neck as possible, with the off side (right) slobber strap running up alongside the cheek piece of your bridle. Keep the tail of your mecate well-organized and out of the way, and bring the slack out of the reins, over the top of his head, just behind his ears (Figure 35). This will take the slack out of the rein that is attached to the right slobber strap.

35

Richard Field Levine

That right rein will come up alongside the side of his jaw on his right side, over his head and then down the left side of his jaw. Buckle the throat latch around *both* reins. You will have a lot of slack between the throat latch and the near side slobber strap that needs to be taken up (Figures 36-38).

Loosen the half-hitch in the near side slobber strap and pull the slack through (Figure 39). No more than the very tips of your fingers should reach through the half-hitch to get hold of the rein you are pulling through. It's safest to *push* the rein through the loop of the loosened knot — from your right hand to your left hand.

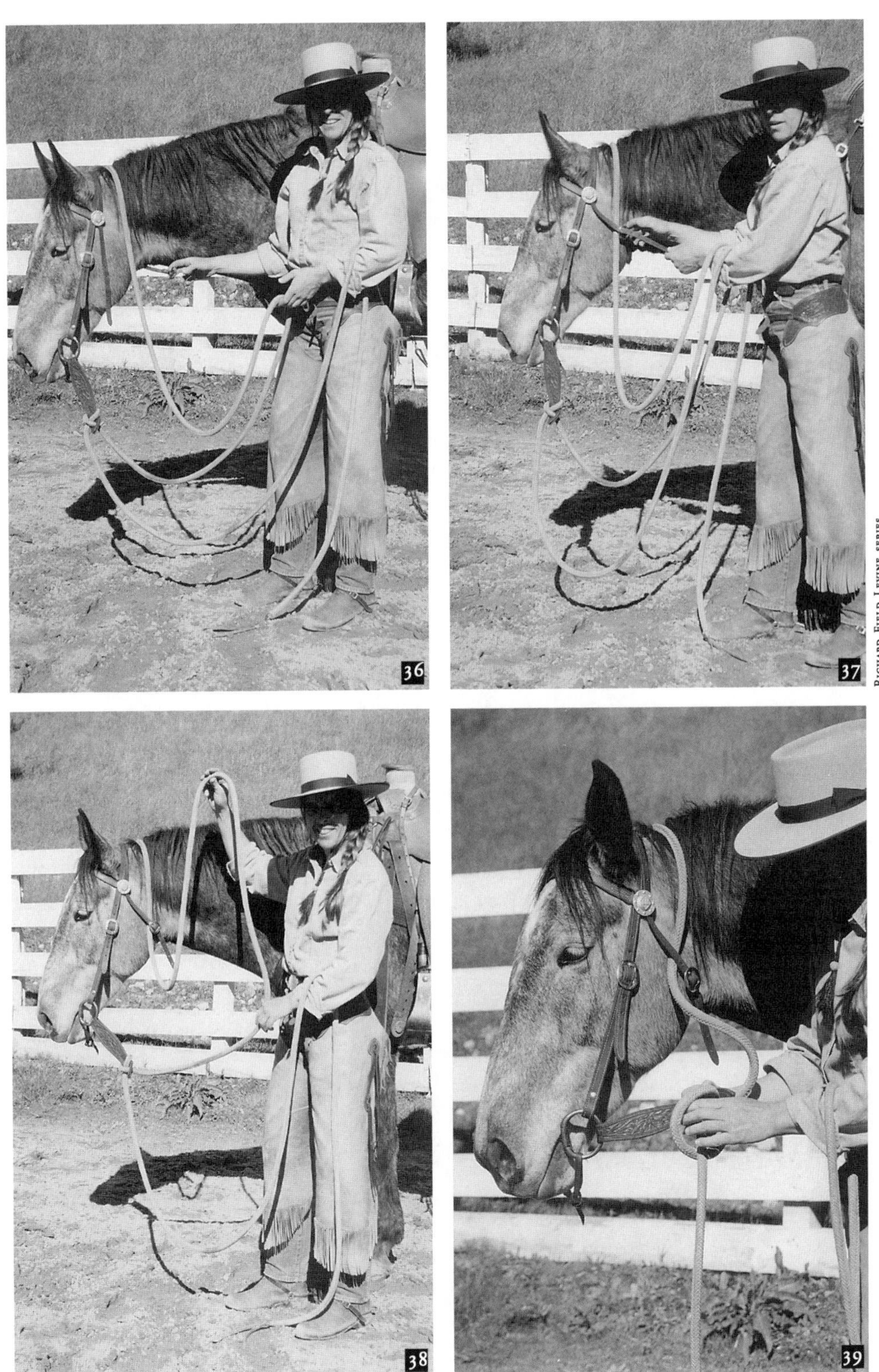

So that you don't tug on your horse's mouth while you thread the rein through the hole in the strap, hold onto the slobber strap as you pull (Figure 40). Your half-hitch is still in place, so just work the slack out of it and snug it up the way it was before.

40

RICHARD FIELD LEVINE

41

RICHARD FIELD LEVINE

When it's adjusted to the proper length, there should still be enough slack in the rein coming over the head to allow the near side slobber strap to hang as if your reins hadn't been shortened up (Figure 41). This is so the feel of your hand on the horse's mouth is still the same, and does not get transferred to a pull that he feels on the poll. You can see in Figure 42 that the rein runs under the throat latch on the off side (right), and the adjustment on the left allows for that better feel we're hoping to establish so it can be felt in the right place. A horse might get confused and inclined to take over with ideas of his own if any more slack was taken out of the section of rein that's between those slobber straps.

42

RICHARD FIELD LEVINE

When there is a need to work your horse up close on the right side (off side), it can help a horse to understand what you want him to do with his feet if you run the end of your mecate under his chin and back through the snaffle ring on the off side (Figures 43 and 44). Before the slack comes all the way out and pulls on the left-side slobber strap at all, just double the mecate over the right-hand snaffle bit ring (Figure 45). Hold it about six or so inches below the bit and use it the same way you would take hold of your slobber strap on that side if your reins weren't shortened up (Figure 46). Adjusting your mecate this way cuts way down on the chance that your horse will get a foot, or a stirrup, through your reins when they're looped over the horn, and allows you the flexibility to feed him out quite a bit of extra line if the situation calls for it.

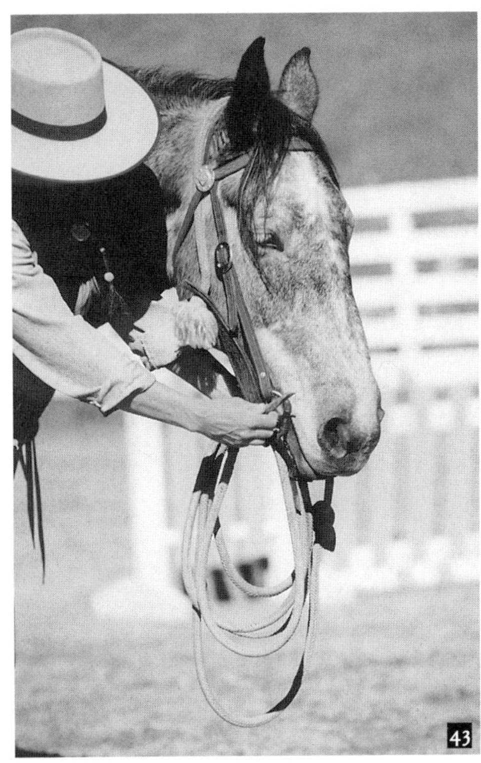
43

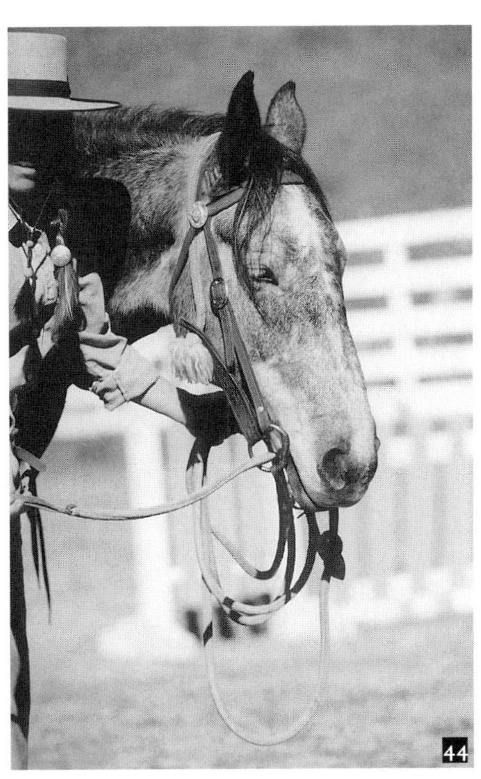
44

Richard Field Levine series

The maneuvers we're about to discuss in Parts 1-7 will help you prepare your horse to have respect for you, and to respond with confidence to your feel on the ground. They'll spark his interest in working with you in almost any other situation.

45

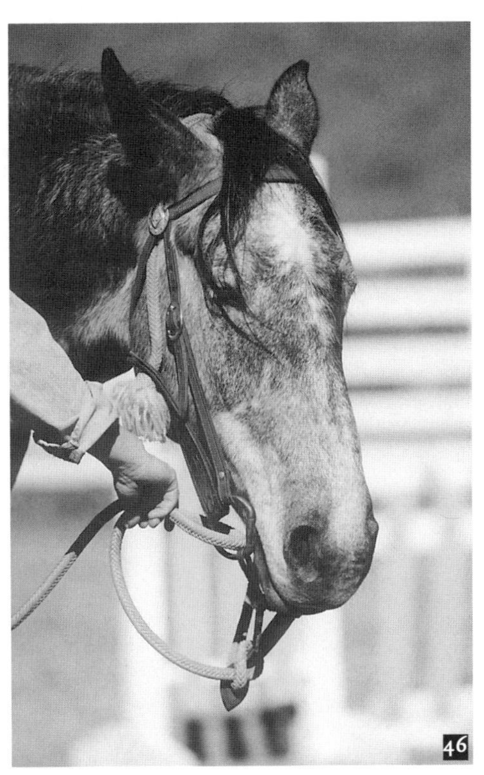
46

Once these exercises have a real fluid feel in them for the two of you, that horse should be a reliable partner with lightness and enthusiasm available for whatever job you have.

In any of the work you do with a horse, be careful that you don't get stepped on, bitten or kicked. To begin, you will use a halter and lead rope. Any type of halter will do, so long as there isn't any self-tightening feature to it, or any hard knobs built in for putting an excess of pressure on the poll area, because those would come under the heading of gimmicks, and those are out. You'll remember to maintain some float in your lead rope whenever possible. (We speak more about float in Chapters 8 and 9.)

Now you're ready to move on to the first exercise, "Teaching the Horse to Adjust His Head Position."

Part 1 — Teaching the Horse to Adjust His Head Position

The exercises in this part are the start of building lightness in the horse in response to your feel. All a person needs for this is a halter and lead rope — any kind will do.

Lowering the Horse's Head

For this exercise, you'd stand on the right or left side of the horse, between his head and shoulder, but not directly in front of the shoulder by any means. If you're standing on his left side, put your left hand on the lead rope pretty close to the halter knot, approximately six inches from his head (Figure 1). Place your right hand on top of his neck, right at the poll, and pull down a little bit on the halter knot or on the lead rope just below where it clips into the halter ring (Figure 2). You won't want to push down much with your right hand, just have it there without much weight on it at all. And for sure there'd be no pinching the horse in back of his ears, because the horse isn't going to know what to do at first. Maybe he'd think he was supposed to lift his head up, which is a real common response.

Diamond Lu Collection

There's one important thing to remember while you help your horse learn how to do this. Be sure to keep your head back a ways from his head, so if he swings towards you a little bit and comes up quick, his head won't bump into yours. There can be very disturbing results for a person who didn't know they ought not stand over a horse's head.

As you present the horse with the feel to lower his head and neck, he'll search for meaning in what you do. The timing of your releases when he makes the slightest try will encourage him to put more effort into his understanding of your feel.

Getting With the Horse On the Start

If the horse's feet are still and his head comes up, keep both hands in place the best you can. Without opposing him with force, just try to keep a constant connection on the halter rope and his neck without adding any pressure — and just go along with that head, keeping contact with him and following his movements with your hands as best you can. Don't try to hold his head down. The important thing right here is that you get with his feel on the start, even if what he's doing isn't exactly what you want. If you don't replace time and a gentle following feel with added pressure, he will end up — I'll say in most cases he will — offering a response in the

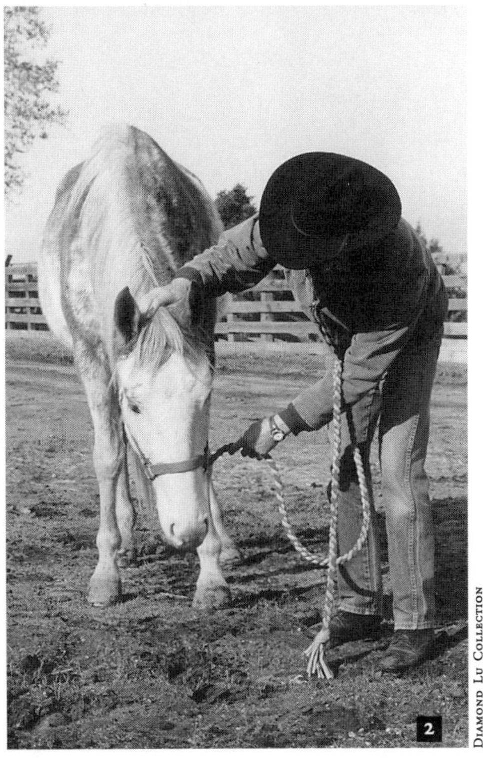

Diamond Lu Collection

neighborhood of what you were hoping for. Then you'd ease off or give a complete release, depending on the horse and the situation. Wait a few seconds before taking a fresh start. This is not a rule, by any means. Where it concerns a person's safety, if the situation changed on the spur of the moment, experience will help you develop judgment about how much firmness might actually be needed.

Your horse will benefit from work at this on both sides (Figures 3-4). Be sure you're not crowding him or putting an excess amount of downward pressure on the halter. Digging your fingers into the top of the horse's head to get him to do this isn't what we're striving to do here. Use a kind of flat hand and take the time it takes. From the look of this mare and her head position, she seems to be quite interested in something over on her left (Figures 3-6). You can see from Figure 7 that she finally started to get with this person a little more and picked up his feel through the halter and his hand on her poll. There's no force used in this whatsoever.

Give your horse the feel to lower his head again and wait for a little change. When he drops his head a little, take your hands off his halter and neck. That is his reward. Wait a few seconds, and then start the procedure all over again.

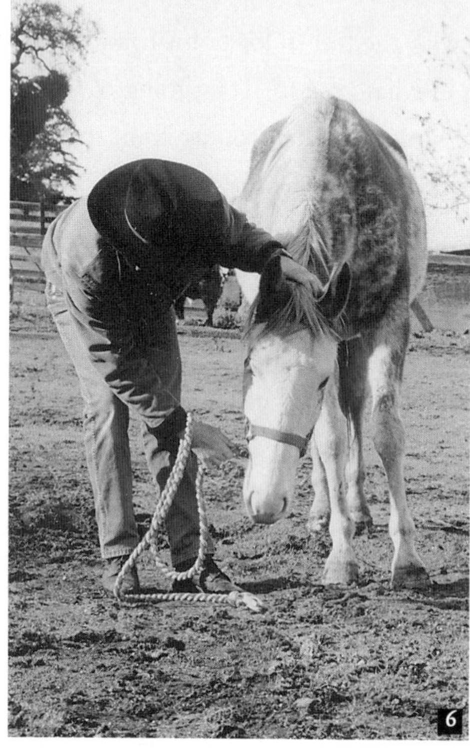

Diamond Lu Collection series

It may take a few tries before you can recognize when the horse is trying. It might take awhile before you can actually see what he's able to show you, his way, when he's trying to understand you. No matter how little he does in the beginning, reward him with a release. This will give him the confidence that he's doing what's expected of him, and encourages him to keep trying to understand you in the future. When that horse is released from pressure on time, each time he happens to hit on the desired response, why he will adjust his future responses to your feel in a way that takes less and less pressure from you. What he does will start to look like the picture you have in mind. When this starts to happen, the horse is feeling of you, and a real good connection starts to get set up between you and the horse. This is what a good foundation goes back to.

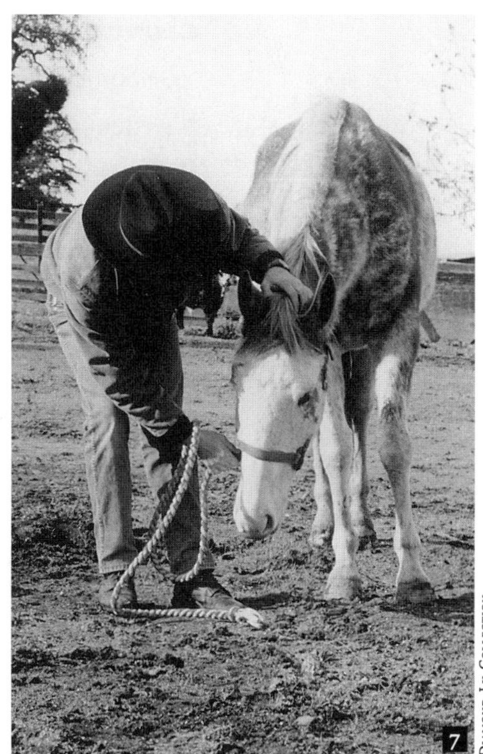
7

Diamond Lu Collection

This approach to the horse's mind is the most important part. You're working to develop his actual understanding — not his automatic response to force with the understanding left out. It can lead a person to the experience of feel with the horse that goes two ways. It (reciprocal feel) *begins* when force and speed are replaced with patience and a different feel that comes when you start to understand the horse's point of view.

Sometimes when you miss the chance to reward the horse's efforts by easing off the pressure, it can take a long time before he's ready to try that same move again. That's because he's pretty sure that lowering his head wasn't what you had in mind. If you don't release that pressure when he gives a little try, then he can't be too sure of what you want. But, he'll keep searching in other areas to see what you expect him to do. If you've missed his tries a few times, then lowering his head might not occur to him to try again for awhile.

Eventually he'll hit on that idea again because most horses want to know what you'd like them to do. It's in their nature to want to get along, and they are curious anyway. To me, it seems that if a person knew this, they might have more interest in waiting for that horse to figure out what they expected him to do. Of course, when a little change shows up, that's when you'd reward him *right away*, by easing off on the tension that's been put in that rope. These releases are how he learns to figure out the meaning of your physical contact and your presence. For this to work, a fella needs to offer the horse a release for the smallest try he gives. And he'd be sure not to get discouraged if he missed on the timing at first.

After the horse lowers his head, watch for him to let his breath out, lick his lips, and chew or yawn. These are all good indications that you and he understand one another. It's rare to observe resistance between a horse and a person when this chewing and licking is going on.

Learning to Follow a Feel — In Practice

Sometimes a horse will hear or see something that interests him and it will take his attention off you and the job you have in mind for him. If you go along with his movements, his responsiveness to your feel will be easier to build in.

In the next set of pictures, this fella's following the horse's head all around there because he's learned how to go with that horse (Figures 8-18). This is how the horse learns to follow a person's feel. There's a fine line there, between a horse getting distracted for a second or two, and a horse taking over with some plans of his own, or responding to his natural instincts of self-preservation. Depending on the situation

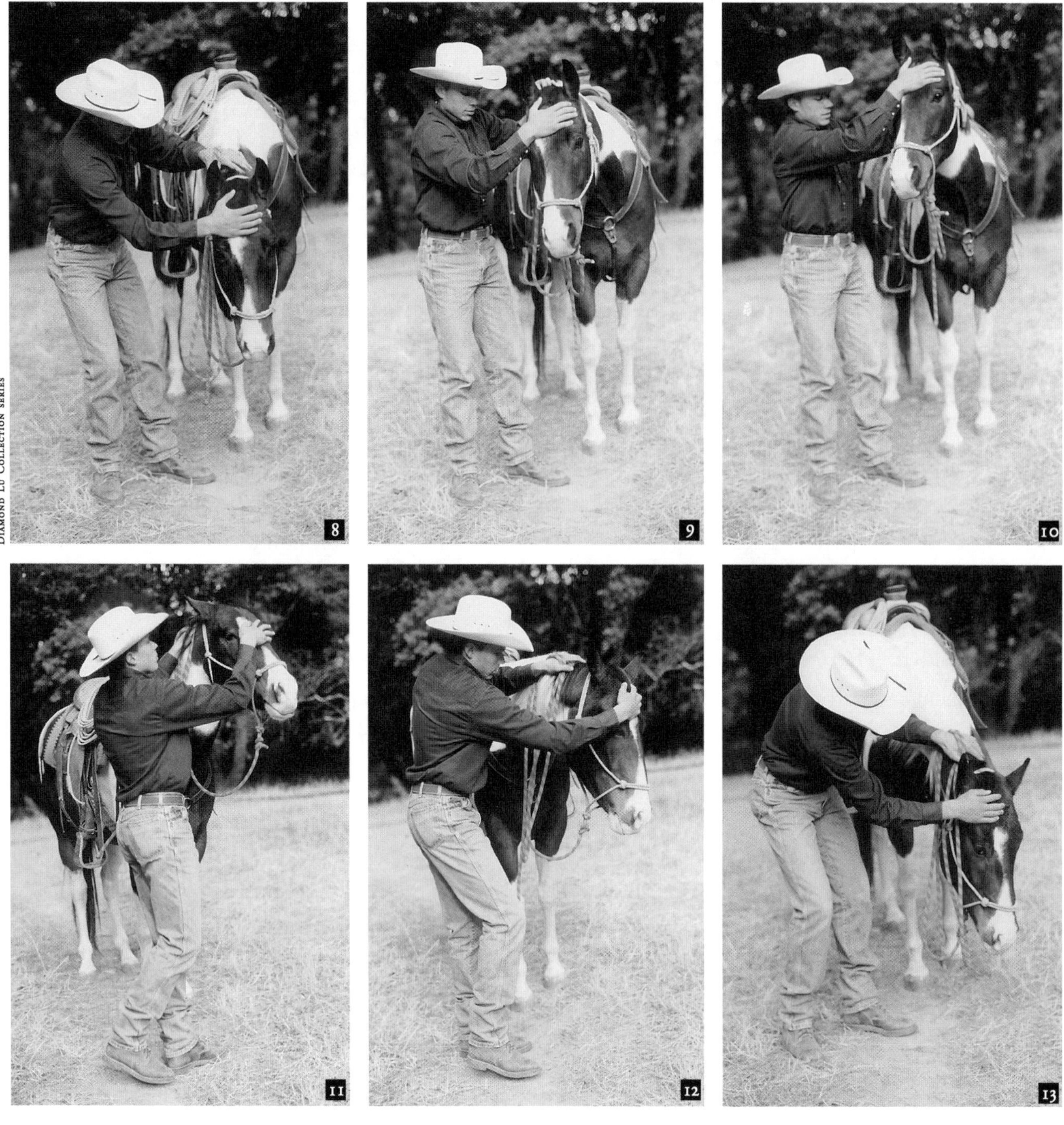

Diamond Lu Collection series

and the horse involved, this could be too far up the line for a person. A horse can get distracted and take over if he hasn't learned how to feel of a person. That's why we want to get the basics built in early.

There isn't any room for force when you're teaching this to the horse. With force in there, why he won't learn what you're hoping he will, but he'd be learning a lot about resisting a person. And, he's liable to be confused about any requirements for him to speed up, if you'd want that, before he understood what's expected when you're going slowly. It's best when your feel and timing meet up together and he can get with your feel, like he's started to do here (Figures 14-18). There is no formula for this, and there's no one thing that a person can do that will work on every horse the same way every time. That foundation a fella builds in there on the start is what he has to rely on if there's some trouble that develops on the job. Without that, he just has self-preservation and some guesswork to fall back on, and that's not always the best.

Diamond Lu Collection series

It's best if the horse is flexible in both directions and can maintain this real mellow appearance when his head is low. It isn't always possible, but we're in hopes of keeping that horse nice and relaxed no matter what we want him to do (Figures 19-22).

After a while practicing at this, the person and the horse will get to a place where they're getting along good together. When it's this way, generally speaking, they have the same idea about things at the same time and many desirable things can happen with a horse that's had this foundation laid in early.

You'll continue this exercise until the horse learns to lower his head any time you present him with that feel. To find out what he requires in order to refine his responsiveness and respect for your feel, why you just keep on with your testing and experiments. You'll take it to a point where he will drop his head down when either hand gives him the feel to lower his head — whether it's on his neck near the poll, or on the halter rope. This is the sensitivity you hope to have available to you when you're sitting on him.

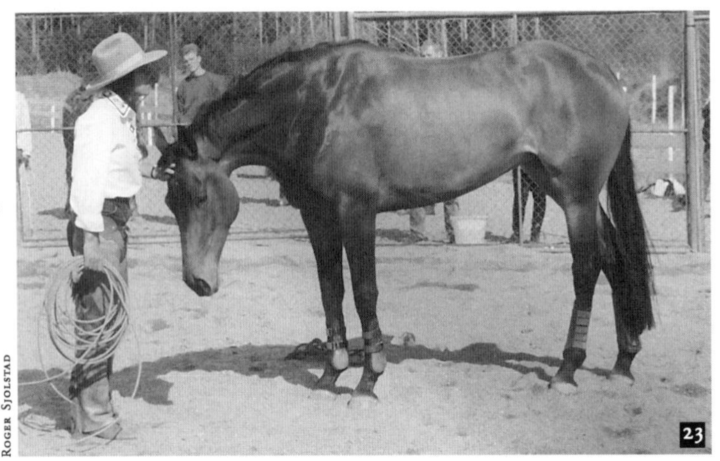

Roger Sjolstad

This horse is relaxed and isn't crowding the person. There's respect between them and feel that goes both ways.

For some things you'll do with the horse he might need to have the ability to move his head and neck to a lot of different places, and for many reasons. The payoff in this comes later on when you can lower his head, or place it anywhere you want to, from his back.

Each lesson has its proper order in the foundation you are building in your horse. When he understands what you want, he will do it.

Bringing the Head from Side-to-Side Real Slow, with the Feet Still

After the horse will lower and raise his head without any resistance, stand just a little bit ahead of the shoulder and ask him to bring his head around towards you, to one side or the other, without moving his feet. You'll want to have one hand on his poll or his neck, and one hand on the bridge of his nose, or you can put one hand on the halter knot under his lower jaw or chin, depending on how big his head is and how his halter fits. Stand out of his way when you bring his head in your direction, and try not to crowd his shoulders or push against him in any way (Figures 24-25). He's apt to resent it if you bring him in real close to you and press on his muzzle or make quick grabbing motions on his face. Actions like that will actually encourage him to pull his head away, which would be his right. Developing a presentation that really feels good to the horse is something a person needs to learn about and *get good at.*

Kim Murphy

Kim Murphy

When you try this on an older horse, it might take longer for him to understand your intentions. That's all right. Older horses can have a pretty big brace developed in their poll and neck and shoulders. You work with those horses right where they are. A fella's experimenting will show him where to stand, and how much or little it takes to connect with that horse's mind. The horse's mental and physical setups work real close together.

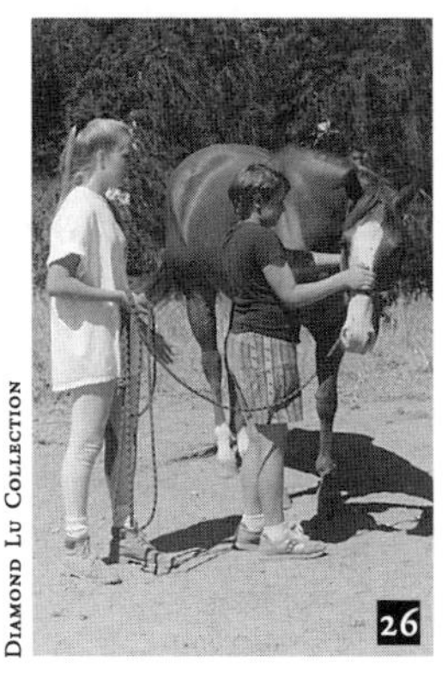

Diamond Lu Collection

26

Diamond Lu Collection

27

This boy is trying to learn the best way he knows how with some supervision. But they've both missed something here — that boy is standing too close (Figure 26). If that horse came forward suddenly, he'd step on the boy's toes or bump into him. This horse is big and could use a little extra room to bend his neck (Figure 27). But these kids are experimenting and they appear to have a nice way of being around horses. His calm expression tells you this.

At first, some horses are liable not to give their heads, but will walk towards you, or do something else. If they do this, let them move around a little and go along with them, but stay in a safe position so you don't get stepped on. If you're liable to get out of position or don't have much strength for some reason, it can help to hold onto the saddle while you're taking his head around and waiting until he can get his feet stopped. Just go with him while he travels in small circles. If you can't keep that head turned towards you a little, keep in mind he might just go straight off or turn the other way and drag you along back by the flank. That could produce surprising results if he was going away from you and you were back there. You'd do your very best to avoid that and one way you could go about it is shown below.

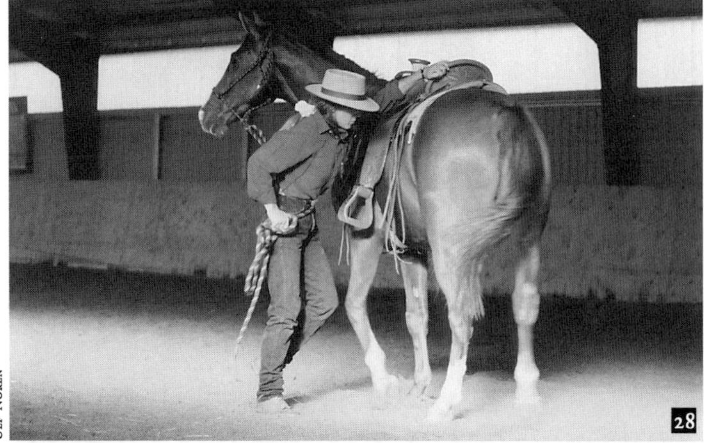

Ulf Noren

28

Ulf Noren

29

This horse thinks he should be moving his feet (Figures 28-29). It could take time for a horse to understand that you want him to just turn his head loose at the poll and bend his neck a little. You'd be sure to release him when he does, but be sure to wait until *after his feet have stopped moving*, and after he's tipped his head in your direction and relieved that pressure on his head.

Learning to Wait

To some people, it might seem like the person in these pictures is trying to get the horse to move his hindquarters over. She is following the horse's movements, and waiting for his feet to stop. This can take time. If she wanted the horse to get these hindquarters to yield, she'd present an entirely different feel and more energy would be going towards that horse to cause him to step away from her. There's a world of difference in that, and it's easy to confuse the two when you're watching.

At this point, you're trying to establish that the horse can 1) bend his neck around real soft in both directions and take his head left or right by bending laterally at the poll, and 2) keep his feet still at the same time. I'll just say that no matter if you are working with the horse on the ground or from his back, it's the feel that you present, combined with the timing of your releases and your body position, that add up to inform the horse about what your intentions are. If you don't release his head when he starts to give to the feel you present, why that horse can become confused about what you had in mind. He might think he should move his feet again to get you to release his head. If he's thinking that, he will try to. At that point, you need to get his feet stopped and take a fresh start. If he moves his feet again, this is a good indication that he isn't clear on what you want. It might take him some more time to figure out that the feel you offered to him was intended to reposition his head and neck, not to move his feet. A person can take another start. Take as many fresh starts as you need to.

Timing Your Releases

Once the feet are stopped *and* his head is still held around to the side, wait until he moves his head towards your hand a little to take the pressure off himself, then release his head. When you want him to bring his head in your direction, it is important that you don't release his head just because he stopped his feet. In the beginning, it will be difficult to remember this. Be aware that when you have his head around to one side and you release his head for stopping his feet, it will give him the wrong idea altogether. Don't worry about this, just focus a little more on the picture of what you want and have another go at it. Eventually the two of you will get this sorted out. This is important for the horse's future.

On the start, your release should enable him to put his head and neck all the way back to a normal posture, so he's standing straight again. To do this, be ready with a long enough coil of rope in your hand to let go of, so you don't catch him up suddenly with a short, tight line in the middle of the reward he's enjoying for doing what you wanted. Further up the line, you won't need to give the horse a complete, full release. Just easing off a little will be enough later on, and you can build on the understanding he has about giving his head. Later is when you'd want to start experimenting with combinations of vertical and lateral flexion. *If you try this too soon, you'd set your horse back in his understanding about feel, so you'll wait on that.*

If a fella was working through feel, he'd not ever tie the horse's head around where he couldn't straighten it all the way out again. After a horse understands that he should give back a soft, giving response, *he needs to be free to take a normal position and think things over right then.* I'll just mention here that the way some people go about getting a horse to turn loose can sure build a real hefty brace into him about turning loose *at the same time.* Or, they get that softness in there that is too soft, and has no connection to the mental system. We aren't wanting any part of responses like this from a horse, *because the feel is missing.*

For best results, these exercises should be tried in the order presented and should not be rushed. Be sure to work from both sides of the horse. The horse has the ability to distinguish between several meanings at once, and a person needs to help him develop this quality. But first a person needs to be able to make those distinctions himself, before he can help the horse. As a fella does this, the responsiveness that he's developing in that horse on the ground *through feel* will begin take on the appearance and qualities of lightness. This will carry over directly to his mounted work.

Teaching an Older Horse to Soften

The next group of pictures show a case where the horse is older and broke to ride without much feel, let's say, so his head kind of comes up as a person goes to gather those reins (Figure 30). Well, he's wondering what he's supposed to do because he's not familiar with any part of what's happening there. And he's apt to think he needs to move those feet and poke his nose out when those reins are gathered up. But, this horse is being taught to flex at the poll while those feet stay put, so it's going to be easier for him to feel of the snaffle bit in the future. In this person's experimenting, she kept the same tension and position on the left rein and grabbed a handful of mane to steady the rein on that side, and moved her feet back in case he stepped forward into the pressure of the bit. She also changed the angle on the rein by slowly lowering her right hand and the horse offered quite a little resistance to that (Figure 31). He hasn't really let go yet, but his searching frame of mind is the start of

30

31

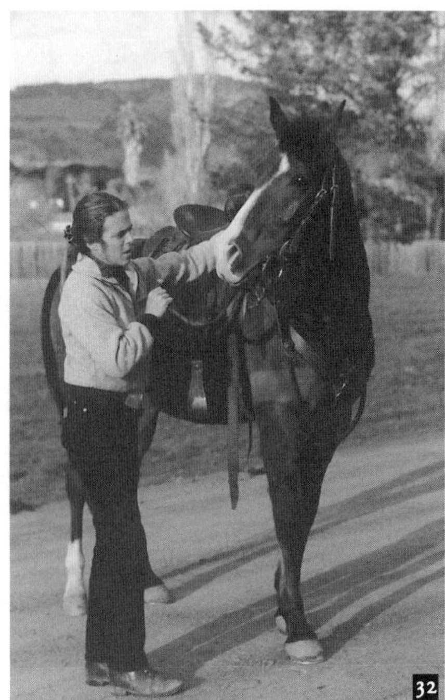
32

Kim Murphy series

33

34

35

Kim Murphy series

it, and then he turned his head loose in her direction. She released the tension on the rein and then took a fresh start (Figures 32-33).

On this try, he picked up a little more feel now and he tucked his chin a little. He's a little more mellow and that's a big start for this horse, or any horse. In the Figures 34-35, he's feeling of that snaffle and real flexed at the poll. He's got a nice expression and there's understanding starting to develop now. He's ready to take a step in any direction because he's prepared to follow a feel, and he could do that from the saddle or the ground. It will be a lot easier for him to learn how to move his feet through feel, because a little foundation is started now.

Taking His Head Around While Mounted

When a horse is just learning to do this while a rider's sitting on him, it's a good idea to bring your hand around to a spot on your leg and push down with your fist (Figure 36). This adds a little stability and sureness to your feel. It's reassuring for a horse to get a rub on the forehead when he gets his head around (Figures 37-38). A person oughtn't slap a horse and think they're rubbing him, but some people do this anyway and say they are petting him. In most cases, that really doesn't fit a horse, and sharp fingernails aren't fitting either. A fella can use either hand for this. Figure 38 shows how the rider prefers to hold the reins in the left hand and keep his hand fixed against his leg so he can rub the horse's face with his right hand. Either way's all right, but if the horse is not apt to stay put, or if things got real active on the spur of the moment, why a fella might be able to present a more consistent feel if he didn't have to change hands on the leading rein. Practice this on both sides until the horse is real relaxed about bringing his head around with a float in the rein in both direc-

Diamond Lu Collection series

36

37

38

tions. It'd help a horse if this exercise is practiced a lot before any thought to not rubbing his head comes in there.

In the next set of pictures, you can see that it'd be no different if you were riding in the hackamore. Take the horse's head to the side, using feel. An observing person would notice that this horse has his attention someplace else (Figure 39). But in Figure 40, he made a change and is sticking close to the feel of the rider, and is relaxed. This other fella's reaching over to rub the horse's face, being careful not to put too much weight over that horse's right shoulder or to twist that saddle on his back by leaning into the right stirrup (Figures 41-42). It's easy to forget that staying centered on a horse's back is real important to the horse.

Diamond Lu Collection

39

40

Joan Glass

41

42

How Softness Can Carry Over

When you're horseback and you want the horse to lower his head, you'd adjust the feel you present through the reins. With your arms a little extended and your elbows coming straight back past your ribs (not out to the side), get the feel of the horse until he begins to get with your feel, and can lower the head a little. Each time he drops down a little, you'd ease off and present the feel again until his head could go real low, with very little effort on your part. One day, the suggestion for this is all it will take — whether the horse is standing still or moving forward.

These pictures show the horse lowering her head in response to a change of feel *coming through the bit and through the reins moving against the neck* (Figures 43-45). Be sure your mecate is tied long enough so that horse can extend her head down as low as you want.

43

44

Jen Simmons series

45

46

47

48

Richard Field Levine series

To take the head around, start with your reins even (Figure 46). Then shorten your right rein without tightening it (Figure 47). The plan is to bring your arm in a wide arc out to the side, past your knee and then up towards your hip (Figure 48). Turning your own head *before* you take out the slack in the rein gets the horse used to the change in your whole body that he needs to understand to make good turns later on. The rein doesn't ever need to come tight when he's been prepared for this on the ground. He'll follow the feel of the float in the rope and turn loose (laterally) in his poll and neck. Don't drop the leading rein when you release the head. This is *too much release* for some horses, and some can get sort of lost and bothered. Release his head *and bring it back into a normal position with your holding arm.* Too much release is just a great waste of a good opportunity for that horse to learn about the meaning in the feel of a person's holding arm, because it has a real important job now, and in the future.

You'd take a fresh start from a normal standing position before taking the head in the other direction (Figure 49). These pictures show the same exercise with the leading — or directing — arm in a different position, which brings the rein in a little closer to the neck. You could use this position on a horse that already had a good start on the basics of feel laid into his foundation (Figure 50). As you progress in your lessons, experiment with how little it takes to get something accomplished. If a person has plans to someday ride with both reins in one hand, there'd be a need to adjust from making a wide arc with your arm, to making less of one.

49

50

51

Richard Field Levine series

As the horse progresses, he should gain confidence in the rider's feel. If the horse is confident in the dependability of the rider's feel and a release doesn't come right away (Figure 51), then that horse is likely to search further for the intended meaning in the feel that's presented (Figure 52). Even though the float was left in this leading rein all the time, that horse knew there was more expected of him because the feel to bring the head back to the middle that came from the holding arm hadn't shown up yet. When the horse turned loose at the poll, then that release showed up and his head was brought back to a normal position by that rider. There's quite a little that goes into this preparation, and I'm in hopes that people will wonder about this part of things. If they do, they might put aside the time it takes to get good at this. It is so important to a horse that they do.

52

Diamond Lu Collection

Diamond Lu Collection

The reason you take the horse's nose back behind the vertical on the start is to build that happy medium once your horse starts to travel out. The horse in Figure 53 is learning how to tuck his chin while he's walking and he's responded to the rider in a supple way. This is an example of vertical flexion where the horse responds well to the feel presented from both of his arms. The horse can sometimes feel of you a little better if you start with one hand higher than the other. You'd wait to present a feel for this until he was used to giving his head freely in both directions.

This paint horse is relaxed, which puts him in position to respond with a real nice soft feel (Figure 54). When he's working he won't come back that far, and you'll leave it up to the horse to find the best spot for his head and poll when he's releasing through feel to those reins. She has good posture and a nice feel to offer that is fitting to this horse. The reins on this outfit look very new and were probably made by hand. This girl will be shortening them at the first opportunity she gets, because they are much too long.

It's a good idea to have all the exercises presented in this book real smooth on the ground before you ride your horse. We just have this one book now, so that's the reason you see people horseback before the next exercise. I don't want there to be any confusion on this, due to the mix-up it can create for a horse.

In the next part, we're going to speak about leading up real free.

Part 2 — Teaching Your Horse to Lead Up Real Free

A horse that doesn't lead up well when you want him to, isn't going to be reliable to ride. When you cannot control the timing and placement of his feet in response to the feel you present with the lead rope, your intent won't be clear to him through the reins either.

These pictures show some horses and a pony that have been taught to lead up real free. There's no confusion about what's expected of them, and they aren't offering any resistance. This is what you want. A horse that's been taught to lower and raise his head, and to move it just about anywhere you want, and to lead up, why that sort of horse can be led just about anywhere, anytime, by the forelock.

The feel to lead up real free carries over to that nice, light feel I'm in hopes people will want to build into their saddle horses. Whether you're on the ground or riding another horse when you're getting a horse to lead up doesn't matter — the results you want are the same. You just have to adjust your presentation, is all. The main thing is that you want the horse to respect

Lori Kline

you, and to respect the horse you're riding if you're horseback. No part of fear is figuring into this whatsoever.

All you'll need is a lead rope and a halter — any kind will do. Or, you can use a snaffle bit, it just all depends on the horse and the situation. The instructions on how to set up a snaffle bit for this were spoken about in the beginning part of this chapter.

If a horse is pretty braced, it's sometimes easier for him to understand the feel to lead up using a snaffle bit, but you'll want to switch back to a rope and halter after you've gotten him to lead up in the snaffle. I'll speak more about this later on.

When you've got a horse leading up real free, you won't have to rely on equipment. You can rely on direct feel applied to almost any part of his body, as long as he understands what you intend for him to do. Your equipment might still be there, but the way you'd use it would feel different to the horse, because once he understood you, the way you'd use it would be different. When a person switches over to working through feel, the focus of their presentation is going to be more about the process, and how their intentions are understood by that horse. Where before, maybe, they might have been thinking about what they should actually do with that equipment to do something to that horse. Well, there's nothing the same in that.

Test Him Out

No matter what you have on the horse's head, you'll first test him out on certain things to see how much he understands. See if he can feel of you to take a step forward or back, like you see this person doing in Figures 6 and 7. If he responds well to your feel for these things — and some horses will — then you'll need to help him refine his responses to get more done using less pressure, until it takes almost nothing to maneuver him forward and back, allowing him to stop in between each step. From there you'll start on some of the other maneuvers mentioned a little further on in this chapter, until you can place any of his feet just about any place you want to.

RICHARD FIELD LEVINE

6

RICHARD FIELD LEVINE

7

If he doesn't step forward and back real smooth, then you'll need to teach him more about respect, and you'll get this working for you by teaching him how to follow your feel to lead up real free. For a lot of people, I'll say most, this idea about leading up real free might not have occurred to them. Leading a horse might bring some different things to mind than what we're talking about here. What I mean by "leading up real free" is a horse paying attention to the feel of your halter rope, or your reins, and following the feel you present by livening up his whole body. The important part in this is that he's ready to move his feet, and will move them, before the float is ever taken out of the rope. And he'll do this without any confusion, and he won't be trying to take over with ideas of his own. No, it would only be in response to your feel to move that he'll lead up with a float in the rope and look for a place to go. What I mean when I say "float" is the slack in the rope, and there's been more written about this in Chapters 8 and 9. It's important for you to understand what float is, all right.

Maintain Float in the Rope

You don't want the rope have to come tight to get him to move his feet, but it might get tight a few times until he catches on. If you're pulling that horse one place or another, why you're just dragging him along then, and that's a miserable feel (Figure 8). It isn't very attractive either, and that's not the worst thing about it. It's proof of the actual fact that a person and a horse aren't really together in the way that matters most to the horse. And if you do have a job to get done, why there might be some surprising things that happen during your project. Or it might not get done at all. But if you know what to look for, why the horse shows you important things about his general makeup and the way he's feeling about even the littlest things you have for him to do, way before you'd get close to any of those bigger jobs. So that's the main reason we want those feet real free, and to get him feeling of you through those reins or halter rope. Because when you need to get going, it's those feet that are going to get you there. They need to be reliable.

8

Diamond Lu Collection

Rather than drag your horse along behind you, this exercise will help you teach your horse how to lead as he should, with a float in the line and confidence about the placement of his feet and their distance from you. There's no resistance and no disrespect in him. But there's a fine line between the two, because if resistance does come in there, and for sure it sometimes will, it doesn't necessarily mean the horse is being disrespectful. It could be that he's aware of things the handler or rider is doing to get him confused and sort of hepped up — things that person isn't aware of. Or something could have startled the horse.

A Horse's Self-Preservation Instinct is Natural

There is always a rightful place for a horse to exercise his concern for self-preservation. It's important to remember that this is the horse's right. When it's up to the horse, he won't do what isn't natural to him anyway, and of course, self-preserving actions are right at the top of the list of things that are natural to him.

Self-preservation is his main job. And it's your job to learn how to handle those situations when they come up, and to get back that better feel you had going with the horse before his instincts caused him to stop feeling of you. That way you can finish the other job you had to do, whatever it was, and when you put the horse up you'd both be feeling good again. And there'd be no need to mention anything that wasn't the best about that horse.

When His Feet Don't Move

As you start experimenting on different horses, you're liable to find that some horses will only follow with their head and neck stretching way out, and their feet won't be too active. A horse can put quite a little resistance in there if he doesn't understand your feel. That's when you take a step off to the side a little ways — about most of the way down your rein or rope — at about a 45 degree angle off in front of the shoulder, and you give a good, firm pull. You don't want to be jerking on that rope. I'm talking about a firm, smooth pull and I'll speak more about this later on, in "Misuse of the Lead Rope."

Depending on how mixed up the horse is about feel, you might have to adjust the direction of that angle towards the back of the horse. But whatever place you start from, you'll do this a few times, being sure to get that body and those feet to move some in your direction each time you pull. Soon, he'll begin to move his feet to follow your feel as the slack is coming out of the line. In the beginning he may want to raise up his head and neck when you lead him forward, but that's all right because he's already been taught to lower his head when he's just standing there. It's the feet you're concerned with now.

If it doesn't seem like the understanding is there, you'll always be ready to give that horse the benefit of any doubt, of course, and not hurry him on the start. You don't ever want to hurry him when you're trying to teach him something he doesn't understand. You'll wait maybe a little while to see if he can understand your meaning as the slack comes out of the line, and if there is any effort at all to come towards you, why you'll ease right off. That is his reward. You'll wait a few seconds, and then take a fresh start.

If he's still unsure, or even stuck there real solid and just stretching out that neck and braced against your feel for him to lead up, that's when you'll have to make another adjustment. And you'll *all the time* be aware that he's learned how to do this by the way he's been handled. There'd be no thought of yanking or jerking on that line when he's braced this way, because he just needs your help. You'll want to have plenty of patience, with no thought on the clock. And in your testing, you might try stepping off to one side a little further, or waiting a little longer for a change to show up. You'll try to make it as easy for the horse to get with you as you can. It might take several fresh starts before your adjustments fit the horse and a change shows up. Or he might be changing all the time to try and fit you, but you just don't see it. Sometimes a person hasn't had enough experience to know what's taking place for the horse, not where those smaller particles of feel are concerned anyway.

Let's say there's no change for quite a little time, except maybe that horse sulls up (that means shuts down). Or he gets to implementing some ideas of his own that cause him to wander off in another direction to graze, or bump into you because he thinks you're in his way. Some horses might think taking off is a good idea. If these things start happening, you're late. Well, I'll put it this way — you're too late to head those things off because they've already shaped up. But then you're still experimenting in all of this, too, no different than what the horse is doing. There's no right or wrong to it really anyway, so when you realized what was taking place, you'd get prepared earlier the next time, and have something for him to do before his plan that didn't include you got underway. What you'd do is just add quite a bit more firmness to your next pull on that lead rope, after the slack is all the way out of it, and you'd hope to get the change that would start that horse and you out on a better track.

You want to present a smooth, firm pull that has no snapping action to it. And just as you give that firm pull, you'll be sure to let your hand open up real quick to remove all pressure from the horse's head. Of course, you'll still have the rope in your hand, held loosely. For this pull to be effective and the release to have meaning, you'll need to cause his feet to move towards you as you leave, and it may take a couple of tries to understand what's required for this to happen. You'd be sure not to block him with your body when he tries to come where you're directing him to follow you. You'd look where you were headed as much as you could, because the idea of actually following is what we're trying to get across in this. And for this to happen someone has to be leading that horse, through feel.

Take the float out of the rope real smooth as you leave (Figure 9). When the slack is all the way out of the rope, firm up as you take off (Figure 10), and be ready to slip some rope to the horse by opening your hand just as soon as he takes a step to follow your feel (Figures 11-12). Be sure you do this from both sides (Figures 13-16). One side is liable to work a little smoother than the other, but you wouldn't worry about that. The main thing is to teach that horse to liven up his whole body and move those feet before the slack comes out of the rope.

Diamond Lu Collection series

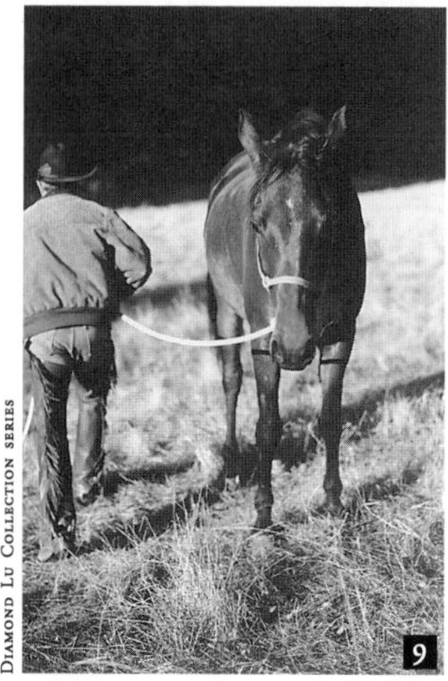

This pulling action may startle the horse a bit, so you want him to have a few seconds to settle before asking him to lead up again. You'll repeat this, on both sides of the horse, as many times as it takes until he can move his feet in your direction before the slack comes out of the rope. Depending on your experience and the horse, you wouldn't expect to get this all in one session. Some horses are faster to catch on than others, and some people can present this is in a way that fits a horse better than others. It's all in the amount of time you have to practice and the different ways you experiment applying your feel. You'll do plenty of speculating as you get this to working for you on different horses, because no two are the same. A fella who really wants to fit a horse, why he sure can, if he's willing to spend the time it takes.

Figures 17-18 illustrate how to make an effective pull to the left. When it's applied correctly to a horse that won't lead up freely, this way of teaching a horse to lead works right away and doesn't cause the horse any pain or upset in his mental system. After a while, the horse will start to arrange his body so he can get his feet moving before the slack comes out of the lead rope. This is real helpful because it carries over to your mounted work when you're handling those reins.

It's best to leave quick and not look back at the horse. Some horses will get confused if you look back, especially if they've had a lot of pressure put on them in certain situations. Sometimes it isn't natural for a person to do it this way, but if the feel presented is effective, then after a few tries at this the horse will start leading up real free, anyway, like the horse in these next pictures did.

13

14

15

16

17

18

Diamond Lu Collection

When you're leading the horse straight, it can take him a few tries before he connects this new feel of a straight-ahead pull with the meaning you had for him when those pulls were off to one side or another (Figure 19). The important part of this is to ease off as soon as he puts any slack at all in the rope (Figure 20). If you gather up the slack and shorten the rope when he frees up those feet, it's not going to work. Some people who learned how to drag a horse will have to unlearn this habit first.

As the horse starts to catch on, it will take less effort to get him leading up. After a few more tries at this, just the firmness of your arm pushing out in front and straight ahead of you as you're going along there should be enough to bring him along at the trot (Figures 21-24). He'll get so he can lead up without any resistance

Diamond Lu Collection series

when you run. Or, he'll be able to trot by you if he's directed to, without the float ever coming out of that rope. He's real responsive to your feel when that happens, and in that is his respect for you.

After a little practice at this, the horse will begin to understand what you expect from him. He'll get ready when you get ready, and he'll lead up real free when you take off ahead of him. On the start, it might take a try or two to get him to lead up real free. When it's built in there on a good foundation like we've been speaking about here, he won't get the idea to bump into your back or even to crowd you, because he'll have learned to feel of you and there's nothing about leading a horse that would cause him to think it'd be all right to do that. We'll say that if he is doing that, then he's not feeling of you and it'd be a good idea to go back down the line a little to a place where you can get him to understand that you don't want him to crowd you. There's a few things you can do to help your horse understand this. Sometimes, I just let him bump into my fist with his nose for general correction purposes. It can happen that he finds the tail end of my lead rope someplace, or I'll generate a little activity in that rope closer to the halter knot, and he finds the limit that way.

This leading up exercise will have quite a lot of value later on when you need to maneuver the horse's feet left and right on the ground, or from his back. When he's already learned how to respond to your feel, and to move his feet freely with some float in the line, the horse is apt to get the message about your intentions for lateral maneuvers without resistance. With the preparation just described working real smooth between you, the horses can usually pick this up right away.

Every horse is different, as I've spoken about before. Some horses are going to maneuver for you real free, but some of them may not understand where you'd like them to put their feet even though they have that willingness. Your planning plays a big part in this. So on a horse like this, you'd spend quite a little time thinking things through and planning ahead, because you and that horse need to get on the same track about where those feet should be. And you want this part to be accurate. With other horses, it might take a little bit longer for them to understand that they even need to move their feet, so maybe you'll have to use just a tiny bit more firmness — but no jerks and no sudden pulls. This goes right against what a horse can understand, and we want to stay entirely away from any moves like that.

A lot of people have a difficult time understanding what an important tool the lead rope is. Because it's real easy to confuse the horse if the rope isn't used in a way that he can understand what you're trying to present, I want to explain a few extra things about that subject now.

Misuse of the Lead Rope

I disapprove of jerking or snapping that lead rope because the horse doesn't have an opportunity to feel of you if you do that. That valuable connection with the horse is lost between pulls when a person gets to sort of jerking on that rope for one reason or another. And that sort of jerking motion is usually connected to emotion in a person that isn't the best. We could call that frustration. When a person is acting like this, a horse doesn't have a chance to get with them, because the feel being offered isn't there long enough to have any good meaning for him. His guesswork and self-preservation will start to figure into things because that jerking will kind of upset him mentally. It comes so quick and fast. The horse can't be sure what it means when a person's feel is excessive and then gets replaced with a full release, and then comes in there again so sharp and so fast, over and over again. I've seen people do this. Some people might think by doing this they're getting something accomplished, but the horse isn't set up to understand what he's supposed to do in response to a feel like this. He isn't geared for this in his thinking.

We want things to be real clear between a horse and the person handling him. We want to stay away from any mix-up for the horse concerning force or fear, so your feel must be applied in a way that he can understand, without any part of force or fear coming in there. Some people might need some time to think over this subject and I'm in hopes they do, because this is so important to the horse. It's also real important to the person's future with any horse.

It's the surprising full release that gets put in there between those jerking motions that gets confusing for the horse, and it can lead to a lot of other problems, too. In most cases *any release* has actual meaning for a horse. But the releases between those unwanted jerking motions, why the horse just doesn't understand these properly. They come right on either side of the moments when the jerked rope gets tight and the horse feels that meaningless pressure, and that bothers him. So that horse tries to understand what actions he made, or is making that he should associate with these real meaningful releases of the pressure on him. What the person usually doesn't understand is that they're applying these reassuring messages to the horse for not doing what they want him to do. *Those releases that are part of any jerking of the horse's mouth or head just encourage more of the thing that person doesn't want.* This type of handling is very confusing for the horse. And, of course, a person who does this is confused about things from the horse's point of view. There's a need for concern in this, because too much of this activity can lead to resentment or fear in the horse, which is usually the cause of dangerous and unreliable behavior in those horses. It's unnecessary and avoidable. If people could remember that any jerking on the horse just erodes whatever confidence he might have had in the human before that, I'm in hopes they'll be willing to try something more fitting to him.

No matter if there is a halter or a snaffle bit on the horse, the smoothness of that other way of firming up described earlier has a lot of meaning to the horse. There's a world of difference in those two ways of pulling on a horse.

25 DIAMOND LU COLLECTION

Using a Snaffle Bit to Help a More Braced Horse Lead Up Free

Like I spoke about earlier, it might help a horse that's braced to understand the feel to lead up real free if he's got a snaffle bit in his mouth, rather than a halter across his nose (Figure 25). But after you'd gotten him to understand your feel in the snaffle bit, then you'd switch back to your rope and halter for general handling purposes. If that rope and halter aren't effective after a person gets him to operate those feet while he's wearing a snaffle bit, why they've gone about it all wrong (Figure 26). I'll say there could be more ideas about equipment than feel taking place in that person's mind, and some force maybe got worked into the practice sessions, too. In a case like that, the horse probably isn't responding to feel the way they think he is, and the best thing to do is get some supervision from someone who has more experience using feel, and who can help other people understand it and get it applied.

26 DIAMOND LU COLLECTION

One Colt that Didn't Lead Up

The horse in this picture was a real interesting case (Figure 27). He was a nice-minded colt — his breed doesn't matter. He had some confusion in two main areas that were connected real close, even though a lot of people wouldn't be able to see that they were. When he was stopped on the ground, he wouldn't get going, and once he got going he didn't want to stop. He'd just crowd right into the person and sort of run them down. That's because he didn't understand the feel to get going or the feel to stop — not either one — and the people who'd been handling him didn't understand either. They had no idea that anything they did with that halter rope or those reins was supposed to connect in that horse's mind to his feet. And that's understandable.

27 RICHARD FIELD LEVINE

BILL AND THE THREE-YEAR-OLD COLT HE RESTARTED IN 1997.

This is a real common problem. Just about every place I've been I see things like this. Most people try to solve the problem with a restraint rig of some type or, maybe if they haven't learned a better way, they're liable to use some other kind of force or fear to get their message across. The girl who was trying to prepare this horse for jumping shows had very little success trying to stop him from bumping into her when he was on the end of the halter rope. She said a crop was used to keep the horse from running into people. And Leslie, she was helping me at the clinic that day, and she had about the same amount of success using a halter and rope to get that horse to lead up — and that wasn't much. So that's about the time when it's real handy to know about the snaffle bit adjustments spoken about earlier, and the way to apply feel using one.

This next picture shows how the horse is ready to take off and he sure did all right (Figure 28). He needed to be shown the limit to that straight away (Figure 29). After he stopped short, there was some confusion for him about taking one more step forward (Figures 30-31). Of course that was understandable, no better than he'd been taught to lead up in the first place. When a person hasn't had an opportunity to learn about this, why they do the best they can with what they know, and this horse had plenty of try and willingness still in him, so they were going to be all right anyway.

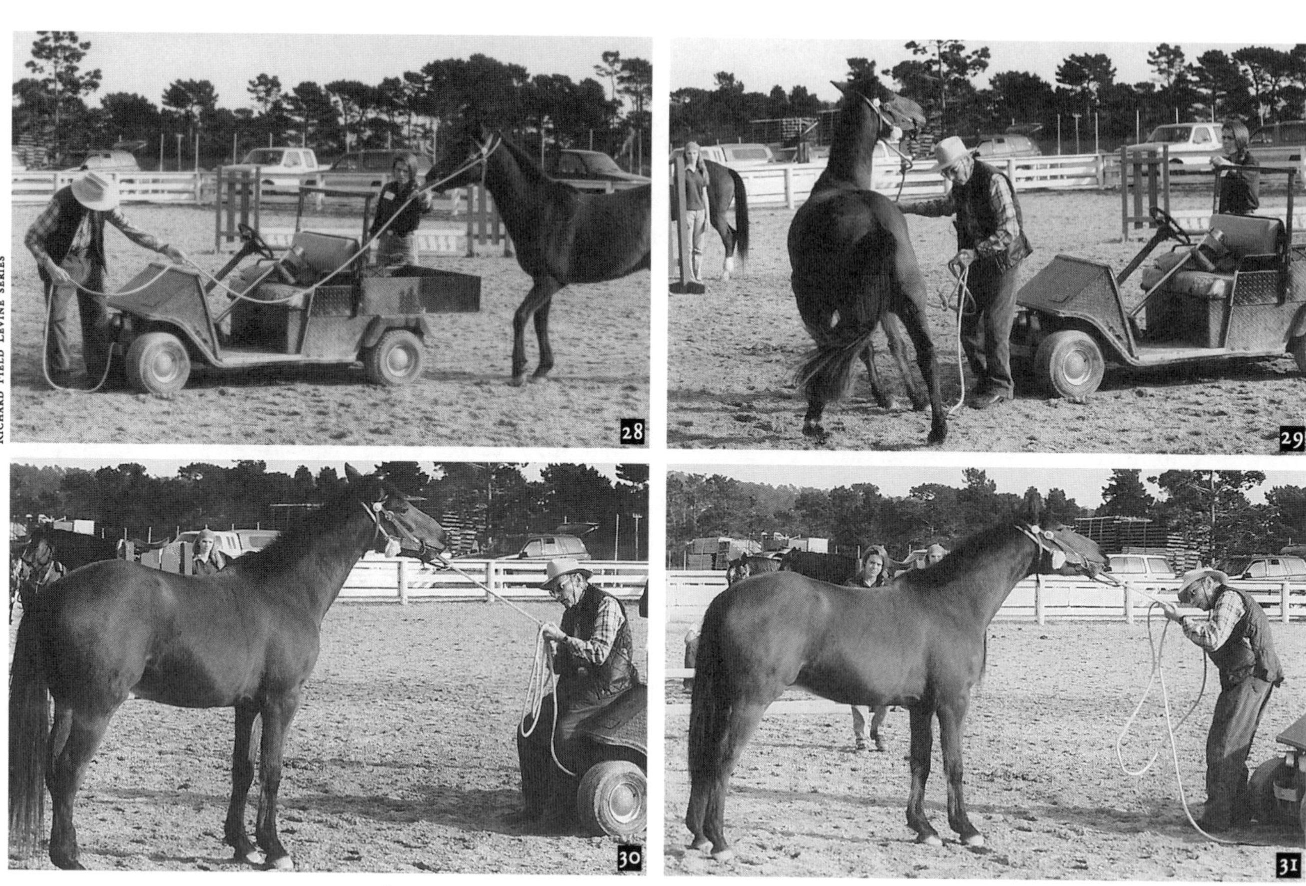

Richard Field Levine series

Richard Field Levine series

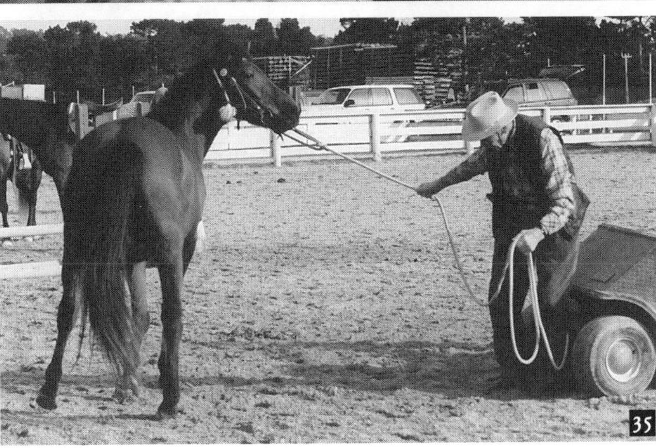

Getting him to take a step forward was part of the testing that needed to be done, and I had to figure out how to adjust my feel in a way that he could understand. When he did come forward one step as shown in Figures 32-33, I eased off. I waited a few seconds and then took a fresh start (Figures 34-36).

So many little particles of feel come into this that can't be spoken about or seen. They can only be felt. Not everyone will feel these particles I'm speaking about on the start, but if people really want to get this, why they will feel some of it eventually. And some will a lot sooner than others. I was in hopes we'd get even more pictures that day because it wasn't long before he did lead up real free and could pass by me in both directions, just following a feel and never taking out the float. That felt real good to both of us.

Well, it's one thing to talk about and another thing to have those pictures. It's best if you can get enough of them accumulated and then line them up like a stopped movie. You'd want to spend a lot of time looking them over because there is so much to see. It's the best way I know of to really see some of the smaller changes that take place between a horse and a person. I realized we should have made a movie that day. But, a fella can get the general idea of things from what we were able to get recorded. It worked out real smooth in the end, but I wished I'd been horseback for that demonstration.

The Clinics at Pebble Beach Equestrian Center

We put on some clinics at Pebble Beach (Equestrian Center), and I was fortunate to have my saddle horse, Beaut, on hand for that. I don't get around so good on the ground like I used to, so she was a big help to me when I was helping the people who had horses that weren't feeling of them.

> There was a mule named Isaac at that clinic, and the man who had that mule had quite a few things working pretty good. But the nicest part about that mule was the way it filled in for that man, because I think he started riding later in life. They got a standing ovation that day for loping. It appeared it was his first time loping, and it made everyone real pleased to see how happy that man was to have a mule that would lope around so easy for him. And he wasn't pulling on that mule either. They really liked each other, and it looked good to me.

Teaching a Horse to Lead Up From Horseback

There were some people at the clinic who had a hard time getting their horses to lead up real free, or getting much of anything else useful done. One horse in particular gave the lady who owned him some fearful experiences horseback. It seems this horse would stop at a spot on the trail and rear and then turn around and run home. This bothered her quite a lot. I was thinking this problem would disappear if we could teach him how to lead up, using feel. And we did that. These pictures you'll see next show what it was like that day with her five-year-old Tennessee Walker, and they show how I started working with him to get those feet freed up. You'll see from these next pictures how I worked this horse from Beaut, first using just a rope halter (Figures 37-51) and then switching to a lass rope halter (Figures 52-61).

Using a Lass Rope Halter

This horse was a case where I needed to build a more effective feel in there, because he had quite a little experience at taking over and doing things the way he thought they should be done. After he got the message, we went right back to using his regular halter because he'd gotten onto my feel and could understand what he was expected to do with his feet (Figures 62-66). Beaut was real helpful in getting this accomplished, and by the end of that session, his owner had a pretty good feeling

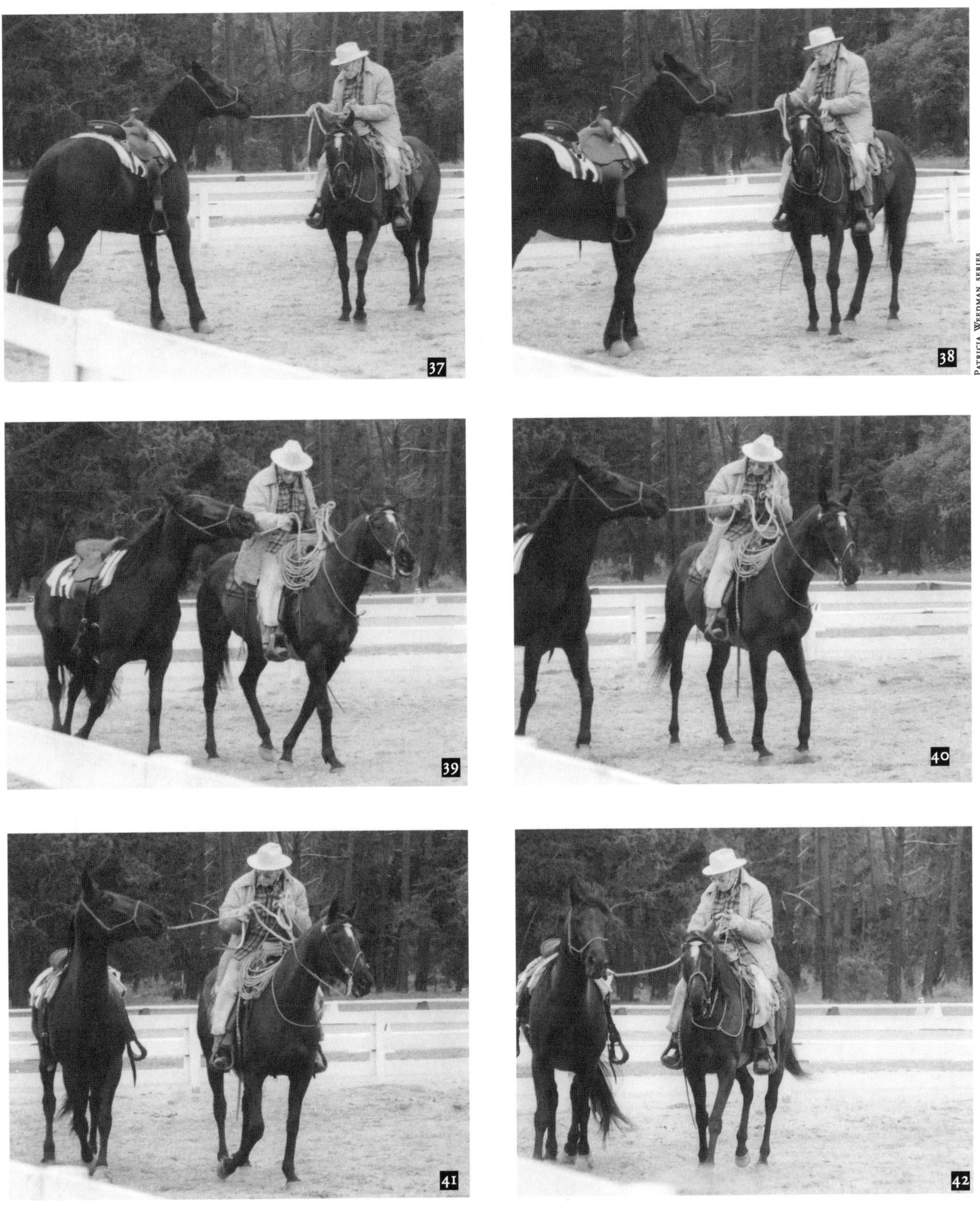

Patricia Weedman series

about the way things went. I'm in hopes that she was, anyway, because it appeared that he was more pleasurable for her to handle and ride after that.

Some people might see this and think this horse is stubborn — he isn't, he's just confused. Beaut is helping me to get this horse feeling of me. He's got quite a brace in there (Figure 37). After he took a step forward with that left front foot, I eased off a little. Beaut is well gathered up in this picture, and is a real help for this sort of job (Figure 38). I waited a second or two before taking a fresh start. We'd made a little progress, but there's quite a little confusion still left in the horse about what I want him to do (Figures 39-42). The reason a horse is liable to be this way is that he hasn't had an opportunity to learn any different from the people who've handled him up to that point. They just didn't know about this.

In these pictures I was offering a little different feel to this horse. By bringing his head around to the right, Beaut and I were able to help him separate his front end from his hindquarters, and put some extra meaning into the feel of that halter for him (Figures 43-51).

If your timing and feel can blend in together just right, it can really help a horse in his understanding of what you want. It takes quite a little experience, and I don't say I get it right every time. Every horse is different and I'm still learning all the time

Patricia Weedman series

43

44

45

46

47

48

PATRICIA WEEDMAN SERIES

49

50

51

and from every horse I work with, about how he needs me to show him what I want so he can understand. On the start, my goal is to fit each horse.

There was a little judgment used here to decide that he would catch on easier if I made a lass rope halter and used it. He had a pretty good start understanding what I wanted the other way, but it didn't take him long to get straightened out on my intentions after we switched over.

Patricia Weedman series

If a person isn't already real handy with a reata, using a lass rope halter is not advised (Figure 52). Even if you're experienced, surprising things can happen and you'd be real careful how you go about this. I'll say most people should not do this without a lot of preparation and supervision from a good instructor. This horse has got an idea to move, but sometimes a horse like this can get too freed up all at once, so you'd be ready for that. I had some coils to let out of my right hand if I needed to give him some extra slack on the spur of the moment (Figure 53).

When he leads up and eases that pressure off himself, I put some slack back towards him (Figure 54). We went along a few steps like that until it was time to take another fresh start and test him out on his understanding of my feel again. A fella needs to be *all the time* adjusting the smallest things he does when he's trying to fit a horse.

He's doing a little testing of his own to see what's necessary to find a place where that pressure comes off (Figures 55-59). It didn't take this horse long to figure out he needed to move those feet to put some slack in the rope and ease the pressure on himself. Right about the time he figured that out was the time he was ready to make another big change, which showed up in his whole body.

Seeing the Change in His Body

There isn't any question that when a horse's mental system registers a change for the better, it shows up in his physical system. There's a real close connection there and this causes the horse's body to take on an entirely different appearance. In Figures 60-61, you can see in these pictures

57

58

Patricia Weedman series

how he's let down and feeling pretty comfortable. There's understanding where there wasn't any before. That's what you hope will happen. Using this approach you wouldn't need to get a horse to work too hard physically for some important progress to be made.

59

After we switched back to his regular halter, he could pick up my feel to step forward without any resistance coming in there. That's when I started to drive him a little, just using the tail end of the halter rope in my right hand (Figure 62). From a walk and up into the trot, and then back down to the walk and through all the way to stopping — that horse could pick up the meaning in my feel and never take the float out of that rope. For whatever we did after that, he didn't need to take the slack out of the rope because he understood what was expected, through feel. The responsiveness in him was based on the respect he had for me and

Patricia Weedman

60

61

Patricia Weedman

Patricia Weedman series

Beaut, and that was based on his new understanding of the feel presented to him through that equipment.This would not have been the best choice of how to move his feet before I got this other response built in. But because he'd already picked up the feel of when I wanted him to move and slow down and stop, well, by this time stopping him didn't weigh anything (Figures 63-66). You'd sure want to get that part good before you livened up a horse like that under these circumstances.

I was real pleased with the way that horse could operate for the lady who owned him when she rode him after that. What he'd learned on the ground carried over for both of them, which is the whole point in a lot of this.

Part 3 — Backing and Leading Up One Step at a Time

When you're teaching a horse to step up and step back *one step at a time*, the most effective position for the hand on the halter knot is with the thumb down, as shown in Figure 1. If the horse tries to take over or is difficult to stop between steps, this position helps to prevent your arm from folding up at the elbow. Because so many people get horses before learning much about them, a lot of horses learn undesirable habits, like bumping into a person with their shoulders and slinging their heads around. If your horse is the kind that's inclined to be pushy, keeping your arm straight in situations like this can help keep some distance in there between you and those shoulders and feet.

1

Diamond Lu Collection

When you're teaching the horse to understand your feel to step up or back, it helps to position his head and neck where they would be normally, before you present him with the feel to move his feet. It's a lot easier for a horse to back up if you tip his nose over whichever front foot happens to be in the lead. It is the motion of his head and neck shifting over to the other side just a little that helps a horse unweight the front leg that's bearing weight. That way, it's easier for him to lift that foot up, reach it back and set it down. In the process of backing, there's a continual shift of the horse's balance and weight — from left to right, and from front to back. That's how the horse arranges his feet for this, and it's no different when he's stepping forward, as far as the shifting and balancing action of his head and neck are concerned. He does what he needs to do for balance. The feet are arranged a lot different at the walk than they are in the back-up though, and this is spoken about more in Chapter 5.

In these pictures, this fella's tipping the nose from the left front foot, to the center and then over the right front foot (Figures 2-3). This helps the horse get ready, and have better balance, when he takes a step back with the right front foot (Figure 4).

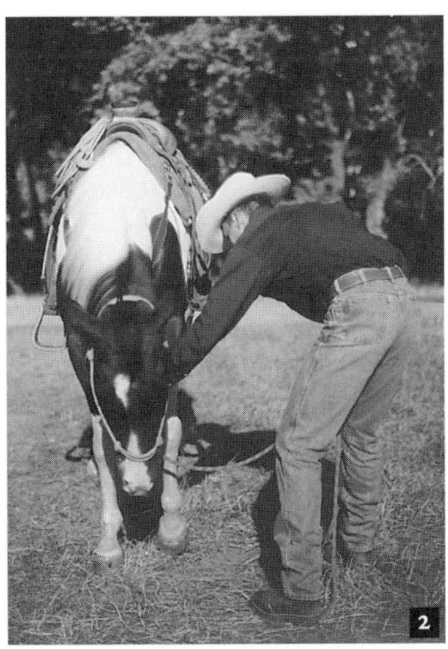
2

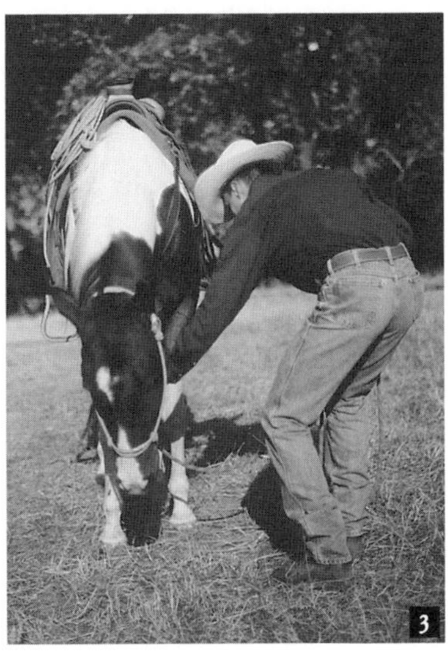
3

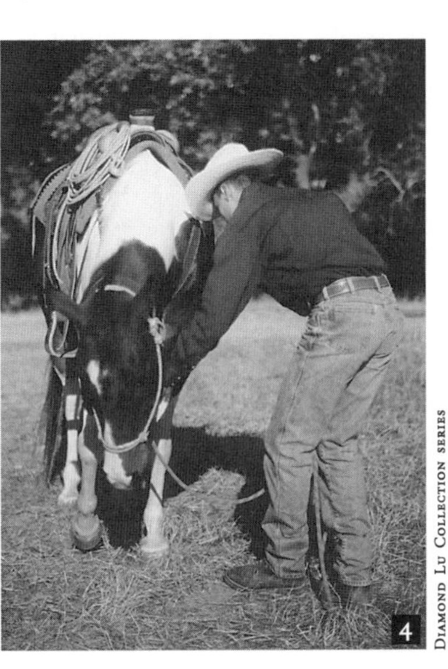
4

Diamond Lu Collection series

To back the horse one foot at a time, first offer as little pressure as it takes for him to shift his weight back without taking a step. It shouldn't take too much, but it could take quite a bit at first, depending on the horse. When he makes a change, reward him by easing off and then try again a time or two — or as often as you need to — until he starts to understand that you want him to take one step back *with one foot.* You'd reward for any move he made to understand your feel, and then you'd take a fresh start. After he steps one foot back, slowly tip his nose back to the center, and then shift it over ahead of the other front foot — which is now the most forward foot — and step it back. You'd like this to be smooth, and after some practice it will be.

After a step or two back, you'd step him forward a step or two. Remember that the front foot that is farthest back will be the one you hope to bring forward. This might seem obvious to a lot of people, but it's surprising how many people just keep trying to bring the same foot forward again, after it's already come forward. They sort of forget about that other front foot. One thing's for sure, that horse didn't forget and he's liable to get skeptical of a person who wants him to do too much of this. When those front legs get stretched out like that, there isn't much he can do with those hindquarters to help himself stay in balance and it's best to not put a horse in any sort of a bind.

At the start of all this, you'd allow him to stop between each step forward and each step back. If you rush a horse through this, he's liable to start holding his breath or tightening up his whole body, so you'd be careful not to go too fast. And where it concerns the idea of drilling him on things, I'm in hopes that you'll stop your lessons while he's still got some interest in what you're doing.

It All Boils Down to You, and the Horse

I'm in hopes that what's listed here is going to help people get a better foundation built in to their horses on the start. If a person takes time to think before he practices with a horse, why he might have an easier time understanding some of the smaller particles in feel. Even if a person thinks they understand what building in feel is all about, he might notice that he'd missed something in his presentation when he tries these exercises. That word "all" takes in so much, and every horse is different, so it's your testing that's going to show you the best way to approach each horse. We've put down some of the actual facts here that describe how a horse learns to understand your intentions, but some things about feel can't be put down on paper.

Building a Connection Between the Halter (or Snaffle Bit) and the Feet

Give him the feel through the halter or the snaffle bit to back his foot up. At first, he won't have any idea that you want this to translate down to his feet. He won't understand the pressure you're placing on his head from the equipment you're using either, because it's not familiar to him. He might try to adjust the position of his head, or neck, or both, because that's where he feels the pressure — right there on his head.

You'll go through his mind to establish the connection to his feet. So it'd be just at the instant when he does move his foot that you'd ease off the pressure a few seconds. I'm not talking here about a full release. It's not that. You don't want to lose contact with him entirely — not where you put the rope down and step back away from him. You'd release just enough so there was meaning in it for him, and so he'd know what he did was right, but you want to keep that connection with him. It's like a conversation you're trying to establish with him, through feel, of course. If you're off in your feel and timing, it may take quite a little time before he can understand. But that's all right.

Lori Kline

5

6

Lori Kline

The rider on the horse in these pictures wanted to experience what it felt like to back up real slow with her eyes closed. She also wanted to see how the neck and head looked when the horse flexed at the poll — and we could say "softened" — in response to a feel on the halter knot from the person on the ground (Figures 5-6).

When the rider started to liven up, the horse could sort out the different aspects of feel being presented for those two things and was able to back up and tuck her chin down and in at the same time. Now that she's experienced what it feels like to be sitting on a horse that can pick up the feel to be this way, it will be easier for her in the future to know if she's in the neighborhood of a desirable response from a horse. It's going to take some time for this rider to learn how to present the feel to back up in a way that brings out the lightness and willingness through that horse's whole body.

When you want a horse to take a step back, your desire for this to happen does not always translate down to the feet. The person on the ground here in these pictures needed to make an adjustment, and so did the rider. They took a fresh start and things improved. The person on the ground eased off as this horse responded to her feel, but she's staying close enough that she'll be able to take a fresh start, without having to make any large motions around the horse's head. You'd want to keep your body out to the side in this exercise and not crowd in on the horse too close in front of here. And you be sure not to ever push or lean on the horse to back her up, either.

The Importance of His First Tries, and Your Readiness to Adjust

It's best if you can observe the first tries a horse makes when he's attempting to understand your feel, because there's usually some curiosity and willingness in those responses. People might be apt to struggle with their horse on these exercises when he doesn't do what they want. They could think he's made a mistake, and maybe think they should punish the horse for doing wrong. That wouldn't be right. Until he understands what a person wants him to do with his feet, he can't do it.

As we've already spoken about, it's in the horse's nature to be curious and to want to get along. An important part of this for the person to understand, is that the horse will actually try to do whatever you want, assuming it's within reason and his physical ability. That horse is going to try hard, through his own searching and observing powers, to understand if there's any meaning *for him* in your feel. That's what he's doing when you want him to take a step back with his feet, and he moves his head and neck around instead. He's searching when he does this — it's natural, of course — and it's no different than when he finally does move his feet. When they do move back in response to your feel, why that's just another one of his tries. In that case it would be a successful try, and the way he'd know it would be when you'd ease off whatever pressure you had on him there when his feet moved. If your timing and feel were understandable, he'd make a connection in his mind to your intentions. He's liable to, anyway.

Or, it could be that sometime he'd just hit on the very thing you wanted him to do right in the middle of some other plans he was making about going somewhere, maybe over to some grass. You'd look for these opportunities all the time you were with a horse. These are real valuable and you'd not want to miss them. Especially if the horse was kind of stuck in his feet, and not wanting to move too much for you on the start. If you respond with a little release for his foot movements — no matter why they moved — why he's really going to notice the release you give him, and take that in for thought.

On horses that are liable to be more confused about what's expected of them — if they've had a little problem with people somewhere along the line, why this sort of horse is always going to be relieved when he realizes he's got someone on the other end of the lead rope who can present something to him that's understandable. Horses want to get along, is why. In most cases they do, I'll say that.

Before you and the horse get things sorted out and working real smooth, sometimes things you don't expect can happen. Most horses are going to be doing a little speculating of their own. Like when you want him to take a step up, and instead he leans into your pull and backs up a step. Or, maybe it's the other way around. You ask him to take a step back and he'd rather push into you, and cause you to back up instead. These things are to be expected until he understands what you want, through feel. And you'll be working at this together a little at a time, building in the basics that are necessary to have in place in order for those better results to show up. And that horse, why he's always deserving of the benefits in any doubts a person has about him.

Your Judgment, Where it Concerns Easing Off, Firming Up and Safety

Now we're getting even deeper into an area where just using words is difficult, because it's so much easier when there's a horse to demonstrate with.

Horses are intelligent enough to find value in feel because they understand it in their mental and physical systems. That's the main value in it, and the main thing you need to remember about feel. Of course, any decision you'd make to release the pressure you had on a horse for doing something you didn't want him to do — why that decision would take in a lot, and you'd be real sure it was safe to do that before you did. There will be circumstances where that is exactly the worst thing you could do. Other times, maybe you'd just go with him, or let him drift a little as he was getting things sorted out, or completely release the pressure you had on him. There are so many things to consider when you want to adjust to fit a horse, and what's best in some circumstances may not be the best in others. That's why I recommend strongly to people that they try to get some real good supervision on this.

With some of those real sensitive horses, and the ones that might be troubled inside about things, there's some judgment that a person develops concerning when to ease off. I'd say that even when there's responses that you don't want, some that you'd think you oughtn't reward him for, well, there's times when just the littlest amount of release *is* needed. It can be very meaningful to let a horse find out, through your feel, that you're with him on the searching and thinking part of things, even if unwanted actions show up on the start. If your judgment and timing on this are effective, then what comes through to the horse is that you acknowledged his try, and not that what he actually did was the exact thing you wanted, in terms of his motions. He can separate this, if you are careful in the way this is done. Quite a little experience is necessary for this to be effective, in most cases.

We're speaking about something now that's difficult to write about, and not too difficult to demonstrate. That's because it's right about in the middle somewhere — between what a horse understands, and what he doesn't — and that's not too hard to recognize when it finally shows up, so long as you're willing to experiment and you have a general idea what you're looking for.

What I'm talking about is connected right to your judgment about his sensitivity and his try. I'm really in hopes that people can understand what I mean when I'm talking about preserving the horse's try. It's not to reinforce the actual steps you *don't* want, *it's to give him confidence that you're with him* in his learning process and that mistakes are just part of it. A horse sure has the ability to catch on, if he's just given a little support and time to sort some things out while you're right there feeling of him, until he can pick up your feel. This takes time.

Of course you'd really appreciate working with a horse that had try, and your feel would let him know you were generally in favor of him and what he was doing — and that'd be his attempts to understand you. And it doesn't mean that you'd let him take over or just run things his way. No, we're not wanting any part of that. You'd always want to be prepared to do whatever was needed to help the horse make some other choices in what he's about to do. A fella will use the better timing he has available for the horse. And to go along with that timing, it might be that the better feel that's needed to take care of this would require that person's full strength. In certain situations, why a person needs to be thinking about this end of the spectrum, too.

For example, if you're concerned about your safety, why then you'd maybe need to use a certain amount of firmness before that horse'd be able to find that place where you'd ease off. And from that use of firmness, he could learn what you wanted him to do, and be a little better prepared for the future. The timing of your release when he understood your intent on whatever it was would be real important right then. And especially where it concerned any extra measure of firmness, why we'd always have the future in mind. If this wider range of things to consider wasn't fitting to your abilities or thinking, you'd do better to hand the lead rope to someone else. In some cases, a person ought to find another horse. It just all depends.

A few releases at the exact right time can really help a horse become convinced that you're going to be dependable for him, especially where it concerns a clear release coming from you for those real small tries he'd offer back to you on the start, before he really understood what you had in mind for him. No matter if it's in the area you hoped for or not, in the beginning of this *the only tries he can make are the ones that actually show up*. He's not going to hold out on you or anything like that, no, it wouldn't be for a horse to do that, but people say this about some horses anyway. Your release is his best reward for understanding the meaning in your feel, as you present it to him through the lead rope, or the reins, or indirectly in another situation. It will carry a lot of meaning for him because a horse can feel your support, and it registers in his mind that he's got a connection with you then. If you've been there for him with that better timing, why in not much time at all, he's going to look you up. It feels good when a horse wonders what you'd like him to do, because there's quite a little you can build on to from there, as you move up the line together.

The most difficult part for people to understand about this is that we are not speaking about anything that's got a formula to it. It's no part of mechanics and you can't just rehearse certain moves you did that worked on another horse — or that you saw someone else do. What we're speaking about isn't something you see someone do and just try to bring over to the next horse with no adjusting figured into things, not if you're wanting to understand and apply this the way we're speaking about. That's why some people call it more of an art, and it sure could be closer to that than to science, all right. But I call it feel.

Many delicate spots will be part of a person's decision-making about how they want to help a horse. Your direct experience will help you to sort out these situations and handle them in the way that's most fitting to a particular horse. One thing to have in mind at all times, is that your horse will benefit a lot more from your efforts to teach him what to do if you are able to arrange things for him so he can succeed — rather than just showing him what you don't want through your corrections. If his decisions don't fit what you have in mind, we wouldn't ever say that the horse was wrong.

Moving Alternate Diagonal Pairs of Feet

After a horse can step back with only one foot at a time, the next thing you'd do is see if he can take one step back with a front leg and the opposite hind leg together. This is the natural position for a back-up step and will be referred to as a "diagonal" from now on. Because this is so important to have in place for good balance, a rider needs to improve his ability to have the horse take only one step back this way.

For this part of the exercise, the horse needs to be as smooth as he was when he just stepped one foot back or forward, and then stayed put. This progression is really fitting to the horse as he gains in understanding. Now, he might have started out this way — moving a diagonal pair of feet when you just wanted a front foot — and that's all right. As long as you got a step and he didn't keep on going, that'd be fine if he moved one, or the other, diagonal pair of feet. When we're speaking about backing this way, whether it's a diagonal pair of feet that move, or just one front or one back foot, *you want him to step down solid,* without offering to go anywhere after that one step. When just one step can be taken, he's waiting for you. Then you have his attention and that's one of our main goals — to get the horse's attention and keep it focused on what we want him to do.

In Figures 7 and 8, the horse is shifting his weight off the right diagonal (right front and left hind) onto all four of his feet. His nose has been shifted over in front of the left front foot. This is good preparation to help him take his weight off the left diagonal for the next step back.

As you teach him to step up and back *just going real slow*, it reinforces what he's already started to learn about the feel of stopping and waiting. The horse should be allowed to take a few seconds in between each step as he's learning this, and you'd remember to do this from both sides. Gradually, the horse will pick up your feel to step forward and back without any resistance at all. He'll be able to stop easily and stand there with no thought in his mind about taking over and doing one small thing more than you asked for. This is important, even if some people don't think it is. To get this real smooth takes time and the process should not be rushed.

Next, you'll shift his weight back off the left diagonal and over to the center, before directing the nose over to the right front foot again (Figures 9-10).

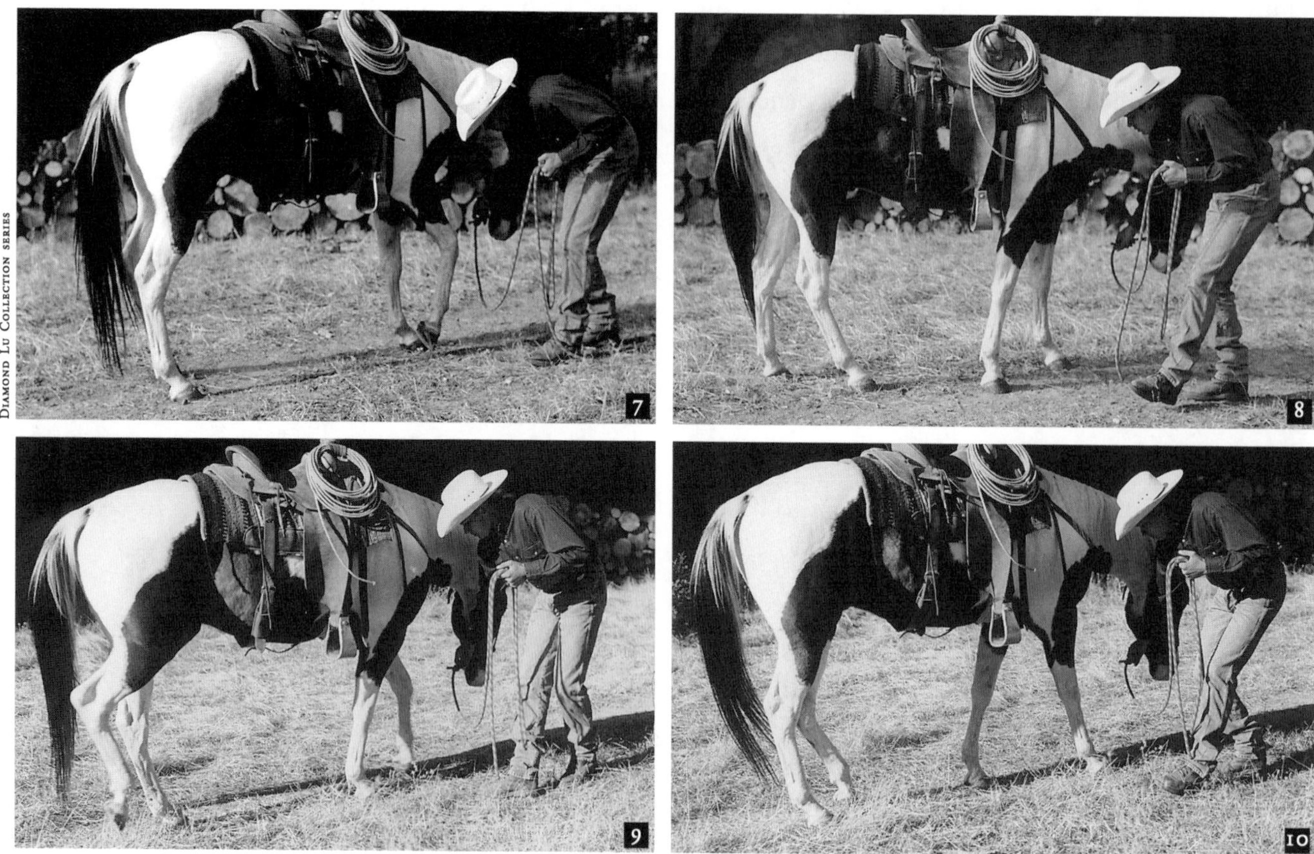

When a person practices this, it's best not to crowd the horse's shoulders because he can learn the habit of leaning into someone or slinging his head into a person. When this gets going, other unhelpful traits can sure develop. I am speaking about this because some people may be learning about this for the first time — and that's if they are new to horses, or not. But there's bound to be some people who've worked around horses a long time who will understand the importance of this preparation at the foundation level. They might think some of this could come in handy in their work with the horse sometime — no matter what job they need to do with him. I can't be sure about this, but I'm in hopes this is so.

Some Horses are Inclined to be Real Heavy on the Front End

Some horses are naturally going to want to unweight the forehand before they shift their weight back, or step the front feet out to the side. Others won't be inclined to do this and will drag their feet on the ground when they step back. The horses that have been handled without much feel are the ones that have more of a tendency to do this. If that happens, a person can elevate the horse's front end just by giving him a little feel to lift up there in his shoulders, before he takes a step back or to the side. And that's if they're on the ground or horseback. Someone without a lot of experience horseback oughtn't try to rework this part of the horse's foundation when they're sitting on him. Those better results a fella needs coming through for him will be a lot more understandable to him and the horse if he can get them real smooth on the ground.

You'd help him do this on the ground by giving him the feel to lift up a little in front, just with your hand on the lead rope or the halter knot, or slobber strap, without taking any step. You'd release when he offers the smallest try to understand what you want him to do, which is to lighten up in front and get ready to lift one front foot up off the ground. It doesn't matter if the head comes up at first. Eventually, after he understands what you want him to do, he'll be able to lift some weight off those front feet when he backs up, and he'll be able to keep his head down as low as you want — within reason.

When a horse that's bad to drag those front feet in the back-up learns how to raise up a little in front, you'd take a fresh start to combine the two things — the lifting up and the shifting back. When he can lift up in front and rock his weight back and forth without moving his feet, then offer just what it requires to lift up a front foot and step it back a little. Any foot that steps back is all right on the start, even a back foot, and you'd try to get his nose over the front foot that's farthest forward to help him. When that's good, then you'll help him step back with a front leg and the opposite hind leg at the same time. That diagonal pattern is real important to keep in place when he's learning to back up. *You want this to be really smooth, and slow.*

Once you understand the way to present an effective feel for this and a change is coming through, this can do a lot to improve the look and feel of a horse when he backs up. A person doesn't want to back a horse up by pushing *any part* of their body against the horse's body in any way. If you do, he'll develop undesirable ideas concerning resistance to feel, and many of these lead directly to bad habits. If the horse did get headed in this direction, well, one of the worst parts about it is that there'd be almost no chance of any lightness being available *when you need it.*

Preserving Try Can Preserve the Horse's Natural Lightness

When a person preserves the try in a horse, the lightness needed for collection a little further up the line in his education will still be there, just waiting to be put to use. There's quite a lot that figures into this lightness being available in a way that's *useful.* Of course, a person needs to have had quite a little experience horseback and handling horses on the ground, too, in order to direct the horse in the best way possible, which includes making the best use of the lightness that's been preserved. There's a lot of benefit to that person in this and, of course, to any of the livestock that he's liable to be around in the future.

The main thing about lightness, really, is whether the horse still has a connection to the spark of life that he came in with, or not. There's some who think he's better to be around if he doesn't have that, but there's a whole lot that people who think this way don't know about horses, and what those horses can do for them.

In some cases, what actually takes place is real unfortunate. That's when a person shows a horse that he didn't do something right by using methods that shut the actual life part of the horse right off. When this happens, it's not the best. And I'd rather think that if they'd seen another way to teach the horse to understand what they expected him to do, they'd have tried it.

When a colt is exposed to too much harshness on the start, it's liable to put his fire out, and of course that puts quite a damper on his try. You'd hope to avoid ever doing that because you'll need that life and try available to you later on. If a fella can just keep a colt busy, without scaring him or overworking him, and give him something to do with all that life and energy he's got available, why it won't be near as difficult to direct him in various maneuvers when he's older. The nice thing about this is if a fella's taken the time to prepare himself and get the colt feeling of him at the basic foundation level, then that horse is going to want to work with him.

If the horse's inborn qualities are still in place, a fella can put those parts of the horse to work for him when they have an important job to do together. It's real pleasing to ride a horse that's been brought along this way. With that lightness and willingness in there, why the combination is apt to produce a horse that has a real nice appearance on the job — even if he isn't much for looks.

Starting to Build in the Stop, One Step at a Time

Stopping is what takes place between stepping up and stepping back. If you go about this in a way the horse understands, you can build the stop in right along with these exercises on the ground. We'll speak quite a little more about this in Part 4. For now, we'll say if the horse has learned to lead up real good — in the sense that you don't have to pull on him at all to free up those feet — then he'll just follow your feel to step up one step. Let him stop, and then step him back the same way. He'll understand your feel to stop if he understands your feel to take one step.

To build in that stop, when you're leading him up a step, just as that front foot is ready to come down on the ground — and we'll say it's the right foot like these pictures show — you'd tip his nose a little bit to the left and back (Figures 11-12). This maneuver holds that left foot on the ground. His right foot has already hit the ground there, but you put a little bit of a backwards feel on that left front foot so he doesn't think he should step forward. Because many times when that right foot hits the ground, why that left front foot will want to come right up off the ground to take a step. But if you hold it on the ground just as his right foot hits, then it's easy to hold it in place. So you'll only get one step at a time, without him wanting to take an extra step there.

11 KIM MURPHY

12 KIM MURPHY

Advance to Backing in an Arc

In your experiments with moving the horse slowly back and forward, one foot at a time, and moving one diagonal pair of feet at a time, you'd always be stepping him straight back and straight forward. When that gets good, you'd start to back him in a little arc. In not too much time, you'd be able to place those feet pretty much anywhere you want to, without resistance and with very little tension on the rope. The feel you're developing in this exercise is an important part of the foundation for retaining the horse's natural lightness.

If it's lightness you want to put back in the horse after certain things had happened to discourage it from showing up in his movements, why this exercise wouldn't be the place to start, not by any means. Going back down and rebuilding from the bottom is what a fella'd want to do in a case like that. By the time you'd reached this exercise in your rebuilding, why there'd be some lightness to work with if you hadn't skipped over the things concerning feel that a horse needs in order to advance.

Shift the nose over the left front foot (Figure 13). After the left diagonal reaches back, shift the nose across the center and slowly back to the right (Figures 14-15). Shift the weight off the right diagonal as he steps it back. When the left diagonal is ready to leave the ground — that's when you'd set his left front foot out to the side by shifting his nose over that foot (Figure 16). We could sure use more pictures for this.

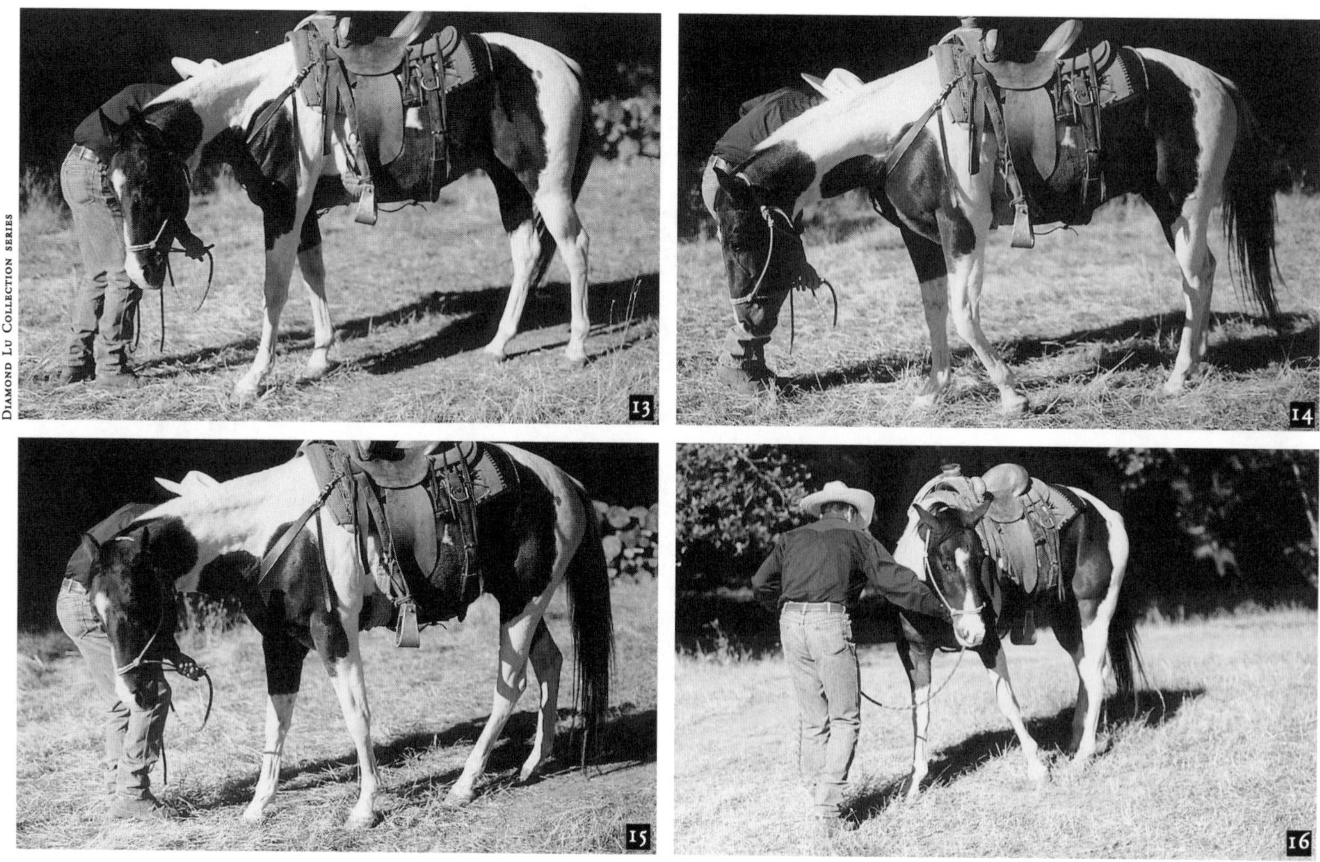

Figures 17-22 show different views of directing a horse in a backward arc to the right. In this maneuver, the horse's forehand is reaching to the right. He's reaching to the left with his hindquarters. When it's done right, this exercise helps to supple a horse and keep him responsive to you. When he understands the smaller maneuvers you wanted, you'd progress to where you could back him all the way around in a circle with your hand on the halter rope, or the slobber strap.

After he can do this from both sides with you up close, you'd try to get this done at a little distance away from him (Figures 23-24). You'd be testing out your connection to him then, to see what he could understand. When you switch sides, a horse is liable to be more responsive on some things, and more resistant on some others. If you've handled him from both sides on the start, this isn't going to bother him.

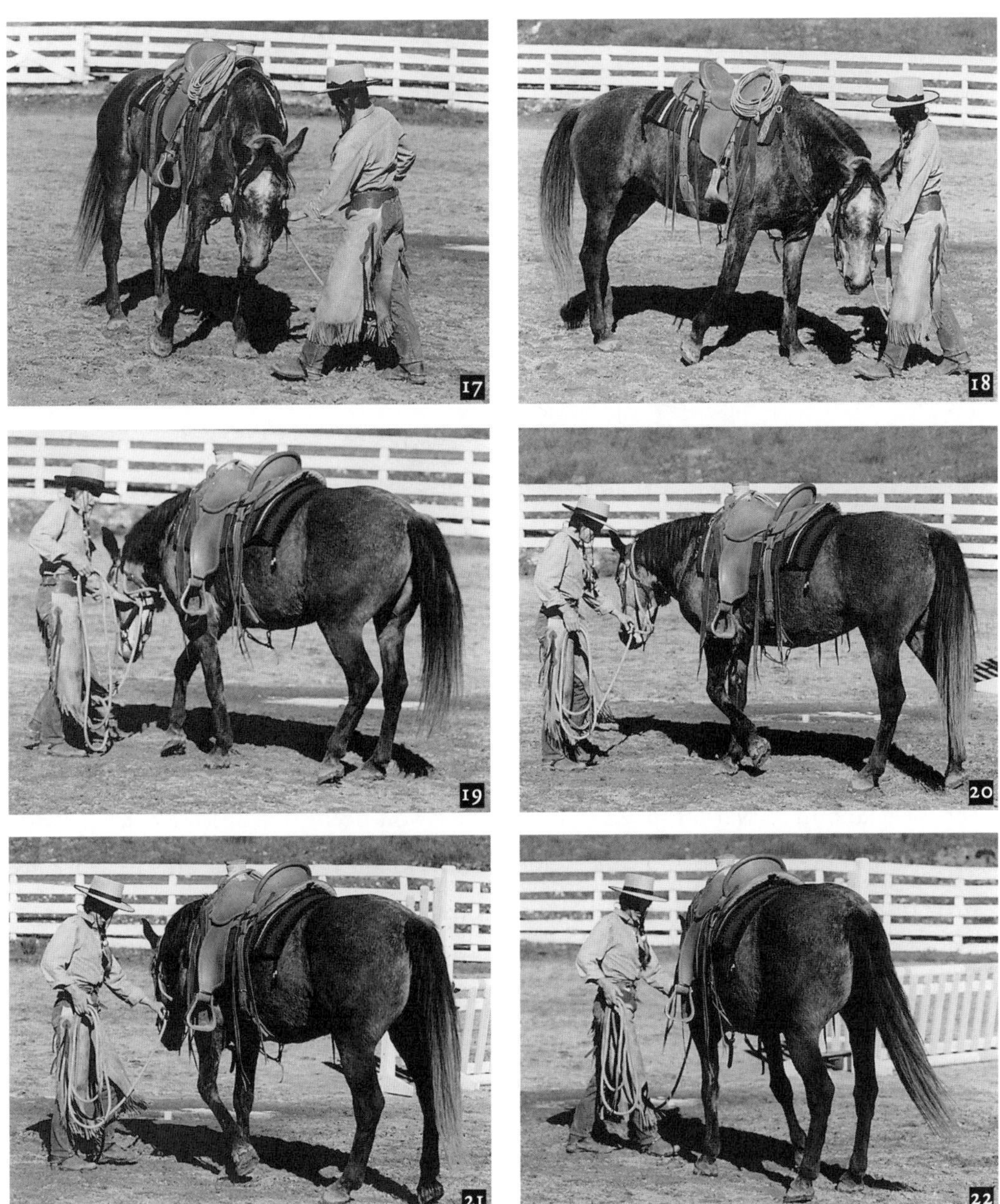

Richard Field Levine series

Not all horses are going to have confidence reaching out sideways with the left front foot if they've been handled mainly on that side. They can get real used to someone being at the left shoulder there, and a lot of horses learn that it's wrong to reach a leg toward where that person usually is. It can show up in the horse as concern, and a brace maybe gets pretty well established in that left shoulder sometimes. Of course, they aren't feeling of you then (Figure 25). Sometimes they'll kind of lurch into a left-reaching step before they can free up and take a backwards step.

Richard Field Levine

Richard Field Levine

You can keep going, or ease off and take a fresh start. Eventually, if there's no hurry brought to this, the horse will relax and his movements will start to flow a little better (Figure 26). There'd be no thought to get after a horse because he was doubtful on this.

If too big a brace comes into the horse when you're working at this, try going back to the side where he's got less of a brace, or do something different to reduce that tightness and get a flow going in his steps again. You can back straight for a few steps, or take him forward, too. As many times as you need to, just lead him forward and back him up, one step at a time, and real slow (Figure 27). Later, maybe work at a little distance from him, change sides, or adjust his head position up or down, or

Richard Field Levine series

do other experiments to see what is going to fit him. The main thing you want is to get that good feel established between you again, and keep far away from any upset. Then, before you try to back him again in an arc (Figure 28), just ease into it by backing up straight for a step or two and the light response will return.

Mounted Work

Before you try to apply these lessons to your riding, it might be a good idea to keep some things in mind, and I'll speak of them here.

Nature provides the horse with excellent balance for the moves he's got to make, at any speed. Whether the horse is traveling straight ahead or backing — or going in any direction — all four feet move in time with the rhythm and swaying motion of his head and neck. The power that he needs to maneuver properly comes from his hindquarters being free-moving and adjustable. This is helped greatly by the swaying motions of his head, neck and shoulders as he travels. Depending on what's taking place, like how fast you're going and *where* his feet need to go, there can be a need for a wide range of movements for this. And another thing — if he isn't able to move his jaws or breathe freely for any reason, well, just about all of his movements are going to be compromised. Under circumstances like this, he's also affected mentally. You'd rather not ride a horse like that.

For almost anything you'd need your horse to do in the future, all the exercises shown in this section are real helpful to have built into a horse's foundation. A fella might be able to turn his horse around or change leads a little easier when his horse can back up in an arc real smooth and easy. This horse is not braced in his body, or pushing in any way against the bit. The main thing here is, there's a connection based on feel that exists between the horse and the person, and it's there for them to fall back on, if they need to. I don't know what could take the place of this — especially if you're speaking about safety for the rider and something that has a lot of value to the horse's mental system, too.

29

Emily Kitching

In Figure 29, the rider's backing his horse straight. You'd want to have this flowing just right before backing in any arcs. There's a good foundation built there, and that rider has a good feel of his horse through the snaffle bit. There's a float in those reins, too, and this is real desirable in any of the work you do with a horse.

To back an arc in either direction, shape your body in the direction you are going to go, and tip the nose over the leading front foot. Figure 30 shows the rider

Richard Field Levine

Richard Field Levine

preparing to back an arc to the right and Figure 31 shows this person preparing to back an arc to the left. No matter which direction you take the head, if you've taught that horse to feel of your arm and leg motions, the forehand will reach towards the new direction, and the hindquarters will reach back, in the opposite direction from where the head is going. This is what makes it a backwards circle. To prepare the horse in the best way for this, it's good to start with small arcs, taking just a step or two, and building from there.

Figures 32 and 33 show two views of backing in a circle to the left. For this maneuver, the forehand steps toward the left, and the hindquarters reach back and to the right. To get this, just move one step at a time on the start, directing and supporting the horse with your arms and legs. Whenever you're on a horse, it's real helpful if you look in the direction you're going. Sometimes a fella needs to look down, of course, and in his work especially, there's lots of time to look down at the ground, and at livestock and all sorts of things. But, if a person isn't real careful about this and *all the time* aware of what their body is doing, why looking down can cause a rider to tip forward much more than necessary. This can

Richard Field Levine

Richard Field Levine

interfere with the horse's body position. He might have to make adjustments that a person might not be aware of, and this could have an effect on that horse's mind and his decisions. In some situations, he might not know what you intend with that weight forward and he might get overexposed from the mix-up that results from his lack of understanding. Too much of this looking down and leaning forward can sure discourage a horse from keeping his weight shifted back in the way that's best for this exercise, or in any work you'd need him to do.

Handling the Horse's Feet

At this point in your groundwork, some good changes are likely to be showing up in a horse that's been approached and handled using feel the way we're speaking about. We're in hopes that the exercises already mentioned have prepared you to present that standing-still-feel to the horse in a way that's effective. If he can stand still and wait until you want him to do something else with his feet, why that's the best time to start getting him real used to having those feet picked up and handled. If you've progressed to this part in your exercises and your horse can't pick up your feel to stand still, something's been missed and you'd better go back down the line a ways.

For some good reasons, handling the horse's feet is one thing that causes many people to get uncomfortable. This is a normal feeling to have, especially if a person hasn't had much experience doing this. A person with no experience at this ought to learn about handling the feet of a horse that can fill in for them. That means he's not liable to be too concerned if they do some awkward things and even make the larger mistakes a person can make getting started on this. When it's another way, and you have an inexperienced person trying to learn this on a colt that's new to this, why in no time at all they can both get to feeling real scared anytime the subject of handling the feet comes to mind, and we don't want that.

What's best is if you can give that horse the reassurance he needs about what you have in mind, and that way it reduces the chance that something will go wrong. If you're using feel in a way that he can understand the intent you have, things are liable to be a lot safer for you where it concerns those feet — and there's always room for the better judgment a person has in this area. Some horses sure give a person reason to be concerned, there's no doubt about that.

Preparing the Horse to Have His Feet Handled Using Feel and a Rope

The reasons a fella'd want to approach handling a horse's feet using a rope can vary, but one benefit is that there's less risk of getting kicked. You'd want to feel safe and be able to reassure the horse with your better feel. This includes knowing when and how much to release any pressure you might have on him, and being ready to adjust in whatever way is going to work out for the best. This will take some time.

If that horse gets upset at any point in the exercise we're speaking about here, why there's no harm in taking a fresh start. There's quite a little experimenting a person can work into this, and they should. The horse needs to stay confident and relaxed about what you expect, and that's most important.

One thing people do, and I've been aware of this a long time, is that they leave a lot of the foot-handling responsibility to the horseshoer. Maybe they don't realize it's their job to get those young horses prepared ahead of time, the way those horses need to be prepared for things to work out. If an owner neglects this responsibility, then when that shoer comes to shoe that horse for the first time, he's at a big disadvantage, and the horse is, too.

But this is a real common situation, and in some cases we'd call it a problem. And it's too bad, because it's completely avoidable. But, maybe some people might not have had an opportunity to learn how to get this part taken care of. Others might think it's supposed to be up to them, and others just may not want the job. Well, I don't know about every situation there is, but it really shouldn't be a horseshoer's responsibility to train a horse in the first place, even if that's what they end up doing.

If some lessons about having those feet picked up are taught to that horse when the shoer's in a hurry, it's understandable. Most of those fellas don't have much time for training horses in the middle of their shoeing job, anyway. I'd rather think though, that if they do get stuck with the job, they're liable to try to get an inexperienced horse prepared the best they know how — using feel, and in a way that is safe and gets the horse ready for the future, the best way they can. If a fella was planning to ever shoe the horse again, why he's sure going to have the future in mind as he goes about things with that unprepared horse, I'll say that.

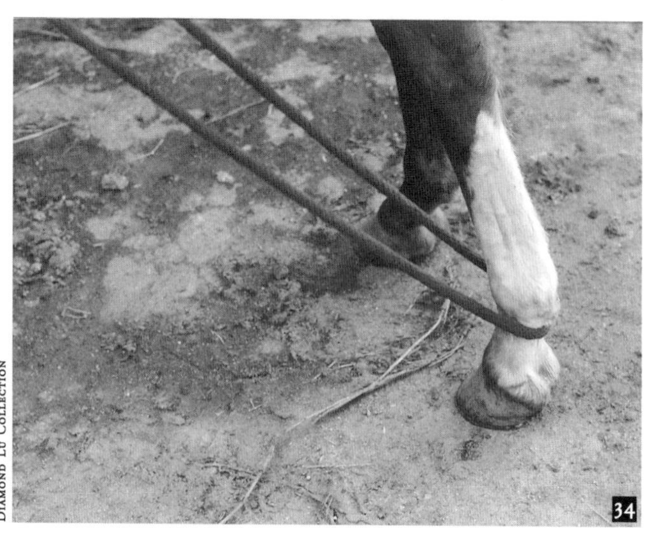
Diamond Lu Collection

34

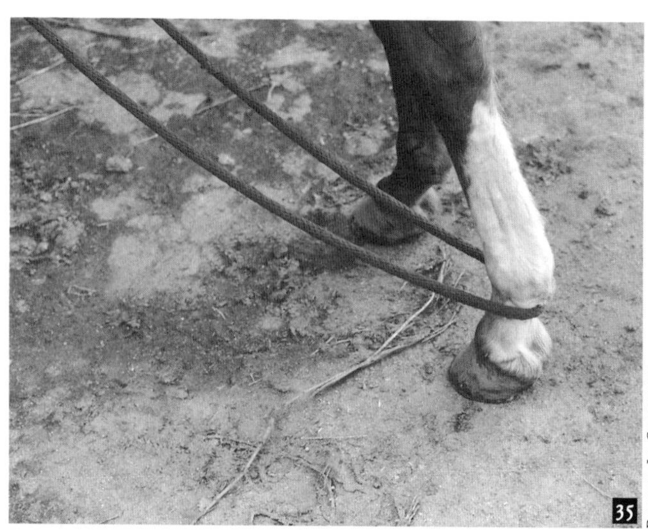
35

Diamond Lu Collection

To prepare your horse in the best way, you'll use a nice soft rope — one of those longer lead ropes is fine — and it doesn't need to be more than about 10 or 12 feet long. If you're going to use it on the front legs while it's attached to the halter, you'll be real careful not to put any unwanted pressure on the halter, because that can be confusing to the horse. On the hind feet, it's a good idea to have a separate rope. You'd want your lead rope that's attached to the halter to be long enough so you can stand back where you need to be, and not take the slack out of it or cause him to shift his weight or step around when you don't intend him to.

To get the horse to shift his weight, you wouldn't need to tighten the rope more than is shown in Figure 34. On the start, that foot doesn't have to come off the ground. For any change in thought or movement that you observed, you'd offer him a release and wait a second or two before taking a fresh start. This horse responded to the feel of the rope and settled his weight back onto that foot when it was released (Figure 35). That's in your better plan.

In this next series of pictures this person was experimenting with different applications of feel until that horse could understand what she expected (Figures 36-40). When he did get onto her feel, why he was more than willing to pick up that foot. There was some waiting involved on the start (Figure 36). It was real helpful to that horse's progress that the slack wasn't taken up when he brought that foot up the first time (Figure 37). When he set it down, he wasn't stepping down into any pressure from that rope either (Figure 38). This would be confusing to any horse. This person experimented using more time and a little less pressure-feel than before, and the horse was quick to pick up the meaning they had for him in that rope. You

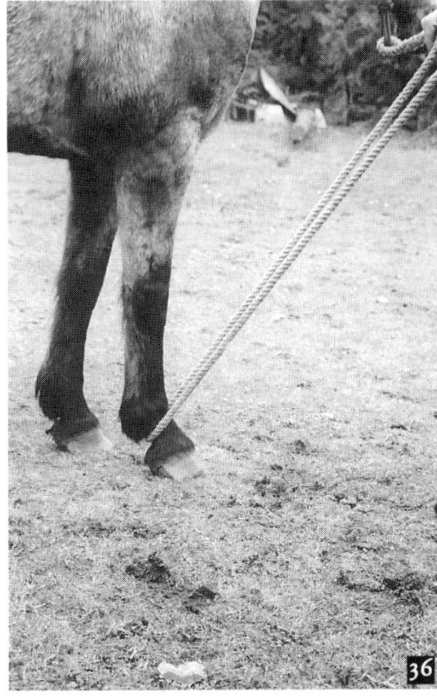

36

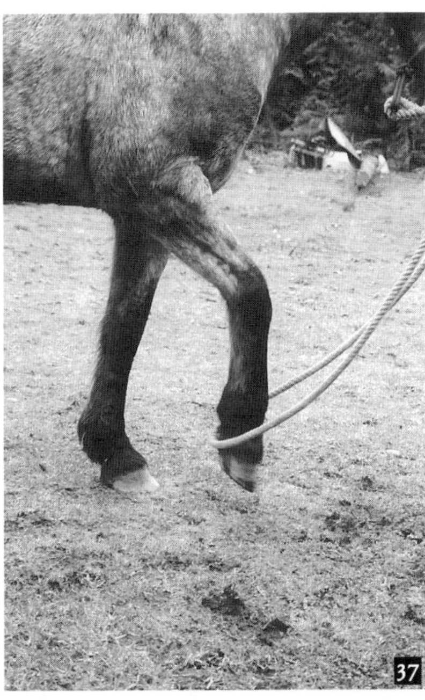

37

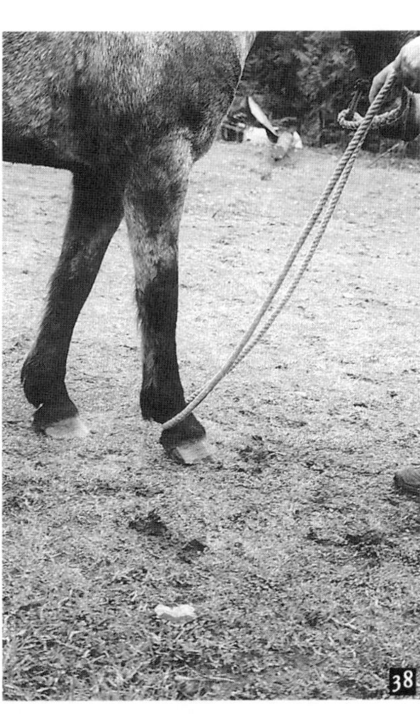

38

Gale Nelson series

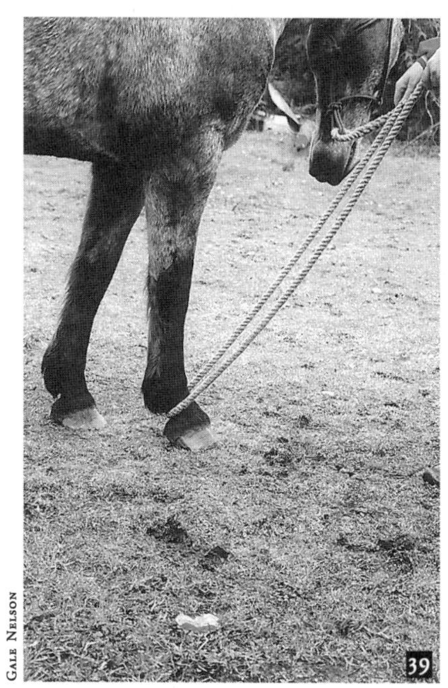

Gale Nelson

Gale Nelson

can see that he really put some effort into lifting up that foot the next time (Figures 39-40). This is due to the better feel the person had to offer. They were in no rush for that horse to learn about this.

When it comes to handling the hind feet, some people are going to take more time than they spent practicing with the front feet. That's fine. There's an idea circulating among people that these feet are liable to be more trouble than any front foot. In a way, they could be right, but there's no set rule for this. There's variations in every horse, of course. But something everyone who's going to be around horses should be aware of is that if certain unexpected things happen, a horse can move all of those feet to wherever he thinks he should, right on the spur of the moment. I'd say most people don't know about the wide range of possibilities there are in that subject.

In Figures 41-44, the approach to take is real similar to the way a person would handle the front feet. It almost goes without saying that we'd not want to use any part of force in this. For the better results, your movements should be calm and relaxed. The feel you present should be in line with what that horse can actually do.

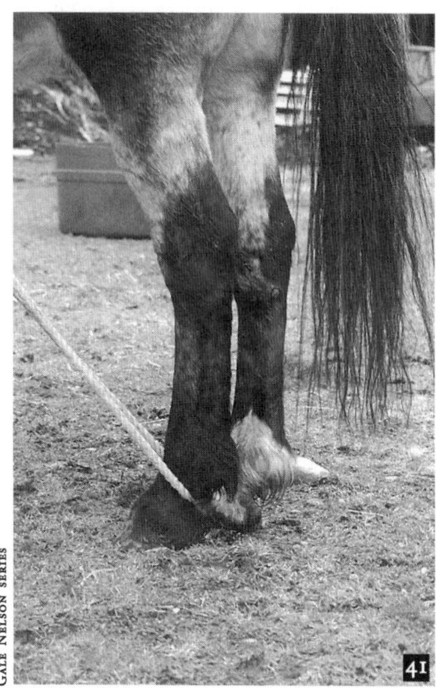

Gale Nelson series

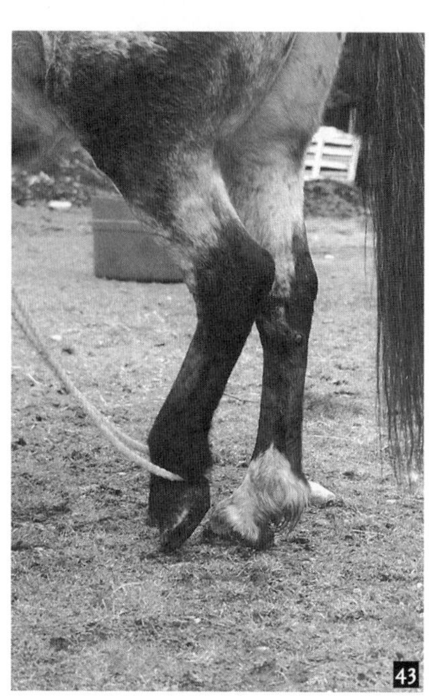

For an example, you won't expect the horse to be able to extend his leg out to the side until he is real comfortable lifting it up and putting it down for you. You'd want him to let you hold it for a while, and swing it back and forth quite a little before branching out into sideways variations on this.

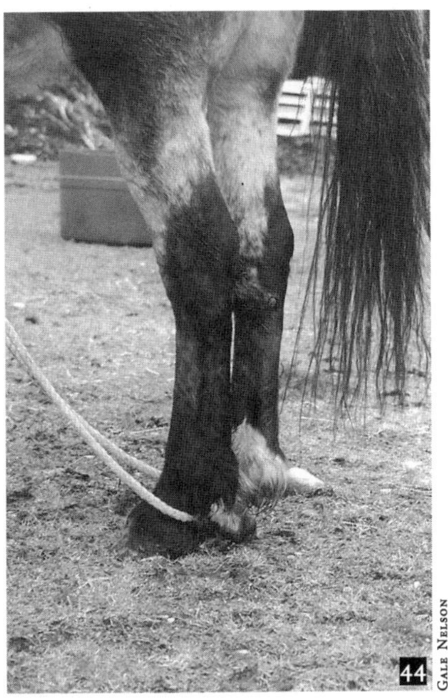
44 GALE NELSON

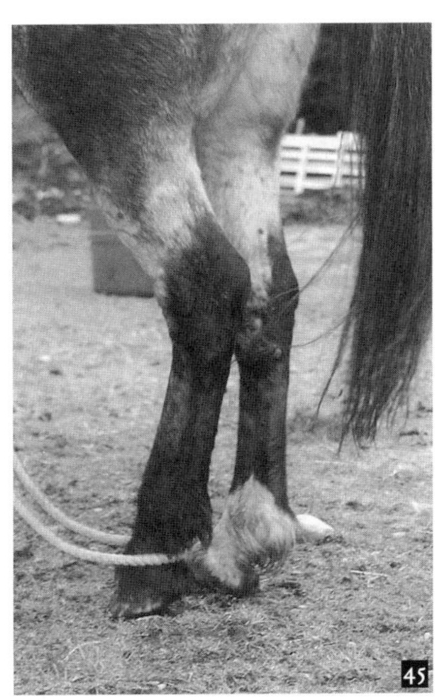
45 GALE NELSON

The timing of your releases should always blend in with his attempt to understand you — and you'll know when that is because you're going to be on the lookout for any little thing he does that even resembles a try. Give him the benefit of the doubt in this, especially where it concerns his feet and keeping him in a relaxed and learning frame of mind. You're going to get the hoped-for results if your feel matches that horse's actual ability to respond right then. If it does, then you'd be feeling of each other, and that foot won't weigh anything.

Once he is real sure about what your intent is, you'd maybe experiment with taking the foot a little higher, or just holding it off the ground a little longer before releasing it back to the ground (Figures 45-50). It might take quite a few applications like this before he gets used to having his foot taken off the ground. You'd want to do this fairly often, but not ever for too long. You'd wait until the horse was real

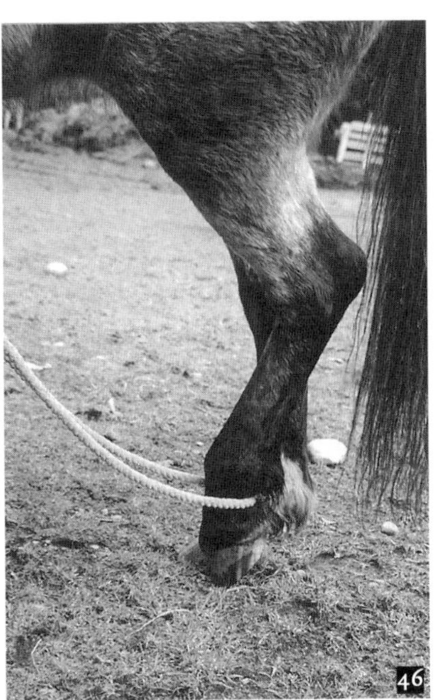
46

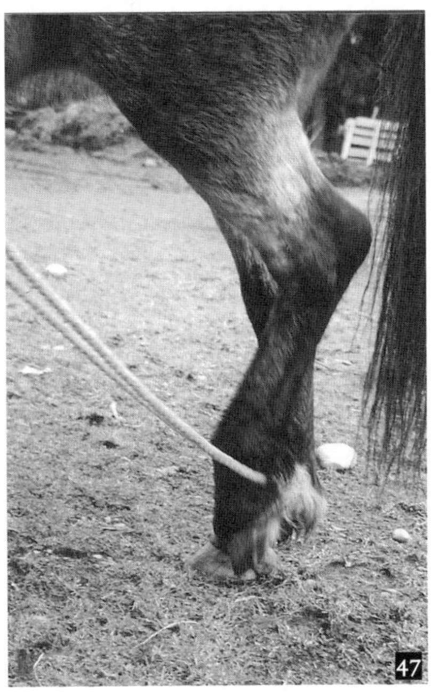
47

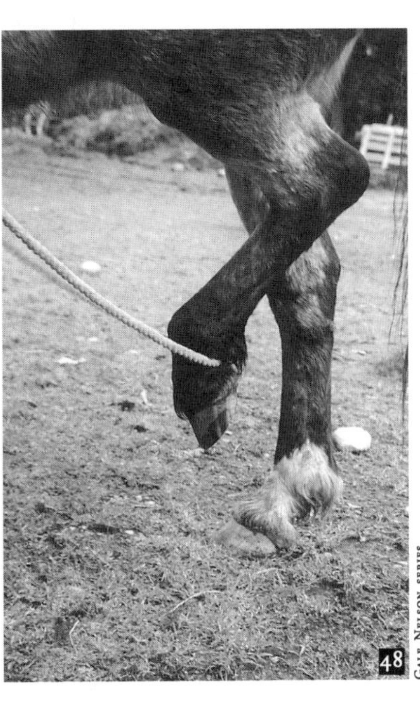
48 GALE NELSON SERIES

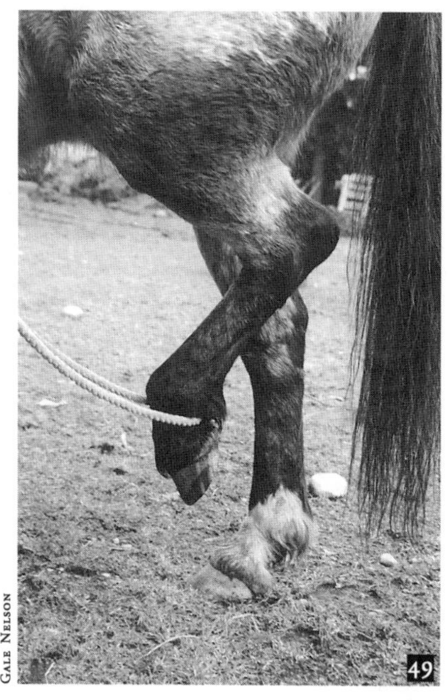

Gale Nelson

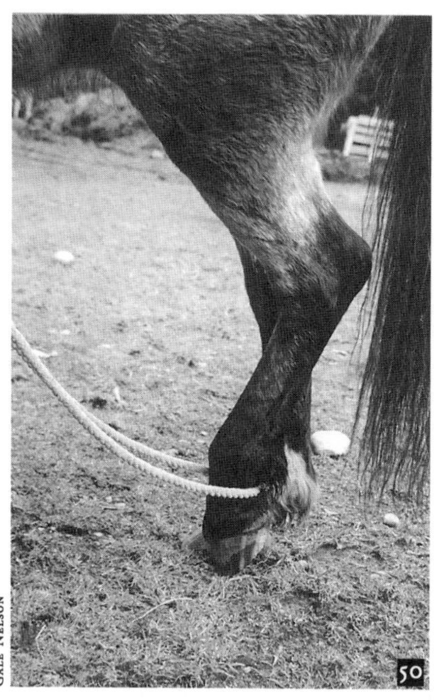

Gale Nelson

comfortable and turned loose to your feel before you'd start to swing his foot back and forward or take it at all sideways. Your timing and the way your feel is applied to handling the feet is so important.

When your feel is effective, the holding-up part of things will be taken care of by the horse. The rope should not be holding up those feet for the horse, not by any means. If this is happening, why that feel being presented is sure not the best, and he'll be learning something about resistance that isn't the best. No, when you teach a horse about a poor feel like that, in just a few sessions he will learn how to struggle or lean on a person. This type of resistance is based in some confusion about feel that can show up at other times, and you'd not want that. If things aren't progressing the way you'd like them to, why it's always helpful to get supervision from someone who has more experience than you do at handling those feet in a way the horse can understand, through feel.

When a person has enough time to teach this to a horse this way, it will have lasting beneficial effects. The horse can rely on it someday when things might not be going too smooth, but of course, we're in hopes this would never happen. But if things got to bothering that horse because his feet were being handled another way — why he'd know how to fill in for someone.

Where to Stand and How to Hold His Feet

When you're handling a horse's feet, where you place your own feet is going to be real important. This should never be a random decision or anything you'd just leave to chance, because it can really hurt when they stomp on your foot. A horse doesn't mean to do it that way, and it's the person's main job to keep out from underfoot. There's times a horse can jerk his foot away from a person and that foot'll land right on a fella's toes. Now when he just takes his foot back because he's startled, or if an undesirable feel had been worked into the approach that was being taken, why he'd mean to take that foot back, all right. But he wouldn't intend to land on your feet. No, I'd rather think a horse wouldn't spend his time thinking about that. You'd just be certain not to have your feet under his, is all.

After he is used to the feel of that rope and can give his feet real easy to that, then the main thing you want to do is get the horse real used to feeling your hand on his legs. A person will take this nice and easy. You wouldn't keep your hand on a leg too long, and you'd get it off of there before he stepped up, or anywhere, because on the start the idea is for him to stay standing. If he moves and then you take your hand off, why he'd think you wanted that. You need him to let you touch and handle his leg, and pick it up. Those are two very separate things there (Figures 51-56).

Go down his leg a little ways, from the shoulder or his hip, just rub him a little more and take your hand off, and do this until he's not one bit concerned about it. You'll test him out, too, on having your hand on the inside of his legs, and all the way down to his ankles and the feet, before you'd start pulling on his leg a little bit. When he's ready, you'd just pull on his leg a little bit, right above his ankle, until he

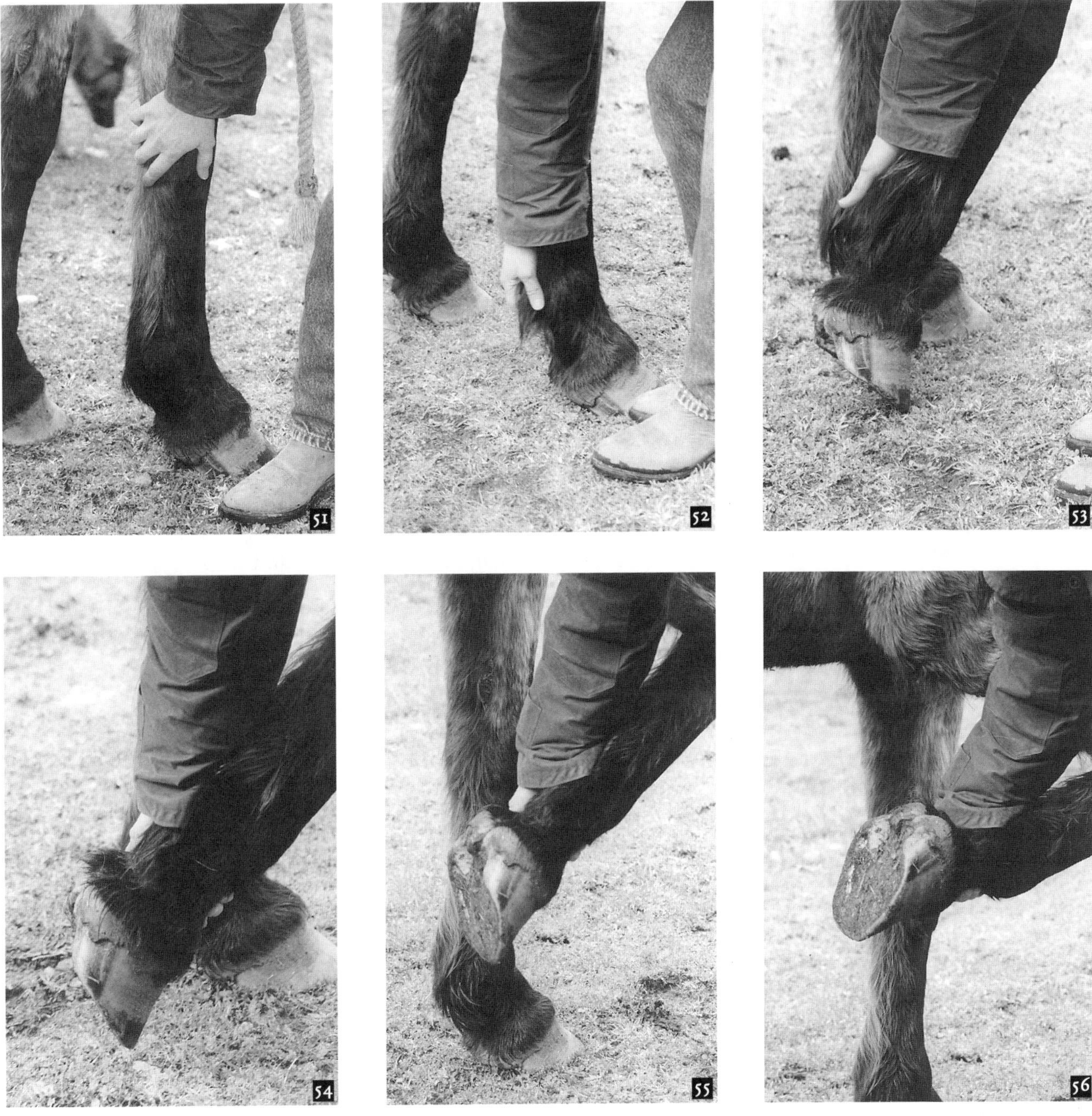

LORI SMITH SERIES

gets so he'll take the weight off. Just a half-inch off the ground or even less is fine on the start and then a fella just has to take it real slow from there to see what the horse is ready to offer.

Some horses will get real enthused about lifting those feet up, and it could surprise a person, so they'd want to not have their face or head too close around the knees or hocks or feet. Some surprising things can happen with those feet, all right, and this is even when the horse had no thought to resist in any way. There's no harm in repeating something here. If a horse is young, or at all troubled, he's going to need slow and careful help on this from someone who's got experience.

But, we'll assume that he's been well-prepared to understand the better feel you'd already offered him through the rope. With that as your foundation, you're going to work his foot back and forth a little until he is used to that. And you continue like that, always looking for the moment when you can release the foot while it doesn't weigh anything. It helps if you can guide it back to the ground with the lightest feel, as he's putting it back down (Figures 57-67). The other way, when it's not weighing anything, and he's holding it way up there and you just let go, well then, that connection is lost. It leaves an inexperienced horse to wonder what's going on.

Sometimes a horse gets touchy about the contact you make with his leg after you've left it way up there, and he's left to put it back himself. On a more experienced horse, this doesn't matter quite as much, but it's nice to get in the habit of following the feel of that leg as it gets set back down on the ground. This way, a horse is less likely to learn that he can kind of grab it back from you when he's got it held up like you'd hoped for. A person will want to keep this in mind when they're riding the horse, too. Farther up the line, this will make sense.

One thing's for sure, if you're hanging onto that leg and waiting to see if he's going to give it to you, you're way off in your thinking and no good thing is going to come out of that. Don't wait to let go until he takes it away from you. When you go at it with this attitude, it teaches a horse how to wrestle his foot back from you. If this is already a problem, there's some planning and thought that needs to go into this, for the better results to carry over for the horse in the future.

After some success at these foundation particles you're building into his understanding, you can take hold of his foot and swing his leg back and forth when you're holding it, and then maneuver that foot a little in your hands. Take it left and right and back and forth. A fella can tap on the bottom of his foot, and maybe around the edges and sides, a little at a time and not too hard. Just do things real gentle so it doesn't startle him and cause him to want to jerk that foot away.

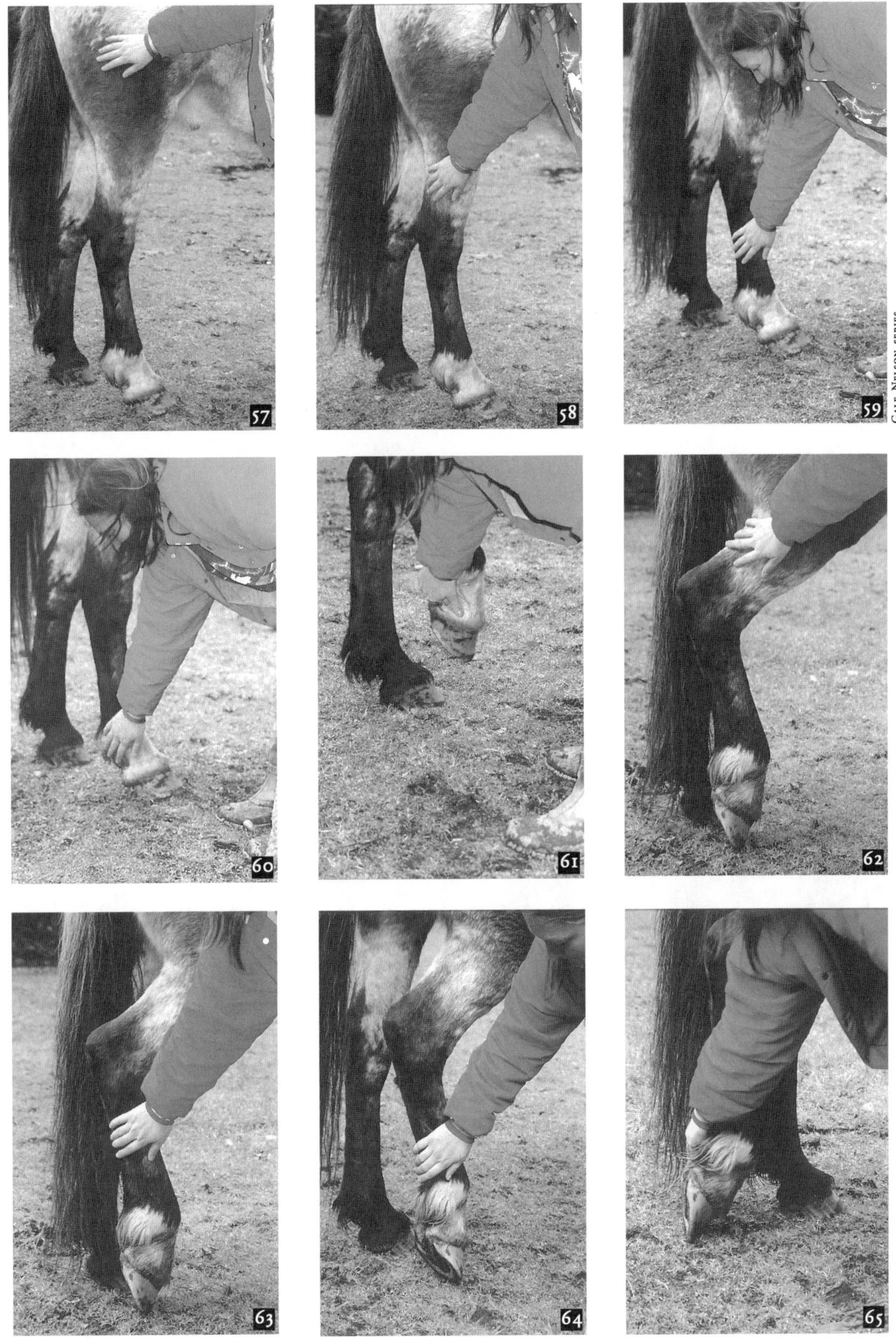

Gale Nelson series

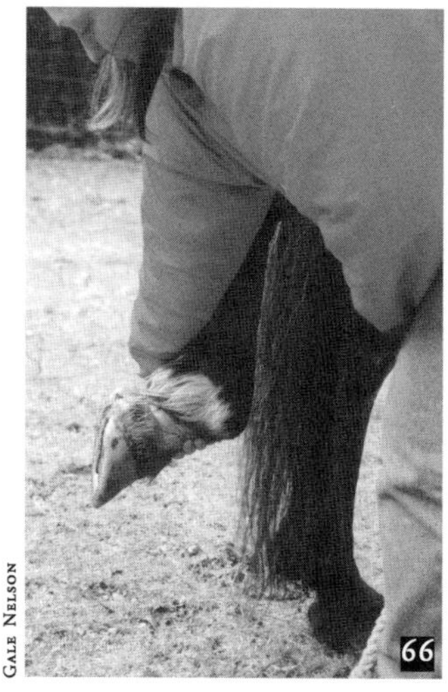

66 Gale Nelson

67 Gale Nelson

Figure 68 shows a shod foot that's got a lot packed into it. When a horse is shod, there's a responsibility the person has to keep those feet right and not neglect their condition or appearance. This is where a shoer can help, and if you can get into the regular habit of checking his feet, there'd not be reason for him to experience any problems with them.

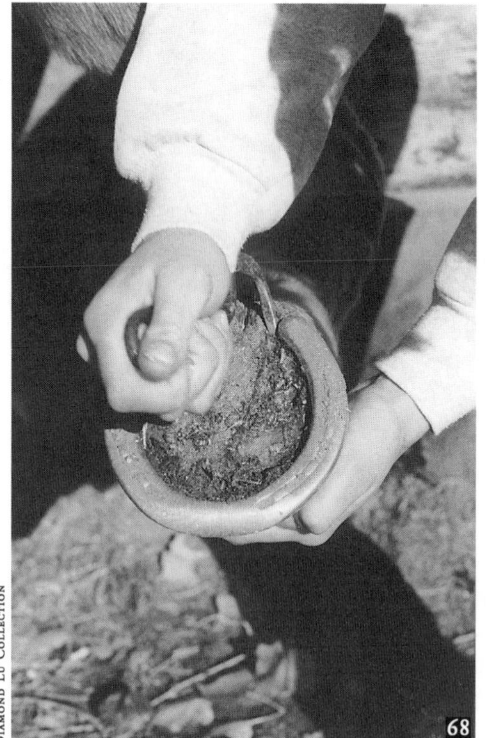

68 Diamond Lu Collection

69 Diamond Lu Collection

This person here in Figure 69 is starting out at an early age and has the advantage of good supervision. Where horses are concerned, it's always the better position to be in.

Part 4 — Teaching the Horse to Stand and Other Important Things

The exercises in Parts 1-3 have prepared you and your horse to understand the feel to liven-up, slow down, stop and stand. These four things are important to know how to do, where the subject concerns horses. There isn't any question that the exercises already mentioned, and the three after this part (Parts 5-7), touch on many particles of true horsemanship. Even though we wouldn't want to leave anything out that's going to be helpful, we have to, because there has to be a cutoff someplace. But, I'd say teaching a horse how to stand is probably one of the most important lessons to get built into his foundation.

In this section we're going to touch on some basics about how to get this done horseback that aren't covered anywhere else in this book. We're also going to speak about many things in this section that might seem to be in a strange order to read. But when feel is the subject, there's so much going on all at once that it's best if you can bring up some things when they seem to fit. This is our first book, and it seems to me that things I'm thinking about will fit pretty good if we speak about them now.

The moving parts of any horse are tied to his ability to slow down and stop and stand still. That sounds a lot more complicated than it is, but it's the actual facts of it anyway. Unless a horse can move, he can't settle and stand, and this part of horsemanship really tends to confuse people. Writing about this here is the best way I know how to put this message across without using a horse for demonstration purposes. Seeing it done, and handling or riding a horse that already has the ability to stand and move built into his foundation, through feel, is the best possible way to help a person learn how to do this.

All of the exercises in Chapter 4, including the three that follow this section, are real important to get working smooth before you'd ever think a horse was ready to ride. But we're going to speak about riding in this part anyway, because there's liable to be some people who want to know about this now. Their saddle horses are maybe going along all right just the way they are for the jobs those people need them to do. Some people aren't going to have the time or the desire to work a horse on the ground and rebuild the foundation. And they might not want to either. Some people who don't get around like they used to could want to know how to apply some of these things in a little different way from horseback, too. We know that. So we're in hopes this part is going to be helpful to them. One thing though, the main features of this section aren't going to translate anywhere near as good for the horse if these exercises spoken about (in Parts 1–3 and 5–7) aren't worked into your plan for the horse. *So there's not going to be anyone thinking that we recommend skipping any of this other (groundwork) — because that suggestion is one we'd avoid entirely.*

Livening Up the Horse, and Bringing the Life Down

You teach a horse to stand, on the start, by knowing how to help him move and having him understand that *you know how to do this through feel and in a way that fits him.* There's a lot of ways this can happen, and a lot of things it could mean. Here are just a few examples of it, and there might be hundreds of others. It's probably more truthful to say there's an unlimited number of variations to this because there are so many combinations of horses and riders, and no two are the same.

Knowing how to help a horse move can mean following his feel when he can't stand still, livening up that horse on the spur of moment, leaving in a collected gallop depart from the standstill, or just shifting the weight back and forward without any steps being taken at all. There is a measurable amount of *life that comes up* in a horse when he's doing all these different things. To the horse and the rider, this feel — to liven up — is real different from other presentations where the feel presented is for the *life to come down.* And before we speak on this subject further, there's no talking about a situation where, to slow that horse down, you'd present "no feel" to him, or have "no feel" coming from him, when you tried to liven him up. If there's a situation spoken about this way, then one of them would be dead. A person should be talking about the actual facts where it concerns a horse and that way there's a lot less room for any mix-ups. There's no further discussion needed on that.

There's also a need to teach a horse to stop, but you'd get the moving slowly part built in first. Moving, slowing down, stopping and standing still are all connected real close in the horse's mind and if no people are around there, why that horse has no problem doing any of those things, any time there's a need for him to.

But whether he can do these things when a person wants him to, just all depends on how his understanding of those things developed for him when he was being handled or ridden on the start. *It's determined by the person who taught him, and that's however much, or little, was done.* If that person was clear in their own thinking about the way these parts of the horse's movement work together, then that horse is liable not to be confused. But it doesn't usually work out that way, and the horse ends up confused because the people who handled him on the start lacked knowledge about the workings of his mental and physical systems. Probably due to them not spending enough time with horses, or seeing what there is to see about them.

If you present an understandable feel to a horse, why he can catch on real quick to the idea that you want him to go someplace. And if you liven him up to go someplace the way we're speaking about, why there won't be any question at all about him stopping for you when you want him to. *He'd stop* as soon he got the message from the feel of your whole body that *you'd stopped* wanting him to move.

The Better Connection Involves the Horse's Mind

When we speak about having a *connection* with the horse *through feel,* what's meant by that word "connection" is *the part that's in place when what you understand and do is directly connected to what that horse understands and does, on account of his physical and mental systems being tied in to yours, through feel.*

The person has got to flow with that horse's movements and understand the intentions in that horse's mental system, the best way he can, in order to get this better connection through feel working both ways. And we've already spoken quite a little on that. I can't think of any more words to use on this, except to say that the way a horse'd be aware of the change in your thinking, and the way he'd know how to get his body lined up to do what you had in mind, is all through feel. That reminds me how some people — when they're riding at the gallop and they want that horse to stop, they just say "Whoa!" and *keep right on riding,* and those horses keep right on going. Those people wonder why that horse just keeps on going and ignores the pulling, but they keep on riding. They fail to see the logical connection there is, for the horse, in his understanding of what they want him to do. No better than they prepared him, he is doing exactly what he thinks he should be doing, in the best way he knows how. His decisions are based on the level of understanding he has, and he is correct in those choices. We'd not ever say a horse was wrong, because how could he be? People might be inclined to say this anyway, based on what they haven't learned yet.

In a lot of people, their thinking is not set up to understand the horse's mind. It takes a lot of time to know about this, and nowadays people don't seem to want to put much time aside for understanding this. But they ought to, and if they really gave it some thought, they'd realize that it's the mind of the horse that makes him what he is.

Well, let's get back to what the horse knows how to do. The horse already knows about slowing down and stopping, and standing still and getting going. A colt has this pretty much figured out on the first day. But it will take some time to get a young horse to understand your feel when he's doing these things, and to get him responding to your better feel when you want him to do these things for you. As we've pointed out in the past, these things should not be rushed if you want to keep the lightness available in the horse. For sure, you might need him to be light in the future for any jobs you have to do on him.

After a horse learns to do these things in response to the feel you present from the ground, the feel that you've built in with your lead rope and your body motions will carry over to the feel you present to him from his back. If your groundwork exercises are smooth and the better results show up in those, well, it means he'd be liable to understand the feel of your reins and your body to slow down and stop, and stand there, or get right to going.

The parts that most people skip right over in their ground work are the three most important ones. The main point in teaching a horse how to lower his head and adjust it in various positions is to teach him to feel of a person (Part 1). The main point in teaching him how to lead up real free is to teach him to respond, through feel, with respect (Part 2). And the main point in teaching him how to lead up and step back one foot at a time, is to teach him to follow your feel to liven up a little, to place his feet, to slow down, to stop and to wait until a feel comes from you to move a foot to one place or another (Part 3). That's after he's waited there for a few seconds, or less, or more, depending on the horse and what was going on around there. There's a lot in that all right. I'd say a person who's missing this is missing way too much, if they plan to ride the horse.

In this first picture (Figure 1), the horse is standing and both the horse and rider are relaxed. Neither one has any plans to do anything other than what they're doing right there. When your horse is prepared to stand like this, you can get him ready to move in any direction on the spur of the moment. This is possible anytime that good feel to stand or move is working between a horse and rider, even when they might have the appearance of just standing there.

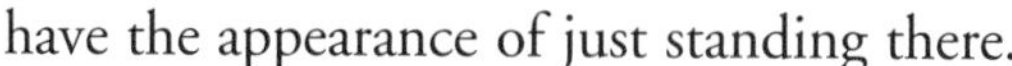

1

Diamond Lu Collection

I'm in strong favor of constructive criticism and the comment I'd offer in that area now concerns the reins in that picture. They look new and homemade, and that's fine. But they are too long. If they weren't shortened, why a stirrup and her foot could get caught in that excess of rope, or a front foot could even get caught up if certain things happened, and we'd sure wish to avoid this. I'm in hopes this girl got that shortening-up job taken care of at the first opportunity. In most of the pictures in this book, we're focused on the better aspects taking place in them. The time when something different needs to be mentioned is when the subject concerns safety.

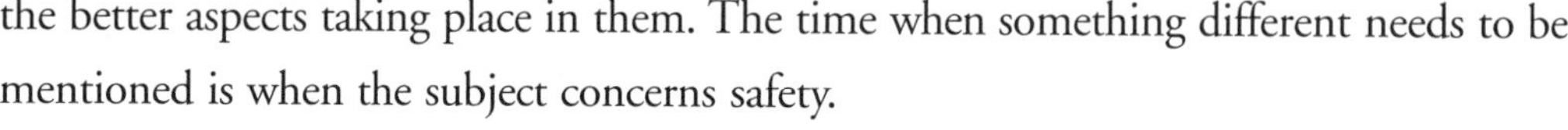

A Person's Attitude and Actions Affect A Horse

Feeling *of the feet* and feeling *for the horse* are two different things that figure pretty heavy in all this. There's a big difference between the two, and it's real important that a person not be confused about them being the same thing. The horse is sure aware of these differences in feel, and it's real important that a person can apply feel *in a way that shows the horse they know about this important difference.*

A horse is apt to look for things to respond to that he recognizes and feels good doing, whether it's lowering his head or backing one step, or any number of these real basic things that turn out well for the two of you, because your timing and feel are fitting. Of course, what fits a horse can change, the same as it can change for a person. What works is always going to be something adjustable. *It just all depends on so many variables — the main one being feel. Due to his natural inclination to want to get along in the world, the horse is all the time going to try to find meaning in what you present to him, and to adjust in the best way he knows how.*

Richard Field Levine

Backing the horse up one foot at a time.

In these next pictures, two small stones on the ground were in a good spot to be a help for seeing and measuring the horse's response to those smaller particles of feel being presented.

The first three pictures of the horse moving his feet are easy enough to follow, but in the course of replacing that left hind foot in Figure 5, several unplanned things happened. If you look at the two small stones on the ground in Figure 6, and compare the placement of his hind legs there to the other three pictures (Figures 3–5), you'll see how he thought he needed to arrange those feet quite a little before he was able to leave that left hind foot there. First, the horse stepped back with his left hind foot further than expected, and then he stepped the left front foot forward, and then he stepped up and took the weight off the right hind foot. And that took care of it.

Preparing to set the right hind foot back one step.

Taking the weight off the left front foot.

Diamond Lu Collection series

The left front foot is bearing weight now, and the left hind is coming up.

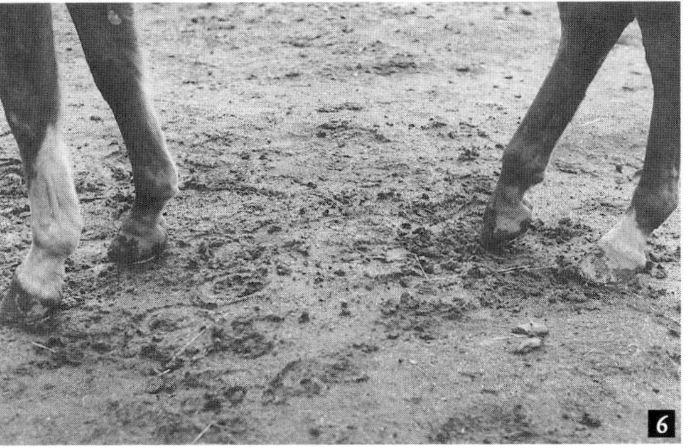

Some unplanned steps caused the horse to arrange his feet like this.

The *main thing* to understand concerning the progress that was made here is that the horse made the adjustments he needed to make in order to feel comfortable. He did it in the best way he knew how, and it worked out. That he did this is natural, and there's nothing wrong in that. He did that because the feel to do something else didn't show up, and it's something worthwhile to notice.

Most people wouldn't think there was anything to notice or talk about in a change like this, because it's so small and nothing bad happened. In a way, they're right. Even though some unwanted steps came in there, the horse wasn't at all pushy and he wasn't too mixed-up about things. He didn't poke his nose out, or sling his head and he didn't back up too far. Of course, the feel and timing that was presented to this horse could have been better, but it turned out all right anyway because he was able to fill in when he lost the better feel-connection that directed those earlier steps.

The *second main thing* to understand is that the horse stayed calm and gentle. He remained very much in that good, learning frame of mind that he started with because the feel presented to him *allowed him to stay that way.* No force or harshness of any kind was expressed towards the horse shown in these pictures. The motions were communicated to the horse using direct feel on the halter rope. What's shown is the actual facts of what happened.

Now we'd not want to assume that just because a horse was cooperative in response to one person's feel, that he'd be this way with another person, or even with that same person another time. Another person at that halter knot directing those feet might get the horse riled up in no time at all. That same person might not get the horse riled up at another time. Many surprising things can happen due to the vast differences there are in people. At different times, it's possible that you'd notice quite a little change in the same person, too. That's due to the general makeup of people, and the way moods and emotions are sometimes tied in there with other aspects. The horse is aware of all this.

We're always on the lookout for the little places where it's possible, and not possible, to bring out a small desirable maneuver or change in the horse, according to our plan. Even if he just shifts his weight from one foot to another — or takes in a big breath of air and lets it all the way out — these are the little things we look for and hope to see. We're on the right track when we begin to notice things at this level. This is how a real solid foundation gets started. To not notice these things, or to ignore them, means the future will be real uncertain from the horse's point of view.

We'd wish to avoid creating a future like that for any horse. There's no room in this for any thought about cutting back on the time you'd need to spend. It takes a lot of time to get this. *What matters most in this is only that the horse and the person are learning to get together, through feel.*

In these next two pictures (Figures 7–8), there was improvement. A little more time was taken for planning, and the person tried to adjust their feel to make a more effective presentation to the horse. It worked out real well. It was pleasing to me to see how little time it took to get more accomplished with that lighter feel and better timing coming in there.

DIAMOND LU COLLECTION

SHIFTING THE WEIGHT SLIGHTLY FORWARD OFF THE LEFT FRONT LEG...

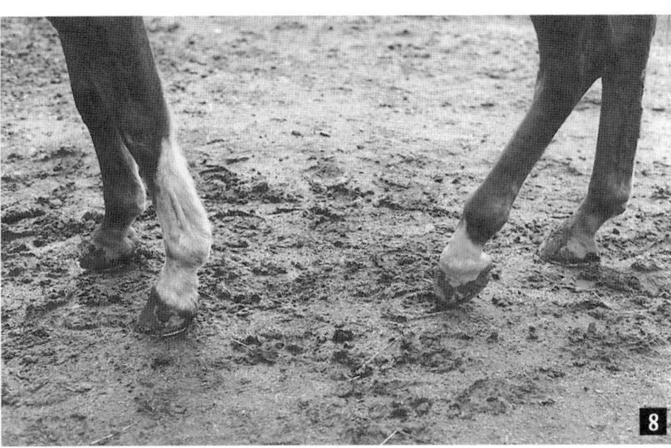

DIAMOND LU COLLECTION

...AND SHIFTING THE WEIGHT BACK, BEFORE PRESENTING A FEEL TO UNWEIGHT THE LEFT HIND FOOT.

Dropping Back to the Basics When That's What the Horse Needs

Now, if a person wasn't understanding how to present this, or they couldn't notice these small movements, or feel the slight adjustments they needed to make to get these results coming through for them, there is something to do that can help the person and the horse. They'd need to back track a little ways right then. That will help to get things clear between you and the horse, and shaped up so you could both continue on a better track.

The pictures at the top of the next page (Figures 9–14) could remind a fella about the importance of rewarding a horse for his try. It's not unusual for a horse to put more effort into something if he feels supported for his attempts to understand what was expected of him. Another horse might have just replaced his foot where it was on the start.

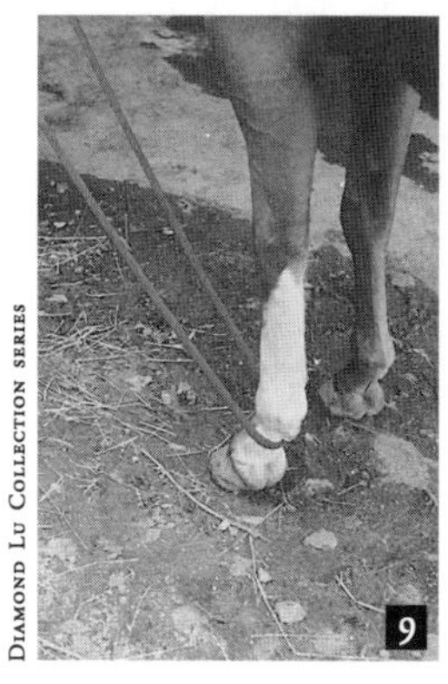

Present a feel for the left foot to lift up.

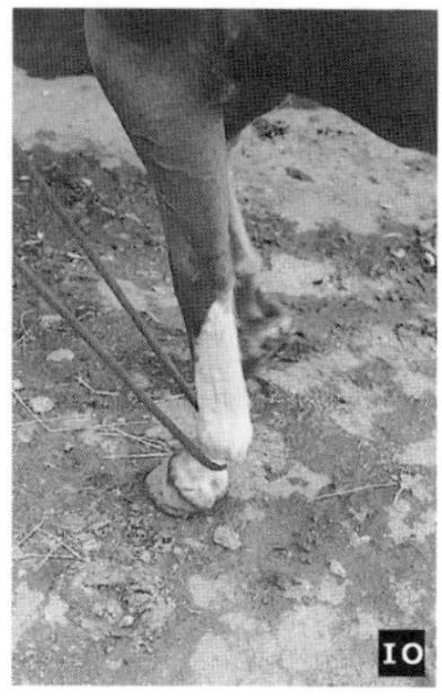

The horse always deserves the benefit of the doubt.

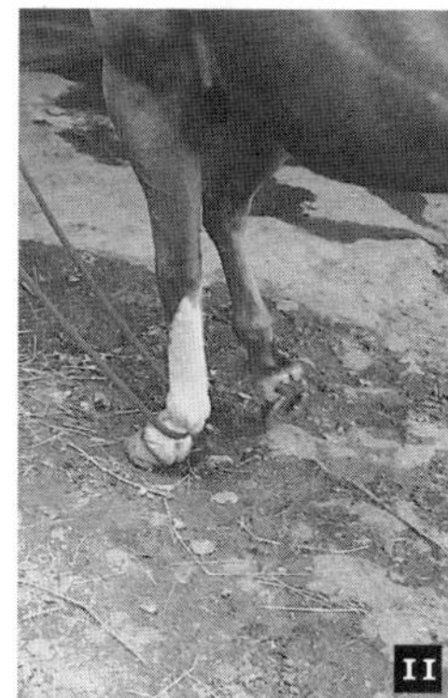

Reward with a release for this try, even though it's not quite what you had in mind.

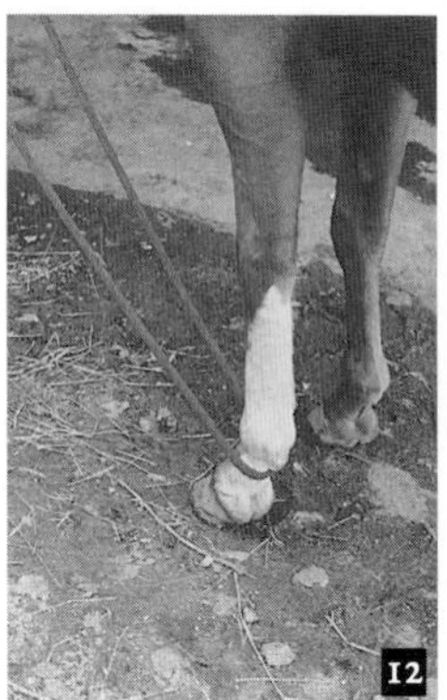

Take a fresh start.

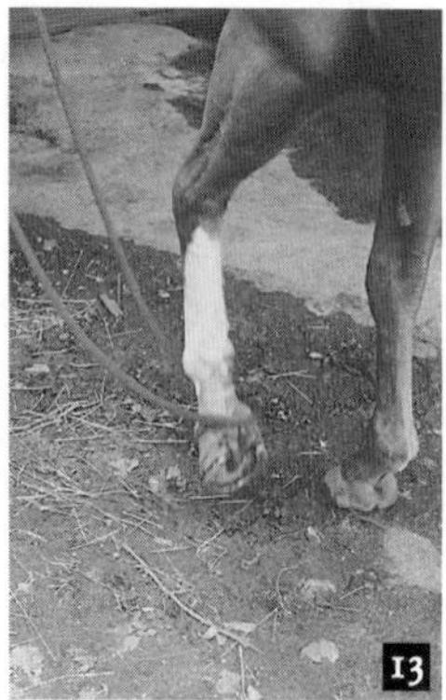

This time, he can lift the foot up real easy.

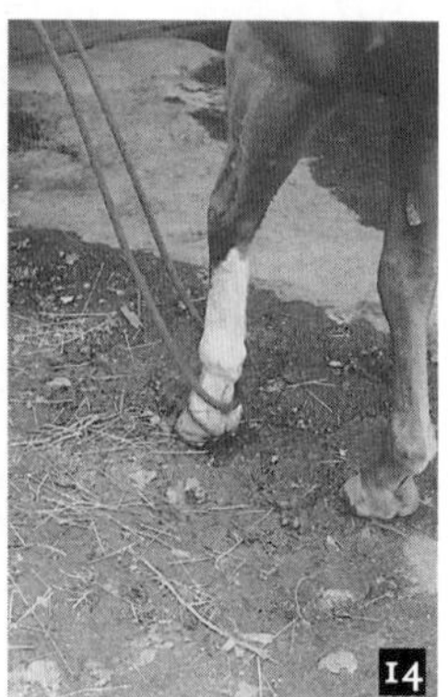

Just replace it and release it, always leaving slack in the rope.

If a Horse Moves When You Try to Get Mounted, Don't Get On

It's interesting to watch somebody get on a horse — just to see how they go about doing it. Most people haven't prepared a horse to stand still before they get on him. And many people are willing to get on even if he's walking off. There is a big problem with a horse that is taught that this is acceptable, because walking off is real close in his mind to other things, like trotting or loping off on the spur of the moment. The horse can find it easy to think these faster movements are going to be all right with a person, and no better prepared than he is, he wouldn't have any way of knowing any different.

If a horse doesn't stand before you get up there and when you're getting ready to get on, why he's liable to be on his way as soon as your foot leaves the ground. In some cases, he might even be leaving a lot sooner than that. *Getting on under those conditions is out of the question.*

What you'd do to help a horse learn to stand while you get on, is to have the reins in your hand when you're getting on and if that horse starts to leave, why you just step back down and ask him with the reins to move one foot back, one step — or maybe a couple of steps. *You'd do this in a real relaxed and easy manner.* It works out best if you can operate those reins the same as you would if you were sitting up on him. Figure 15 shows some of this, but the horse and the person are about at the size limit for this maneuver to be effective for them. For a person no bigger than she is, and a horse that's any bigger than this one, why that person would need to hold those reins about six to eight inches back from the bit and below the neck, not as she is doing in these pictures. But either way you held them, you'd need to spend a few minutes working real calm and relaxed to get that horse connected to your better feel again. When the horse can stand quietly, you'd take a fresh start at getting on.

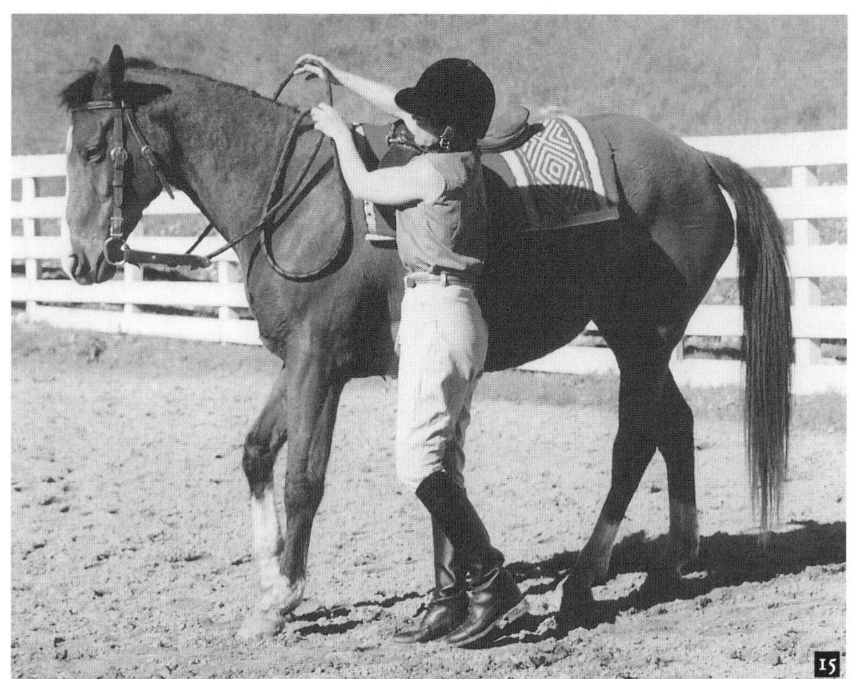

15 RICHARD FIELD LEVINE

Shaping Up Your Horse's Feet So He Can Stay

The horse in these next pictures (Figures 16–18) has a basic understanding of standing and waiting for a person to get on — in the way that I'm talking about now. You'd like your horse to be able to do this with a float in the reins, if you can. This won't always be possible, so you're going to make adjustments as they're needed. But you're going to try and stay on this better track with safety in mind, and head in the general direction we've spoken about above, using feel.

If you're ready to get on, like the person in this picture (Figure 16), but you aren't sure where your horse's feet are, you'd be sure to look down at those feet to see if that horse was going to be able to balance good enough for you to get on without him having to move his feet. If you

16 JEN SIMMONS

thought he couldn't stand still without getting off balance while you pulled yourself up there, why then you wouldn't continue getting on — you'd step down right away.

To help a horse get his feet shaped up when they're out of position, you'd take the saddle (by the horn or the pommel) and sort of rock it back and forth. When you push it away from you and then pull it towards you a little, a horse that's at all off balance is generally going to shift his weight from one foot to another to adjust his balance. Maybe he'll take a step, and that's fine if he does, because you want him settled and real stable when you go to get on. If he's been feeling of you in the exercises covered up to this point (Parts 1–3), then he's not liable to need to move until you get ready to have him to go somewhere. If he takes more than a step and gets to traveling around there a little, why you'd go back to practicing those exercises listed earlier.

Jen Simmons

17

Jen Simmons

18

Some Safety Considerations

Some people aren't going to be as handy as others when it comes to getting on a horse, and those people might be liable to get hung up in the stirrup, or hang on to that horse's mouth if they lose their balance getting on or stepping down. That'd sure overexpose most horses and you'd try to avoid doing that if you could, because a situation like this can turn disastrous.

A fella'd want to take some precautions and the best way to go about this is to just stop about halfway up — and for sure before he starts to swing his leg over that horse (Figures 17–18). Even on a horse that's gentle, a person would want to be in the habit of hesitating a little as he gets on, because he might not ever know ahead of time if something isn't right. If it isn't, why he'd have it worked into his plans ahead of time to step right down so he can take a fresh start. That person would have in mind to keep balanced when he got on the ground, so he doesn't jerk those reins by mistake while getting off. It's real important to avoid doing that.

Surprising things can happen when you don't pay attention to some of the smaller messages that come from a horse. That's why you'd want to be in the habit of always being sure that the horse *and the whole situation* was as right as you knew how to get it before you put your leg across his back. That word "whole" takes in a lot, but there's three things it definitely includes and that's making sure your saddle is cinched up, making sure the horse can stand still, and *not having any pressure on those reins to keep him standing that way.*

When you get to be my age you really appreciate one of those benches for getting up on a horse, and a fella can build one of these pretty easy. They're good for most anyone to use when they need to get those younger horses used to seeing someone above their heads. You can stand next to them up there and also get them used to your rain gear and your rope and things like that. It's also helpful to have a bench or platform so you can teach a horse how to pick you up from either side. And on some of those much bigger ranch horses, it can sure feel like a platform would be helpful, because sometimes what you have to do in the process of getting on the horse throws him off balance a little, and that can cause him to move his feet. You'd always want to avoid that situation.

Picking Up the Second Stirrup

It's real helpful to get in the habit of picking up the off side stirrup — or the near side stirrup if you get on from the right side of the horse — as if you were always getting on a real sensitive horse. After you were halfway up and had your leg coming across his back, you'd sit down and put your foot into that other stirrup in a real careful way. These last two things (picking up the stirrup and sitting down) can happen at the same time, or one a little before the other, and it can work out fine in reverse order, too. It all depends on the person and what fits them and the situation they are in right then.

Sometimes a fella decides to just ease onto that horse's back and he'd want both feet already secured in those stirrups, but I've seen it done both ways by some of the better riders. Whether your foot is secure in that stirrup before you sit all the way down or not, it's real close timing of whichever comes first anyway. But one thing is for sure, the details just mentioned in connection with getting on and having that horse stand still are real important.

There's a little technique I use to pick up a stirrup. I sort of poke my heel out away from the horse as my leg is coming down and I'm settling into that saddle. I bring my toe into that stirrup at an angle, so there's no chance of startling or confusing a sensitive horse. I'd not ever want a horse to get the wrong idea about what I intended him to do on the spur of the moment, and before I was ready to go with him. I kind of think most people don't appreciate the full extent of how important this really is.

Giving the Same Signal for Many Things Leads to Big Mix-ups

One thing needs to be mentioned before we go much further with this. It's amazing how people can mess things up for a horse on the subject of stopping and standing still. Many people do pretty much the same thing to get a horse stopped as they do to get him going — they give the same signal for starting, stopping and standing. Of course those people don't *think* that's what's taking place, but it sure is. What makes it so difficult for the horse is when a person lacks a basic understanding of how their *smallest unaware actions can affect that horse.*

Eventually, enough of this confusion and unaware actions — pulling on the reins to mean different things, for example — will cause a shift in a horse's judgment and decision-making. Of course, he's still only trying to adjust the best he can to what he's not able to understand. After he's had enough of this he'll just stop relying on any guesswork he might have been using up to that point. Unless something comes in to change his mind, he's going to switch over to relying real heavy on his instincts of self-preservation.

Well, pretty soon, he's going to get *real sure* about taking over with ideas of his own. Once a horse reaches this point in his thinking, he's pretty much given up on making sense out of the feel presented to him through the reins and other places, too. He's going to proceed at whatever he thinks he should be doing, the best way he can. This isn't too pleasing to most people. Some will even get the idea that horse is doing something *to them* that he oughtn't be doing. When they think this way, they usually say things about a horse that shouldn't be said. These people just don't have any idea what's really taking place — they just *don't know.*

I'm really in hopes that this book will help those people. And we're also putting all this down in print for a good many people who really do get so close to getting the right things applied. I'm in hopes this information about the smaller particles of feel can be useful and really make a difference to them and their horses, too.

When the Horse Stands Still, But Only Until You Get On

Sometime on a horse that has trouble standing still, you can get those feet to wait just long enough to get up there, and then before your feet are in both stirrups, before you're able to offer him a feel to start and before you have a chance to get with him on leaving, why he's on his way. When this happens, you'd get him stopped as soon as you could, right then, back him up a step or two — and then ease off. If he starts off again before you'd offer him the feel to start, then you'd just pick up on the lead rope or the reins, and stop him, and then back him up a few steps again. If this is presented right, that horse gets so he learns to understand what it means to wait for you. Of course, it's best if you build this in ahead of time, on the ground.

There's plenty of people who'll try to get this taken care of from his back, and there's a few who can. But not many can, not if they're wanting to get the results we're talking about. I'd rather assume that those people who can already have a pretty good feel of their horse on the ground. Well, if a fella's horseback and he's trying to help a horse get rid of this undesirable habit, he ought to have another important thought in mind and that is, he doesn't want any part of bad timing coming into this that teaches that horse to take over. There's a real fine line there, because that's exactly what will happen in this situation if a fella's timing isn't the best. No, if it's that way, it can sure set a horse back a ways, and the person, too.

I've seen a lot of people correct a horse that had difficulty standing, and I've seen some of them go at this with an attitude of force and punishment that is entirely out of line, and we aren't talking about that, not by any means. But as long as the person is learning to communicate with the horse through feel, and has an interest in getting his ideas across to that horse this way, there's sure some hope.

Getting With the Horse When He's Ready to Leave

We just spoke about a horse that takes over and has to get moving the minute you get up there. Some horses will be able to stand there after you're on, but some of them sure can't stand still for long at all. It seems like some people figure a horse ought to stand there forever and when he doesn't, they try to make him stop, right when he feels like he needs to move. Well, when they work with the horse this way, he's bound to learn some things he shouldn't. Those things are liable to turn into habits that aren't the best. In this situation, a horse can get real disrespectful and take it from there. A person needs to remember that this can lead to dangerous situations that are avoidable. Even without any wrecks showing up, this tendency in a horse is a real poor reflection of his basic foundation. I'd rather most people would get off a horse like that and work with him on the ground to build in some feel that went both ways, before they ever got up on that horse again.

When you're getting on a lively horse like that, it's a good idea to get ready to leave with that horse *before it becomes his own idea to leave.* Don't wait for that horse to take over and leave. If a fella tries to keep this lively kind of horse standing for too long, pushiness can come in there in no time at all, and that horse'd be sure to take over and get going on his own. No matter what the rider did, a horse like that would think he had to go — and if the horse needs to go? He will, and this is his right. No part of force is the answer to this, and to fight him with those reins at this point can lead straight away to something undesirable. There's just no question about that.

The timing of your feel comes into this and is important on this real lively kind of horse. The best part about it is it'd be one of the simplest jobs you'd have. When he can no longer stay *then he's ready to leave, and you'll just go with him.* Just ride the horse as he goes. Like anything else, it'll be simple for some people, and not for others. But that's one of the main ways a fella can fix up a horse that can't wait, and turn him into one that can.

On the start, when he's feeling of you to liven up, that's when you take him somewhere and the two of you go together right then. There's a fine line on the timing here. If you're in tune with the feel of the horse and have learned how to get with him on the ground first, your chances of developing the better timing horseback are real good. You're teaching him to respond to your energy. That real slight movement, and the life that he needs to associate with it, comes up in your body. He feels that.

You'd adjust your body in a way so he can feel you get in time with the feel of his body, and you'd do this exactly at the time when he's shaping up to go. You'd use your legs with just a real slight movement as he leaves, just to get him used to it — to get him used to being asked to go *when he's ready to go.* Do just enough, but not too much, and you'd do this *when* he's ready to go. You're experimenting will tell you just how much is enough for a particular horse. We call this getting together with the horse, or "blending in."

This feels just right to a horse that has trouble standing still because he doesn't want to be held back. Just like you don't want to be pulling on those reins when the horse is standing, you'd sure want to be real careful to not pick up the reins when he starts to move off, because that interferes with the part of his understanding about what the rest of your body is doing. It also sets him back in his understanding about the meaning you want to build into the feel of those reins, for turning and stopping.

A horse doesn't like the feeling that he's leaving alone when there's someone on his back who's not with him. Depending on many variables that can enter into this, that uncomfortable feeling in the horse can lead to certain actions that will result in him leaving alone all right. There's a good chance that the rider will be alone, too, and they'd maybe wish they'd learned how to get with that horse on the ground a little earlier, when being on the ground had an entirely different meaning.

It wouldn't be right to punish a horse if this happened. It's just something that happens, and it's really nobody's fault. A fella'd do a little different the next time, is all.

If you don't pick up on those reins as a signal for your horse to go forward, and instead use your legs, pretty quick that horse will learn how to compare what you do when he's standing still with the feel of what you do when you ask him to leave. A person's better judgment should give that horse the proper feel to move after he has stood there as long as he can. The most effective way to prepare a horse to understand your feel of these two things is on the ground, way before you plan to get on him.

If He Can't Wait for You, Adjust Your Timing and Help Him Go

The main point in all this is to learn to feel of the horse and help that horse feel of you, so he can understand *what the difference is* between your feel to liven up and your feel to slow down, or stop. There should be no mix-up on our part about the difference between the feel of those two things, that's for sure. If there is, then the horse isn't liable to figure it out and he'll just revert to self-preservation maneuvers that a person might wish to avoid.

If a horse is persistent in his eagerness to move before you're ready, then one adjustment a fella can make is to present him with just the slightest feel to leave *before* he leaves. You'll get ahead of the horse on this, and you'll get him ready to leave. Then, after a little of this, he can wait there a few more seconds. If he's a nervous horse, why you'd better settle for three or four seconds rather than to expect him to stay there for five minutes. If things go the way they should, and you progress with this in a way the horse and you can both make sense of, then you'll catch onto the way you'd *get him ready to get ready* to leave, and there's measurable progress when a fella can do that. He's feeling of you then.

The horse's feel and the way he's reacting will tell you what to do, and how long he's going to stay there. If you can get onto the feel of that from the horse, and make your necessary adjustments to get him going before he takes over, it will mean your timing has improved. Everything you need for this will come to you from the horse through feel, and with practice you'll get with his readiness to go. A horse like that will start to catch onto the feel of your readiness pretty quick. And you'd not forget to use your reins and your legs to direct that life in the horse as it started to come up.

You'd always want to have in mind, ahead of time, a place for a horse like this to go because a horse like that *needs to have a place to go*. You'll make plans ahead of time about where you'd direct him and the adjustments you'd need to make all depend on the particular horse. If he's already moving and you don't have a plan, why that will cause him to think he ought to have one, and you can be sure he's got one, all right, but his decisions on this might not be pleasing to you.

Unsticking the Dull-Sided Horse and Generally Livening Up the Other Kind

It takes so much life in a horse to maneuver. If he doesn't have much life in him, he won't have much feel. It's natural enough for a lot of horses to be a little on the slow side and not too enthused about doing anything, because if it were up to them, they'd be out with the other horses eating grass and standing around. And some horses just don't want to move.

There are a lot of reasons for this. One reason is that they've not been taught to move through feel. And some of them, no better than they've been handled, *have been discouraged from moving.* That problem is generally due to a person kicking the horse and pulling back at the same time, or just hanging on that mouth because they haven't ever learned how to ride a horse in a way that fits the horse, and that takes in a lot of people. If a horse doesn't understand the feel to move, these horses are usually the ones who haven't got the first idea about the feel to slow down or stop either. When a horse gets onto the better feel a person has to offer, problems like this don't exist, and that's our goal. People have devised many mechanical ways of dealing with this that we don't need to dwell on, because we're a lot more interested in getting our horses to feel of us. I'm in hopes that someday certain items won't be so popular.

Diamond Lu Collection

19

You can see the life in these two people, but you can't see the horses they've just livened up because they ran out of the picture.

On the start, we have to teach that horse to liven up a little bit when it's necessary. If you don't, he won't have enough life in his whole body and his feet to make the maneuvers we'd like him to make. So in order to get him to liven up when there's a need for it, we need to get him sensitive to our leg. That's where the gas comes from, is down there, at your leg. Later, you can refine that quite a little and this is talked about further up.

The sensitivity I want people to get built into their horses can be developed rather quickly — and I'd rather assume they aren't inclined to pass over the beneficial effects of the groundwork exercises mentioned earlier. If things are following a course where timing and feel are working together for those better results, and you have no thoughts of rushing things, why in almost no time at all you can reach a point where the horse can pick up your feel for a gallop depart by simply wiggling your big toe in the end of your boot. No one will see this, and they'll sure be amazed.

I know of several ways to do this, but I'm going to speak about two main ways. That's using one leg, real firm, and the other way I call the "pressing in" method. People use this approach, but I like the first way because it leads quicker to those better results. You'll give the horse time on this. There's a lot of other methods people use to make a horse liven up that create a brace. It's quite common to see whips or gimmicks and threatening ways used to get the horse to operate. We won't have any part of that, and no further mention of it will be made.

Livening Him Up with the One-Leg Method, Real Firm

We don't have any pictures that show this being done like we're going to speak about here, but you'd *use only one leg for this*, for the better results. The reason for using only one leg is that when you bring two legs in real quick and meaningful against the horse's sides at the same time, it can create confusion and mix-up for him that just prolongs the time it takes to teach him this. Two legs coming in there at one time is too much. When he's learning how to liven up, I leave it up to the horse where he goes, and this is a real important part because what you're after here is for that horse to liven up in his feet. When you've got the life in those feet working for you, it's a lot easier to direct them.

As far as an ideal response to all of this is concerned, when you do tap that horse with your leg to get him to liven up, his whole body livens up. There's no direction for him to go — no special direction. Just anywhere he wants to go is where I let him go. I let him choose the direction at first, because I don't like to distract him anymore than I have to from the job of first being able to liven right up when he feels my body liven up. When he livens up, I go right along with him, I'm not just sitting there dead in that saddle. I'm ready to go with him when he moves. This is what can give him the confidence in you to go when you ask, because you allow him to go. A lot of people want this from their horse, but don't seem to like the idea of letting him move after they get him livened up, so they pull back on the reins as he starts to go. This gets real confusing to a horse after awhile, and some horses get real resistant to your leg. That's when you know it just isn't working out for the horse.

Getting Him Straight

Just as soon as he learns how to liven up, when he's reliable at that, then I start giving him a feel of a direction to go in. I might just line my body up towards an object, a tree or something a good ways off, and see if that horse can stay right under me, just to see if he can head right where my body is headed. Pretty soon he'll follow my feel. I do whatever it takes to keep him on line there. It takes very little sometimes, after he gets hooked on to my feel. I travel with him and I direct and support him as we go. Of course, by this time, I've learned how to tell where his feet are under me, and when I make these little corrections to his direction, I'm careful not to do too much. I do just enough to keep that line, then I let him keep on it until he can't stay there. Then I'll put him back just when he begins to stray off it. The idea isn't to hold him tight with both reins to make this happen. It is the correction in one direction or the other that lines him up so that straightness can come in there.

After a little practice, he'll understand the slight feel you offer him to liven up and go. And due to this other practice just mentioned, why getting him to go straight someplace isn't liable to be any trouble at all. He'll liven up if you're real careful not to pick up those reins when he starts to leave. From these next few pictures you can get the general idea of how this is done, but the young person here is just learning so we're going to mention a couple of things she'll need to work on, because we don't want people to get confused by what is shown.

Use only one leg to liven up your horse.

Diamond Lu Collection

20

This pony is stuck at the gate (Figure 20). A lot of ponies and horses are liable to think this is a nice place to be. Experience shows them this is so. In the best way she knows how, this young person is experimenting with offering that pony the feel to liven up. After a couple of tries at this, the pony trotted around, and she caught on to how to get with him as he got going (Figure 21). He didn't offer to buck, and he had no history of bucking people off. He's the kind of pony that really wants to get along, which is one reason he was a good choice for a smaller person to learn this on.

There's always a chance when a person is starting out that they'd be inclined to hang on those reins and jerk the mouth in the testing stages, so that problem was avoided by just not putting any bridle on the pony in the first place. Sometimes a horse needs reassurance when a new feel to do something is presented, and rubbing them on the neck and all over where you can reach without losing your balance is really helpful to them. After several tries at this and a lot of rubbing his neck and his butt (Figures 22–23), he was able to walk right out and make turns and stop and liven up to go, through feel. By the time things died down and the lesson was over, this younger person could just straighten up in the saddle and wiggle her foot just a little and that pony could liven right up and lope out, and then get back down to the walk in a stride or two. He stopped kind of in the middle of that round corral when she was ready to get off, which was one thing they were trying to get accomplished that day.

Diamond Lu Collection

21

These are the actual facts of what happened. I wasn't there but I was told about this by people I know who were. I thought there might be quite a little value in this for certain individuals. It really pleases me to see someone so young as this getting started using feel, especially when they can get results like that.

When a person has a lot of the basics working for them, it's always a good idea for them to be able to leave real smooth in a gallop depart on either lead. There's quite a little written about this in Chapter 5, but the main thing I wanted to mention about this is the need to use one leg instead of two for the better signal a horse can receive for this. But the fella in Figures 24 and 25 was at a disadvantage on this because I wasn't there that day so we could visit about it first. It's always best if you can talk things over. This horse looks to be a real stout and athletic kind, and there's a real precise look to the way she livened up into the gallop for this man. When they have this look, I'd always prefer to see the whole horse.

This fella is getting ready to liven up his horse.

This is a gallop depart on the left lead from a standstill.

I don't like to keep picking on a horse all the time to get him to do something. When I want a duller sort of horse to liven up, why, on the start, I just turn my toe out away from his side and press down in the stirrup, quite a little ways out away from the horse. I bring that foot right to him in a way that has some meaning to him — and I bring it right to the place where my leg would hang. I like to bring it *way out away* from him before I bring it in, so he can tell the difference between that and other motions that have less meaning, or different meanings.

On some horses it only takes once or twice, and they'll get ready to liven up right then because they can feel when you're ready to make your move. You'll have to find out how much it takes. It might be hardly anything and then it might take a lot on the start. I like to take my leg clear off to give more meaning to it when it goes on. After he gets so he maneuvers well, then you can do a little less and still get that life up in his body. This feel is real useful to have built in. It'll be real different from any other feel you present to him.

There needs to be a lot of starting and stopping. When he feels your body liven up, his whole body livens up and that's when his feet are ready for you to work with. That livening-up message from the person is real important to a horse, and he'll notice it. If you're consistent, he'll remember it and he'll get real good at recognizing the difference between the feel to liven up and the feel to slow down.

It's not so complicated if you know how to get your horse prepared. You're not going to *make* the horse do it. You're going to have to *fix it up for him*. You can put him in about any position and when he's prepared, he'll be able to feel of it, and feel for it, and he'll take the lead you ask for, or do whatever else you want.

Maybe you'll need to give him more time to understand. Or, if the horse has a lot of fire in him and wants to go way too fast all the time, you'll have to spend some time on getting that horse to slow down for you. No, if he has an abundance of life he'll sure need to learn to slow down first, through feel. *Then it doesn't matter if he's too fast or too slow — the horse is going to know what you want and be able to respond to you.*

That respectful, accurate response is what we need for safety when a fella's horseback, and he needs to get something done.

People want to know about using spurs for this. Well, it all depends on how sensitive your horse is. Some horses wouldn't pay much attention to just your leg. *It also depends on what sort of control you have over your legs when you're up there, and if you really know where your legs are all the time, or not.* If you can operate your legs by using one independent of the other, you'll have an advantage at this. I like to use a spur, but I like to use it as little as possible. The main thing is to get your leg away from him right after you come in with your spur. That's what works best for me, not to have that leg hang down pressing on him after he's livened up. When I need more life in the horse I like to just liven up my leg. But there's other people who have success just pressing a leg into their horses, and if the horse is sensitive and that works out, then it's all right.

The Pressing In Method

Some people do it another way, by pressing, but the horse can get confused when you leave your leg on there. Pressing doesn't mean raising your heel up and grinding that heel into his ribs, and leaving it on there so every steps gets another deep grind from your heel with no relief. This is what some people have a habit of doing and it's one of the less attractive habits a person can get into. A horse doesn't seem to respond well to that grinding-in feel, but the pressing way can work. It just depends on how it's applied.

Constant Pulling or Pressure on the Reins

One of the biggest problems horses have is the way some fellas just kind of hang onto those reins. It really bothers a horse when someone keeps steady pressure on his mouth when he's just standing there, or when he's walking and moving faster, too. Generally speaking, a person who does this hasn't got very good balance on a horse, or they haven't learned about the importance of being able to operate their arms independently of how they sit on the horse. There's a lot that can go wrong if a fella isn't onto this, especially on a more sensitive horse.

We've included enough pictures of horses that are bothered by an excess of pressure on the bit that we don't need another one here to show you how bad it looks. We want to show something that has a better appearance than that, because we really want people to get the right idea about feel and how it's going to look when it's applied in a way that the horse can travel to a stop with a float in the rope or the reins. And when he comes to a stop, why you'd hope to have the reins weigh almost nothing in your hands.

Figures 26-27 show how the rider's slight adjustment in posture and feel brings the horse down to a stop from the walk. That horse understood what the rider expected, is the reason it worked.

Richard Field Levine

Richard Field Levine

I want to speak a little more about how a rider's posture can affect the horse when they want to collect him up and slow him down, too. That's coming further up in this section. These next pictures (Figures 28-36) show some ways a horse can look in the walk, trot and lope, and traveling collected in those gaits, too.

Diamond Lu Collection

These young people and the pony are in a lively, extended walk.

This horse is in a pretty good walk, and the rider has her gathered up a little.

29

Lori Kline

Jen Simmons

This horse is relaxed in an extended walk.

Patricia Weedman

This horse is in an extended trot and the rider has good posture. She's not interfering in any way.

Every now and then, you want to travel with more tuck than you need, like the horse shown in Figures 32–33. This keeps the horse knowing how to travel and operate under par, and able to maintain a posture that's not got anything to do with pushing up against the bit. But you wouldn't want to hold this for more than *a second or two* or you won't strike that happy medium we're hoping to develop in his head carriage. When people get in the habit of riding like this, it's called hanging on the mouth. That habit sets up a lot of undesirable patterns in that horse's mind which

Jen Simmons

Jen Simmons

Jen Simmons

Emily Kitching

Emily Kitching

he'll sure put into action if a fella doesn't make a fast change in his ways. It can also really alter the way a horse appears when he's under saddle. Figure 34 shows the same horse at a slower, collected trot. Figure 35 shows a horse in a relaxed lope. The horse in Figure 36 is in a collected lope. The rider has his leg underneath him, and he's looking ahead.

One Habit That Isn't the Best

When a fella's in the habit of hanging heavy on the horse's mouth, he's liable to just pull on those reins a little harder *when he wants that horse to liven up and go some place*. This messes up just about everything — *especially the stop*. But a horse responds to the feel he's presented with. It's not hard to understand the horse's point of view. If he's all the time expected to stand still with steady pressure on his mouth, and he's always been presented with a pull on his mouth when he's supposed to leave, why then any meaning he was supposed to understand about stopping when those reins came tight after he's got up some speed, why it just wouldn't be there.

By the time a horse that's been handled this way is running at full capacity, he doesn't have one thought about stopping when those reins tighten up. As far as he knows, he's only doing what they taught him to do when they pulled back, which was to move his feet. How could a horse that's been prepared this way know about any part of slowing down? There's not much chance of that. But they sure want him to stop anyway, and they sure hope he will when he's heading straight towards an oak tree, and there's plenty of them in this country. No, what's on people's minds when they've got this to contend with is usually limited to whatever physical strength they have, and maybe the bit they're using, and whether or not they're going to get hurt. All of this is real understandable. We sure don't want anyone to get hurt.

When a person isn't geared to think about slowing down except when the horse is galloping, well, they haven't given any thought to his mind or his feet at the right spot in his education. That was the part that got left out of their education is why, but you start right where you are, and go on from today. *If a person takes time to think about this from where the horse is, they might switch their thinking around to favor the horse and just limit what they expect of him to what he can actually understand and do.* I'll put it this way — it will be a lot safer and more pleasurable for them in the future if they do.

The stops we're talking about would proceed from a walk slowly down to a stop, and then you'd rock the horse's weight back. After that was good, you'd take the horse from the trot slowly to the walk and then ease down to the stop from there. Later he'd get so he could trot to the stop, and just stand still, or you'd keep a feel on those reins and have him still light and collected and step him back before you eased off and let him settle. You'd take the same approach using the transitions when you wanted to stop from the lope. It wouldn't just be where a fella is going full steam and pulls up quick and forgets about the preparation. Not ever that way. The horse needs to understand his own progress, and be sure of the footwork he's expected to do. And before you expected him to understand how to lope to a stop on the spur of the moment, why you'd have it set up so when he was asked to trot to the stop, that came real easy. There'd need to be plenty of real slow work ahead of that, so there wasn't any doubt in his mind about what you wanted him to do. He'd understand through your feel what to do, and he would do it.

Maintain Softness all the Way Through the Stop

When you walk the last step down to a stop, using feel, try to keep softness all the way through the last few steps to the stop, and then maintain that light feel and rock him back, or even take a step or two back. There is a slight change in the rider's body at the stop, which you can see in Figures 37–38.

Jen Simmons

37

38

Jen Simmons

When you practice trotting to the stop, it's best if the horse has a relaxed appearance and stays soft all the way through to the point of stopping, like this horse in Figures 39-40. Variation is important, and you wouldn't back the horse up every time. It's important to experiment with your posture and the feel on your reins.

Jen Simmons

39

Jen Simmons

40

The boy in these pictures has a good feel to offer the horse. They are both learning how to stop. The rider's body has stopped riding forward, and at this stage of their learning, why that horse's head being in a below normal position is all right (Figure 41). Head position is secondary to the horse actually slowing down and stopping. The better he gets at slowing down, the more normally he'll be able to carry his head — it won't be so low and overflexed.

Diamond Lu Collection

41

On the start it's good to have that extra tuck, though, because once the horse really learns how to stop those feet, he'll hit a happy medium in his head carriage (Figure 42).

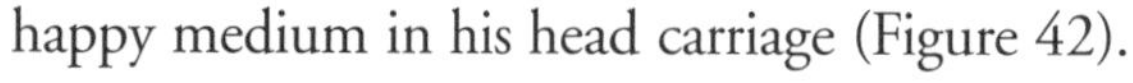

Diamond Lu Collection

42

In Figure 43, the rider is stopping from the lope and isn't using a bit to get the job done. He's just using his lass rope around the base of the horse's neck, is all. When the horse is prepared through feel, he knows what you expect him to do with his feet. Buck is sitting deep in the saddle like a person wants to be. This is real important if a person's plans include making the best use of their posture to help the horse keep his weight shifted back. You never know when you might need the front end of the horse available for a maneuver — and that could be the very next moment, it just all depends.

Diamond Lu Collection

43

Separating Balance from Dependence on the Reins, in the Better Posture

Balance and timing and feel can come together for a person a lot better when their posture isn't working against them and the horse. This won't be a complete discussion of posture and its beneficial effects, not by any means, because entire books have been written about that. It's an important subject all right, and we're just scratching the surface. What I want to do here is show some basic examples of how the better posture appears, and to speak about a couple of things a person can practice to keep on the right track.

I was first thinking that we oughtn't have any pictures where we didn't show everyone in proper Western saddles and the complete right gear, and all the things a cowboy would use and wear. But, where this is a book written on the *actual facts of true horsemanship through feel*, I got to thinking that the horse doesn't care what type of saddle you have on there. And really, if people are interested in the same things we are, which is getting along better with our horses, most of them aren't going to care about that either.

Diamond Lu Collection series

There's no advantage to a fella sticking his feet way out front, or too far back either. He's a lot better off with his legs hanging down underneath him, like this picture in the middle shows.

Diamond Lu Collection

47

What all these pictures have in common and what I like about them, is that the people and the horses are feeling of each other and, to my way of thinking, this brings out the better appearance in all of them.

Diamond Lu Collection

48

This rider is learning how to ride without stirrups or reins (Figure 47). The young girl is leading with a nice float in the line, and the horse is filling in. In the next picture, the rider and the horse are going along just as nice as can be (Figure 48). This is good practice for the future. She's just carrying her halter and lead rope there, and it appears that she's steadying herself by pushing down a little with her hands. Neither of them seem to have a care in the world. The other rider is trotting around there real relaxed and has good posture and balance, too (Figure 49). Once a person can keep their balance at the walk, trot and lope, sometimes they'll do a little experimenting to see if there's room for improvement a little further up the line. This horse is jumping the creek, and the rider is sitting there nice and relaxed (Figure 50). Her left hand is resting nice and gentle at the base of the horse's neck there. The other young person is learning about the better place a person could stand to be sure that things work out.

Diamond Lu Collection

49

Diamond Lu Collection

50

The rider is learning how to adjust the reins and present a feel for the horse to tuck his chin, and soften (Figure 51). She already has real good balance from learning how to ride bareback.

Diamond Lu Collection

51

Richard Field Levine

52

This person is looking ahead (Figures 52-53), and walking along, real relaxed. That horse has enough room to extend her neck down and step down off that place. The rider kept her balance and didn't tighten up those reins any.

Richard Field Levine

53

The Importance of Review and Taking Enough Time

It's always a good idea to drop back and review some things with a horse that the horse and the person can do well together without confusion or tension of any kind. There'd be no drilling in any part of an understandable review, of course. With a little break in things, and a little practice doing what the horse can understand, why the confidence and good feeling that comes from doing that for a few minutes is liable to get him back on the right track for anything that he didn't understand just a little further up the line.

It's really no different than being a kid in school. It took a year of kindergarten just to get you halter broke, and then there's eight more years you had to be there just to get out of the eighth grade. When they expected you to move ahead on the new material and you didn't have a grasp on things that were spoken about earlier, why you were liable to not feel the best when pressure like that was any place around. What a kid in that situation needs is help.

In one way it's not any different for a horse. In another way it's a lot worse. So many of those horses get all those lessons crammed in so fast and they have to sort things out in only a few months, when they aren't even three. No part of what's taking place in those lessons is natural to a horse anyway. And some of the people involved in this, why they haven't got much idea about the inside workings of a horse, or the basics that a horse *needs to rely on in the future*. And where feel is concerned, a good many trainers haven't heard anything about that, and the horse is forced into things. We're in hopes that if they read this book and don't think much of it, that they won't get discouraged or turn away. The reason being, I want to encourage all the people who work with horses to improve. If a person reads over these things a second time, I'm thinking that they might see things in a little different way. After they'd had some time, maybe they'd discover some useful things. Sometimes all a person needs is a little while to soak on things that are not familiar to them on the start.

I want to help them right where they are in their understanding of a horse. When they worry about how "good" they are — well, the horse will let them know whatever they need to know about that. But some people worry about it anyway, and where it concerns an instructor, or anyone they might go to for supervision, sometimes a fella can forget that it's the response he gets from his horse that matters the most. It's what that horse thinks and feels that is our greatest concern. Or it should be anyway.

Now, there's three more exercises coming in an order we listed for the better results to show up. A person is always going to make adjustments, of course, and we're in hopes they have some ideas now about what to do if they run into little spots that aren't working out for them.

Part 5 — Stepping the Hindquarters Over

If a horse is going to be dependable for any purpose, the main thing that has to be reliable is a person's connection to the horse's hindquarters, through feel. Positioning the hindquarters helps the horse stay light and keep his footwork accurate.

Before a person starts teaching a horse to step his hindquarters over, the basics that are spoken about up to this point (in Parts 1-4) need to get built in and be working real smooth. We'll assume that a person has spent quite a little time applying their better feel in these exercises and that the horse is ready to start on this part. He'll have a real flexible poll and neck, and if he doesn't, we're in hopes a fella'd not go much further until that's taken care of. That's because in order for a horse to step his hindquarters over without a brace, his head and neck need to go up and down, and sideways and all the places in between, real soft. That's basic. Without that reliable response built in, things aren't going to work out for too long.

Some of the other beneficial effects of a person's better timing and feel ought to be showing up in the horse by now, too. That horse ought to be able to lead up real free, stand still, shift his weight onto or off of any foot, step back, and take a step forward without any resistance at all showing up. Keeping that horse as sure as he can be about what's expected of him needs to always be at the front of that person's thinking. The idea of slow and steady progress with the horse has a real big part in this, too, because when a horse is rushed, many things can happen that slow down his understanding.

Flexibility is Natural for the Horse

Most people can't imagine the flexibility that's required for some maneuvers a horse needs to make. When they are working up the line beyond what that horse can understand, their presentations to the horse appear rough, and to a horse that's not prepared, they *are* rough. No better than some people present their ideas to a horse, they just bring out resistance in him. From there, a person may feel the need to continue presenting some things to that horse in a forceful and demanding way. When a horse is on his own and has reason to be flexible, some maneuvers come real easy to him. But these could sure amaze a person if they were sitting up there, all right.

For example, no one taught the horse shown in Figure 1 how to do what he's doing. It's just something he *can* do. Of course we'd rather he not do that when we're sitting up there on him. The main thing a person needs to be thinking about concerning this move — or any maneuver the horse is inclined to make — is that it is the *feel of something* that caused the horse to want to get in this position in the first place. And from the look of this horse — twisted right around there like he is — it was probably the feel of something not too good. Nature has fixed it up for the horse so that when he wants to get his teeth on a spot that needs scratching, he's able to operate in this real agile and adjustable way, and right on the spur of the moment, too. You can see there's a good amount of flexibility all through this horse — from the poll and his neck, and down through those ribs — all the way back to his hip and leg.

Some people may not see the connection in this picture to the exercise we're going to talk about. But to my way of thinking, it's really beneficial to observe the way a horse's mind and body respond when he's decided to get something taken care of. This is tied real close to what he'll do for you when he decides to operate the way you want him to. And that's based on what his body can do naturally, and what his mind can understand from the feel you present. That's as deep as we need to go on that for now. We need to talk about some other things that concern a horse's hindquarters, and the way people are apt to view a horse in some situations. I also want to go over some of the real small things a person wants to be aware of when they try to accomplish the maneuvers described in this part of the book.

LORI SMITH

1

A lot of people might have heard that a horse needs to be soft and giving, and real flexible throughout his body. Seeing the move that horse in Figure 1 is making, they might suppose it meant that horse is real adjustable, and they'd be right on that. If they didn't know any better, they might think he'd be ready to ride, and try to saddle him. Or, if they could see that he was saddled, they'd maybe think they could just get on and go for a nice ride someplace. But there's a precaution that could be beneficial if a person's plans include riding a horse they don't know about. *A saddle on a horse can be real deceiving. If he's not prepared to be ridden, through feel, why there's a good chance that saddle is something he's just packing around.*

If a fella went to saddle this horse and the presentation he offered to him was fitting, he'd sure be started on the right track. But if he lacked feel and timing, or if his balance wasn't too good, he might be surprised at how stiff that flexible horse could get when he tried to turn him, or get him stopped by pulling straight back if he started running. A fella could think he wasn't going to get too far with a horse that was difficult to bend. And he'd sure be right on that. But, it's easy to see why a person could think it's fine to just pull himself up there and start going — and it's really no one's fault if they have that idea.

This young fella is getting his horse prepared for work he wants to do in the future (Figure 2). The horse is learning to follow the feel of the rider's leading arm on the rein. Because a lot of the basics needed up to this point have been taught to this boy and laid into that horse's foundation, it might not be too long before the motions of both his arms will be able to influence the proper placement of that horse's feet.

2

Diamond Lu Collection

If the Horse isn't Ready, Take More Time

At any point in your practicing, if a horse starts to hold his breath, or get at all rigid through his body, you'd want to hold off. Just stop right there. Struggling with a horse can sure bring out the less attractive self-preservation aspects in him, and we'd rather he didn't need to rely on those when we're anywhere near him. When there's a lack of feel being presented, sometimes a horse can do things that will surprise a person if he's pushed further at this point.

There is no point in going further if the things you need to have in place have been passed over. Go back and catch the horse up on the things you missed. If there's any hurry in this, it won't be fitting to any horse. It's when a person rushes a horse's progress that people are inclined to make comments about that horse being what they'd call a "problem." If they say that, they sure aren't working with feel. People who use and understand feel in the way we're speaking about aren't mentioning that word "problem," not if the subject concerned horses anyway.

There's quite a little that a person can miss and still think they've got a horse that should be working at things further up the line than he can really understand, *through feel.* What I'm talking about is shown in these next pictures (Figures 3-4). This horse is kind of mixed up and he's tight. His whole general appearance says a lot about what he's not understanding in the feel that's being presented. He's got some stiffness in his body and he holds his head up in the air, so I'd say there's quite a little room for improvement. This person is setting things up so that horse can discover there's a better way for him to go about things. It will bring out the best in the horse when he realizes this. But right now, he's not too sure there's anything taking place that's to his advantage.

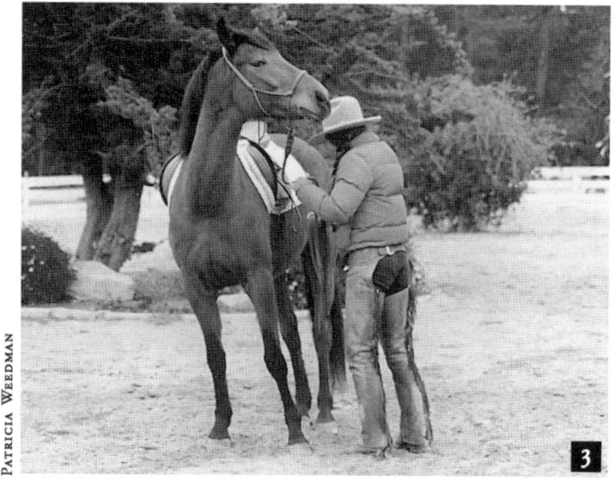
Patricia Weedman

3

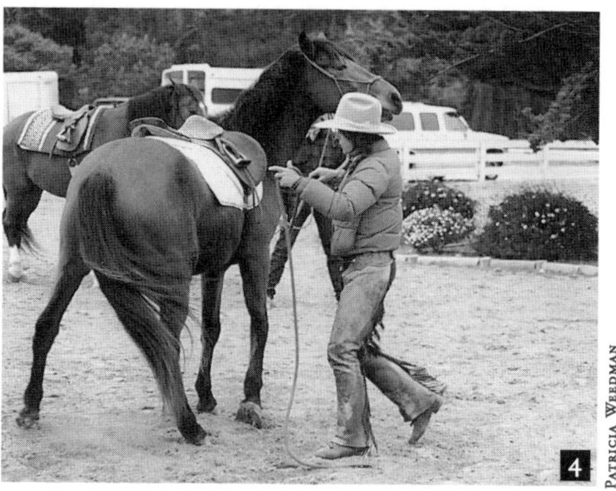
Patricia Weedman

4

If a horse has already been saddled and ridden quite a little, it's easy for people who don't have a lot of experience at this to assume he knows how to maneuver just like they want him to. That includes putting his feet in different places, running around fast, stopping or turning real good, or standing still as long as they want him to. Of course, this is understandable because the ideas that many people have about horses are based on something they learned, all right, *but they're not always based on the actual facts.* When they ride that horse, a person who assumes these things is going to find out straight away what the actual facts really are. I'd rather those people get their information in a way that's not apt to lead to any discomfort for them or the horse.

The next two pictures show this bay horse is trying hard to do what he thinks this person is asking him to do. His foundation isn't the best, not by any means, but he's got a lot of willingness available for the job. In the first picture he's tipping his nose to the left, and not offering too much resistance to her feel in his head or neck, considering how he was prepared (Figure 5). Even though there's a bend to the left in his poll, and a little bend in his neck, what there is to notice here is that there's a pretty big brace in this horse still. But he's a real agreeable sort of horse anyway. He'd maybe go along like this and be fine, until he wasn't. You'd not be in a hurry to ride one that couldn't step across any better than that. So long as she doesn't ask him to step any deeper over towards the right with his left foot, he'd hang in there as long as

Patricia Weedman

5

Patricia Weedman

6

he could, or it seems he would. Figure 6 shows how the little bit of give and flexibility that there was in his poll and neck just disappeared as soon as she wanted him to put a little more effort into stepping over behind. This horse needs to be caught up on several aspects, but it's good to see that he's got plenty of try and hasn't entirely lost his confidence in people. A lot of things will start to turn around for this horse and the person who owns him, when the feel that's presented helps him to get a better understanding of what he's expected to do.

Before You Get On a Horse, Test Him Out

It's easy enough to find out if a particular horse is going to be responsive to you before you get on, and that's if he's saddled up, or not. With the lead rope or the reins, just see if you can take his head around real slow, to one side and the other, and see if he can leave his feet still. If he can, then see if he can step over a little with a hind foot in either direction and still keep his head around towards you, without taking the slack out of the rope or rein. If he can do that without taking a forward step, or crowding into you, then try it on the other side. If the horse can step one hind foot across the other one, and keep his head around with a float in that rope or rein, why then he's got a little start of feel established there. It's enough to continue with and build onto. If he can't do these things, you wouldn't get on.

If a horse doesn't understand something, he's able to let a person know about his confusion pretty quick, especially if the person's inclined to hurry his progress at all. Any hurried motions or impatient feelings a person introduces will just change the meaning of everything they do with the horse into the wrong idea, *for the horse*. If these exist, we'll assume that person's going to get such motions and thoughts switched around. What a horse is able to do, and what he's going to do, can be two different things in some cases. *It's real important that people can understand and recognize the difference, through feel.*

Position Yourself to Help the Horse Succeed

Stepping the hindquarters over is one of the more difficult maneuvers for a person to get the hang of, usually on account of they haven't got the right feel built into that horse in the areas already covered to this point. But it might just be that the person hasn't figured out yet where he should be standing so the horse can step his hind feet over.

Be sure that where you stand doesn't prevent him from bringing and keeping his head around and keep it there. There's going to be quite a little variation to this because no two horses are the same, and no two people are, either. Generally speaking, the best place to stand is to the side of the horse, just a little back behind the shoulder, and facing the general girth area at pretty much the center of the horse.

Diamond Lu Collection

Diamond Lu Collection

When you're in that position, liven him up a little and have him step his hindquarters away from you. The shorter person in these pictures is learning how to stay in position and get in time with those hind feet as they step across (Figures 7-8). Good supervision can really help a person get started on this exercise in a real effective way. You'd be sure to always practice this on both sides of the horse.

Learning About the Smaller Adjustments

The next pictures show the progression this ranch horse made when he was presented with the feel to take a step over behind, from left to right (Figures 9-16). To get this working smooth, a fella needs to get with the timing and feel of that horse right on the start, and this calls for quite a few smaller adjustments from the person. A horse needs to learn how to adjust to the feel that's presented, and he will, when he understands the intention behind each particle of feel from the person that's directing and supporting him to do what he's being asked to do. This requires a person to be trying as hard as possible not to miss those smaller particles of feel coming across from that horse in all of this. *Because they all have meaning.*

It's up to each person to get their message across in a way the horse can understand. There's quite a lot of variation that's possible in the feel a person might need to apply to make these exercises effective, and that's true for all people and all horses. It could require a fella's full strength someday, or just the littlest motion that an observing eye might miss. And that's a motion that's really just produced by thought. It's the very lightest touch that goes along with a feel like that. *There's a lot of difference in a fella's variations of feel that the horse will notice.* That's kind of deep to speak about but if it's mentioned, or not, that's the level a person will need to reach if they want to be effective at applying feel. A fella might have to be around a lot of horses before his powers of observation and his sensitivity reach a level like that. But it can be done, that's for sure.

Of course, you'd remember to always ease off a little for a try, and you'd be sure to allow the horse to stop between steps before you asked him to step away from you again.

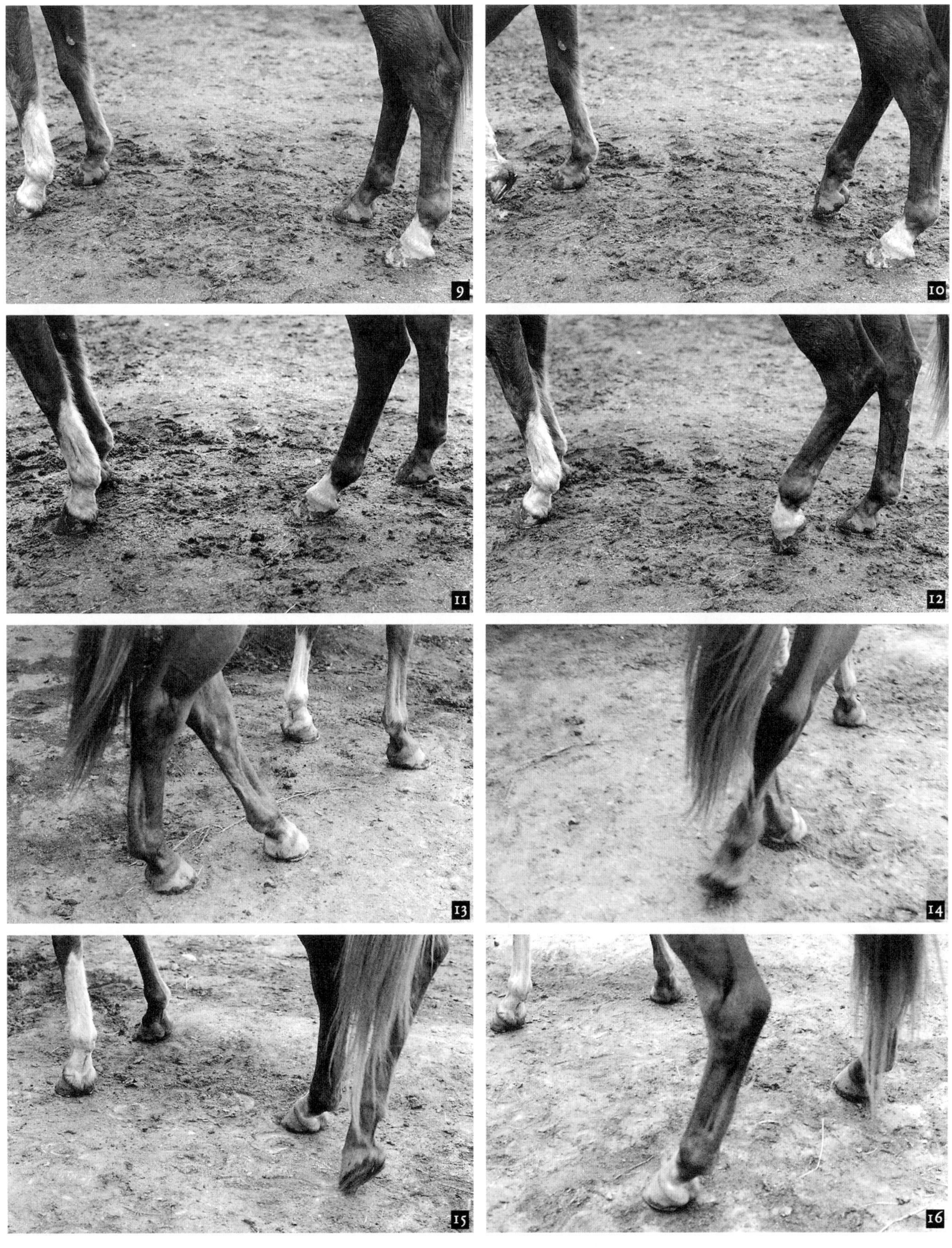

Diamond Lu Collection series

You Need Clear and Flexible Plans and the Horse Needs Time to Experiment and Think

When you want a horse to step away from you, it might not be at all familiar to him, but since he'd like to know what's going on, he's liable to be doing a little experimenting. If a fella presents a feel that allows the horse to do a little of this, then that horse is apt to try a few things to see what's going to relieve the pressure that just came in there. A person will be hoping to see this interest from the horse, and be ready to reward his littlest tries to understand what you expect of him.

He might put that foot somewhere that you don't want it to be, or he'll maybe need to move all four feet. Or, he might shift his feet forward or back, or step around. He'll experiment to see what meaning there is that could be a benefit to him in your feel. You'd reward him as much as necessary to keep him moving in the right direction. It's the process of getting good at this that helps a person develop their better feel.

You might decide to help the horse just shift his weight back or forward and this is not the same thing as taking a step. You're going to help him just shift his weight a little, and maybe he'd even place and replace his feet, if he needs to, in order for him to do what you want him to do. If you have a clear idea of what you want, that's the start of it. It's helpful if that real patient aspect of yourself is part of your plan, too, and if you can work that into whatever the horse might be doing while he's figuring things out. That's the mental part of *blending in with the horse* that's going to produce a change for the better. This takes time.

If the horse is the excited kind, and he's eager to keep stepping away from you but doesn't seem to want any part of stopping, well, you'd do your best to help him get ready to slow down. *He needs to experience the getting-ready-part of slowing down that happens before he actually can slow down.* This is one of the most important parts of getting with a horse's feel, so he can pick up your feel. For a nervous sort of horse, this "getting ready" part sure has to happen and be comfortable for him before any part of slowing down or stopping will exist in his mind. Then, you'd work on the slowing-down-part until it was real obvious that he was ready to stop. Then your idea to stop is there to match his, through the feel you present to him through your body and through that rope, too. If your timing's been right up to that point, that stop will be there. That's one thing I'm sure of.

We've spoken quite a little about stopping already (Parts 3 and 4), and a person could refer to that if things weren't shaping up to go that smoother way.

These pictures show how someone can direct the life in a horse that doesn't understand how to step over behind and slow down his feet to a stop (Figures 17-18). A fella plans to stay out of that horse's way while he's searching for a place to

Rhonda Smith Briano

Rhonda Smith Briano

stop. By holding onto the cant board (cantle, or back of the saddle), he can stay in position, feel how much tension is on that lead rope, and watch those feet. Experience will show a person how much tension on the rope is needed to keep the head around and still help the horse to take *forward* steps.

Blending In With the Horse's Steps and Timing Your Release

There's a spot where a fella can really mess things up. Sometimes this will happen before a fella's too far along in his progress on this, and before he's figured out the best way to teach this part to a horse.

I'm speaking now about not letting the horse develop some bad habits, like taking over, and learning to make some undesirable motions with his head. A horse that roots his nose out or slings his head to get the rope loose from you isn't safe to be around, especially for a person who doesn't have much experience. You'd want to be sure to avoid getting a horse going on that, and there's a way you can set it up so this isn't likely to happen.

Once your horse shifts his weight forward to free up his hindquarters, you'll keep his head around to the side until his feet have stopped moving. There's a reason you do this, and that's so you can retain all the benefits of that good cornering feel you started to build into the horse in the first exercise. It's not hard to get a start on this and then lose ground, because there's always a lot to think about and sometimes things can come up that can set you back. That's fine, you just keep going from where you are. This way of doing things adds a lot more meaning to the horse's knowledge of stepping over behind when you need him to.

On the start, you'll go along with that horse the best way you can and try to stay out from underfoot. To help him slow down, step your own feet around there, just a tiny bit slower than he's moving his feet because, really, you're following his feel. It can help to get the right timing for this if you match your legs up to two of his and stick with that timing he's on for slowing down. When he takes that last step, you are ready to take the last step, too, and you stop together.

On extra sensitive or mixed-up horses this could be confusing to them at first. You might wonder how long it's going to take for them to figure out what you want. But those horses always seem to figure it out in the end. So you'd plan to be in the frame of mind of knowing it was going to work out for the best, and you'd be on the lookout for as many little indications as that horse might have for you about when that last step was coming. Before you'd release his head, you'd wait until all four feet came a stop. You want him to be standing still when you release his head, and you'd want there to be some float in the lead rope. He doesn't have to stand there for long, just a few seconds. It can even require less time than that, and other times he's going to start moving those feet again and searching for what he thinks you want — thinking that he's missed your meaning, even if your timing was pretty close. Just go with him again if that happens, with his head held around, following his body movements like before. Again, you'd wait until he found a place where he could settle and stop his feet, and then flex at the poll and release a little slack back up that rope in your direction.

When you know those feet are still and there's slack in that line that the horse put there himself, you release a coil of rope long enough to let him return his head to a normal standing position. The horse learns a lot of valuable things when it's done that way.

On a slower horse, your testing and speculating might cause you to think you ought to push on the horse's hip, or slap him with your hand, or lay the tail-end of your lead rope over the top of his rump or even on his flanks. Some people even swing at the horse with their lead rope right around his hocks. This will teach the horse to move away from you, all right, but those actions and his responses aren't going to connect in his mental system about the meaning you want your leg to have when you're on his back. That's because your legs aren't going to be touching him that way or in those areas. We hope not anyway. Use your stirrup for this because it's hanging right where your leg will hang when you're on him. If he's not saddled, why then you'll tap him on his side with your rope, right where your leg will hang down. And a person will experiment to see how little they can do to get him to step over.

Sharpening Up Your Observations

When you want a horse to step his hindquarters over to one side or another, you'll watch to see if he takes a forward step with his inside hind leg, or a step back, or if he takes a little a step sideways — right up close to that outside foot. There's a world of difference between all these steps. The results could be real surprising for a fella if he thought a step back or sideways was the same as a step forward, especially if things got all sped up or confusing for that horse, and he was horseback. No, you'd be real careful in your understanding about the look and the feel of maneuvers he can make with his hind feet. Any of this work a fella wants to do horseback will be a whole lot easier if the lessons for this go real smooth for him and his horse on the ground, first.

When you're working on the ground and getting used to the feel of getting his hindquarters stepping over properly, the horse could step back or sideways on his own, or you might have caused him to do that by something you did. Just keep going with him, or try again. Sometimes it's best to just take a little break in there and let him rest. His actions will let you know what will be helpful to his learning progress at different times. What's going to take place just all depends on the horse and on how far along and observant the person is. Remember to praise the horse, and rub his neck or shoulder a little to reassure him.

If there's a lot of tries at this and the horse still isn't stepping his inside hind leg across the outside hind leg, why the chances are real good that you've either let the head loose as he starts to move, or you're holding him too short on the rope and having him move when there isn't any float left in that line. When you do these things, or if you get out of position as you present him with the feel to liven up his feet, it will cause a horse to step backwards or step sideways, and even onto his own foot. In these less desirable positions he's liable to not step across that way I'm talking about.

The way a horse's feet are placed on the ground tells a lot to an observing person about what that horse is understanding in the feel that's presented. When you want him to step forward and across with a hind foot, he will, when it's clear to him. When a person is sure about what they're after, and has had a little practice staying in the better position that's required to achieve this, why it all takes on much a nicer appearance (Figures 19-20).

When you get with the horse's motions and you're waiting for him to find a good spot to stop his feet, you can take advantage of some of those sudden things he might be wanting to do, whatever they are. Experiment by drifting along with him a little, but remember that there's no part of force in drifting with that horse. Like

Emily Kitching

19

20

Emily Kitching

anything else we hope to be able to do with those horses, the main point of this procedure, is that you are *all the time* looking for opportunities the horse gives you to shape and direct him. But not because you tried to force him to give you those opportunities, or to change. It's through feel that you can teach a horse to slow down and stop, and do most anything. And that last step the horse takes before he stops, or any of the last few steps leading up to that stop, why they don't weigh anything. There's just the weight of the lead rope or the reins in your hand, when it's right.

You'll build on his ability to step those hind feet over in a responsive and willing way until he can step part way around in a circle. Eventually, he'll be able to make it halfway around in a circle. Then, when he can step across behind for you real smooth with his head down low and around to the side, without pulling away or pushing against your hand at all, why he'll be able to step clear around when you want him to. Of course, he won't always be relaxed and able to make smooth, slow steps on the start. Later on, he'll be able to place and replace all four of his feet just as nice and calm as can be, with real even, smooth and slow steps, and his body will stay real relaxed and flexible during this, too. Your lessons don't ever need to be too long.

For most people, it's going to take time to get good at this and see the value in it. I know a few who are pretty good now. It's really something a person needs to hear about, and watch, and spend a lot of time thinking about. A lot of time to practice and soak on things is real important, too. No person is born knowing any of this. But some can figure it out, if they're willing to take the time and they have the strong desire.

We included two more pictures here for general purposes. They show some of the younger people practicing this and learning to improve on their timing and position (Figures 21-22). I'd say this exercise of operating those hindquarters is one you really can't get too good at. Everyone's trying to achieve the same thing here, and the results are showing up in different ways. I'm real pleased to see things shaping up for the horses who are handled by people just starting to learn about this fitting way. This is promising for the future.

Diamond Lu Collection

21

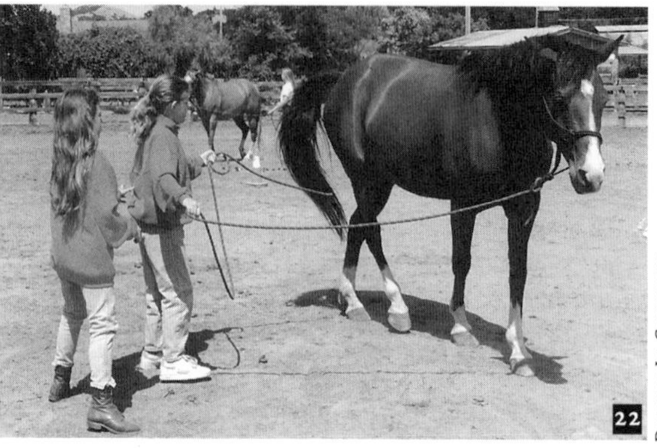

22

Diamond Lu Collection

Be Real Particular About How the Horse Takes the Pressure Off Himself

One thing a fella wants to get real clear on is this: If a horse steps over real good behind, but pokes his nose out or slings his head after his feet are stopped, why there's still a big job ahead that needs to get taken care of. There's no good part of feel in that, not when a horse is disrespectful and taking over that way. You want some float in the lead rope between the halter knot and your hand, and you want the horse to put that float in there himself. That way, he doesn't get the idea he can just stop those feet and push against the halter to get some relief from the pressure. It's natural for him to want that pressure to come off there, all right. But you'd prefer to have him learn how to ease off that bothersome pressure-feeling by coming towards your hand. The payoff for that will come when you're riding him somewhere and he knows to soften when you take up the slack, instead of poke his nose out and run off someplace. The people who let a horse just jerk some slack into the rope after the feet have stopped, and do nothing to correct it, well, they're missing a real important piece of this and the rides they have might not be the best.

When the horse takes all the pressure off the lead rope by flexing at the poll and bringing his neck around in your direction, then you'd release it back to him so he can stand with his head and neck straight out in front of him, in his normal way. *This is one way he learns to separate the meaning of the feel in your rope from the meaning you want him to understand about the energy and movements you present to him using your whole body.* The horse needs to know the difference. Understanding this difference is real important to getting a job done horseback, and to your safety while you're doing anything horseback.

If you only let that line out a few inches, or stopped his head halfway back to the normal standing position with an unexpected jerk, or if you tried to get him to step over again before you offered him a *meaningful* release — well, any of those things are going to confuse that horse. If that poor feel is worked into his understanding of things at this stage in his learning, why he's liable to have no idea what the actual lesson was supposed to be. The lesson he got may not be the best, but time will show a fella what that lesson was.

Mistakes are always going to be a part of learning, there's no getting away from that. No matter if the horse did what you expected that time or not, he's always going to need some time to "soak" — and we call it that because he needs time to let what just took place sort of soak into his mind. And a person could sometimes be thankful for a little break right then, too.

The Experiments and Adjustments a Person Makes

You'd not fight a horse at all, or firm up too much if things don't go as planned. It's the last straw when that happens and a person who's liable to be this way can think of other things to spend their time on. It's real important for a person to understand that what the horse does is because that horse either didn't understand what it was you expected, or because he did understand. In either case it means there's more thought a person needs to give to their role in things. You might not be inclined to think what you did caused the horse to do what he did, unless you had some good supervision available. Sometimes it takes another person to help us see something that we do.

The general run of horses really wants to get along with people, and it's up to us to see how to fit each horse the very best we can by not confusing them. We can't help doing this on the start. But we sure can help that horse by not punishing him when he gives a correct response to that thing we *didn't* mean to ask him to do, whatever it was. When a fella practicing this has a better idea of what he's looking for, and gets closer to the presentation a particular horse can understand, why then he's liable to find that horse knows exactly what's expected of him. And that horse will do it, if he's been rewarded for trying to understand up to this point.

There's quite a little to this, but it's not always going to take near as much as just got mentioned here. No, on some horses, they'll catch on to what you'd like them to do right away, and some will fill in for you, too. Others might not catch on so fast.

It might happen that a horse will tip his nose towards you a little, and because of the kind of horse he is, and what the two of you have gotten done together up to this point, why maybe for starters you'd call that little try good. Or, maybe you wouldn't, and if you didn't then you'd take your hand, or your rein or the rope out to the side, and put a little life into it and you'd step like you wanted that horse to move. And if he did, then you might call that good. Maybe he'll just take real little steps in front with his head clear around to the side in your direction, but when he stops there's float in the line and he's understood your feel to yield those hindquarters and done just what you wanted, and that was enough. *When you take time at this, you'll know.*

Moving the Feet with the Reins

There is a time and place in your work with a horse where you'll want to be able to move all those feet — and then move one foot at a time, too — just by picking up on a rein. But that's further up the line. *Doing this too early and without enough experience, can lead to many big problems for the horse.* We won't speak about those here, except about that real big problem you'd plan to avoid, and that's when your horse starts moving when you touch the reins. Generally speaking, that sort of horse doesn't get slowed down or stopped when you pull back because about that time he's liable to be gathering up more speed. This could cause a fella to get concerned.

It's one of the worst things to get a horse going on, and it's one thing you'd never want to teach him to do. It doesn't mean that a horse won't learn to do this anyway, because all horses sure can. You can get this straightened out, but the best approach is to never get them started on that in the first place. Horses that run faster when you pull harder haven't been shown this other way of thinking and operating, through feel. And that's because the people haven't either.

Stepping the Hindquarters Over From the Ground Connects Right to Your Mounted Work

As you practice stepping those hindquarters away from you, you'd want to be thinking about how the groundwork ties into mounted work in the horse's mind. It's the adjustability in the hindquarters — and whether you're able to influence the speed and direction they can maneuver in response to both types of feel, when the horse is anywhere around you, connected to you or not — that determines a whole range of things that can take place.

You'll be sure to have the horse prepared to step away from pressure that you put on his side, just a little behind the cinch, right about where your stirrups hang down and where your calf would be. You could use the tail end of your mecate or lead rope for this, or if he's saddled, you could use your stirrup to bump him a little. Just do whatever it takes to get the idea of stepping over going for him, so long as whatever you do is through feel. Pushing and leaning on that horse won't bring a person or that horse any closer the goal of maintaining lightness. But, eventually, a person's going to learn this actual fact through his experimenting anyway.

If your groundwork has been real effective to this point you wouldn't need to actually touch that horse's body at all to achieve this. *But you sure don't want him to misunderstand your meaning if you do.* If there is any confusion about this, then when you go to ask him to do this same maneuver in response to your calf or your heel, some things can happen that might really surprise a person.

In the next set of pictures, the foal is going around real smooth and understands what's expected of him in the first place (Figure 23). That girl is in a good position to direct and support him around in that circle, but there's a slight problem she might not have noticed. In the second picture, nothing changed much in the girl's posture or position, and because of that this colt has no idea what he's expected to do (Figure 24). When he felt the tail end of that lead rope come in on his side there, why it caused him to pop his head up and stiffen his whole body including stopping his feet

23

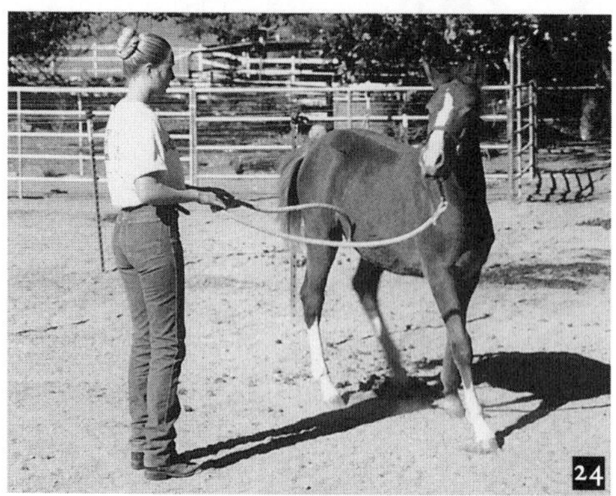
24

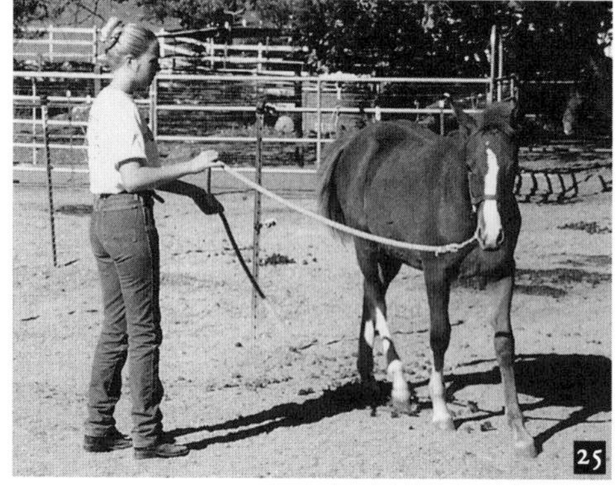
25

right in their tracks for a second there. He didn't connect a meaning to it is why he responded this way, and it was real startling to him. Now, there's no crime in what took place of course, but when he's just going along there real smooth and calm and where he wasn't prepared to know how to adjust to it, why she overdid things a little. He wasn't bothered or in a hurry beforehand, and he was real alert and willing to do what she wanted. In the third picture he got started up again, and continued on (Figure 25). This sort of thing happens, and when it does, why we hope to notice the little things, and adjust for the next time.

People sometimes don't realize that their habit of swinging the rope without bringing any extra life into their body causes a horse to ignore the feel to liven up. These smaller things make a big difference to a real sensitive horse, until they don't, and when you get a horse dull to your feel to move away from your rope or your steps towards him, it's not the best situation at all. The lesson in this carries right over to your mounted work. No, I'd say that one of the worst things you can build into a horse you plan to ride or handle much in the future is to make that horse dull-sided. But plenty of people do it and they just don't realize what they are doing.

This is just one of the smaller things that can happen and be forgotten when someone isn't right there handy to take a picture. Most people might not think it's worth speaking about, or noticing. Maybe they don't know about this part yet.

Timing Your Legs Up with the Horse's Steps

Nothing you do on the ground to get him to step over behind should prepare the horse to expect that you are going to grind your heel into his side, or jab him with a spur once you're up there. It's quite amazing to me that many people even leave their heel or their spur pressing right in there, even after he moves his feet. This will sure confuse a horse, and it fits right in with the way a lot of those same people just hang on a horse's mouth. You won't get the horse ready to expect either of those things from you. You'd try your best not to anyway, because that builds in resistance, and we don't want a horse to develop *any part* of that.

26

27

28

Kim Murphy series

The next group of pictures shows a young horse walking away with his right hind foot coming off the ground. First, that fella gets his own mind and body in time with the horse's feet, and then he can get with the motions of those feet to demonstrate the timing of when to bring his lower leg in against the horse's side. He wants to do this as the right hind foot is coming up off the ground, since he's planning to corner that horse on the right anyway (Figure 26). That's the best time to present a feel for the horse to step his right hind leg across the left hind leg. When the rider can feel the right hind foot about to come off the ground why he just helps that horse by cornering the horse a little to the right and brings his right calf in against the horse's side, just a little behind the cinch (Figure 27). It doesn't take much. A little direction and support is all that's needed when a fella's presenting the feel to step over behind to a horse that's been prepared. Of course his leg feel was released as soon as the horse responded (Figure 28). That way the horse knows he did the right thing.

This Maneuver Prepares the Horse to Step His Front End Across

One reason getting those hindquarters real adjustable is so important is that it's a lot easier to maneuver the front end later. If the back end is active, the weight can stay on it easier and the front end isn't so apt to get stationed solid. When the forehand is heavy like the horse shown in Figure 29, that's a sure sign that the hindquarters are hung up. In an undesirable situation like this, the horse's range of motion is hindered by having too much weight on the leading foreleg, which could have been avoided if the right front leg had come in behind it, and not across it.

If you can maneuver that hind end where you need to, why the front end isn't going to be too much trouble to operate. It is the action and position of those hind feet that makes the front end want to move freer. This is an actual fact, and the benefits to this are spoken about and shown in the next part of the book.

Jen Simmons

The hindquarters need to be available and adjustable for any maneuver. This horse is backing an arc to the right.

Diamond Lu Collection

This horse is taking forward steps in a small circle to the left. This horse is flexible, and prepared to do what's being asked of him.

Part 6 — Stepping the Front End Around

The Foundation Must Be In Place

Before you begin practicing this maneuver, you'll want to be sure you and your horse have a good foundation laid in place and you'll get this foundation by practicing those exercises we spoke about earlier, in Parts 1-5. Of course, one of the first things a horse ought to learn is to follow the feel of your arm, and that'd be *any* place your arm goes. He'll get on to this when you've taught him how to raise and lower his head, and when you can take it around while he's keeping those feet still. That's the start of it. From there, teaching the horse to follow a feel with a float in the rope or the reins is one of the main goals we have in preparing him for this maneuver — and for any job you might have for him in the future.

I want to remind people of the actual facts concerning the front end of a horse now because it's so important to the horse.

Horses are designed to move and the hindquarters are set up to figure into all of the moves a horse makes. When you need a horse to move his front end, he will give you his best performance if he's allowed to use those hind legs the way they were designed to be used, as supporting structures that are placed and replaced, time after time, as the need for maneuverability and lightness in any part of his body requires. And this need is *all the time* changing.

Before you're ready to work on getting the forehand to step around or away from you, be sure that you can stand at your horse's head and step his hindquarters around slowly, one foot at a time, using the halter rope or the reins to direct the placement of his feet. If you can't easily place and replace those hind feet, then the horse's hindquarters aren't being used the way they were designed to be used. You'd want to go back down a ways and get them operating correctly, so a fella might read over some of the things mentioned about stepping the hind feet listed in Parts 3 and 5. We're going to assume that you can do this nice and smooth, and with this foundation in place you have what's needed to move on up the line.

Practice from the Ground, on the Start

The horse has a much better opportunity to show you what he doesn't understand when you're on the ground. If you get horseback too early, you aren't going to be in the better position to help them, I'll say in most cases, and that's especially true on this maneuver. I'm speaking about this now to remind people before they get on, to spend enough time on the ground practicing all the basic maneuvers that come before this, *from both sides*. Then you'd be ready in the best possible way to step the front end around the hindquarters.

On the start of this, you'd practice stepping the forehand around one step at a time, and you'd want to be up pretty close to the horse. Get that real accurate and feeling good to both of you, through feel, and then take a few steps back and experiment to see how effective you can be at this from a little distance.

It's good to have a clear picture in your mind about this, of stepping those front feet around in one direction and then the other. Present the feel to him that you want him to just be yielding away from you a little, but still paying real close attention to what you have in mind. The person adjusts as much as he needs to so he's going real slow and accurate with each step, and is always ready to stop and wait. This is what it's like when he's feeling of you. There's no limit to what it's like when he's not.

Give the Horse Clear Signals to Avoid Confusing Him

A horse can easily get confused by a person having both hands in this blocking position shown in Figures 1 and 2. If a person presents a feel like this to a horse, it can cause the horse to back up or appear to be sort of stuck. If that horse gets startled by something behind him, why he might even be inclined to come forward and bump into that person standing there in front of him. I know this has happened.

Lori Smith

1

From the person's point of view, a fella might think the horse doesn't want to move.

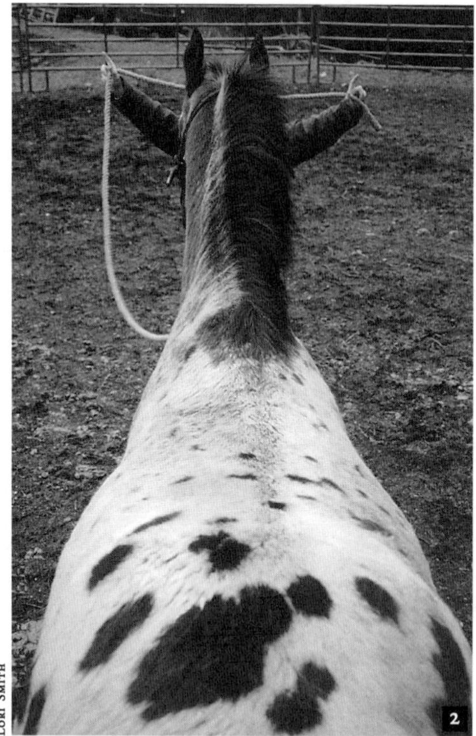

Lori Smith

2

From the horse's point of view, he isn't sure what that person wants.

When a fella's preparing to step the forehand back and then over in one direction or the other, it's a big help to the horse if the directing arm comes down a little bit lower than the supporting arm. In those last pictures you can see that the person's arms are just about at eye level, and she's blocking that horse on both sides. It's a big help to the horse if he knows which direction to take. If the person lowers the leading arm to make that opening clear to him, he's liable to get the message (Figure 3). Of course, you'd remember to rock the horse's weight back to free up the front end first, and then you'd tip his nose over the leading foreleg before you bring up enough life to move him (Figure 4). He won't be in balance to do this maneuver if his weight isn't rocked back.

Lori Smith series

In Figure 5, the horse has picked up the feel to yield his head and neck to the left in a real soft, responsive way, but he's missed the feel to rock his weight back, due to the message from the person being a little late, or just not there so the horse can understand it. Since there's no rush to any of this, that's fine. When some life comes up in the person shown here, why her left arm is in a good position to support the horse so he can rock back onto his hindquarters, or take a step back. This is the preparation he needs to get in so he's at an advantage for stepping in behind the leading leg with the following leg.

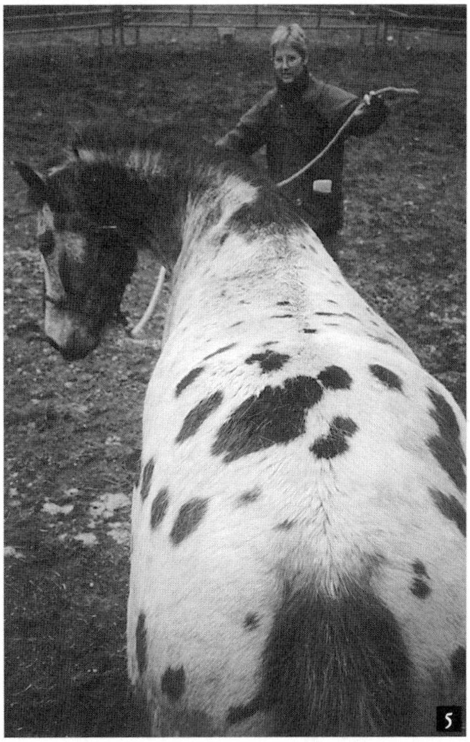

From this foundation, the horse can reach in the new direction with the leading leg. Then, if you were stepping him back and around in a small turn, you'd give him an opportunity to use himself properly and feel his way around a turn, or any part of a turn. You need to help the horse keep his weight rocked back *while* he's maneuvering the front end. To help him understand the feel of this on the start, step his hindquarters back just a little as you offer him the feel to move his front end, so it doesn't get hung up.

It confuses a horse when his front end gets heavy, because he knows what it feels like to move correctly, the way he came in knowing how to operate his feet. You sure want to avoid doing anything that will cause that front end to get heavy. Those hindquarters operating the way they should is what keeps the front end the way it needs to be — real light and freed up. And that's if you're mounted, or not.

Lori Smith

Lori Smith

In these next pictures, the person put a little distance between herself and the horse. Figures 6 and 7 show two views of how this lady positioned herself to help the horse go around in a circle to the *left*. For starters, the horse will step back and to his right, which is towards the person's left — and that's true whether the person is on the ground or mounted. When she wants the horse to step the forehand in the other direction, she'll adjust her arms and the way she's facing, so she can step his forehand back and to his left, and then he'd be able to head out around her in a circle to the *right*.

Switching Directions

When you're teaching a horse to switch directions, or when he's learning anything new, it's important that you allow him to stop in between steps and soak on things for a while. Just a few seconds will do. Going slow like this, and rewarding him with a rub on the forehead, helps the horse stay calm and relaxed and in a learning frame of mind (Figures 8-9).

This fella's preparing to take a new circle to the right (Figures 10-11). The horse has already shifted his weight back and stepped in behind the leading foreleg with his right front foot. This is due to the feel being presented, which includes the person's

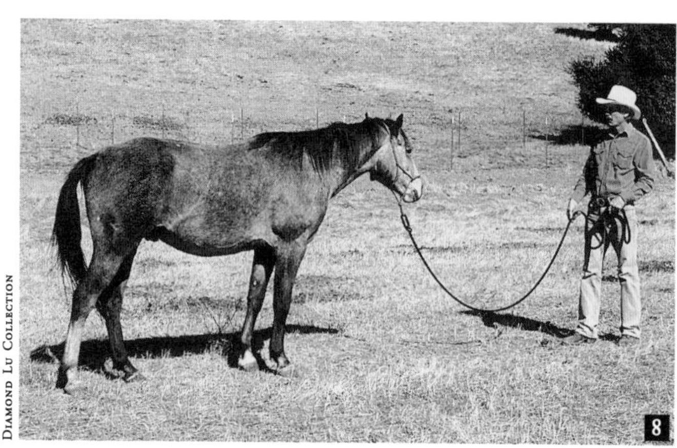

Diamond Lu Collection

Diamond Lu Collection

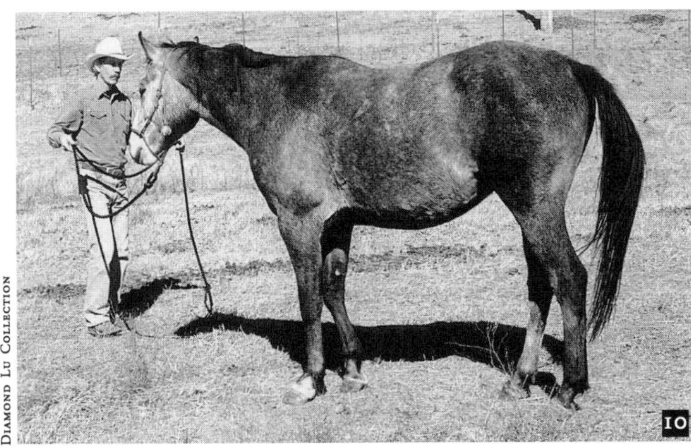

Diamond Lu Collection

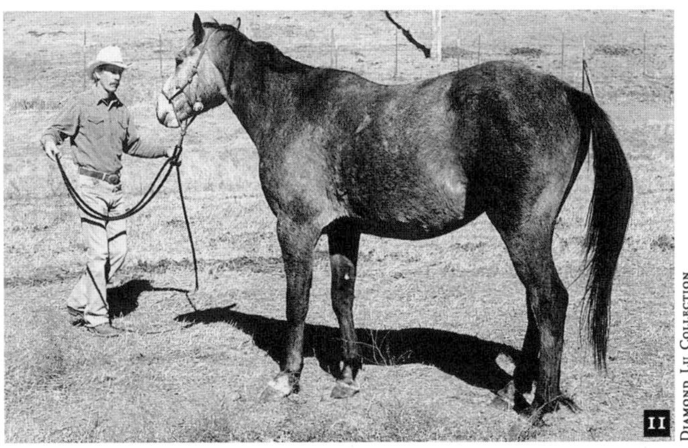

Diamond Lu Collection

position and his timing. Of course, he livened up his own steps a little, and it's this livened-up indirect feel that causes the horse to think he should respond with life, too. Sometimes the things to notice are quite small.

We'll assume that a lot of people don't want their horses to operate heavy in front (Figures 12-14). Even if the weight is back on the start, when a horse reaches across the leading foreleg with the following leg, it puts weight on the leading front foot, which is the one that we're trying to unweight in the first place. He can maneuver another way for better results.

Diamond Lu Collection series

The reason we want our horses to step in behind the leading front leg with the following front leg is because it frees up the leading leg for that lighter,

maneuvering purpose you have in mind. Compare Figures 12-14 with these other pictures, Figures 15-18. I'm in hopes a fella will see what's happening.

When a person is learning to not interfere with a horse as he's preparing to step the leading front leg in a new direction, there's a variety of adjustments he can make to help the horse. In Figures 19-20, direct and indirect feel are used to get the

15

Diamond Lu Collection series

16

17

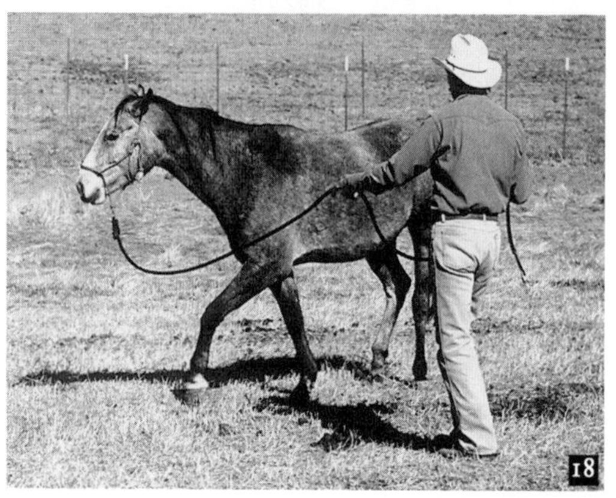
18

message across. On the next page, the older gentle horse is filling in for that young person who is learning how to step the front end over (Figure 21).

You might offer the horse a feel to leave in one direction or the other, and he'll maybe want to walk forward to where you are in the middle. You'd be ready for this and maybe step towards his shoulder a little. The shoulder nearest you will become the inside shoulder of the circle. As you present him with enough (indirect) feel from your body to help him want to leave, you can also liven up those feet a bit by changing the feel in the lead rope *just a little*. You'd like the horse to step back a little, step in behind the leading leg with the following leg, and then reach the outside front leg away from you to start the new direction. If he's already going around there and you want him to travel in a larger circle, you'd skip the stepping in behind part, because

19

Diamond Lu Collection

20

Diamond Lu Collection

he'd already be traveling forward and this wouldn't fit into that maneuver unless a lot of other things changed in your plan. But if you think about these things and do them, one thing's for sure, that horse isn't going to get mixed up about whether he's supposed to walk right to you, or right into you. No, he won't do either of those things because your preparation is going to eliminate any moves like that from his thoughts.

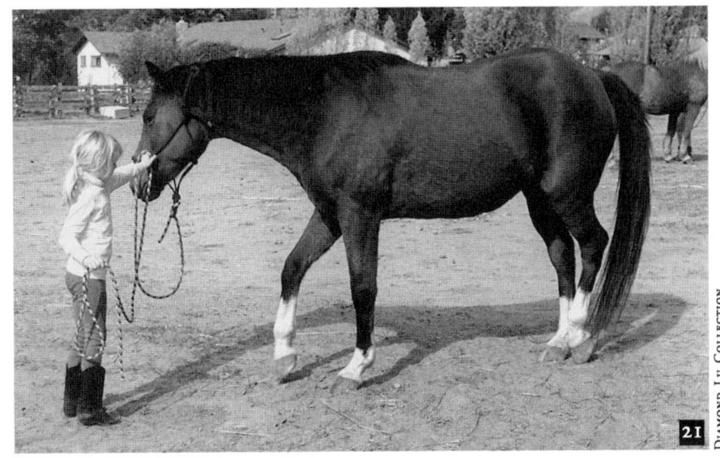
21

Diamond Lu Collection

The young person shown in Figures 22 and 23 is practicing some maneuvers with an older horse that has a good idea how to fill in for her when it's needed. She wants the horse to pass by her and leave some float in the lead rope. She's doing some experimenting with her timing and feel to see what's going to fit the situation and this horse in the best way possible. In Figure 22, she isn't livened up much and it appears that the horse is making a decision to move slowly to his left to avoid walking into her. She has her weight back and the horse is heavy on the front end. He's changing directions at a point in the stride that isn't as convenient as it could be for him. In the future, she'd adjust her timing in a way that'd be more helpful. When his left front foot is just about to come up off the ground, she'd tip his nose over in that direction and liven him up a little to get him re-routed on a little better track. After some practice at this, her experiment with livening up like I just spoke about was a little more effective, and the way he's responding that respectful way to her is real pleasing for me to see. You can see in Figure 23 that she livened up as his weight came off the left front foot so he could set it over to the outside a little. This widened out the circle he was making around her to the left, and of course this gives her an opportunity to slow him down and stop him a little further away from her. *We don't want any part of teaching those horses to come into the center on their own for stopping or*

22

Diamond Lu Collection

23

Diamond Lu Collection

changing directions. It's apt to result in surprises for people, and especially where you have beginners and younger people involved, that's out. And I'd say I'm firm on that.

One thing a person wants to be cautious about also comes into the sensitive area of good sense. When you lack experience, you need to be careful how you approach a horse that hasn't been taught to feel of a person. If you jump into this exercise we're speaking about now, without the step-by-step preparation we've already listed and explained here in this book, a horse is apt to resist flowing in any direction he's asked to go with his forehand.

Surprising things can happen if an unprepared person takes a step back away from a horse when they are attempting to maneuver that horse's forehand in a new direction —and this is especially true if they have any inclination to take the slack out of the lead rope when they do step back. It doesn't matter whether they want the front feet to reach backwards in part of a little arc or step out to the side a little and walk past you. This poor maneuver just described can lead to nothing good and so we'd state this as a caution for beginners and younger people and everyone else, too. Of course we can all make mistakes sometimes, but this is sure one you'd like not to make.

Maybe people wonder about this, and it's understandable. Well, the reason you take a precaution in this is because this is a maneuver where it's not difficult to encourage a horse to push right into you with that shoulder nearest you, and maybe step on your feet. If feel isn't applied in a way that horse can understand, why a horse that's already been taught some pushy habits is liable to have only one thing on his mind, and it won't be stepping that forehand away smooth and slow and accurate the way you'd hope he will. It's when you hurry any of these practice sessions that he's liable to resist your feel to move, and of course, this will interfere with your ability to place those front feet as light as possible on the ground.

No, if he comes right in there, it's due to the pushiness and misunderstandings in him that have been taught to him by people who lacked the feel we're talking about. Well, it might take up to your full strength and some of your faster and most inventive ideas right on the spur of the moment to get that situation straightened out. On the start, most people aren't going to be equipped with the better plan on how to handle this, so that's why I'm mentioning it, and encouraging people not to skip over what comes before this.

It might be a fella can take care of this just as it happens and that's fine. It may never show up again for him, or for another person either. But in most cases, when it's taken care of just that far up the line — and where a lot's been missed in the foundation — other things are liable to show up now and then. We're in hopes that you'd take the time to go all the way back to the place where there wasn't any sign of pushiness or mix-up, and start him on the basics right there. You'd move along and when you got back up to this exercise we're talking about now, why there's very little doubt in my mind that this original problem would be gone if everything below this had worked out when you rebuilt that foundation.

To some people, the need to go back down below where that horse can understand your feel and do what's expected of him will not make sense or be obvious. Not all people are geared that way in their thinking. But, the others who take their time at this and try what's listed here when they get into those tight spots, well, if they can get this applied without any part of force or fear or resistance coming in there, the chances are pretty good that they'd not be inclined to ever say anything about a horse that they shouldn't, and I'm sure in favor of that.

We've collected some pictures here of a horse that has no idea about feel or yielding, or much of anything else useful where placing his feet and having any respect for a person is concerned (Figures 24-26). You' d be always better off to work with the horse where he is, or some things are likely to show up that you might wish to avoid.

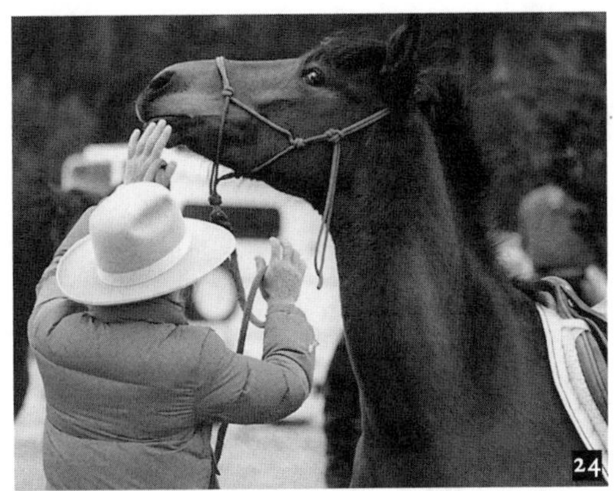
24

25

Patricia Weedman series

26

Now, depending on the circumstances and the horse, a fella can be too close or too far away to be effective. And that's probably true about a great many things. It's important to know that so a person doesn't get his thinking stuck on an idea that this can only be done one way.

There's bound to be problems coming up for some people when they approach a horse with rigid ideas they're expecting him to fit into. The actual facts of things concerning a horse could appear to those people to be this rigid way, but if they're thinking like this, they haven't got things understood from the horse's point of view — and I'll say *yet*. You'll learn about your horse's point of view by spending time getting to know him and seeing how he responds to your feel, because feel is what makes it possible for him to understand what's expected of him. What we want to keep right at the top of our thinking is to have the horse's attention on what we're doing and needing him to do, and to have our ideas clear to him in every way. I can't think of another way to get this across any stronger. Except, maybe, to follow with our main idea for this book about true horsemanship, which is through feel, and which has already been stated here in print many times and explained in various ways.

I am still looking for ways to improve on how this could be put across to people, because there is nothing more important to the horse than feel. It's what they look for in other living things, it's how they live and, maybe, it's the reason they're still around.

With everything nowadays as speeded up as it is, I've often wondered if there isn't something real important that people can learn from the way horses interact. When feel is operating in the horse the way it was set up to work, there's no part of it that's got anything to do with mix-ups about force, or fear or resistance. They understand each other, there's no question about that. I'm not sure on this, but I'd rather think there's something the horse has to contribute to this world that's a little further up the line in thought than just having someone sit up there on his back, or having people use him in those other ways they've found for him to get their harder work done.

One real reliable horse taught me how to make the best use of what he had to offer, and that was during the faster work I sometimes needed to get done horseback. He was a strong little horse and he was real fast. He could get out of my way before I had time to interfere with him, and looking back on it now, I realize that horse did quite a bit of filling in for me. That horse's name was Patrick. There isn't another horse I've ridden that handled as smooth and accurate as Patrick did. I'd say that I was able to handle the horses I've ridden since then better on account of what I learned from him, and that's due to just everything there was about him. He was so fast I didn't have time to interfere with him. It was really something, the way he could use his hindquarters to set the front legs up to maneuver free and light — for anything we needed to do, no matter what it was.

In the years I had that horse, he never missed a cow or a move that I can recall. Patrick was the best horse I ever rode.

Jen Simmons

Stepping the Front End Around the Back End

In these pictures, the horse is using his hindquarters to support his weight while the forehand reaches in a new direction (Figures 27-31). This is a maneuver that a fella needs to have real reliable and light on the ground in the rope halter, or snaffle bit — way ahead of when you want to ride him through this maneuver. If he's not hurried or confused when you practice these exercises on the ground, his natural lightness will be part of that respectful response you've taught to him, and that'll carry over when you ride.

This horse has her weight shifted back, but her left hind leg isn't set up in the best way for a tight turn (Figure 28). If this maneuver is a set up to just step off and walk out in a new direction, then it's all right. You'd remember that the position of the head is secondary in importance to the accuracy of footwork.

IN YOUR PRACTICE, YOU'D AVOID HAVING HIM REACH OUT WITH A FRONT LEG IF THE FOLLOWING LEG WASN'T IN A GOOD POSITION TO OFFER ENOUGH SUPPORT TO KEEP HIS WEIGHT SHIFTED BACK THROUGH THE TURN.

There's three main things to improve on in this picture (Figure 29). I'd say the fence is the first thing to change, and you'd do that by getting far away from it before asking that horse to step his front end around. Due to the room that rider is trying to give the horse for the right shoulder and that leading leg to make it through, she's a little off center and that's something we'd like to correct in the future. There's plenty

Gale Nelson

Jen Simmons

29

Jen Simmons

30

31

LORI KLINE

of float in the reins and the horse isn't thinking about pushing on the bit in any way — and that's fine. But I'd work to slow this maneuver down some from what it is. And, it'd work out better in the future to lower the holding arm. This will help the horse through the turn a little better, by keeping the weight further back and the head and neck in a better position. When you're learning to apply feel, there's quite a little to remember.

In Figure 30, the rider was able to follow some of these suggestions made earlier and these are reflected in that horse. You'd want to notice the general setup here: Right hind foot back and right front foot forward — ready to reach. A fella can easily see from this how backing a real fluid circle to the right on the ground fits into the foundation you'd need for this. You'd work on refining the head position in this maneuver further up the line, after some other things were solid.

In Figure 31, they're just turning right around, is all. There's always things a fella could notice — like that grass being in the way of those feet so you can't see them. But in a case like this, everything you'd need to know about that footwork is obvious by the way the horse is shaped up. And it's all right, because they've turned and they're going someplace now.

Combining Your Recent Lessons

Let's just review a few things here by saying there isn't any *making* the horse do anything. It's real important that a person and the horse understand this. We aren't going to make him stand or stop, like we've already spoken about, and we won't be rushing him or forcing him to turn or to stay straight, either. It's not a difficult thing to do, but it's not so easy to talk about. For some people, this really won't make sense right up until the second that it does, and then you won't forget that feel — and the horse won't either.

To straighten a horse — and always through feel — there's so much that can get accomplished by thinking about the hindquarters and the front end, and the way they operate together when that horse is going in one direction or another. That straight place is just the place that's in between right and left. You aren't going to give that horse a feel to go to the left or to the right when you want to go straight, anyway. And, if he's been taught to feel of you the way this book was set up to show you, well, then your horse would be lined up straight. No matter if you were mounted or handling him on the ground, the feel of straightness will be the same. Your speculating and testing will help you determine which things you'd need to do with a particular horse so he could understand that feel of straightness.

Generally speaking, it's a good idea to combine standing or stopping with keeping the horse straight. When he's stopped and he's straight, a horse that's well prepared in the basic maneuvers we've been speaking about here, why he can do almost anything that's asked of him, right on the spur of the moment. And, when you wanted that horse to turn, why you'd always remember to do your best to keep the life up in him.

Part 7 — Changing Directions, Through Feel

If you want a horse to be *reliable and light* when you ride, it's important that you can operate both ends of the horse separately, before you teach him to change directions. If he's not hurried or confused when you practice these exercises on the ground, his natural lightness and this respectful response you've taught him will carry over when you're riding, there isn't any question about that.

This last part of the exercise section is mostly pictures, because so much has been put down earlier about the little things a person needs to think about and notice. In your practice sessions on any horse —if he's young or old, or troubled, or not — well, there's things that will come up and be interesting to talk over. Some things I find interesting are shown in Figures 1-9. One of the most interesting things to me, is that this mare, Annie B, still hasn't picked up the feel to maneuver quite as smooth as she ought to when it's needed. And that's fine. There is no rush in any of this now, or ever. The person needs to be aware of this and try to gain confidence as they learn how to set things up right so the horse can understand how to do what they want. That will carry over for the horse, later on, when he's able to fill in for someone who's got a presentation that maybe isn't the best.

Annie B is a three-year-old that came in for some help a few months ago. She was headed for slaughter, just like my other mare, Beaut. The nice lady who knew about Annie B called me up and we talked things over. She got her re-routed up here just in time. She's just a real gentle horse and wants to get along, but some people can't even get along with a horse like that. There's all kinds of people in this world.

In this series of pictures, the person is using a good approach and Annie B can understand each part of what he's wanting her to do, which is to feel of the snaffle bit by bending to the right, shifting her weight forward to untrack the hindquarters, and then shifting her weight back to follow through with her front legs. She is able to keep a nice expression on her face and follow the feel to lead without taking the float out of the rope.

In the experimenting a person does for this, it's going to be real important to practice making manageable coils in the end of your longer rope, so it doesn't ever get tangled up. It can help to practice with another person on the end of the rope to learn how to feed out the coils one at a time by opening up your fingers. There's many variations in the way people like to handle equipment, but one thing that's real important is to always know the feel of that rope, and where the end of it is and how those coils lay in your hand there, so if things speed up on the spur of the moment, you and the horse aren't going to get caught up in it and get a rope burn, or something like that. Practice dropping those coils one at a time. A person sure wants to be good at that.

Diamond Lu Collection series

Diamond Lu Collection series

If you've gone about all these exercises in this chapter in a way that fits the horse up to this point, that horse is just pleased to be there and try to do whatever it is that you want. If you haven't prepared him for the future, that'll be real clear right now. We're showing this next run of pictures (Figures 10-15) so people can compare them with the first group. This is to give people more of an idea of the little things that can affect a horse in a way that isn't the best. Of course, there's an endless amount of things that don't work, and I'm not ever in favor of focusing too much attention there. But, there's a certain thing people are liable to do without knowing it can make things more difficult for the horse to understand. I thought it might be helpful to point out the smaller things a person might like to avoid on the start.

In this demonstration, you can see that the fella's starting to walk before that mare is prepared to follow the feel on that rope. But they're getting along the best they both know how, and this is for demonstration purposes anyway. The horse is a little confused about the pace and the feel of things, and she is filling in a little, even though she isn't sure what to do with the rope as tight as it is around her that way. Slowing things down just a little will put more slack in that rope and give her some time to figure things out. A little different feel on that rope could be real beneficial, but things turned out all right anyway. That's because this fella has a lot of try in him, and the way he is around a horse favors the animal in the first place. Horses can sure sense when people have the right idea about them, especially when their attitudes towards learning how to feel of a horse are this open-minded way. Annie B discovered in this situation that she could adjust to some things that hadn't shaped up in the earlier session.

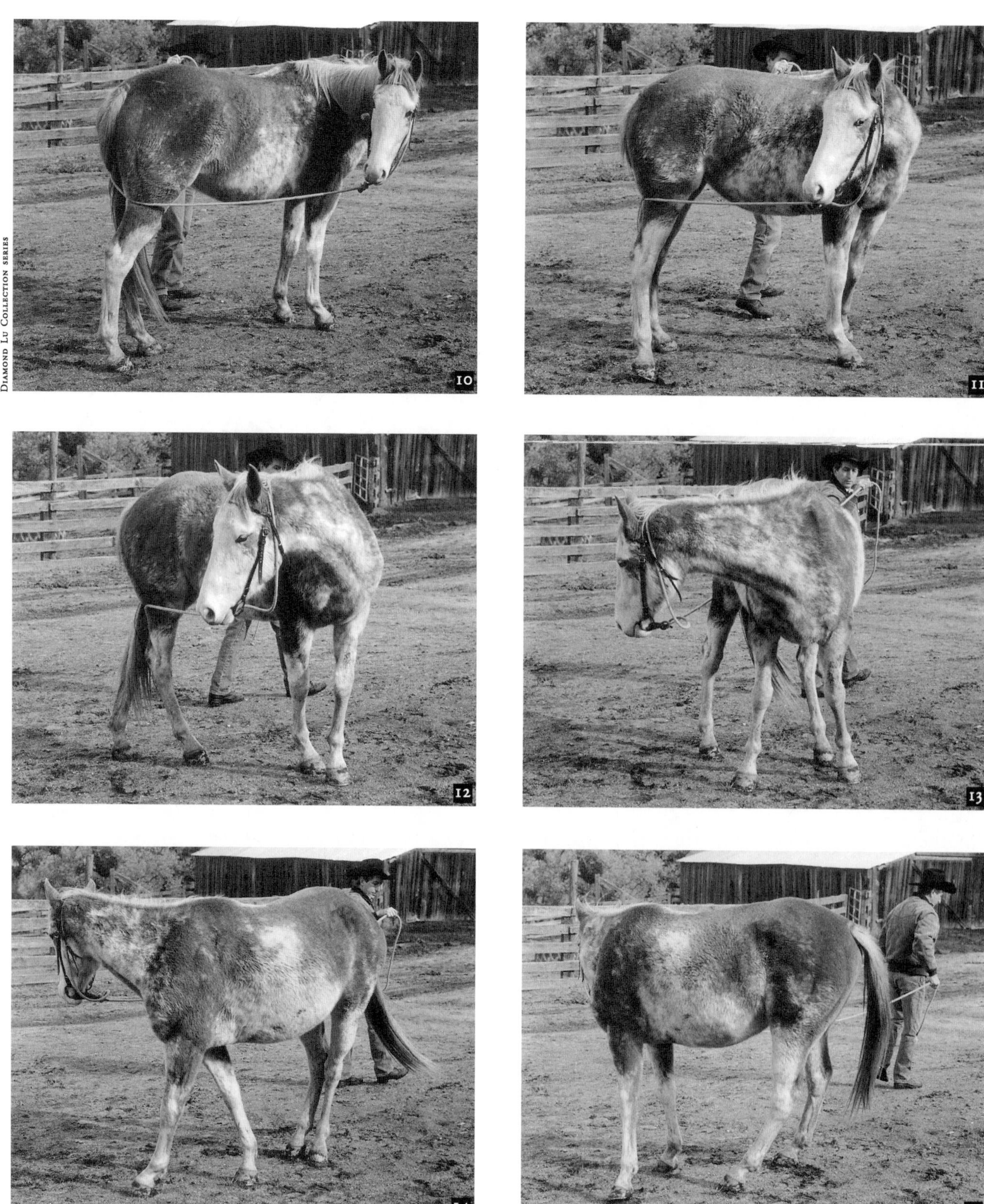

Diamond Lu Collection series

It Takes the Time it Takes

A fella shouldn't worry about anything when he's handling horses. Just get with the feel of that horse is all — that's what's most important on the start. Pick up the horse's feel, so that horse can get with you, and give no thought to the time it'll take.

If a person needs more time in some spots to clear up his understanding of things, he'd be pleased to spend that time. If his plans include advanced maneuvers of any kind, that time investment will pay off for him later on. Improvement will show right up in that horse once your feel and timing have meaning he understands, and you can progress from there.

When you're working a horse on the ground, it's best if your plan of how you want the horse to operate takes into consideration things like the way the ground is slanted, and if it's uphill or downhill from the way you want that horse to maneuver (Figures 16-23). It's easier to do some things on level ground, and to do some other things on a little hill. Just the same as some maneuvers are going to come through for you better if you're heading home than if you're going away from home. Little things like that really have a lot to do with how you can get the horse's mental and physical systems operating with your ideas.

Diamond Lu Collection series

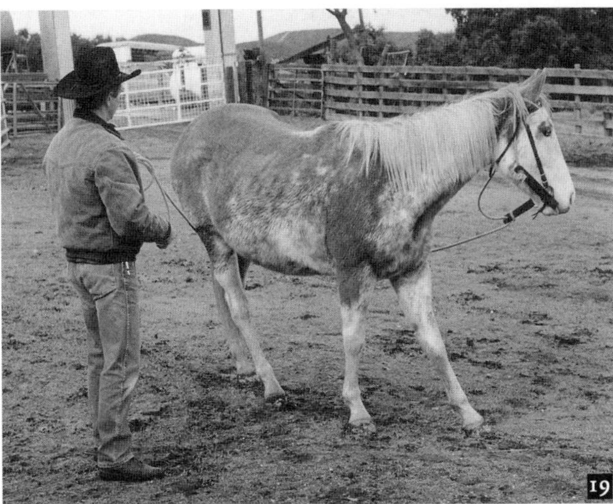

Diamond Lu Collection series

Sometimes it's helpful to switch sides, and when there isn't a flat place to work, why you can set the horse up to take his first forward steps towards the downhill side of a slope if you need to. That way, it's easier to help a horse understand how to make good use of those hindquarters. And there's other adjustments a fella can make, it just all depends on what's going on around there. The more time you spend with the horse trying to fit the situation in the way he needs to have something presented to him, the more likely you are to start seeing certain aspects you hadn't noticed before. A fella wants to make good use of those new things he's picked up on.

You'd want to remember that a mixed-up horse is just missing something important in his foundation. You wouldn't worry about this at all, because it's real easy to miss some things. I'd say most everyone does miss out, here and there, as they're learning, because there are so many variables coming in all the time to remember and observe. And that's *anytime* you're with a horse.

If a fella's learned how to make the best use of his better feel at the foundation level, then he can help a horse work through one sort of mix-up or another so his intent gets through real clear to that horse. When this happens, it's because he figured out through his experimenting how to present his feel in a way that fit that particular horse. That's what I call *true horsemanship*.

The few people who really understand this, in the sense of *being horsemen*, could be a big benefit to an unlimited number of horses by helping others in their learning process — and that'd be in classes on using feel and applying it in a way the horse can understand. This is something I sure like to think about. If the better instructors got onto this approach and could see those better results start to show up in their own horses, why I'd rather think they'd want to see it show up for their students, too. I'm in hopes this is so. Where a person's not had an excess of instructors, or time for practice, there's always something he can learn from another person if someone's around to demonstrate things that another person might not be as well acquainted with.

In Figures 24-50, I'm just taking care of some little things, because Annie B had pretty much stopped feeling of this fella, a little more than I thought was necessary. Some important things sure had been missed in her foundation, of course. That's not open to question.

Well, there was a little tuning up that had to take place on Annie B that day, I'll put it that way. After she got onto my feel and understood what was expected, why she started to fill in a little while that fella tried some new things he hadn't been exposed to before. It was real pleasing to watch the progress they made together that day, and they got to really understanding each other after that — through feel, of course.

There's a few things that bother me about this next run of pictures, and that's the ones we didn't get. I wanted to show how a fella can take that long lead rein on the snaffle bit and be on the off side with it, and flip it back over the top of the horse and come out with it just right on the near side. In all of the pictures we got for this book, those didn't show up. I was disappointed, because there's a little technique in that maneuver that a fella could use in the future if he'd had a chance to see it. This was between Figures 32 and 33. We had a little trouble finding the right pictures to fill in between Figures 37 and 38, too. And for Figure 76, we took Figure 80 and flipped it around. The horse looks good but the rope's on the wrong side of the saddle, and that fella's not left handed.

But we're in hopes a fella can get the general idea from studying these anyway. He needs to get used to the feel of that rope and send it out a ways as he brings it up and over the horse's back. A fella'd want to be sure he gets the hang of managing that rope so he doesn't hit the horse in the head or on the ears as it's coming over the top.

It'd be good to do a little experimenting and get accurate at this maneuver before you'd actually do it using your snaffle bit. You can attach a halter to a fence and practice sending the rope up and over without a horse being anywhere near there.

It can be helpful to have a ramp to work from and it can be real beneficial to adjust the snaffle bit like this for your ground work when you're working with certain horses. Feeding out those coils at the right time and gathering up that rope in a way that doesn't give the horse an unclear message — why it takes a lot of experience to get this sorted out, and you aren't going to get it working real smooth on the start. No one is. This is one of the actual facts that's so helpful to have worked into your thinking before you even get to where the horse is. A lot of times if you just get an opportunity to see something done a new way, and see how to get that real effective feel applied, why you can catch onto it right away and build from there.

24

25

26

27

28

29

30

Diamond Lu Collection series

31

32

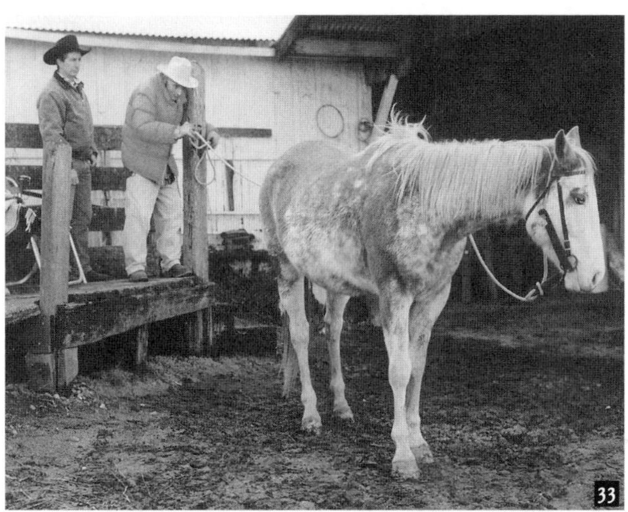
33

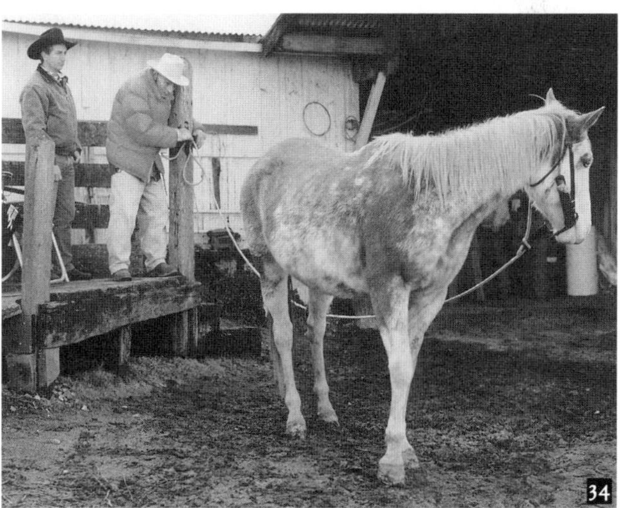
34

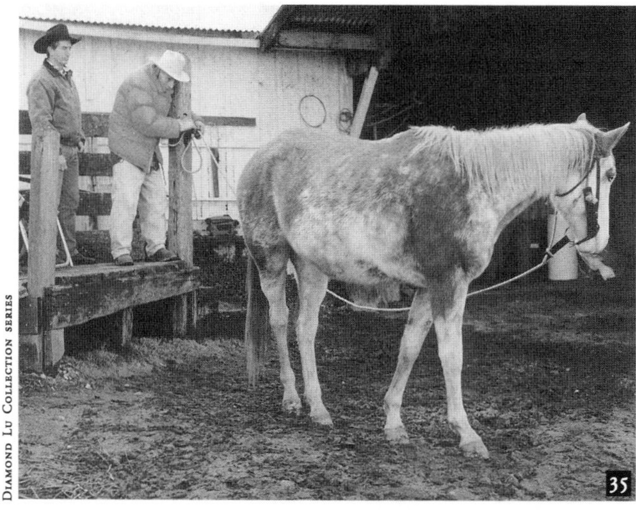

35

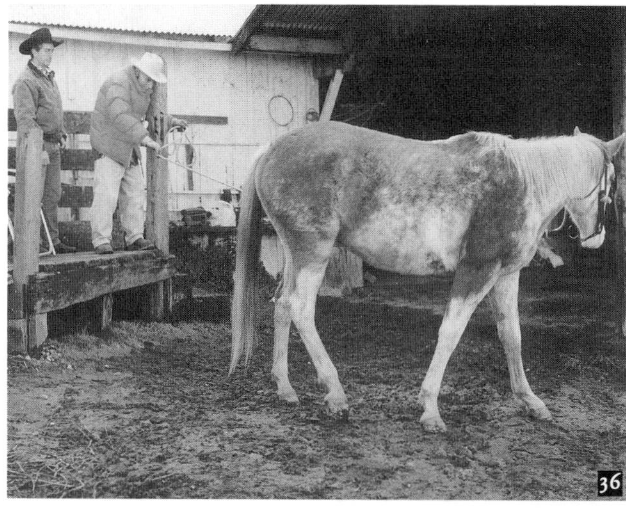

36

37

38

39

40

41

42

Diamond Lu Collection series

43

44

45

46

Diamond Lu Collection series

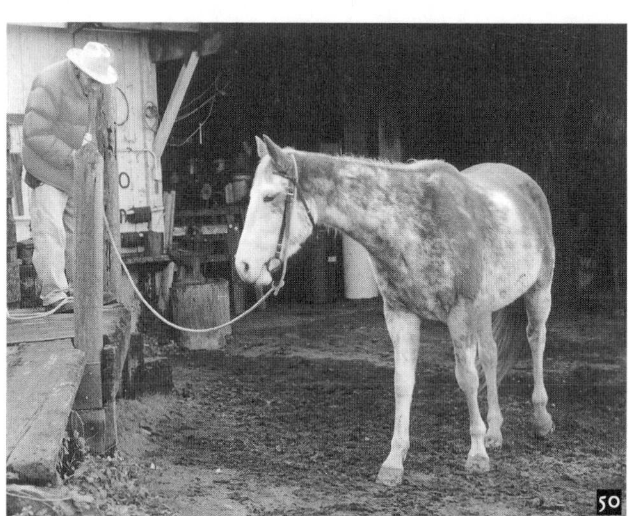

I'd say this fella has a real strong desire to learn about handling horses through feel, and we got a lot accomplished that day (Figures 51 - 65). Through his more careful observations, he caught on how to present Annie B with a real effective feel to operate her forehand and hindquarters this way. After a few tries, she started to move in smooth and correct motions. Generally speaking, these pictures show how the forehand supports the horse's weight while she adjusts the hind feet to follow his feel for a new direction. This positioning sets her hindquarters up in the best way to provide good balance as the forehand reaches in a new direction.

There's a lot taking place in these pictures, more than most people are ever going to notice if someone doesn't help them realize just how much there is to see and be aware of, from that horse's point of view.

It's all right to let a horse take a step or two away from you with the forehand on the new line of travel and then stop before going on (Figures 60-62). It's the better choice to make if the horse is uncertain, because the alternative might be for that horse to crowd you or, in some cases, a horse might lose their mental connection

51

52

Diamond Lu Collection series

53

54

55

56

57

58

59

60

61

62

63

64

Diamond Lu Collection series

65

with you and just take off — and that's if you were on the ground or sitting up there. Either way, a situation like that is undesirable, and there's quite a little advantage to having a horse that's willing to wait for you and see what the best thing is to do next. I'm in hopes that by now people can have this idea already in their thinking pretty solid — whatever a horse can do for you, no matter what it is, *it's based on the lessons and exercises you both learned up to this point.*

On the next page, the bay colt in Figures 66-72 had only a little exposure to this way of being handled and is doing pretty good, considering. There won't be a need for a whip any place around that horse anymore, because he's got a start now on operating entirely through feel. There's still a little mix-up in him though, and a person can see this. It shows up in the tightness he carries in his body, and the expression on his face. And it's in the way he's elevated his neck and head and got those legs braced. Still, you can see quite a little improvement. There's no hurry in this anyway. I'm in hopes this horse is going to make it. The young girl who brought him to the clinic has a *real* strong desire to learn about this more fitting way. If she's apt to encounter any resistance in the future, from any horse, I'd say that she's going to be willing to make an adjustment, and put quite a lot of thought into the approach she's going to take. No, she's capable of bringing out the best in any horse she handles.

Patricia Weedman series

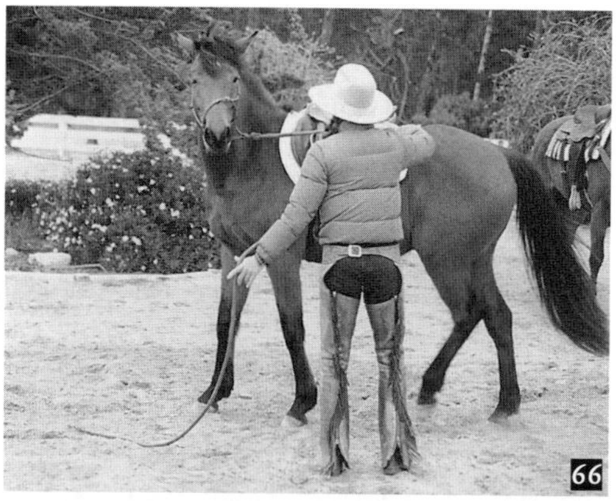
66

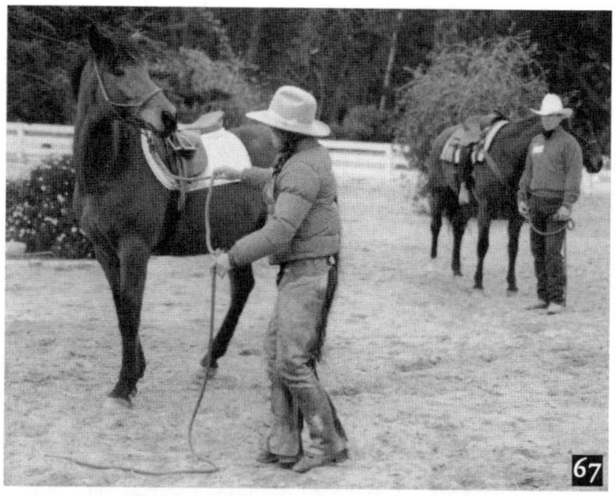
67

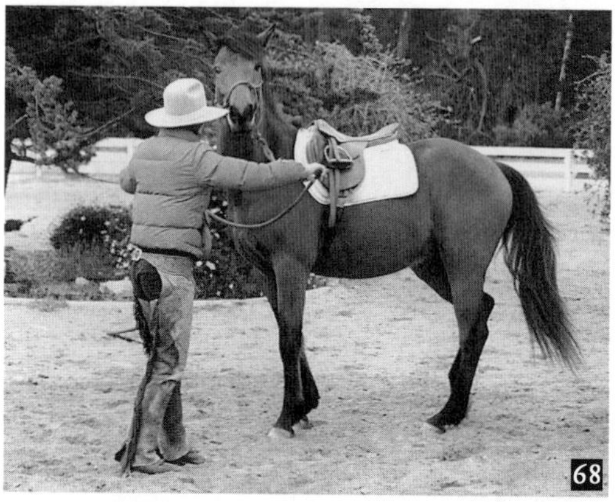
68

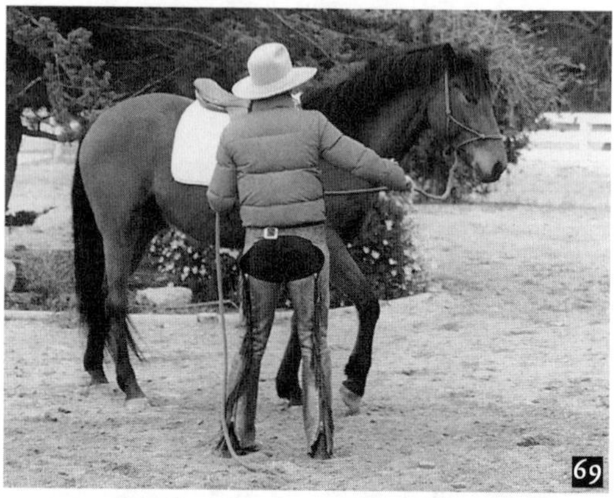
69

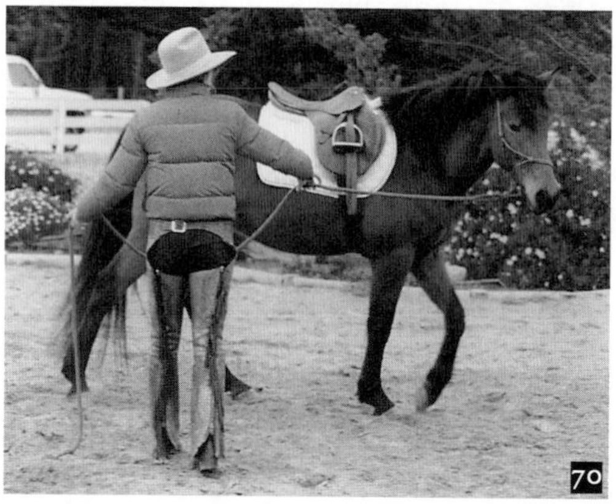
70

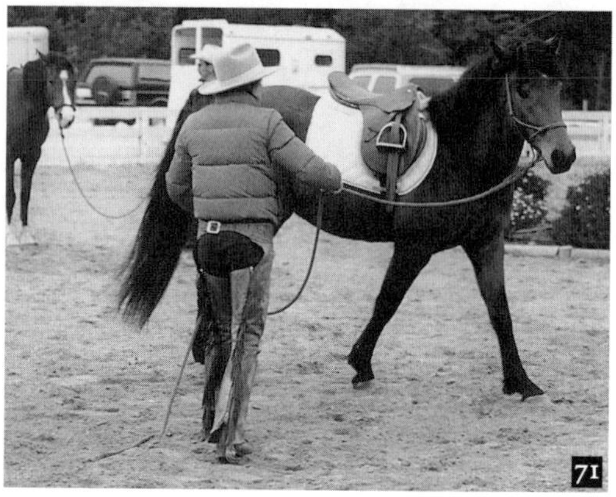
71

72

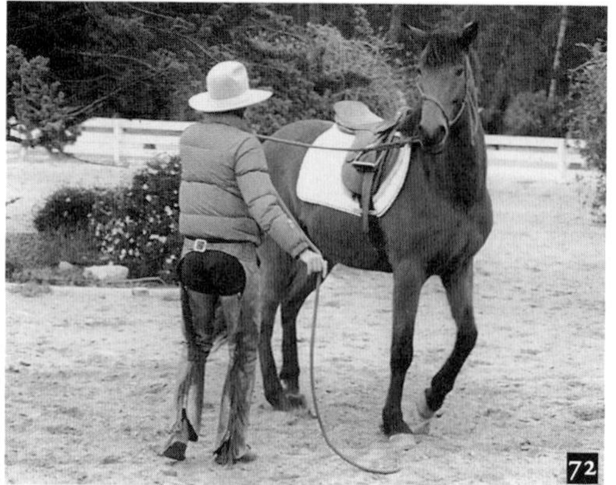

The pictures of the paint horse (Figures 73-80) show a little better flow in the horse's movements. He has nowhere near as much concern as the bay horse had about what might be about to happen. That's due to his positive experiences with this young fella and the presentation that's been made to that horse, through feel, up to this point. His calm and relaxed manner are also on account of the young girl who handles the foal in the next set of pictures, because she owns that paint horse and has spent quite a little time at this. When younger people start learning this, there's some real hope for so many horses that are coming in the future. This is so pleasing for me to think about.

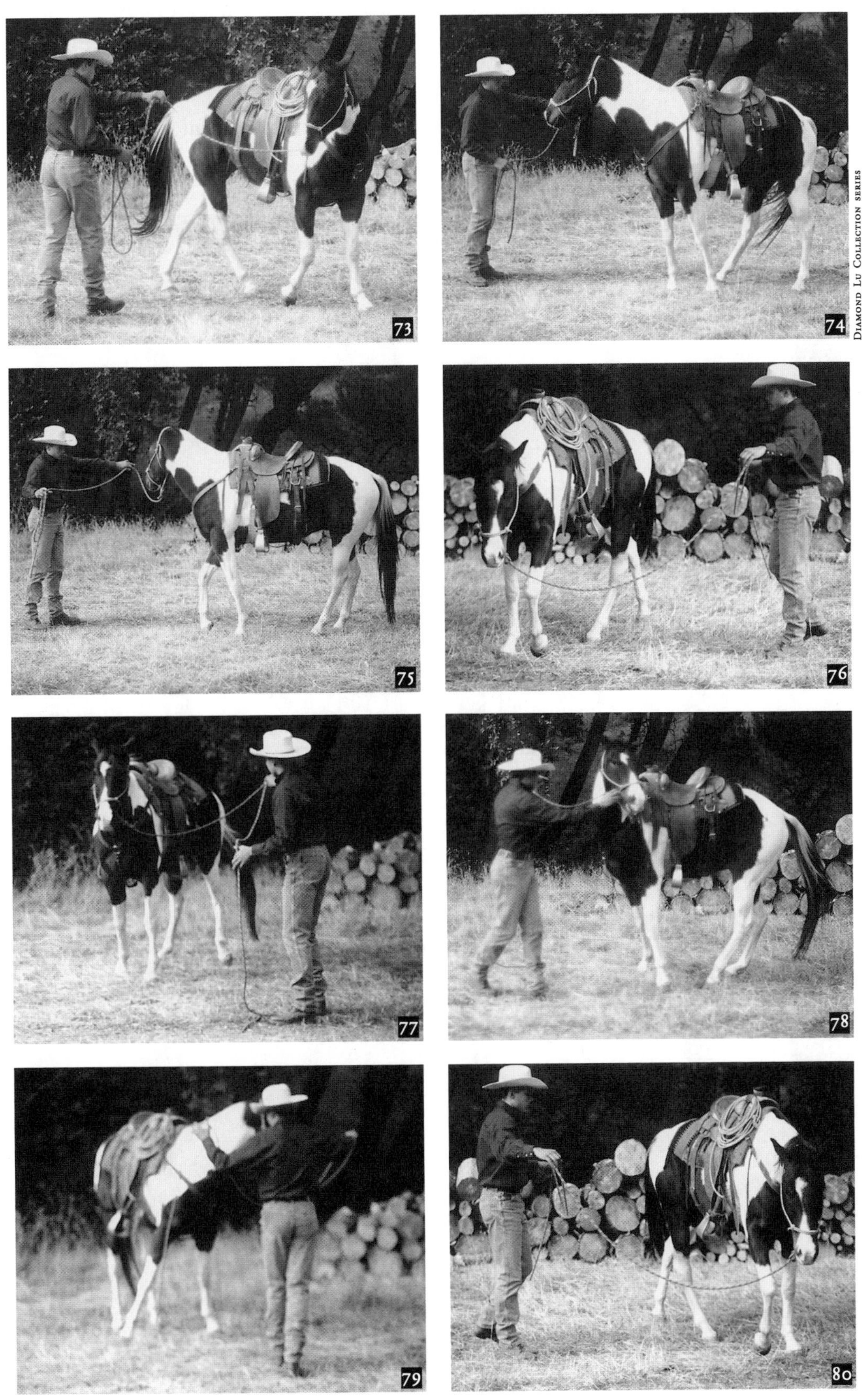

DIAMOND LU COLLECTION SERIES

When horses are young, it's real important to establish their responsiveness to your feel on the ground, way ahead of when you want to ride through this maneuver (Figures 81-94). Those foals need to learn the feel of waiting, and how to not crowd a person. That way, the part where the horse learns to take over with ideas of his own, just because he's moving near a person, will never come into his mind. There's no part of a pushy horse developing when you offer that nice, relaxed feel that he can understand and follow.

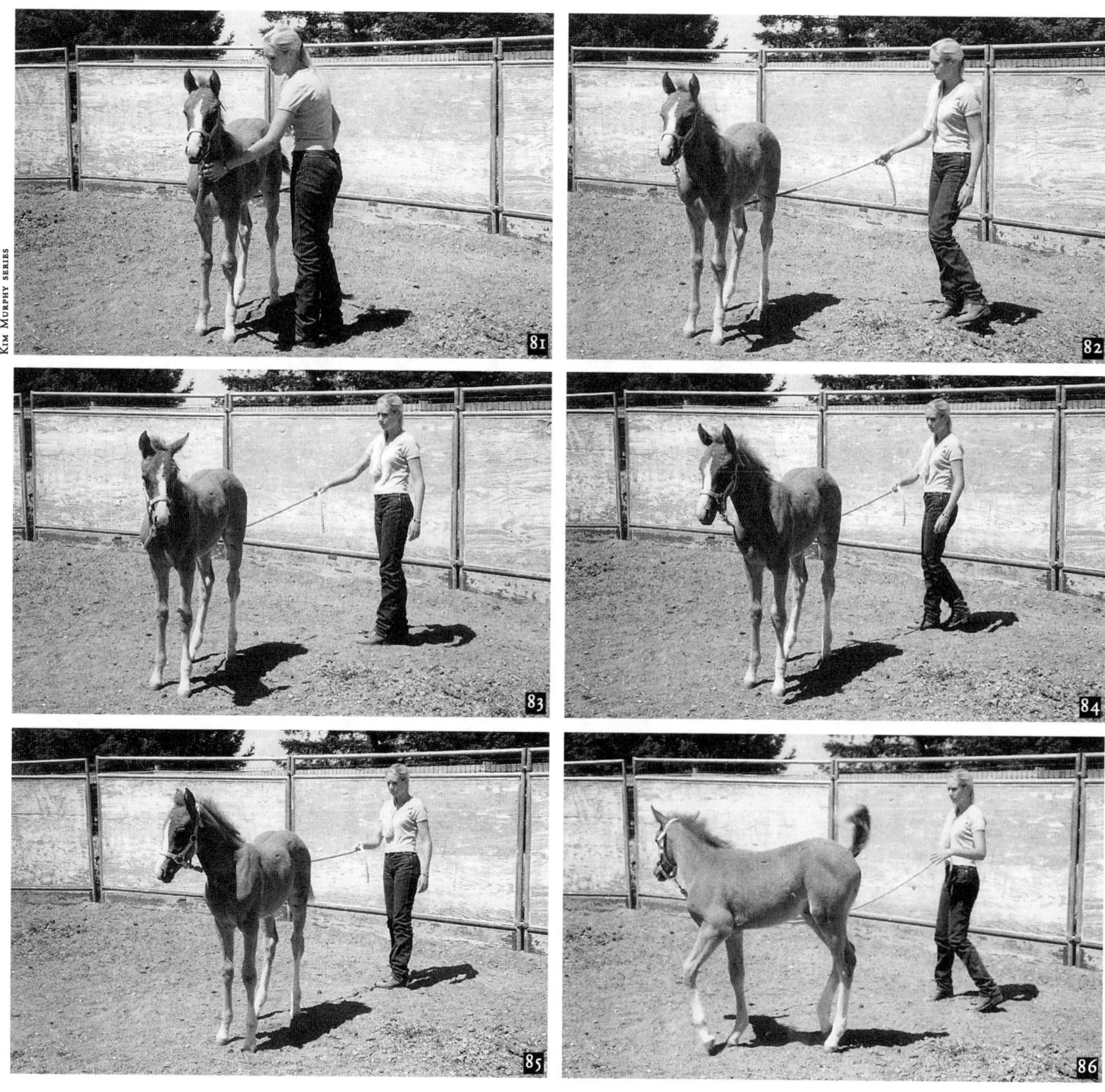

Kim Murphy series

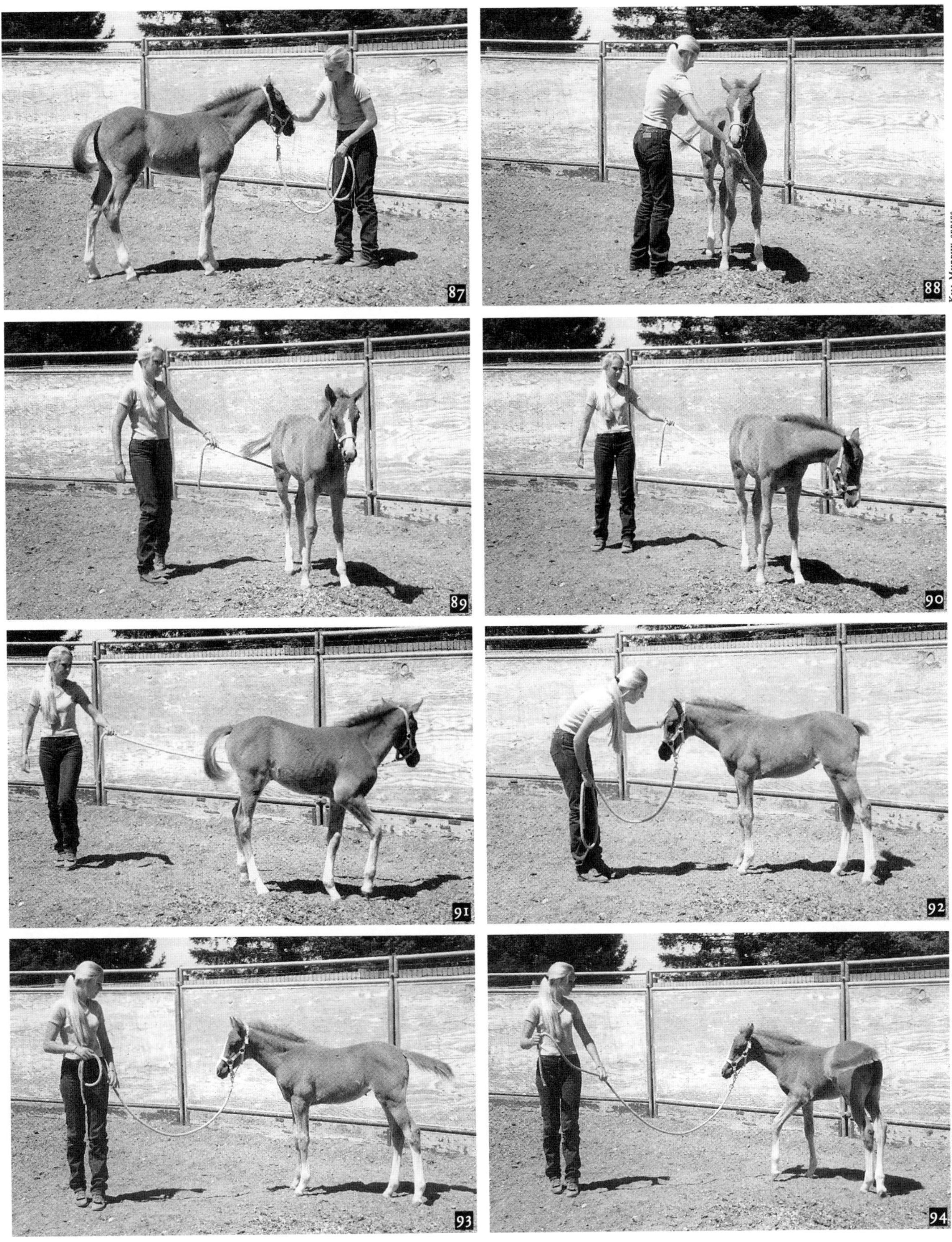

Kim Murphy series

Diamond Lu Collection

95

Changing directions, using feel. This rider is feeling of his horse, and the horse understands what to do with his feet.

The next subject we're going to speak about concerns the way a horse places his feet at the various gaits. Our goal is to make this information accessible to people who maybe never gave some of these things much thought before. It almost always occurs to me when I read something over that there'd have been a better way to say something. Usually, there's another word that could be used that would seem to fit in there better. When you want to make it easy for people to understand things that are so difficult to explain in print, if it's only words you've got to explain this, why it's good to have pictures. In this next part, we added some diagrams to go along with those pictures because this area gets a little too deep. If this subject and these diagrams are helpful, well, that was our plan.

Chapter 5:

FEELING OF THE FEET IN DIFFERENT GAITS

IN THIS CHAPTER WE'RE SPEAKING ABOUT THE ACTUAL FACTS as far as the placement of the horse's feet in the various gaits is concerned, and that's whether you're sitting on the horse or not. It's real helpful to learn about how a horse's feet move at the different gaits, and to learn how to place his feet wherever you need them to be. And it's best to get real knowledgeable about where those feet are liable to end up on the spur of the moment, too. If a person doesn't know about this, surprising things can happen when a horse needs to move those feet.

You'd maybe not notice the things that a horse was missing in his foundation until you'd like him to do something he isn't prepared to understand. This could be anything: stepping into a trailer, slowing down, changing leads or just standing still. Whatever a person presents to the horse, what he learns to expect from their feel, that is what he will do. If a horse hasn't been scared too badly or had the try taken out of him, then at the point when he understands where and when and how fast you want him to place his feet, it's usually only the limits of his physical capacity that will prevent him from doing it. *The right thing is obvious to a horse that's been prepared through feel, and you'd not ever need to force that horse into any maneuvers.*

There's no point in speeding things up or trying to finish a horse when he's missing the basic understanding of how to shift his weight from one foot to the other *when you want him to.*

It Helps to Observe Horses Moving Freely in All Gaits

Getting in time with the feel of a horse's feet can be accomplished when you're on the ground or mounted. A few things are taking place beyond the up and down motions you feel when you're sitting up there. Those feet lift up, reach forward, step down and then support the horse's weight while his other feet get arranged to come off the ground for whatever he's going to do next, which could be most anything. A person can break this down into even smaller particles of feel and motions if they want to — and some of them will if they decide to advance up the line that far in their horsemanship.

If you have the opportunity and the time, it's real helpful to observe horses when they're moving freely in all the gaits. In those situations, you'd do this for long periods of time. You will start to pick up the little things in a horse's movements that show those decisions he makes about his own balance *before* he places each foot on the ground. His footwork is always changing in response to the actions of other horses, or even sometimes the weather, because the ground he's on can play a part in this, too. And it can sometimes be that some unpleasant conditions in his own body, like stiffness or a sore foot, will affect the way he moves. When I get the opportunity to spend a little time around a horse, I always watch those feet.

Get a Little Help With This On the Start

On the start, it's best to learn about the placement of the feet while you're being led on a horse with your eyes closed. That makes it pretty easy to understand. I've spoken about this earlier — the feel of those feet and his whole body movement comes right up through the saddle. There's a lot to sort out about that. It's best if you can do this without having to think about other things, like directing him around holes or away from low branches.

Walking Straight and in an Arc

Get someone to lead the horse at a walk straight ahead and then have them arc off to the right and left, or walk him on tighter corners. When that feels all right and you want to add some variation to it, why you can ask them to just speed up a little and slow down when you're walking straight and through some turns. This way you'll have a wide range of ideas and sensations to think about, and the feel of those things will help you understand how the horse moves. You'll feel that there's a lot going on and it's important for you to learn about this, because his movements affect the way a horse is set up mentally, and his thoughts about what you want him to do are tied right to his feet. Before a person's riding ability can advance, they'd need to learn about the timing and balance that's required to stay with the feel of that horse. That's an actual fact, regardless of what anyone says or thinks that's different, and there's always going to be those who do, all right.

Backing Up

If the person leading the horse has enough experience to present a feel to back that horse up a few steps, I think doing this is something the rider will benefit from — just going straight back and then backwards in small arcs in both directions. It's nice if you can get familiar with the feel of the feet doing that before you'd take those reins and expect him to understand something you wanted him to do going in reverse, especially when you have no idea what it actually feels like when the horse is going backwards in the first place. No, it's important to try to preserve the horse's natural inclination to try to understand a person. Backing maneuvers can really mix a person up on the start and we'd try to avoid having an inexperienced rider try to back up a horse too soon. It can cause the horse a lot of confusion if the rider doesn't understand the feel he needs to present to that horse to back up one step at a time, real smooth. I'm in hopes that people will understand my thinking on this, because it's going to benefit them in the future, and that's what we need to have in mind all the time, where horses are concerned.

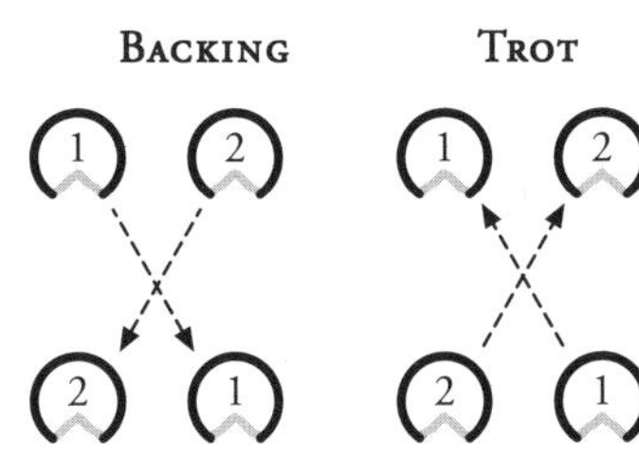

Nature made sure the horse has good balance in reverse.

In Chapter 4, we spoke about how in the trot and the back up the feet actually move in pairs the same way, but the horse is going in different directions. This diagram shows how the horse makes use of alternate diagonals in the back up, just like he does in the trot.

Footfall at the Walk

The walk is a four-beat gait. (See the diagram on page 226.) You can see from these pictures that at any point in the stride, the horse has two or three feet on the ground. It's easy to feel the feet moving if you spend some time at this. It's too bad these pictures can't show the many particles of feel there are to notice between the steps.

A horse doesn't ever want to step on himself. At the walk, if the left hind foot just stepped down (Figure 1) the left front leg has already reached forward to step out of the way. The horse has most of his

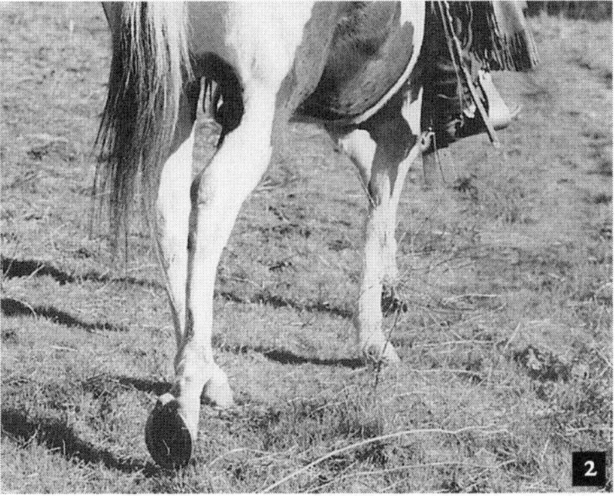

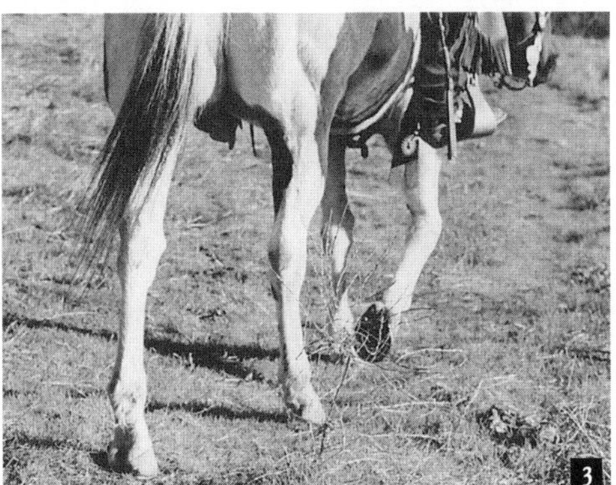

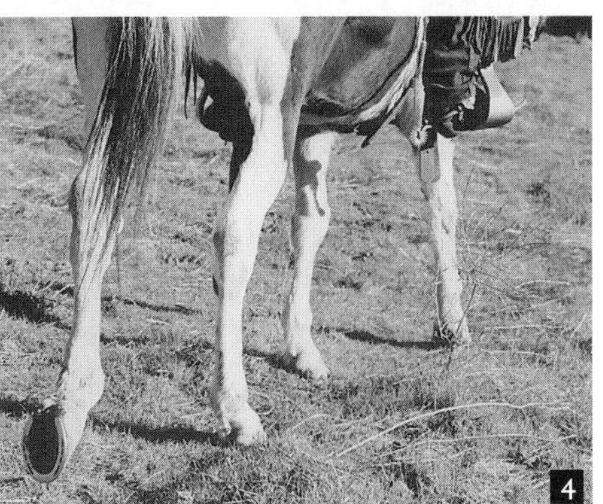

Diamond Lu Collection series

Footfall at the Walk

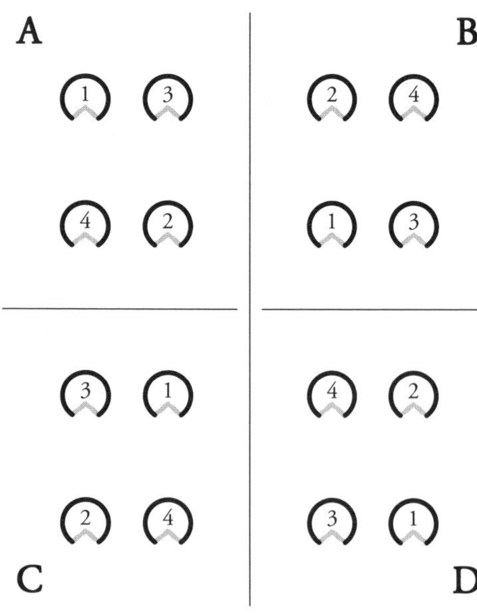

weight on the right front and left hind leg in this picture. Depending on their physical setup (conformation), some horses will lift up the front foot quite a bit before the hind foot on that same side sets down. This sometimes makes an oddly-appearing step, but the actual pattern and order of stepping is the same anyway. Other horses, why some of them just barely miss stepping on the back of their own foot, and some don't miss. Usually this is due to the influence of the rider on the mouth, or a shoeing job they had done that wasn't the best. Sometimes those feet just get neglected and grow out too much.

No matter which foot starts the walk stride, the pattern is going to be the same. You will hear, see, and feel the rhythm of the feet like this: front-back-front-back, or, back-front-back-front.

As the left front foot steps down, he lifts up the right hind foot and gets ready to step up underneath himself with it (Figure 2). Figure 3 shows how the right hind steps down after the right front foot gets picked up. That pulls his weight forward off the left hind and onto the left diagonal (left front and right hind legs) which is doing most of the supporting as the right front foot starts back down (Figures 3-4). We'll speak more about diagonals when we get to those faster gaits. The motion of stepping down on the right front foot draws the left hind up underneath him, and in order not to step on himself with it, he'll move the left front out of the way again (back to Figure 1). That starts the stride over. These are the actual facts of how a horse places those feet when he's walking sound on good footing. It can really pay off when a fella listens to this, I'll say that.

This picture shows two horses, just walking along and looking relaxed. They are both feeling of the rider and understand what's expected of them. The foal is about to step down with his right front foot. The next foot he will pick up is the left front. It's the opposite for the horse on the left. They are going along in an extended walk.

5

Diamond Lu Collection

In a picture of the extended walk, a horse could look like he's trotting, but the stride still has four beats, and not two, like you have in the trot. The horse in Figure 6 is in a lively extended walk, and so is the horse in Figure 7. This shows two examples of the way the reins can be handled, using feel. The rider on the paint has a nice connection to his horse through the reins. The fella on the nice-appearing roan horse has him shaped up, through feel, in the hackamore. An extended walk is one of the nicest ways I know to travel

Diamond Lu Collection

6

7

Emily Kitching

when you're horseback. The fella in Figure 8 is cornering his horse at the walk. I like the way he handles a horse that's in the bridle. The horse is about to bring the left hind foot forward and step down on the right front foot.

8

Diamond Lu Collection

Footfall at the Trot

In the transition from a four-beat walk up to the two-beat trot, the *actual job* of the front feet and the back feet is the same — and that's to speed up. At the trot, the one-two stepping order of the front feet stays the same, but the number of beats in the stride gets reduced by half because those back feet need to catch up with the faster rhythm of the front feet. This is what puts a "double diagonal" into the trot, and it's good to have it that better-balanced way. Except for the times when the horse has a springy trot, and he extends the trot to where he's got all four feet off the ground for a second in between steps, why he's always got a solid pair of feet to step down on in the trot.

Generally speaking, this is a real good gait to travel in. Most horses can stay comfortable and dependable at a trot in a lot of situations. But there is a down side to the trot, the main one being it can be so bouncy on some horses that a fella might have to make big adjustments in his riding to travel like that. New blue jeans are about the worst thing to wear if you plan to trot a long ways, and the best cure for the chafing you're bound to get from a day of trotting is to put on some long underwear.

When we speak about the name of a certain "diagonal" (left or right) at the trot, we're speaking about the side of the horse that the front leg in that diagonal pair is on. Even though there's a hind leg on the other side of his body that's moving at the same time, that leg just isn't mentioned for some reason. If a fella was mentioning his horse's right front and left hind leg for any reason, he'd just call it the right diagonal and people would know he was including the left hind leg in that.

These next pictures (Figures 9-14) show many of the different things there are to notice about a horse when he's trotting. There isn't enough room in this book for all the pictures you'd want to have or things there are to say about the trot. But from the pictures we did put in, a person can get ideas about how the horse moves when he's on his own, and when he's mounted. I think it's quite amazing that sometimes what's most important to notice about the way a horse does something is a little detail that lasts for a second. It is so small and then it's gone. There's so much to notice.

The mare in Figure 11 is in an extended trot. She's got a nice, big stride. But her shoulders are kind of low because she's got that head up, and she appears to be a little tight. Right here I'm going to let people know how dangerous it is to leave a halter on a loose horse. They can lose a horse to a broken neck if they stay in that habit, all right. The horse on the next page, in Figure 12, is in an extended trot that has a different look to it. This horse has a springy stride and is trotting out real relaxed. He's about to come down on the left diagonal.

The horse in Figure 13 is trotting out real free and has a relaxed stride. He's about to step down on the right diagonal. The horse in Figure 14 is also in a trot, but he's collected up and feeling of his rider, with plenty of life available. He's shifting his weight across the right diagonal and reaching for the next step in the trot with his left diagonal.

Walk to Trot Transition

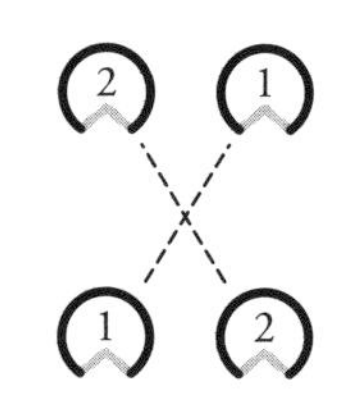

Back feet catch up

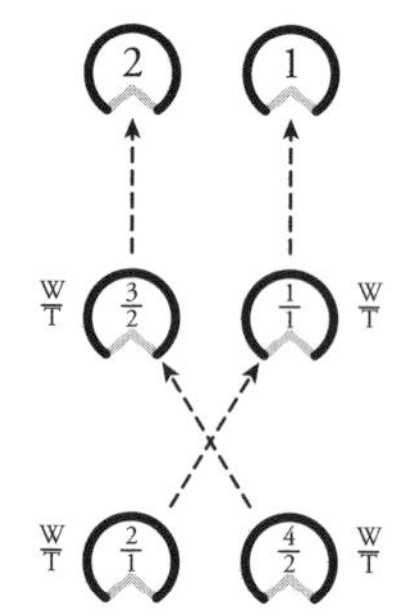

Front feet speed up

Walk

At the walk, the front feet travel in a 1-2 rhythm. When they speed up to a trot, the rhythm doesn't change, but the back feet have to hurry up to get in time with the front feet. That's how four beats turns into two.

Trot

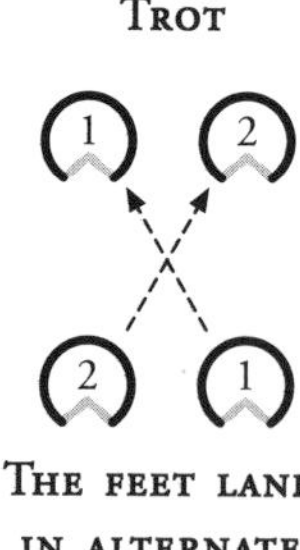

The feet land in alternate pairs, called diagonals.

This horse is trotting and his weight is on the right diagonal.

Diamond Lu Collection

In this picture, the horse's weight is on the left diagonal.

Diamond Lu Collection

Diamond Lu Collection

Emily Kitching

Footfall at the Lope

Diamond Lu Collection

The lope is a three-beat gait. Listening to the sound of the feet when you move up from the walk to the trot, and then from the trot to the lope, makes it a little easier to sort out what's going on. Listen for the difference between the 1-2-3-4 beat of the walk, and the 1-2 beat of the trot. The walk and the trot sound sort of crisp. Then there's the 1-2-3 sound of the feet hitting the ground at the lope. That's real different and a person might wonder about only three beats because that horse has four feet, so that's apt to be confusing on the start. A fella might wonder what the horse is doing with that fourth foot, if the listening and counting he'd done up to that point had made sense to him.

Two Feet Get New Jobs

When a horse lopes he keeps one of the diagonals he had at the trot and he gives up the other one, so those two feet can advance into different jobs. The hind leg of the freed-up pair really takes on two extra jobs — that's in addition to the support function it had before. Now it's going to push off, and also help to slow him down when he lands on it and needs to collect up. Its job is to support him and to help him slow down at the same time he needs to keep moving forward. This purpose of the hindquarters is visible in *all the gaits*, if you know what to look for. In the next run of pictures, Figures 15-17 show the hindquarters doing their job to support, slow

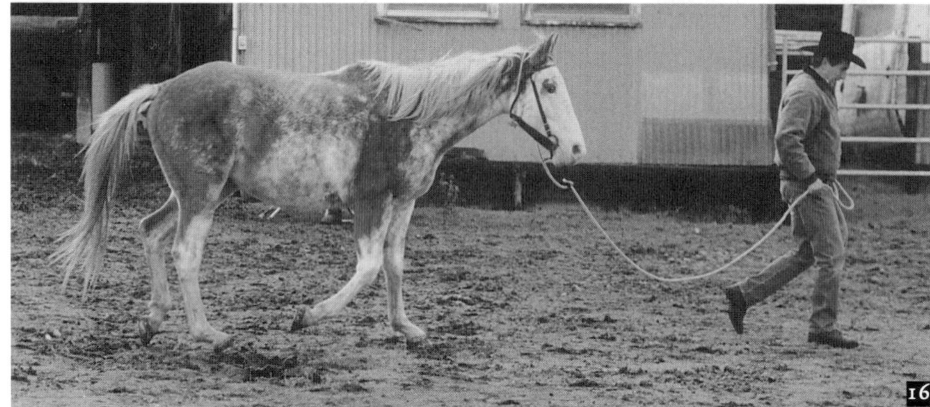

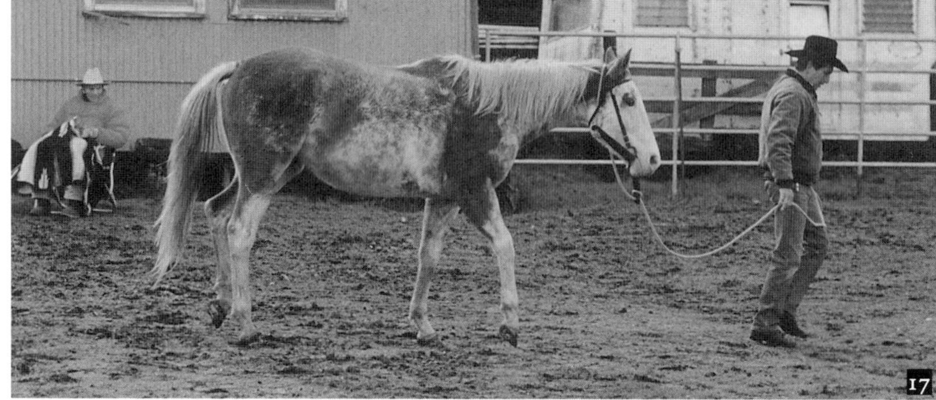

down, and keep the horse going at the same time in a downward transition from the trot to the walk.

In Figure 18, the right front foot is preparing to go into it's leading and supporting job at the lope, while the weight is being transferred across that supporting (left) diagonal. The left back foot is getting ready to start the stride over again, because it has those three jobs to take care of that were just listed a few different ways. Of course, like the left back foot, the right front foot has to be there to slow the stride a little too, especially in a situation like this. But even with all these specialized little jobs they have, it's the actual facts that all the legs need to be available right on the spur of the moment to work to the fullest extent in *any* maneuver, whatever it is.

One thing I like about this picture is it shows how the hindquarters are set up to take care of the horse's balance and a person's safety. And another thing I like is those reins aren't pulled tight. And, this horse is real relaxed but alert and focused on the job, which is always good. If the natural lightness that the horse was born with is left in there, why this feature of the hindquarters can give a horse an extra nice appearance in any gait, especially when a horse isn't much for looks.

If a person can learn how to ride in a way that doesn't interfere with that hindquarters being *all the time* real dependable and adjustable, why a horse can get can get pretty handy at changing directions for a person, and making those faster adjustments with his foot placement. This is desirable to some people, of course. It is to me. But I'm thinking that the general run of people who keep a horse maybe don't care too much about it, and I'm in hopes this will change.

18

Gale Nelson

More About Loping and Leads

In the first step of the lope, when one of his hind feet step down, the horse needs to have good balance. The good balance he has available to him in the second beat of the stride is due to the other hind foot landing at the same time that the front foot on the opposite side steps down. This real beneficial diagonal pattern is held over from the trot. It's one aspect of his footwork that helps to keep him steady when he has to speed up in a turn, or make a sudden stop.

After that, his other front foot steps down. That's the third beat, and whatever front leg that is, that's the lead the horse is on. There is a short time after this when the horse has all four of his feet in the air, and that's just before he steps into the next stride.

One real handy thing he can do is change leads when he's got all those feet up. This is a valuable thing to know about his natural way of maneuvering at the lope. He can also change leads when the hind leg steps into the stride and both front legs are in the air, or even when the front leading leg is still on the ground and both back feet are in the air. Those are the three main ways a horse can arrange his legs when he's going to change a lead. Sometimes, he might only get the job half done, and when that happens the leads are working separately. That's called a disunited lead and we'll speak about that a little further up in the book. One thing though, they sure don't feel the same as when he makes a complete switch in front and behind. And, it doesn't feel near as good to the rider when he changes first in front, or first behind, as it does when he changes leads as nice and smooth as can be, right between two strides.

When the leading front foot is on its way to the ground you want to be sure to *not ever jerk on the reins or twist your body around up there at all.* You can scare a horse by doing that. If a person was going to make a habit of moving that way, he'd have a good start at building a real big brace into that horse when he loped, and at other times, too. When that leading front foot steps down on the ground, the whole horse and the rider are balanced on it. A person wants to do all they can to help the horse when he's in that situation. The main help they can give him is to not interfere with his balance. A lack of understanding about the horse's balance could throw the whole outfit way off.

I've seen people inspect the hoofprints a horse makes in the soil after he's loped by a spot. I've done this, too. It appears that one pair of legs on each side is landing ahead of the other, and when you see a horse lope from the side, it sure does look that way. In a way, this is true. One side of the horse does step down ahead of the other side at the lope when his feet are in the correct alignment for whatever lead he's on.

But the legs on his left side don't land at the same time, and the legs on his right side don't either. In the dirt it appears that they do, and watching from the side a person can sure get this impression. But the actual facts of his body motions are set up a little different than that, for the reasons already listed.

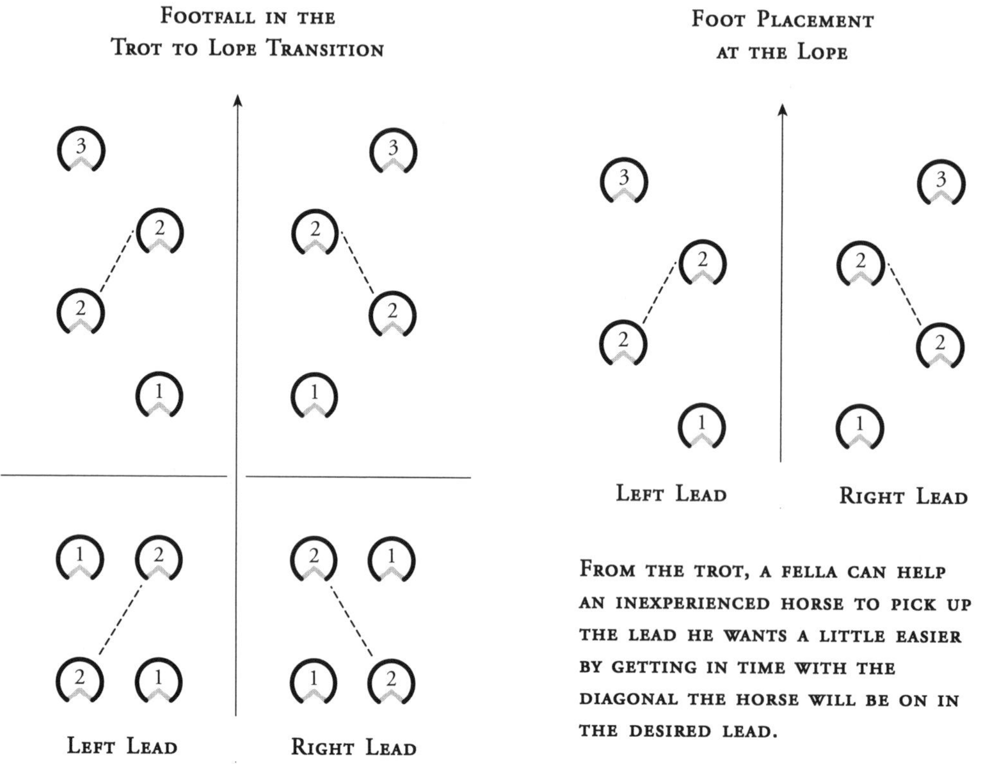

FROM THE TROT, A FELLA CAN HELP AN INEXPERIENCED HORSE TO PICK UP THE LEAD HE WANTS A LITTLE EASIER BY GETTING IN TIME WITH THE DIAGONAL THE HORSE WILL BE ON IN THE DESIRED LEAD.

Preparation for Loping and Lead Changes

The preparation you and your horse need for loping and lead changes should be built in far ahead of the time when you'd have a need for it. This could mean days or weeks or longer. It really all depends. To prepare a horse to lope on a specific lead, or to influence a lead change, a rider must understand what to feel for and how to present what they want to the horse in a way that the horse can understand. To change leads real smooth without causing tightness in him, the horse needs to understand *what* he's expected to do with his feet, and *when*. He can't know this if the rider doesn't know where the horse's feet are, and how they operate in all the gaits.

It's important for the rider to know the look and feel of both leads and really be sure of what's going on. If the plan is to switch leads while the horse is loping, it's best not to be relying on too much guesswork. Of course, people are going to do whatever they think they should do, but when the subject is changing leads, the lack of preparation can really get a horse mixed up, and not just about lead changes. It can carry over into a disappointing situation just in loping, generally, regardless of what lead might be involved. And this can be difficult to straighten out.

Once a horse loses his confidence about this maneuver, it can bring out some resistance and self-preservation in the horse when he's asked to do it. For me, the sad part in this is that changing leads correctly is an inborn ability that's tied right to the horse's self-preservation on the start. A lot of horses would keep that ability if people understood the importance of this preparation.

Get the Horse Comfortable at the Lope Before You Try Switching Leads

Before I present the horse with the idea to switch leads, I want him to be confident about loping along on both leads at an extended lope, and collected, too.

I like it best when the lope shows up after he can do the exercises mentioned earlier, and I'd prefer that any horse I'm riding can do all of these exercises in a relaxed and confident way. It's best if he can do them all real slow, and still have plenty of life available if I want him to lead up free and travel past me on the halter rope, and that's in both directions. Or, when I'm riding and have a job to do with him. I want him to be able to stop from the walk any time, and be able to make the shift down from the trot to a stop in a stride or two, and then move back up to the lope real smooth, with softness throughout his body. One thing I don't ever want him to do is push *at all* against the bit. Sometimes the lope shows up a little sooner than a person thinks it should, but no matter when he's ready to lope, it's best to try and go with him and not to interfere.

In the beginning, I like to ride him from the trot up to the lope, on either lead he chooses, and then slow back down to the trot again. We might only stay in the lope for a stride or two at first, or maybe even a few strides. We ease up to the lope, and come back down to the trot, then down to a walk, and finally we come slowly to a stop. I like to keep the horse feeling settled and pretty soft in my hands, but still completely attentive and responsive to me throughout his whole body. After he's stopped, I want to be able to rock him back a little, or step him back, without losing that softness. I'm feeling of him then and he's feeling of me. It's good for the horse's confidence when a person can lope a horse like this, and they'd do what they could to keep that good feel between them.

From there, we might leave again at a fast walk, in a slightly different direction. To do this, I just rock him back, or maybe take a step backwards with him, and then I open the new way up for him with my leading rein and leg. He should shift his weight back and reach a foreleg in the new direction opened up for him to take. My holding arm has a role here, of course. This reinforces an idea I want him to have, that he'll always want to wait to see where I might want him to go. It's not ever helpful to have a horse that overdoes the anticipation when it comes to leaving after you've stopped. Then we start out again at a real energetic walk, move up to the trot and then just ease up to the lope again. This doesn't have to be for too long. Really just until he can lope comfortably in any direction, on either lead. We aren't talking about drilling or "training" the horse here, this is just to expand his experience carrying someone on his back. We just want to have the horse feeling real comfortable while he moves out at the lope or the gallop, that's for sure.

I don't push him to stay in the lope. And I don't correct him if he's loping to the left on the right lead, or loping to the right on the left lead on the start — that comes later. When he's traveling like this, it's helpful to remember that his body is shaped where his mind wants to go, so I just get with him. When he's on a lead that isn't natural for him, considering the direction we're going, I'm there to support him the best I can so he doesn't get confused or upset as he's going along. If there's not much room for us to change directions and lope in another arc *so I can fit the lead he's on*, then I'll ease him back to the trot so he doesn't get any tighter than he already is. And he will be tight because he picked the wrong lead for the way we're going. If he was with me in the first place, then he'd have picked up the correct lead. My main concern here is getting together with the horse mentally and physically so he's *ready* to take the right lead, if he can, on the next try.

It always works out better if there's a lot of space for experimenting whenever you're starting to lope those young horses, or any horse that's at all bothered about loping or turning. So I'll assume there's plenty of room for us to lope or gallop around there when he's on the wrong lead. My job is to get with the horse, and I just look over towards where he's wanting to go. At about the same time, I adjust my leg position to fit the lead he picked and then I use my reins just as gentle and smooth as I can to support the message my legs give him, so he can just drift over to whatever direction fits him best for the lead he chose.

This way he learns that whatever lead or direction he decides to try is okay with me, and he can also learn two other things. The main thing I want him to know is that he's not in any trouble with me if the lead he's on doesn't feel quite right to him. And second, he learns that if his balance isn't how he needs it to be so he can stay in the lope, I'm there to help ease his body into a more comfortable position for him, to better fit the lead he thought he should be on. There's no time I'd ever want to present a poor feel to the horse because he chose one lead or another. Another thing I'd do a lot, is help a young horse slow to the trot so we could take a fresh start, or just bring him all the way down to the walk if that's what he was needing to do, for any reason. After he was settled and maybe had a few minutes to catch his breath, we might try loping again, or not. I want people to know there's no good reason to hurry a horse on this.

I want him to feel real comfortable loping, no matter what. This could happen in an afternoon, or in the course of a few days. Or it could take a lot longer. Really, it all depends on the horse, and the rider, and whatever is going on around there.

Each Lead Feels Different to the Rider

The leads feel real different from each other, and they also feel different from horse to horse. After I've ridden a horse a little on both leads and have gotten comfortable with the feel of each one, then I make sure he's feeling of me enough so that I can depart on either lead, slip back into the trot and then pick up the other lead. When that's good, then when we're loping around there, if he's not on the lead I prefer, why then *I just ride him as if he were on the lead I want him on.* If I've prepared him to feel of me, then riding him that way usually takes care of it, and the horse just goes over to the new lead.

When I'd like him to change leads again, I ride him the way it felt when he was on the other lead. If I haven't skipped those steps the horse needs in his groundwork and his mounted work to prepare him for this, then he will usually just follow the new feel over to the new lead as soon as I stop riding the other one.

One thing I'm pretty careful about on a horse that's just learning to get with me, is that I don't ever want to surprise him with the feel for quick stops or sharp turns. Those are liable to upset him. So, a person'd try real hard not to do that under any circumstances, but especially when the horse is uncertain about carrying them at the lope and changing leads.

Diamond Lu Collection

The preparation for a lope depart gets built in through feel, ahead of when it's time to try it.

Diamond Lu Collection

The horse steps into his right lead with a push from the left hind leg, and travels across the left diagonal. The (right) leading front leg is up and about to reach forward.

Emily Kitching

Side view of three feet on the ground in the right lead.

Lori Kline

The horse is balanced on the left diagonal and will step onto the (right) leading front leg to complete the stride.

Emily Kitching

23

This horse is taking the last step in a stride of the lope on his right lead.

The next six pictures show different views of a lope depart on the left lead.

Diamond Lu Collection

24

Starting from a standstill, this fella has gathered his horse up a little for a lope depart on the left lead.

Diamond Lu Collection

25

He steps into the left lead with a push from the right hind leg. He is about to step down on his supporting right diagonal.

Diamond Lu Collection

Side view of the left lead at almost the same spot as Figure 25. The right diagonal is about to step down.

Diamond Lu Collection

The horse's weight is being transferred from the right diagonal onto the (left) leading front leg.

Diamond Lu Collection

This shows a side view of the lope. His feet are just a little ahead of where they are in Figures 27 and 29.

Diamond Lu Collection

Another view of the left lead on a horse that appears enthused about going someplace.

Lead Changes aren't Mysterious to the Horse

Many things determine the lead a horse chooses when he's on his own. The main concern he has is to adjust his balance to fit each situation he comes across. For the most part, a horse is going to pick the lead that will keep him balanced.

Generally speaking, if he's balanced in a turn at the lope, he's going to be on the correct lead for that maneuver. Only some interference from the outside would change his natural tendency to be balanced in the best way. That outside influence isn't always a person by any means. He can take some less balanced steps if he runs across poor footing or if he needs to adjust his feet to avoid a hole, or maybe something he sees or hears startles him. There's no limit to what can distract a horse and cause him to suddenly change his leads on the spur of the moment. No, anything can come into a horse's awareness that a person might not even know about because it was so slight. But usually that horse will stay upright and things will work out good for him. Sometimes a horse might fall, and sometimes a horse might fall and not ever get up, but it's fortunate that this doesn't happen too often.

When the lead he's on doesn't offer him the best support for wherever his feet are about to go, a horse will switch leads naturally. If you get a chance to watch a lot of horses moving around, you can see how easy they switch the lead they're on when there's a need for them to adjust their balance. I'd say the way they can do this comes somewhere under the heading of "instincts," but there's decision-making figuring pretty heavy in there, too. In most cases, a horse will just walk or trot up to the lope. But in your preparation, you'd sure want your horse to be able to leave real smooth from a standstill into a lope depart on either lead. You'd depart from a gallop on either lead from a standstill, too — and get that real good and smooth before you'd ever want the horse to change leads for you while he was loping.

Like I spoke about earlier, horses are born with the physical ability to change leads and the mental capacity to judge when they should. It's not our job to teach them how to do this. People take a lot of different approaches when they try to get a horse to change leads and the subject confuses them. Sometimes the confusion they have about this shows up in the horse when he's asked to switch leads, or even just when he's loping, because he anticipates that he'll have to do this in a way that's difficult for him. I'll say that the best thing to do before any lead changes are put to the test, is to get a horse comfortable loping on both leads from the trot. When that's good, then make a lot of simple lead changes by slowing down to the trot and loping again after that.

The Way a Horse Changes Leads can Vary

When a horse changes leads, it might be that he switches in front or behind first, and then in the next stride he'll catch up with his other legs to complete the lead change.

It feels the best to me when the front and hind legs switch their jobs at the same time, and the second-best feel is a lead change that is started by a hind foot. The order of changing I don't much like is a front-foot-first lead change, but that's just a personal preference. As long as the horse stays balanced and relaxed, and doesn't need to speed up or get tight in the change, it really doesn't matter too much how he goes about changing the lead.

When the front and hind pairs of legs switch leads together, that feels real smooth and some people call it a simultaneous lead change. This happens when no feet are on the ground between the last beat of one loping stride and the first beat of the next one.

Simultaneous Lead Changes

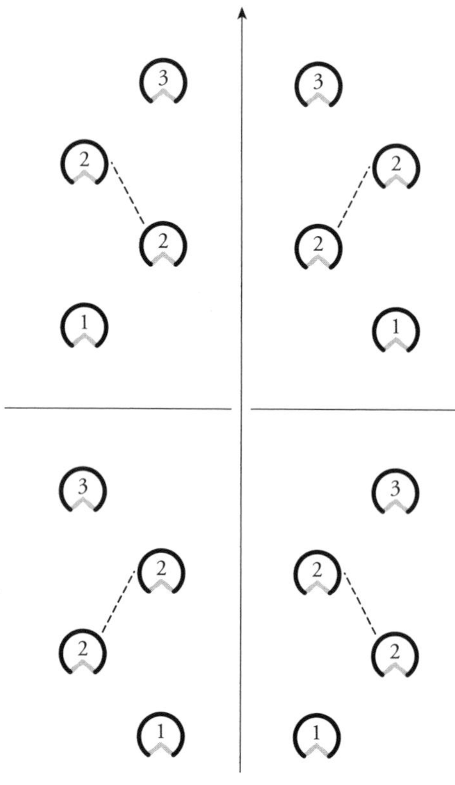

From Left to Right **From Right to Left**

The paint horse in Figure 30 has his left front foot on the ground and he's ready to bring the right hind leg underneath him again to take another stride. If the horse and the rider were prepared to change leads at this point, he could start the next stride with the left hind foot instead, and he would look just a little different than it does here, if that was his plan.

If the feel to change leads has been understood by the rider and the horse, then when the horse is at the best place to change that lead, he will, and it's usually when the horse can put down whichever back leg is best for the balancing job he's got ahead of him. As long as the feel to change the lead goes all the way through the horse, the front legs will change position too and then there's no problem with him ending up on two leads. When a person's just starting on all this, it's helpful to know that the horse is liable to pick the best lead for him to be on because nature set him up that way on the start. But, people have a habit of needing to see if they can just come in there and get a lead change when they'd like it to. There's nothing wrong with that, so long as that horse understands what's expected of him.

Diamond Lu Collection

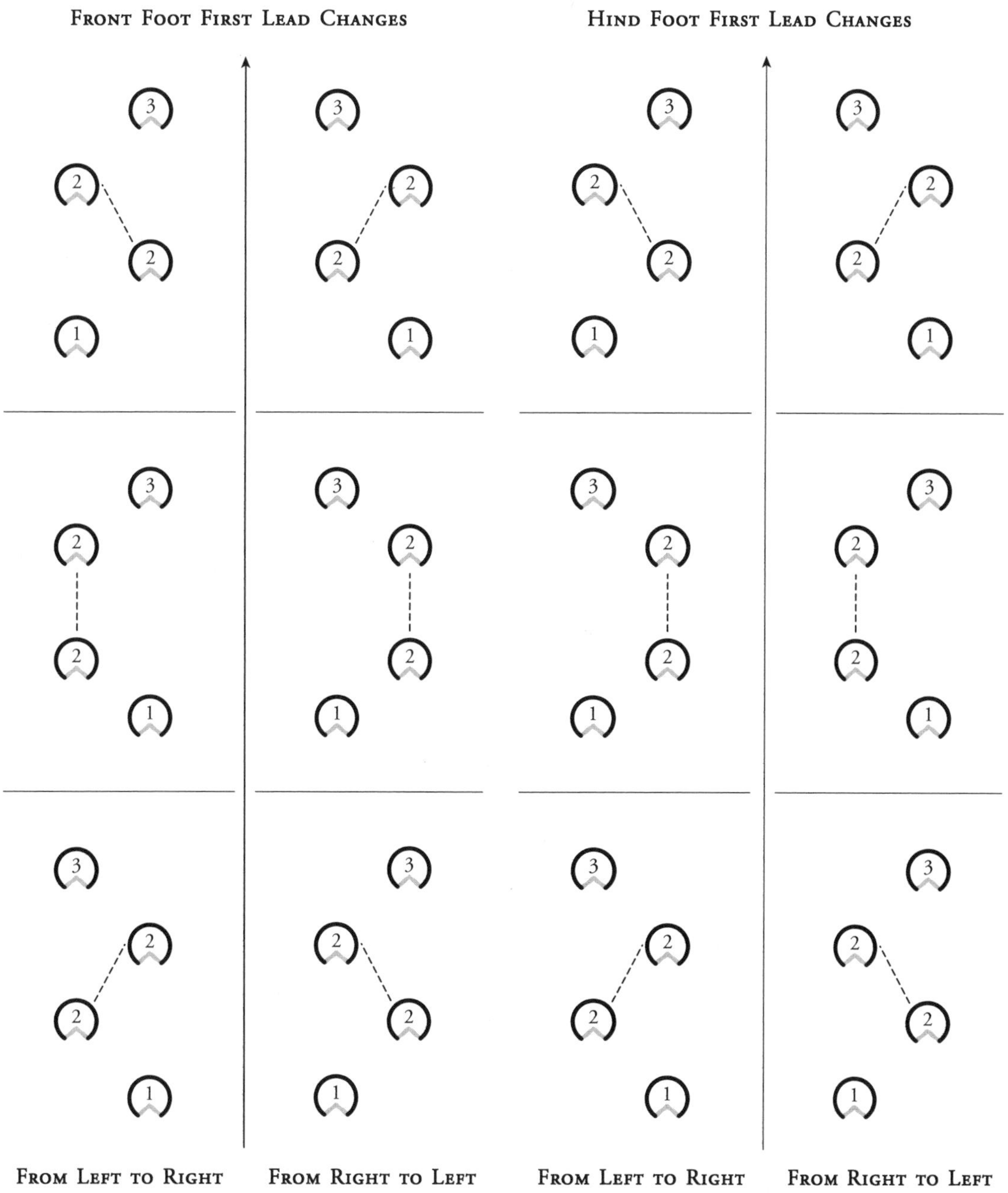

Front Foot First Lead Changes | **Hind Foot First Lead Changes**

From Left to Right | **From Right to Left** | **From Left to Right** | **From Right to Left**

In Figure 31, the horse in front is at a spot where the leading leg is about to come off the ground. This horse is on a right lead, and appears concerned about the motions of this other horse coming up on her left side.

31

Diamond Lu Collection

The thing to remember about leads changes is that in order for the horse to keep his balance at the lope, *if one leg switches functions, then all his legs must rearrange themselves* to give that horse the stability he needs for the job he has, at the speed he's going. There's a change of lead only when the front legs and the back legs change their position. This creates a new diagonal to support the horse in the lope.

One thing about the horse's balance in the middle of each lope stride is that it really helps him to maintain (or regain) his balance, and his straightness, even in those real tight turns. But another interesting aspect is that some horses like to travel at a slight angle in the lope. Maybe it'd be helpful for a person starting out to know that this angle has a natural place in the way a horse carries himself as he goes along. That way they won't think they ought to correct this. A horse can sure be taught to travel real straight at the lope, but you'd wait on that.

In some horses this angle is real noticeable. If it is, or it isn't, a fella should make sure his own body is heading straight towards where he's wanting to go, and not try to take on that angled way of riding, because if that gets to be a set pattern for him, it could hinder him and his horse further up the line. Depending on what foot placement is going to be needed on the spur of the moment, if you're riding a horse that's bad to switch leads or gets on the buck for some other reason when he's at the lope, why sitting with a twist or a slant to your posture could unbalance the whole shebang and unseat you pretty quick. And if someone's riding two-handed and sitting this way, well, the reins aren't going to be even for one thing, and the slack won't get taken out evenly when a fella stops his horse or turns.

This can be confusing to a horse, and limit the sensitivity he could have available for that rider one day. No, you'd hope to be sitting right in the middle of your horse, with your body as even as you can be on both sides. When that's how you sit on your horse, he will have a much better chance of staying with your whole body feel. Good balance is what gives a horse the most confidence when he's loping, no matter what job you have for him.

Balancing at the Lope and the Gallop

A horse's self-preservation instincts cause the horse to want to stay on his feet most any way he can. It's usually only interference from a human that causes him to keep maneuvering in an unbalanced way. For an example, if he's traveling on one lead with the front legs and the other lead with the back legs, why that's not natural. It isn't too safe and the horse knows it, due to his instincts of self-preservation. When your horse is on two leads, one in front and one behind, they say he's "disunited" at the lope.

If only the front legs or the hind legs switch position at the lope, this throws the horse off balance. That's because the supporting diagonal he used for balance in the other lead is no longer available until his hind legs switch their position and their job. When they do catch up, then there will be a new diagonal available to him in the new lead. This awkward way to lope can also happen when the back legs change jobs and the front legs stay the way they were on the old lead.

When the feet land this undesirable way at the lope, it's a problem in the turns because his main way to stay balanced is missing entirely. It's not safe to lope this way. Another reason you'd plan to keep the lead intact is that the horse is balanced on only one foot in two out of the three beats in every stride. This is an actual fact the horse knows about. He needs to keep his balance in *any* forward, sideways or backward movement, not just at the lope. Imbalance can occur on a straightaway, in a turn, when the footing changes, if the rider loses his balance or just about anytime — and you'd wish it wouldn't.

Well, there's hope, because there's no need for this lack of balance to show up in a horse that's well prepared, through feel. No, a person's going to prepare his horse to lope without this problem. And that word "problem" won't need to be mentioned, not when the subject concerns loping, or a horse.

When the Horse Lacks Balance, He's Going to be Short on Confidence

Generally speaking, a horse is directed to change leads only in front, or only in back, when his rider lacks feel and has poor timing, or when the rider's balance isn't the best. When this happens, the horse may travel crooked like that for a little ways just to keep from falling over. What's amazing to me is that the first step he takes like this might be what's necessary to keep him from falling right then, and the second stride he takes this way, if he doesn't get that lead corrected, can cause him to fall down. It doesn't always happen this way, of course. It just all depends on so many variables.

When the horse is loping disunited because his front legs changed leads first, he might be able to catch up his hind legs to match the new lead of the front legs. If he can't, why a fella should never force that horse to change leads — he can just drop back to a trot and take a fresh start. Or, if he keeps on going along there, that horse might be able to regain his balance by getting his front legs changed back in time with the leading position and rhythm of the lead that those hind legs were in. This is just a general observation of what can happen, but for every horse, of course, there's variations that will take place.

The drawings and pictures on the next page show what can happen when a horse changes leads only in front, or only in back, without matching up the other pair of legs. Figure 32 shows how a horse's feet land on the ground when he's loping with his leads disunited. In this picture, his front legs are arranged in the same way that they'd travel on the *left* lead, but the hind legs set are set up the same way they'd be if was loping to the *right*. In Figure 33, the horse's front legs show their position in a *right* lead, and the hind legs are set up as they'd be if he was loping to the *left*. These foot placement setups show a lack of balance. Of course, this is an example that we set up at the standstill especially for these pictures. A person would need to have some imagination about how it would feel to be loping on legs that landed this way.

Foot Placement for Demonstration of Disunited Leads

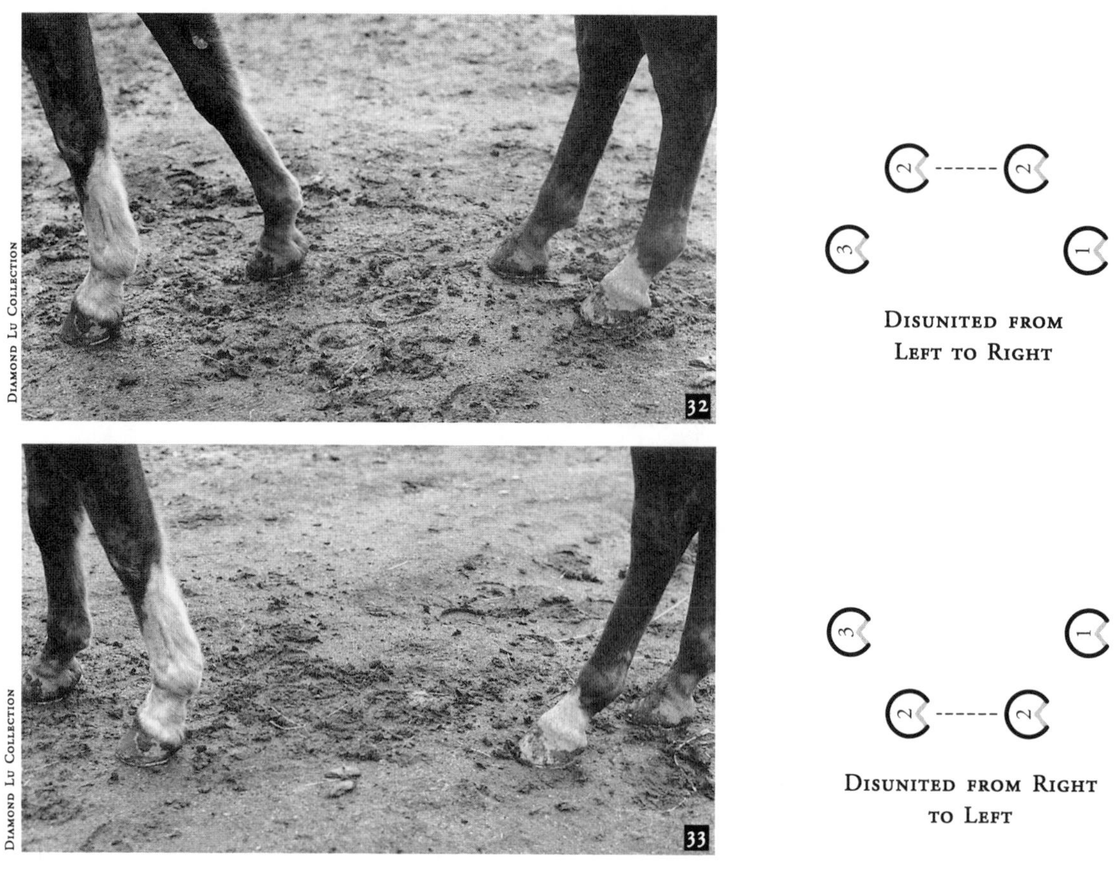

Nothing is out of the ordinary about a horse standing this way. But at the lope, we'd rather it was a little different.

It's not the best to lope too many strides when the horse is disunited. If the horse isn't able to unite his leads, why a fella wants to drop back to the trot for a stride or two, and just help him *get ready* to step up to the lope again. This is called making a "simple lead change" or a "drop-to-a-trot" lead change, and a horse needs to get confident doing this. When a horse regains his balance, this gives his confidence in the rider quite a boost and his sureness about traveling at the lope gets fixed up quite a little, too.

Footfall at the Gallop

The gallop is a four-beat gait. Regardless of which lead your horse is on, when the lope speeds up to the gallop, the supporting diagonal disappears on its own, because each foot lands separately. That's because the second beat in the lope stretches out and turns into two separate beats. That's how the three-beats of the lope turn into four. The hind feet land first, one at a time, and then the front legs come down, one at a time, and they get picked up the same way. That's because the horse is pushing a lot harder with the second hind foot when it lands and this is what gives him the extra reach he needs in the front legs. He can cover a lot more ground faster that way. In some ways the gallop is no different than the lope, meaning whichever lead the horse is on at the lope will stay the same at the gallop, until it doesn't. And that could be for a lot of reasons, but the extra speed required for the gallop will not cause that lead to change, or make it unstable for the horse.

While a horse is galloping, he will have one foot, two feet or three feet on the ground. Or, you might happen to look when he has no feet on the ground at all. That'd be the time just after the leading leg leaves the ground, and before the opposite hind foot sets back down again. You could say there's a cushion of air under him then, because for a second there is. Some horses have a real good feel at the gallop, especially when there's good footing underneath them.

FOOTFALL IN THE LOPE TO GALLOP TRANSITION

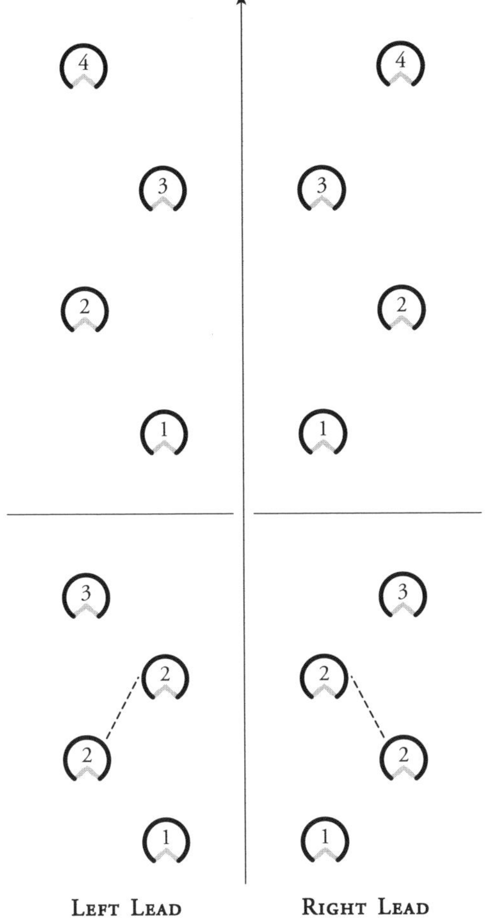

DIAMOND LU COLLECTION

FIRST STEP IN THE GALLOP, LEFT LEAD. THE FEET LAND ONE AT A TIME, AND COME OFF THE GROUND THE SAME WAY.

DIAMOND LU COLLECTION

SECOND AND THIRD STEPS IN THE GALLOP, RIGHT LEAD. THE WHITE HORSE IS ABOUT TO START A NEW STRIDE AT THE GALLOP, RIGHT LEAD.

Diamond Lu Collection

Second, third and fourth steps in the gallop, left lead. This horse is learning to take off in a gallop in a stretched-out position. The reins are in good position and the rider is balanced, so he's not interfering with that horse.

Diamond Lu Collection

Fourth step in the gallop, left lead. In the time that follows this step — when the horse's feet are all off the ground — the horse will continue to arrange his back legs to push forward into the next stride. The right hind leg is already getting in position for this.

Diamond Lu Collection

All four feet in the air, between strides at the gallop, left lead. What a horse in this situation really appreciates is a rider who understands feel and knows a lot about what's going on. And where it concerns placement of those feet at a gallop, why those words "a lot" take in a lot.

When you slow down to a lope again, why that slower motion puts the diagonal pair of legs back in there, and those three separate beats of the lope can be heard again. This provides the horse and the person on his back more stability for turns or anything else that they need to do.

Generally speaking, the horse's balance doesn't get too far off at the gallop unless he's on the wrong lead at the lope to start with. If this happens, it sure isn't the best situation. When he's traveling this way, you'd better get him slowed way down. Take him all the way back to the trot before you'd ever *think* about trying to double him. There isn't any question about that. A fella oughtn't take that risk because he's liable to get bunged up, and that horse might get hurt, too.

Exercises to Help Prepare You and Your Horse for Lead Changes and Other Maneuvers

- Prepare your horse to follow the feel of the halter rope and the reins so you can place his head and neck anyplace he's physically able to, within reason. That'd be up and down and around in both directions, and by combining lateral flexion and vertical together. This brings out the better appearance in most any horse.
- Get your horse to lead up real free. You'd want to be able to liven up the horse on the spur of the moment, and also take the time it takes to step him forwards and backwards going real slow, one step at a time. Be sure to allow him to stop in between each step. Both of these things are important to have built in real solid on the ground and from the horse's back, if your plans include true horsemanship through feel. A good many people will be amazed when they realize that their horse has been waiting a long time for them to get onto this. It's one thing to gain an understanding about feel, but getting it applied in a way that the horse can understand is altogether different. We're in hopes this will work out for them, because nothing I know of compares to this, not where it concerns horses. My main goal is to help people learn that if their horse understands them, there's not much he won't try to accomplish for a person. This is the most important thing I've learned so far.

39

Diamond Lu Collection

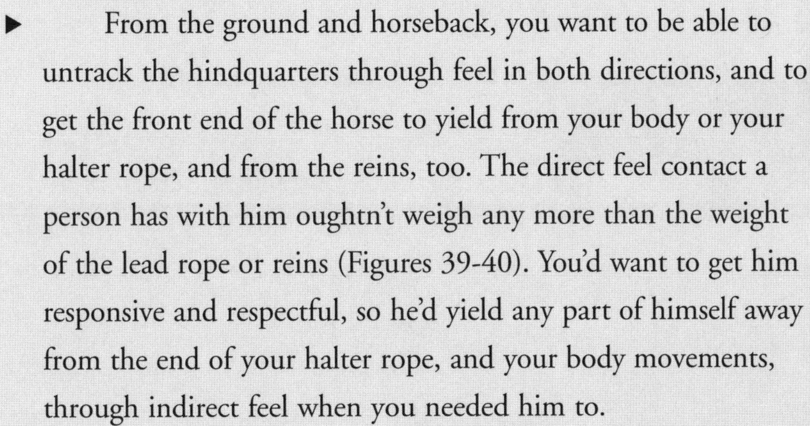

- From the ground and horseback, you want to be able to untrack the hindquarters through feel in both directions, and to get the front end of the horse to yield from your body or your halter rope, and from the reins, too. The direct feel contact a person has with him oughtn't weigh any more than the weight of the lead rope or reins (Figures 39-40). You'd want to get him responsive and respectful, so he'd yield any part of himself away from the end of your halter rope, and your body movements, through indirect feel when you needed him to.

40

Diamond Lu Collection

- You'd hope to have a horse with light and sensitive responses. When something interferes with that progress, you'd want one idea at the top of your thinking, and that'd be to *not do too much*. At the same time, *you'd always be ready to do whatever was needed* even if the firmness that was required took your full strength. If those firmer actions were needed, a fella'd want to remember that the timing of his release after that would be real important, even more important than at other times. Of course, he'd be wanting to time his release the best he knew how, anyway. And the idea about doing less, whenever he could, would always be in a fella's mind if there was a horse around.

▶ Ride with feel as you practice making those smoother transitions. Ride from the slow walk up to the fast walk, into the trot and then up to a fast trot. Then you can let it fade a little. Let it die down some, and he'll pick up your feel for slowing down. No pulling whatsoever is involved in this. Then, you'd feel for that life in him to come up and forward. From a walk, through the trot and then, maybe, up to the lope just for a stride or two, and go back down again. Go real easy, until you can adjust your feel of him to go a little faster, or slower, or at any speed in between. That horse'd stay right with your feel, on account of his willingness to do so and your desire to have it that better way. A fella's going to need to get this in place real solid, and in both directions.

▶ Practice a lot of simple lead changes. Come out of a turn at the lope, ride him back to the trot, and then ride straight ahead for a little ways, and *when he's ready*, ease up to the lope and come out on the new lead.

▶ Before I'd try to get the horse to change leads I'd figure on a lot of starting and stopping. This is real gradual work. You'll build in a lively walk from the standstill, and you'd want that horse to have plenty of enthusiasm to trot out from a standstill, too. When that's good, then you'd lope from a standstill. He needs to be able to leave at the gallop, on either lead you want. And in all the gaits, you'd be sure he was real comfortable, if he's collected, or not.

Diamond Lu Collection

▶ Praise the horse often, but not with feed. The best way a person can show their good feelings to the horse is through feel — that's praise enough. Well-timed releases mean the most to a horse. And rubbing on their necks and shoulders, or scratching anywhere that feels good to them, why, it's real important to a horse that a person has some knowledge about this.

Chapter 6:

TRAILER LOADING

I KNEW A FELLA WHO USED TO BACK HIS HORSE TRAILER into the barn door and in that area behind the trailer — 30 or 40 feet or so — he'd drive those horses around with a broom and they got to looking for a place to go. If they didn't stay in the trailer, well, when they came out of there, he'd just keep them going around in that area until their self-preservation made them look up a reason to go in that trailer. Like putting cattle in the chute. You might have a horse that doesn't think that chute looks too good, but you wouldn't force him in, you just keep him real busy in the pen and he'll start looking for someplace to go where you'll leave him alone. This is sure one way of teaching a horse to load.

To my way of thinking, a fella has a great responsibility to the horse whenever the subject concerns trailers. There's another way to go about this, and that is by using feel. This is the approach I prefer to take because the horse understands it. Some things you can do are specific to trailer loading and these are most beneficial to the horse and the person if they are practiced ahead of time. Trailers can be real dangerous places for horses, and for people too, because it's quite unnatural for them to be in a trailer in the first place. Getting into a trailer is where the horse needs extra direction and support from a person, and it's important to prepare him for this real slow — a lot slower than a person might imagine.

KIM MURPHY

1

KIM MURPHY

2

FOALS HAVE A NATURAL WILLINGNESS THAT IS TIED TO CURIOSITY.

Preparing the Horse to Load

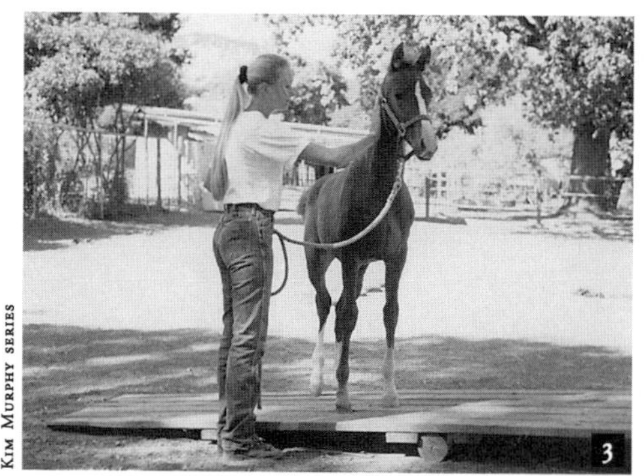

Kim Murphy series

The leading and backing up exercises we spoke about in Chapter 4 are good preparation to help your horse feel comfortable getting in and out of a trailer — any kind of trailer. After he can lead forward and back up one step at time, you can introduce some objects that will help prepare him to be more at ease in and around the trailer, like these pictures show (Figures 1-12).

A rub on the neck will reassure the horse. You'd want to get his attention back in your direction before he makes plans of his own.

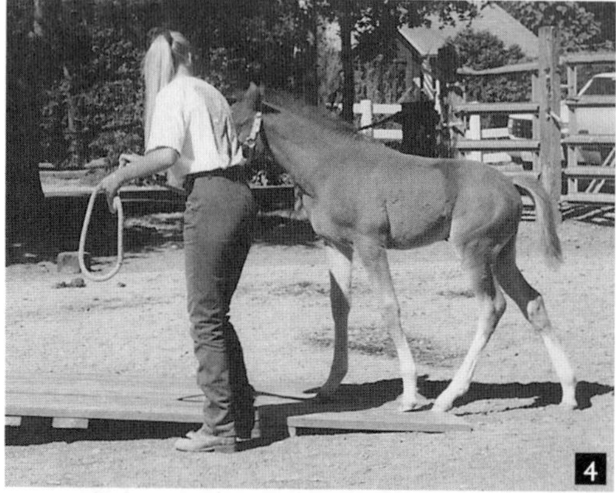

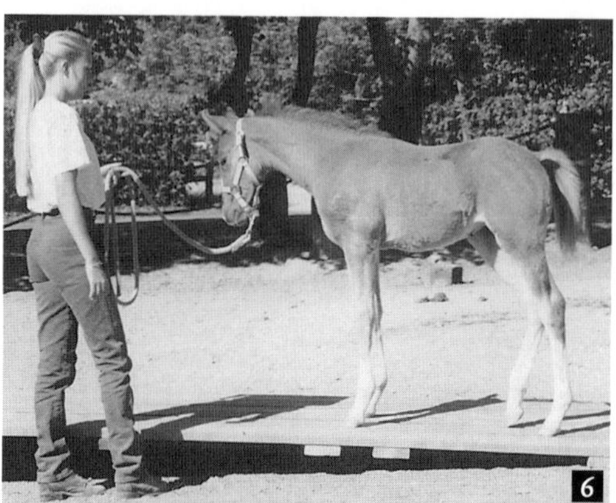

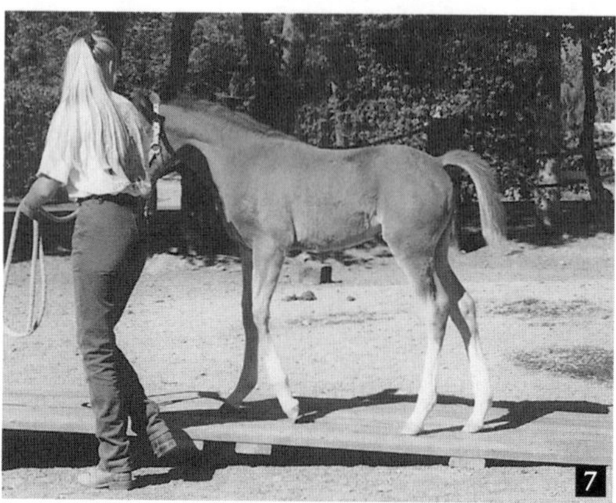

The feel you build into leading and backing helps a foal gain confidence to try new things. With feel built into his foundation, a horse is more willing to put his feet on strange objects. You'd take plenty of time with him here because it's so important that he learns to feel comfortable in strange surroundings. If things didn't go smooth for him in the trailer, he'd have some good experience to fall back on.

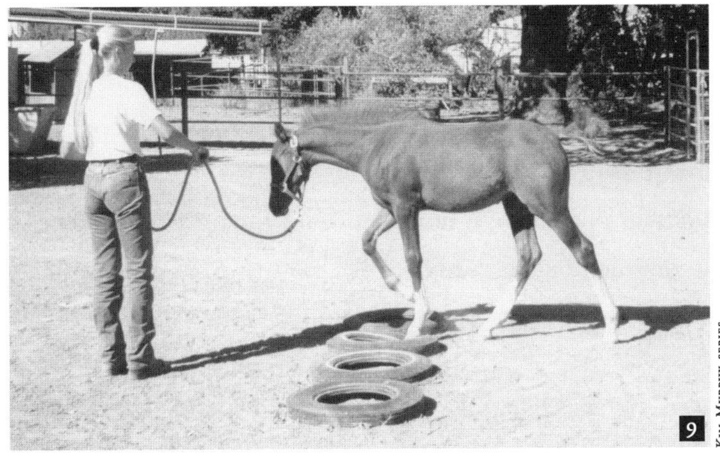

Kim Murphy series

Soon he'll be comfortable walking just about anywhere with a person who's learned to use feel.

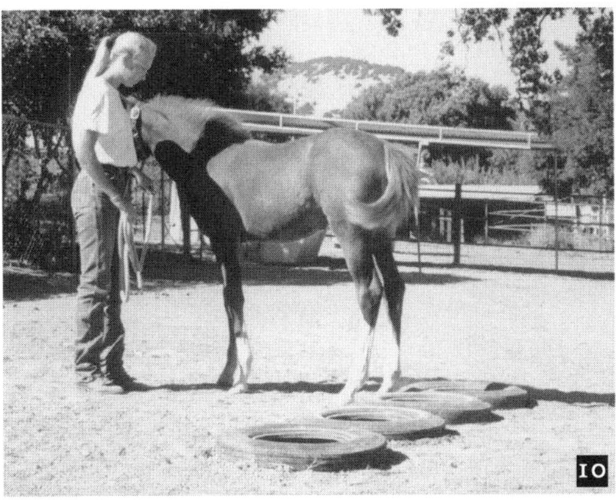

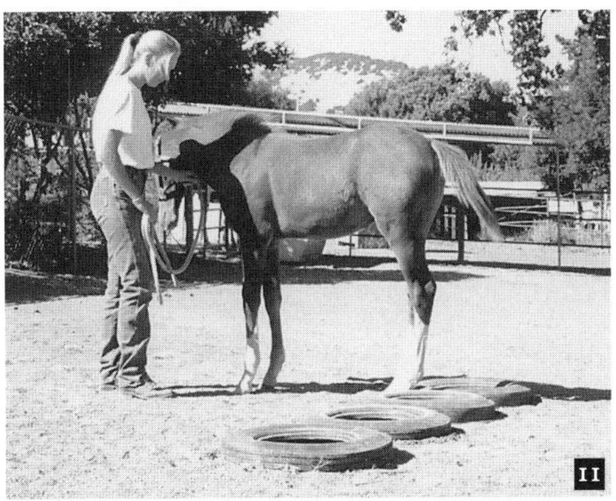

Take your time teaching him to back on and off small things. He should learn that he can do this before he's asked to back out of a trailer. No force should come into this whatsoever, because that foal will go along with your plan if it's presented to him so he can understand. This preparation will pay off later on.

Working in a Corner

Once your horse is feeling of you doing those exercises in Chapter 4, you can do a little more work to prepare him for trailer loading by working in an "L"-shaped corner. All you need is a halter and lead rope and a little stick, about three-feet long. You'd not do this with a horse that's liable to kick you — you'd go back down the line a ways to get him better prepared for this, through feel.

Position the horse in the corner so his hind end is toward one part of that "L" in the fence and his right or left side is alongside the other part of that fence. If you're right-handed, you'll position the horse with his right side along the fence (Figures 13-15). Later, switch him around and drive him up with your left arm. You need to stay safe, so don't crowd him. Your position is also real important and at first you should be in a position to drive him forward — *and be sure to allow him to go forward when he tries to move.* If you stay in the right position and don't rush this, the fences will discourage him from backing up or going out to the side, away from you. Put a little life into that stick, or give him a little tap on the top of his butt with it, just enough so he gets the idea he's supposed to step forward. This will carry over later to motions you make toward him with the lead rope instead of a stick. He'll be getting the idea that when you move toward his butt with life in your body and that lead rope, he should be making plans to move forward and straight ahead, straight away. This is real valuable to build in.

Lori Smith

13

When he goes forward, kind of go with him, even if he goes fast. If you've got him feeling of you from doing those exercises in Chapter 4, he oughtn't go too fast as long as you don't hit him too hard. You'll go with him on the start until he gets onto the idea of moving forward, but you never let the slowing down part get too far away from him, because you don't want to teach him to escape from you, or to anticipate anything you might want him

Lori Smith

14

to do because he's liable to set his own schedule for it. *There's just a real fine line in there.* To head this off, you wouldn't tap him, or even make a motion like you were thinking about it, after he made even a small try to get going forward along that fence.

15

LORI SMITH

Another thing we don't want a horse to do is hop in and out of the trailer. To some people, it might look like the horse loads real good when he goes in this way, but what they don't think about is he probably unloads about the same as he goes in, and that can be dangerous. To be safe and reliable, the horse needs to step in there and back out real slow, one foot at a time. *That's how you want it to go, regardless of the horse's age or his past, and no matter which side he's loaded from.*

When he steps up forward, why you'll just give him the best feel to stop that you can, through your lead rope, and then back him up one step or two, real slow. This is similar to those exercises in Chapter 4, but the "L" shaped corner's going to feel real confining to him, just like the trailer will. And, generally speaking, the corner will be a safer place to get this working for you. Be sure not to put too much pressure on him, and don't crowd those hindquarters and put him on the defense about this. If he's that way, you're doing too much.

Teach Him to Back Up by Pulling on His Tail

It's best if your horse will stand in a straight-ahead trailer after the butt chain is down and wait for you to pull on his tail to back out. He's learned to wait and to feel of you when he can do that. Once in awhile, you might have to help a horse up at the halter to get him started back out. Some horses will want to fly back out of there and with that sort of horse especially, you'd want to get him used to taking little steps inside the trailer, forward and back, without ever getting to the back edge of the trailer. You'd want to spend time preparing him to back out safely one step at a time long before you lead or send him into the trailer.

You can teach him to back up like this in the corner, stepping up there beside his butt and gently pulling on his tail (Figure 16). Of course, you'd not do this with a horse that's inclined to kick at you. On a horse like that you'd first need to help that horse get more comfortable with you back there. And if he's all right with you back there, then you'd lift up his tail a little, and just as he shifts his weight back, then you'd ease off any pull on his tail. A person would continue to build on this until they could just pull on a few of those tail hairs to get him to back up.

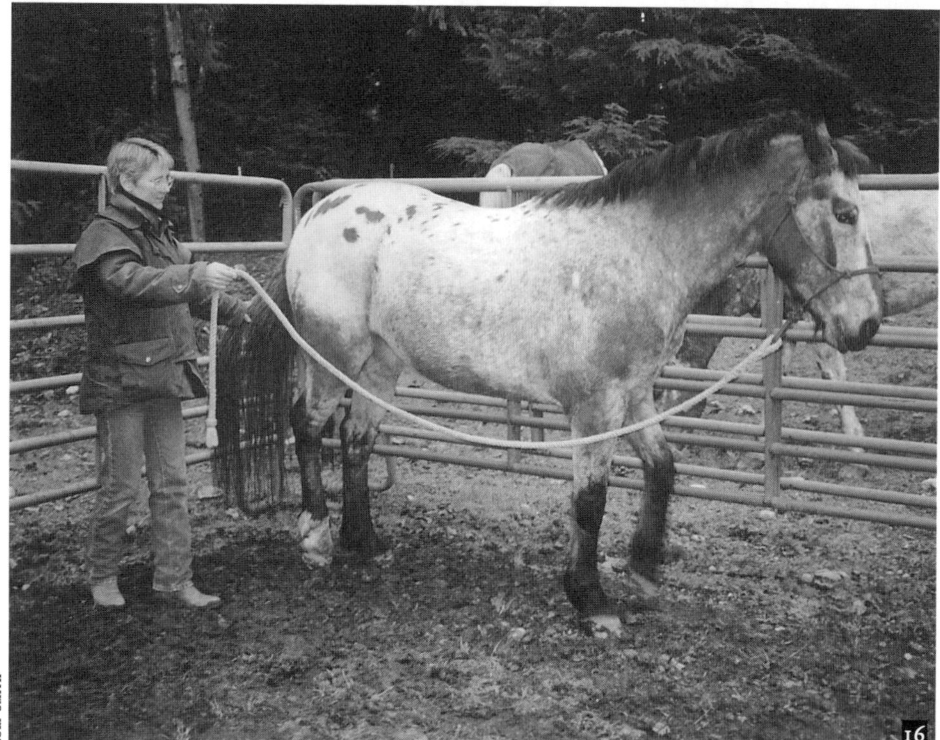

Lori Smith

16

After he can step forward and back real nice and slow in that corner, why he'll be ready to go over near that trailer.

At the Trailer, You'll Build on His Willingness to Move

Lead your horse over to the trailer and line him up a little ways back from the open trailer door. Put a little life in your body and the lead rope — or stick, if you're still wanting to use it — so he steps forward. Make sure your body or the arm that's holding the lead rope is not blocking the trailer entrance. You'll build on his willingness to step towards the trailer by easing off when he shifts his weight forward or takes a step up to the end of the floor or the ramp. And then you'll just do like you did in that corner, and back him up a step or two. He's apt to want to smell in there a little, or poke his nose around inside, and that's all right at first. He's testing out the situation in the only way he knows how. You'd go along with a little of this as long as he was feeling of you. *Don't put the whole horse in the trailer on the start.*

The Horse Needs to Get Comfortable, One Step at a Time

When he's close enough to step a foot into the trailer, a fella's going to come out way ahead if he just works on getting one front foot in and out. On the start, you don't want to let him go all the way in. *He needs to learn how to get out as he's learning how to get in.* There's no advantage whatsoever to a horse that will get in the trailer but has no idea how to get out of there safely. As you teach him how to take one step in and then

17 18 19 20 21 22

Joan Glass series

take a step out, you'll want to be able to stop him anytime. In your experimenting, which ought to take place on the slow side where a trailer is concerned, the horse needs to get used to standing there real calm with half his body in the trailer and half outside. He needs to get comfortable with three feet in and one foot out, too, in all combinations and with different front feet going in on the start. If you'd rub that horse on his neck, his shoulder and his butt from time to time while he's learning about this, it's helpful. Some horses need quite a little reassurance at this so they're safe to handle in and around a trailer. Unfortunately, what gets so many horses bad to trailer is people having no idea that the horse has no idea about any of it.

If a person is inclined to skip over the basic preparation a horse needs to have before his first exposure to the trailer, they might also be inclined to rush a horse through his first introduction to the trailer, too. The main reason is, some people don't think they have the time. That's what some of them say. Others say it isn't necessary. Well, surprising things can happen when a person goes about things this way, and they probably will. No, when they rush a horse through the trailering part, there's a big chance that in the future they'll get real familiar with spending that time they thought they didn't have before. If this happens, I'm in hopes that these people will get right to work on the basics.

Some people are going to try to fix a trailer loading problem by applying a lot of extra pressure to the horse at the back of the trailer. If they do this, why they've still missed it and quite a little more time will have to be spent if they are going to help that horse get a clear understanding about what he was expected to do on the start. If luck figures in there for them, they won't get hurt and the horse won't either. Of course, not everyone who's skipped the basics on this can say they had luck. The good part about all of this is that if they get properly prepared, they oughtn't be in need of luck.

It's real important that he can lower his head for you and that he's feeling of you here, because when he gets his head started in that trailer and stops, which most horses do, he might raise his head and bump it when you pull on the lead rope a little bit to back him out. Once he's bumped his head a time or two, he's liable to just fly back out of there as fast as he can at the next best opportunity he finds. It's a terrible thing when this happens, because it's entirely avoidable. It's a hard habit to get a horse over, so it's best to head that one off before it ever gets started. *You'd do all you could to prevent that horse from getting anywhere near an episode, or another person, that will scare him in or around a trailer.*

A horse needs to get comfortable shifting his weight from one foot to another and stepping up and back inside any trailer. This will help to head off any inclination he'd have to hurry out. As he steps back out, you want to get him calm and mellow, so you can stop him any place, and lower his head. Then step him forward, or back him up again. The adjustability of the horse's head and neck, and the handler's ability to maneuver those feet in the trailer and anywhere around it, is what ensures the safety of all parties involved. Two horses at different stages of development are shown backing out (Figures 17-22).

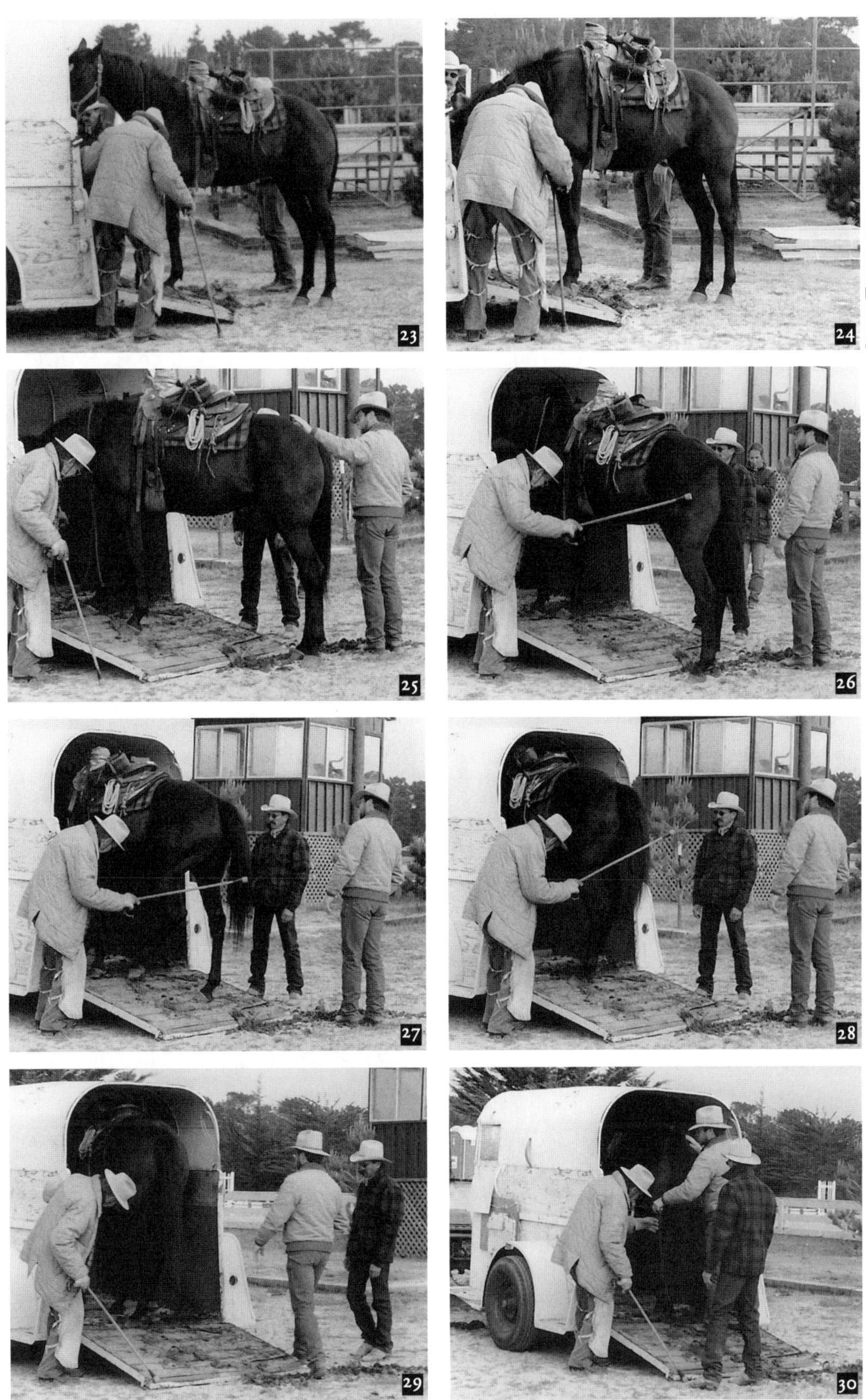

Patricia Weedman series

There isn't much room for Beaut in my trailer, but she can still fit in there with a saddle on. A fella wants to be sure he uses those saddle strings to tie his stirrups up over the top of his saddle before he'd try to load a horse this way.

When a horse is skeptical about a situation, it helps to reassure that horse by rubbing them on the butt with your hand. I got Beaut real used to moving up along a fence when I tapped her on the butt with a short stick, so she knew what to do when I tapped her with my cane. And I think a horse sometimes has a different outlook depending on if you're leaving home or not. But, that shouldn't make a difference in the results — only in the feel and how you adjust to fit the horse right then.

Once you get him stepped up all the way in there with all four feet in the trailer, why you've got to be careful that tension doesn't come into your lead rope and get him started backing out unless you're wanting him to come out. And don't let that lead rope get on the floor in there where he can step on it. Maybe he'd pull his head up real fast and hit the trailer roof with his head. This experience should be avoided.

When the Horse Gets Sticky

You can see from these pictures that this horse isn't too comfortable with the idea of getting in the trailer. It can be real difficult to load a horse that's had some bad trailer experience when you're alone, and when there isn't much time. But these conditions are quite common, and a fella has to do the best he can.

31

Kim Murphy

The horse in Figure 31 is halfway in and could step up or back depending on what the person felt would work best here.

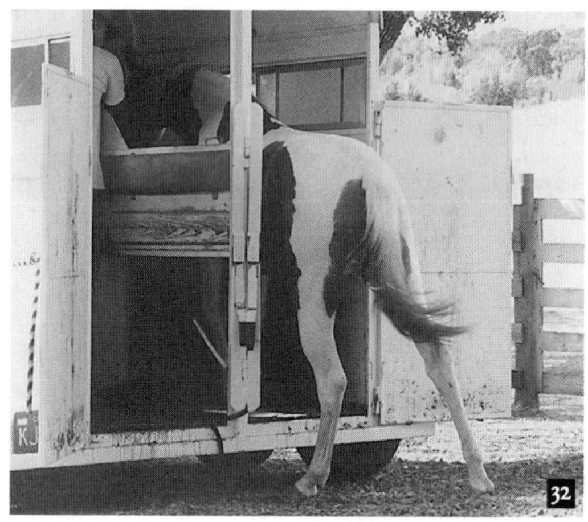

32

Kim Murphy

In Figure 32, the horse stepped forward with his left hind foot, and then moved the right hind foot back, and this gives him a real unsure appearance. There's activity in that tail which could just be from flies or a breeze. I don't know because I wasn't there. It could be the horse is thinking he might need to fly back out of there, and if he is thinking that, why a kink could have come into his tail, all right. That lead rope somehow got dropped on the ground, and sometimes this is unavoidable when you're working alone. You'd always try to keep track of it so that horse didn't step on it and get scared.

You can see in Figure 33 that the horse's balance improved some after he brought that right hind leg up underneath him quite a little more, but he's got that tight look to him and here's where you'd maybe have some other things in mind for him to do with his feet besides standing there much longer.

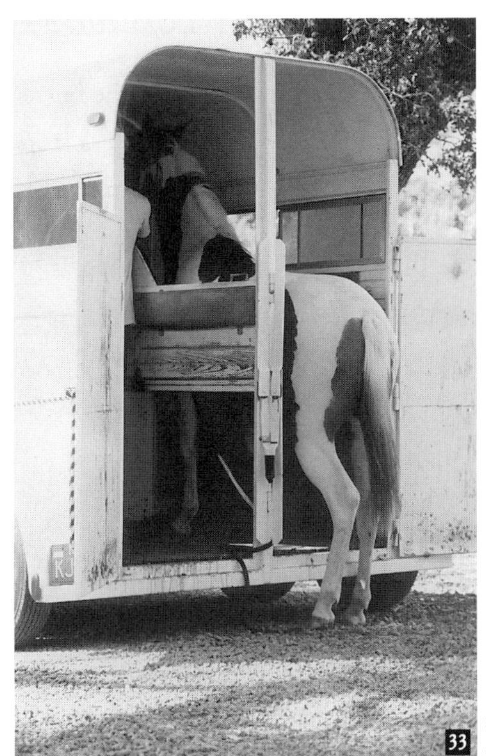

33

Kim Murphy

He's repositioned those back feet again in Figure 34, and it seems this horse might be ready for a step back now. The young fella has gathered up that lead rope and is offering the horse some reassurance up in front of the trailer.

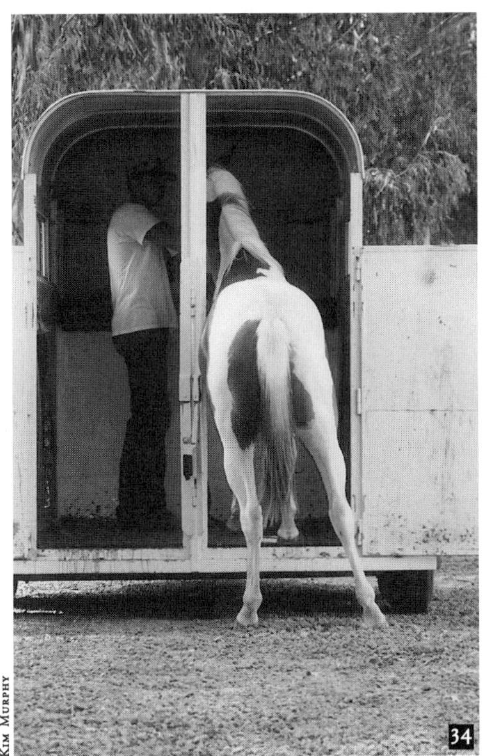

34

Kim Murphy

One thing that's not the best about still pictures is that you can't be sure about so many of the little things that are taking place. But, from how that horse is standing in Figure 35 it looks like he might be the kind to benefit from a little feed being in that manger. If there wasn't any feed to put in there, you'd have some the next time. He does seem a little more relaxed than he was in some earlier pictures. We aren't sure how much practice the horse had shifting his weight back that day, but at least it appears that there was some improvement along the way and no sign of roughness at all.

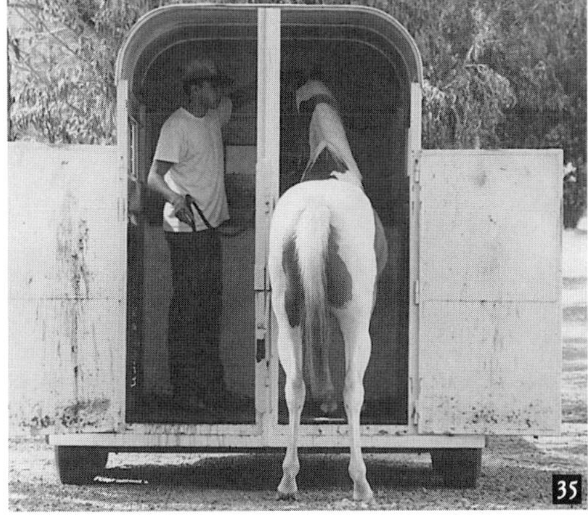

35

Kim Murphy

Loading from a Distance

After the horse has a foundation built in to where he can liven up his feet, slow them down to a stop, and move in one direction or another when you want him to, then you can offer him the direction and support he needs to load from a little distance (Figures 36-41).

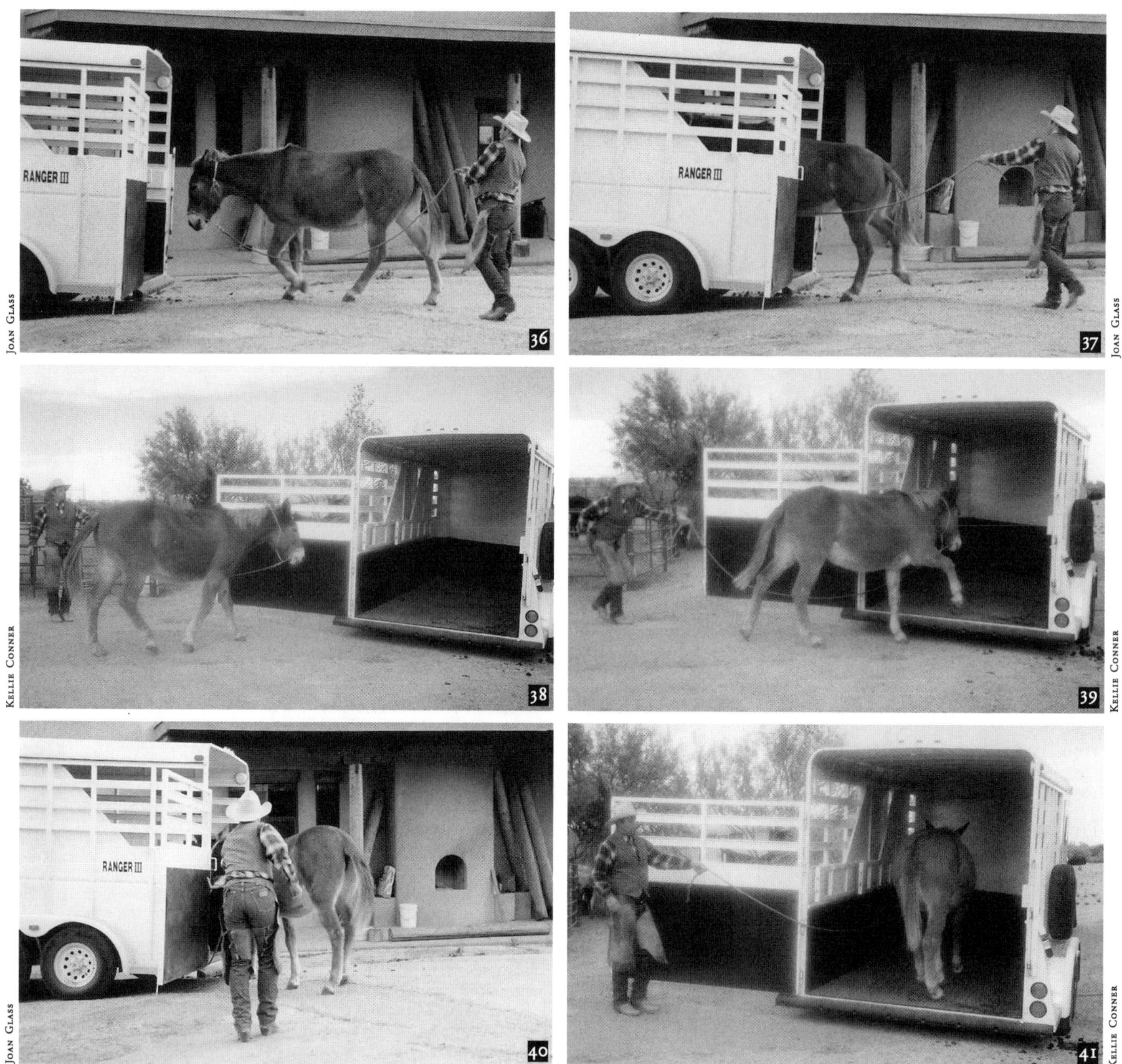

This fella has his mule lined up for a straight shot at the back of the trailer. Way before this, the preparation was in place for that mule to know how to get in and get out of the trailer safely.

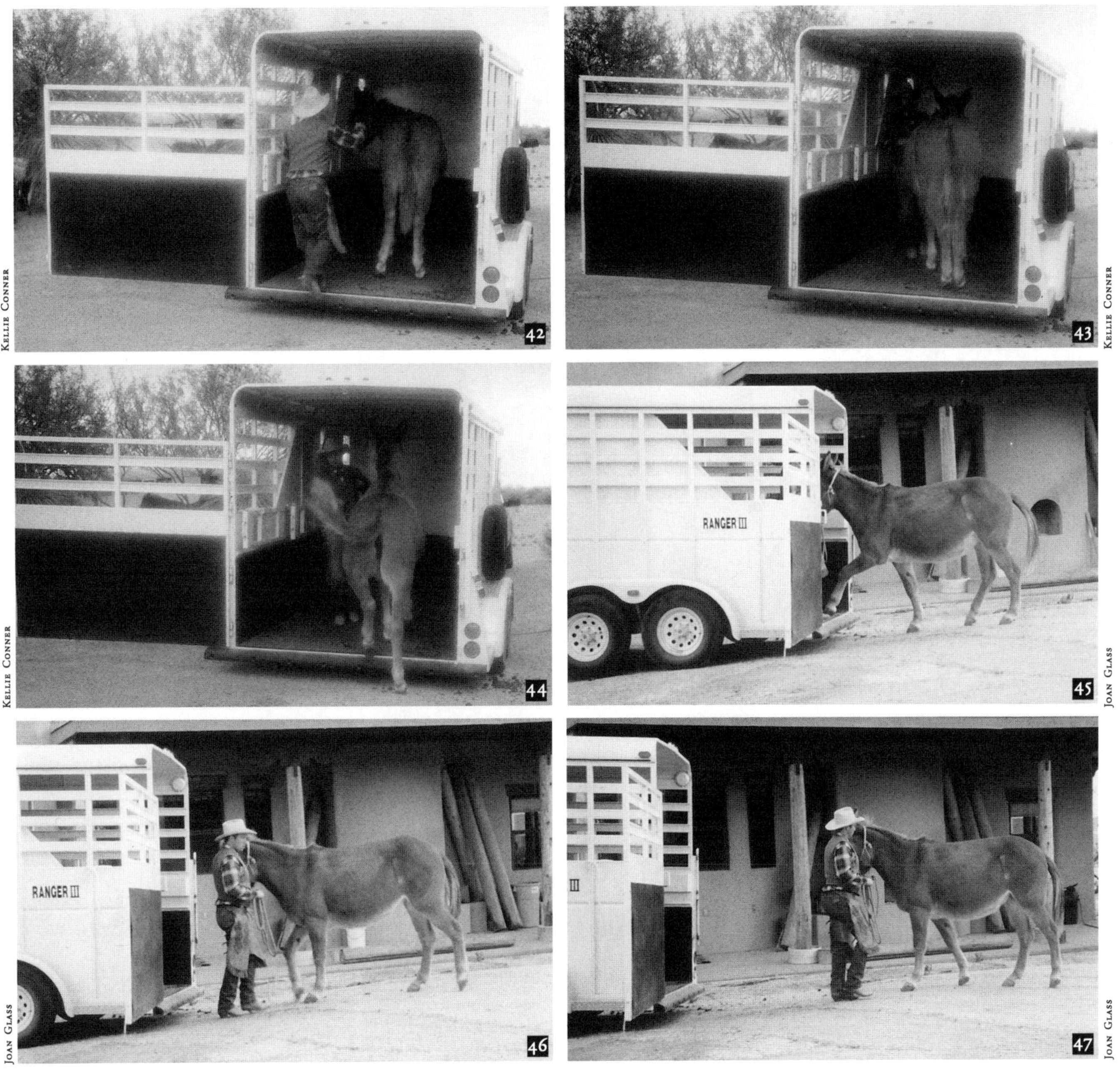

These pictures show how the mule has been taught to load into the trailer and then to stand and wait until another feel to move those feet is presented to him (Figures 42-51). This ensures the safety of the animal and the person, too. Special care is taken here to back the mule straight, slow and easy once he's outside the trailer, and this is a real good habit to get into. That way, he's not liable to think he should start turning around when he's halfway out, or bump into a person after his front feet hit the ground.

Joan Glass

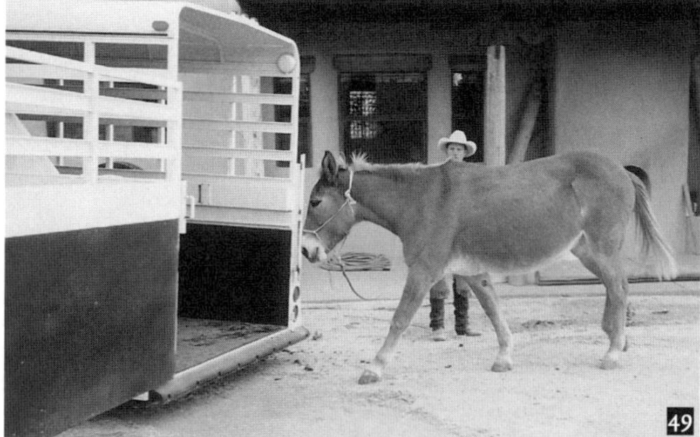

Joan Glass

Kellie Conner

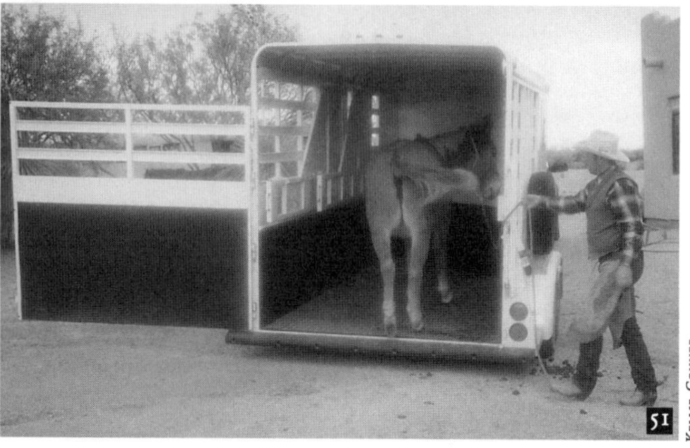

Kellie Conner

If you've worked your horse from both sides on the start, trailer loading is possible from either side. That mule is alert and offering no resistance to the idea of getting in the trailer, and this looks real good to me.

Turning the Horse Around to Step Forward Out of the Trailer

There's no harm in teaching your horse to follow you out of the trailer this way, *but a lot can go wrong for a person, and a horse too, if feel hasn't been taught to him on the start.* He should know how to step down and up, of course, he should be able to do this when he's going forward. But I'd rather a person got the backing good on the start. This way a horse won't think he's supposed to turn around to get out of a two-horse straight-ahead trailer. It's real dangerous when they try to do that.

Joan Glass

Different Types of Trailers
Straight Load, Slant Load, Step-Up, and Ramp

Horses aren't too enthused about being in a place where they can't go on through and come out the other side. That's why I like to put a little feed in the manger of those straight-ahead trailers to make it worth their while to get in. Just a taste of some hay or grain, enough so they can get a good mouthful or two. But there's not going to be any offerings by hand to motivate the horse into that trailer. No, that small amount of feed is just up there for him to enjoy when he makes it — it's more of a slight reward than an incentive. It's a little more satisfying for the horse to have something to chew on when he's in a space that's so confining, and these two-horse straight-ahead trailers are sure that way. In a slant-load or stock trailer, you wouldn't put feed or hang hay nets in there because it's not so confining. I ought to mention there's some other undesirable things that can happen with those hay bags tied right close in their faces — where there's liable to be horses tied right close together, too. There can be a fast wind blowing all that hay around when you're going down the road.

There's all kinds of ways to help a horse get into a trailer — like having another horse tied in there helps if a horse is skeptical about getting in. But that doesn't guarantee that he'll go in if there isn't a feel that he understands on the front end of that lead rope. I've seen horses that are real used to eating in there, but they won't stay in long enough for you to get the door shut. Or they won't load if another horse isn't already in the trailer. This just goes to show that it has more to do with the feel presented to him than it does with food, or another horse being in there before he is.

I've seen all kinds of horses and all kinds of problems people had getting them loaded. Not so much nowadays as 40 years ago. I think those gooseneck trailers have made a big difference — there's more room in those. Some of them have windows, so there's daylight on the side, and they just don't seem so confining for a horse, even from the outside they appear to be a little more inviting than some older-style trailers. In trailers that have a swinging divider or gate, you can swing it over to one side to give the horse a little more room, so he doesn't feel so confined, and for a horse that is skeptical, why that'd be a good thing to do in a straight-ahead or slant-load trailer.

Step-up trailers are not so much of a problem as the trailers with ramps. It seems a horse will step up a little easier than he steps onto a ramp. Those ramps make it a little harder for a person to position themselves, but it can be done all right.

Preparing Him to be Tied

There'd be no reason to tie your horse in a trailer until he can stand quietly in there, and go in and out real calm, and stand a while waiting for you to present him with the feel to do something else. Even then, I'd rather not tie him up until I get the butt chain across. In most cases, it will be safest if you don't tie him until you raise and secure the ramp or close and bolt the door. Of course, your judgment plays a part in this, because adjustments to the normal ways a person goes about things might be necessary. This is true especially where trailers are concerned, because even the good habits a person is liable to get into won't fit every horse the same.

Chapter 7:

KNOTS THAT ARE NEEDED FOR TYING YOUR EQUIPMENT

Some equipment doesn't come with a buckle where you'd need one, and knots work better in some cases anyway. There's not always going to be someone around to show you how to tie a knot, or do it for you, so the best thing to do is just to learn to tie these three basic knots for general purposes — a half-hitch, a bowline and a slip knot. Then, when you're on your own and you need to tie something up for some reason, you're in business.

What's listed here and shown are the steps to tie up the snaffle bit reins if you need to tie your horse someplace and you don't have a halter handy. Then there's instructions on how to tie the lead rope you'll need to have along when you've got your horse outfitted in the bridle. I call that a lead rope, but some call it a pull-down rope and maybe they've got other names for it, too. Whatever a person calls it, I've found that it's a real good way to lead your horse when he's wearing the bridle, and that method has been in use a long time. The last knot demonstrated is the slip knot, which is the best knot to use for attaching the bosal to the forelock. After you'd tied on your lead rope and attached your bosal to the forelock, you'd continue bridling the horse, and that is shown in this chapter too.

Tying Up the Mecate So You Can Safely Tie Your Horse

These pictures show you how to tie your reins up on your snaffle bit, so you can use the tail end of your mecate to tie your horse when you don't have a halter handy. If you can tie the half-hitch and bowline knots properly, they will make it safer for your horse and easier on the equipment when you tie him. Don't tie your horse with the tail end of your mecate when your reins are looped over the saddle horn, or buckled through your throat latch. This can hurt your horse and tear up your gear. I'd rather a person got some practice tying these knots real good and understanding how to get them undone and re-tied pretty easy before they'd ever need to rely on them when it involved a horse.

Start with your reins as far over to the right side of your horse's neck as possible, with the near side (left) slobber strap running up alongside the cheek-piece of your bridle. Keep the tail of your mecate out of the way, and bring the reins towards you *under* the horse's throat. This will cause the rein on the left slobber strap to snug up. Run the folded, looped end of reins, from back to front, between your snugged up left rein and the horse's neck and back through itself. This is called a half-hitch. (Figures 1-2). With your left hand, make a coil in the tail end of your mecate just below the point it exits the near side slobber strap (Figure 3). (Note: The rope should intersect at the top of the coil; the tail end of your mecate should be directly under your left thumb, and the piece of rein that travels back to the slobber strap should be on the bottom side of the coil you just made, held in your fingers.)

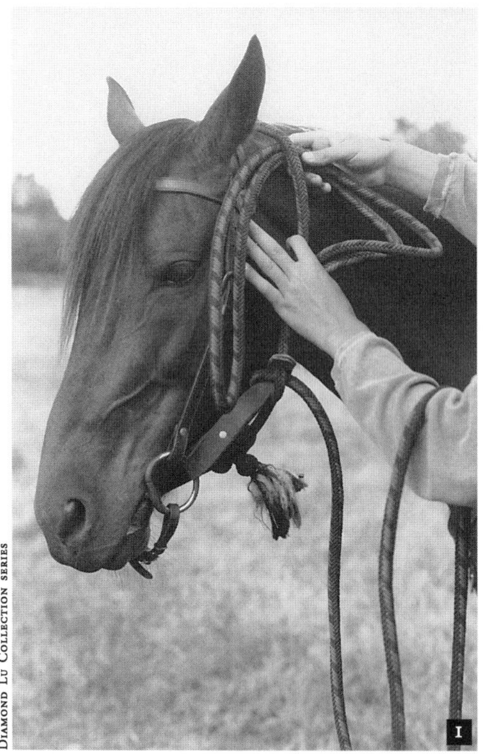

1

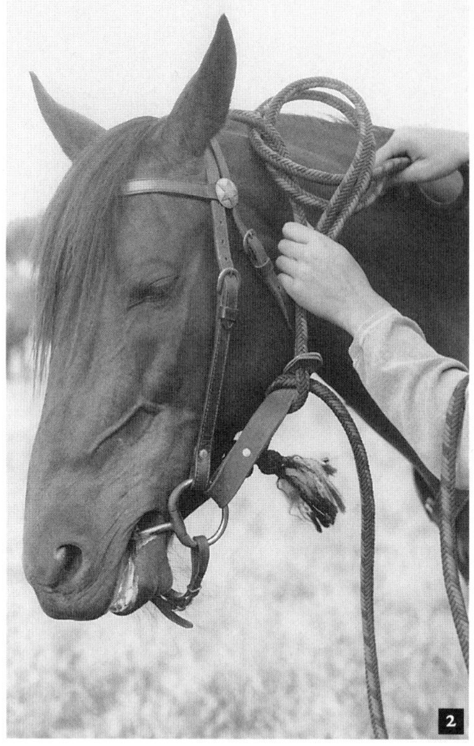

2

3

4

Put the end of the folded rein down through the coil, from the top, and bring the reins through and towards yourself (Figure 4). At any point, you may want to switch hands on your lines. Pass the end of the reins to the right, and back around the tail of the mecate (Figure 5). Then, run the end of the reins towards the front and up through the coil they just passed down through, and right alongside the section of reins you put through from the top (Figure 6). You will have four pieces of line through this coil now. Snug this up, and you've tied a bowline.

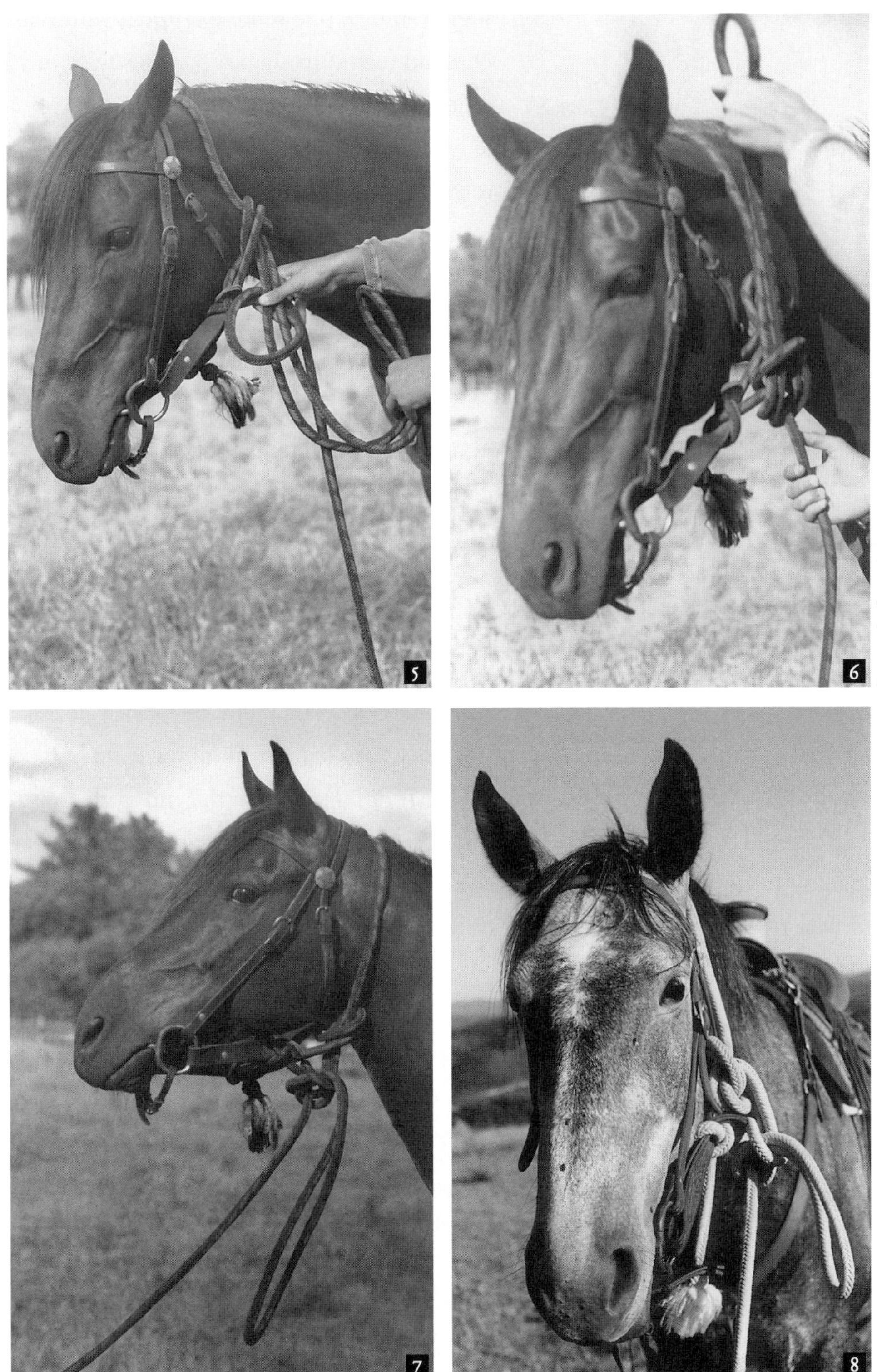

Diamond Lu Collection series

When the reins are tied off like this, there's still a place where the front feet could get caught in this loop (Figure 7). Even a loop that was this small (Figure 8) could present a problem because it could get caught on something, so a fella'd be sure he tied the horse to something higher than his head to prevent a hoof from getting in that

Diamond Lu Collection

loop. Or, take one more half-hitch with that end and tuck it in (Figure 9). This way, you'd reduce the risk of an accident even more.

Check to make sure that any pressure on your lead rope won't raise the bit in his mouth, or shorten up any of the lines around his neck. Now you can use the tail end of your mecate to tie your horse.

Tying Up Your Lead Rope

Your lead rope can be a horsehair rope, or cotton or made of something else. It shouldn't be too thick either. On a smaller horse a rope about 12 feet long will get you by, but on some of those bigger ranch horses 15 feet is about what you'd need.

To tie off your lead rope when you aren't using it, you tie a loop around the base of the horse's neck and coil up the extra lead you have, and then tie that up with your saddle strings. First, have the end of the rope in your left hand (Figure 10). You're going to tie a bowline here, because a slip knot could choke a horse depending on what took place. Here's the review on how you tie it. With your right hand, make a loop, with the coil going just like this fella has it

Diamond Lu Collection

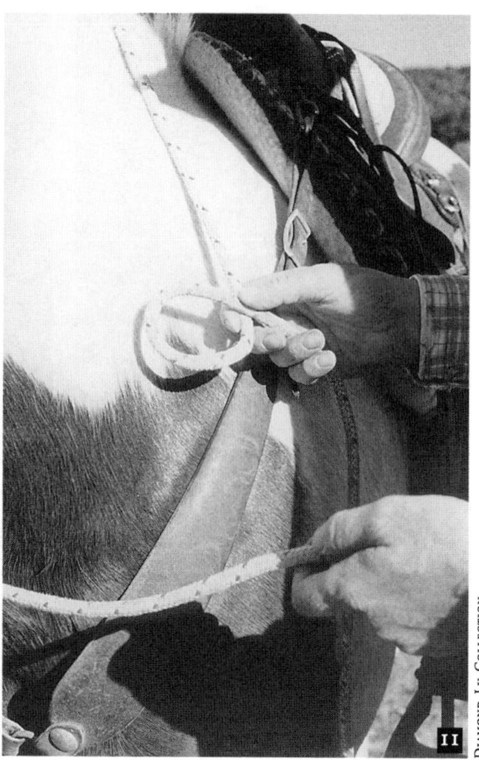

Diamond Lu Collection

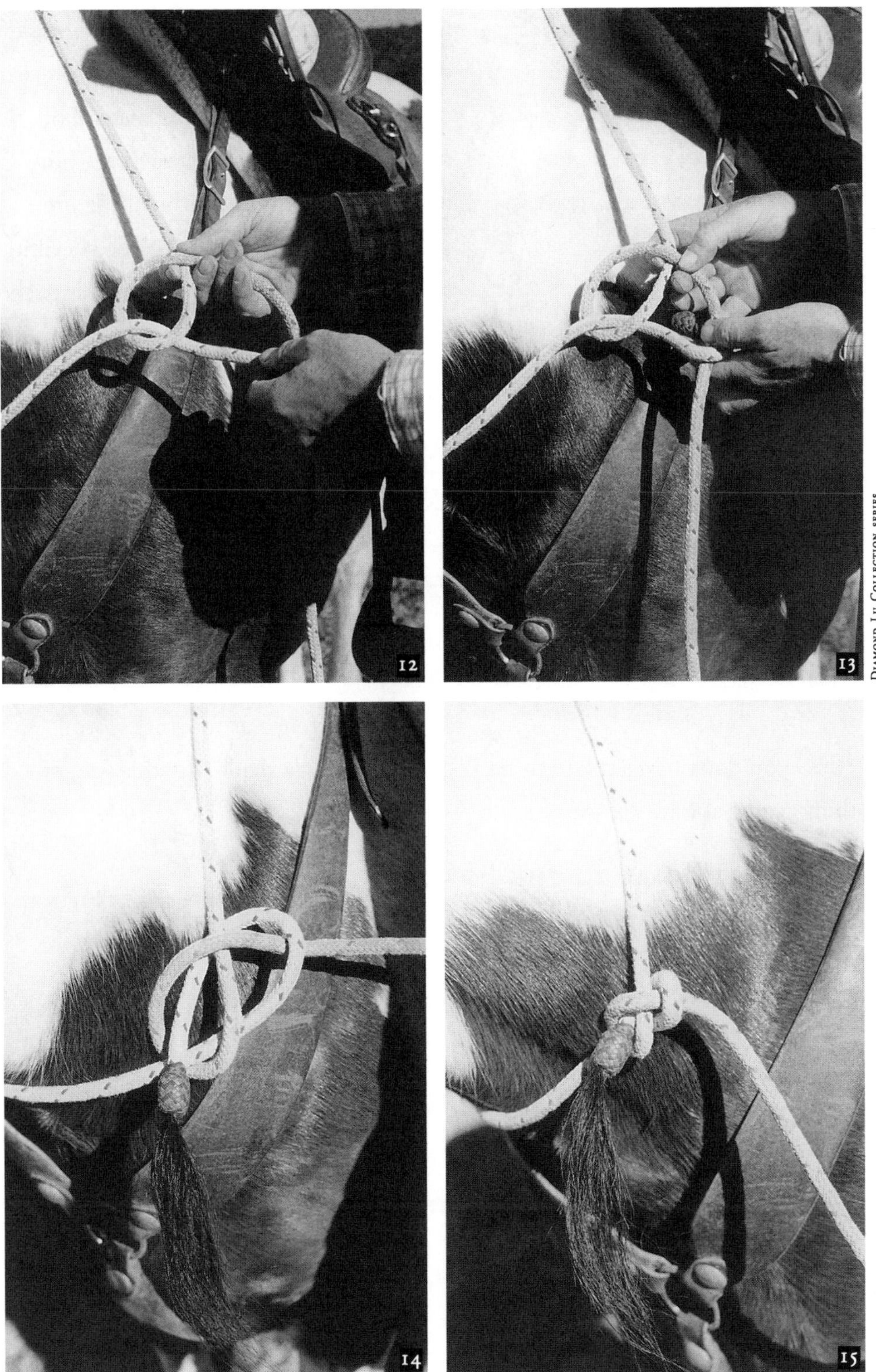

Diamond Lu Collection series

(Figure 11). Run that end through the loop that was just made (Figure 12). Bring the end back around that other piece of rope and then take it back through the loop you just put the end through (Figure 13). This time you're heading in the other direction with it. Now it's right alongside that first pass through there that you made. Figures 14 and 15 show how it looks before and after you take up the slack in the knot.

Diamond Lu Collection

To lead the horse, untie the lead rope from your saddle and put the end of your lead through the bottom of your bosal (Figure 16). Then re-tie the bowline up a little higher on his neck.

On a horse that's been taught to feel of you, why this is just as effective as having a halter on him, and it's safer than trying to hold on to your mecate or bridle reins while doing some jobs that you might have to do on the ground, like fixing fence or moving a lot of things when you don't have a place to tie your horse. I'd say that's why this way of doing things came about.

Attaching the Bosal to the Forelock and Bridling Your Horse

Diamond Lu Collection

Slip your bosal over the horse's nose and draw it up to where it sort of settles on his face at an angle. It's best to have the heel knot hanging down just above his chin with the sides of it not too close to the corners of his mouth. You'd rather it wasn't pressed up into those face bones either. Your bosal should fit close but not tight.

Take the leather thong up to the forelock and wrap it around a few times, snug, and start your wraps just where the hair grows out of his forehead (Figure 17). You'll wrap tight, and take your wraps towards the end of the forelock, being careful to lay that

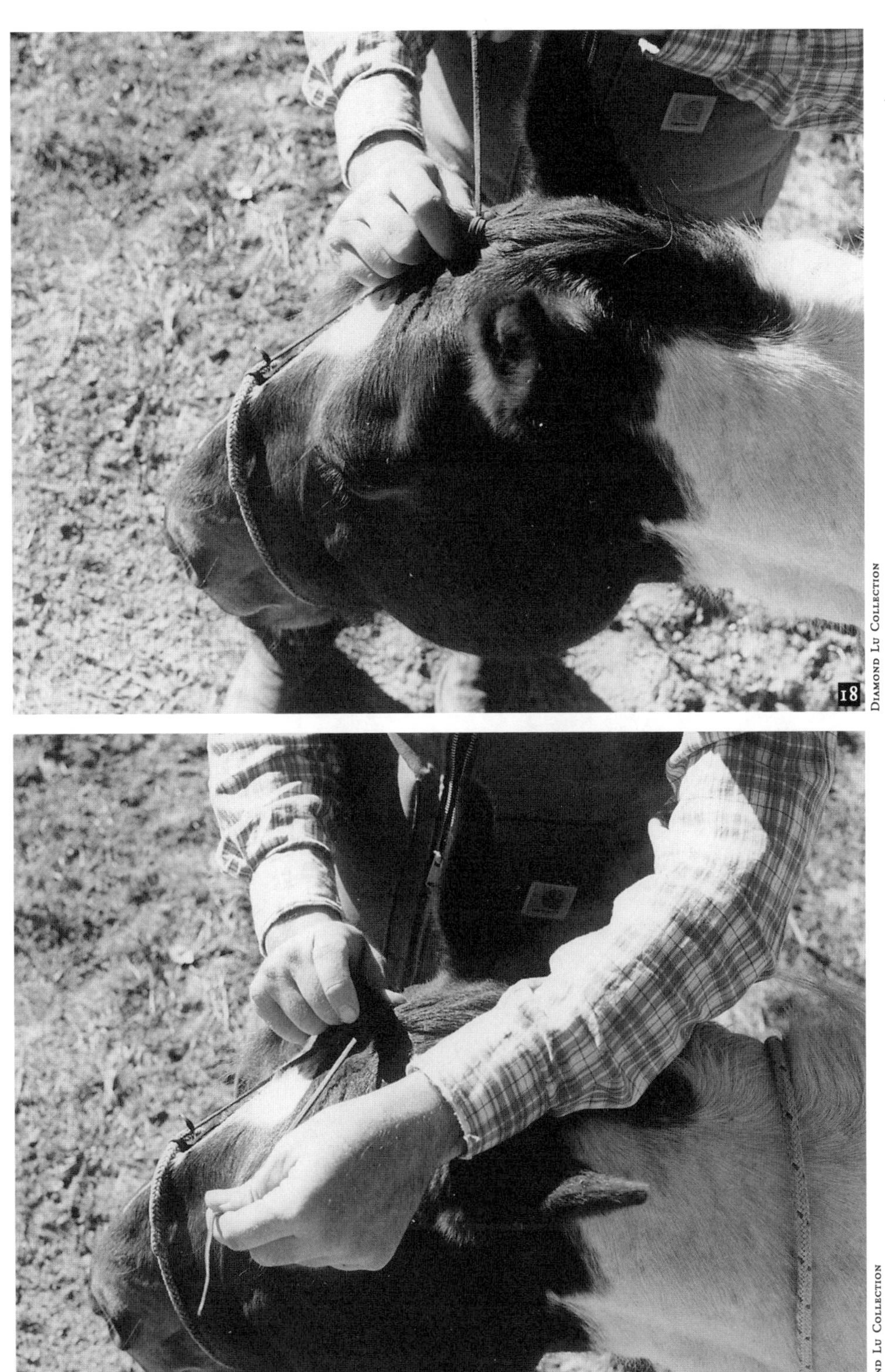

Diamond Lu Collection

Diamond Lu Collection

little leather tie piece in real close and neat and accurate (Figure 18). Before you get to the end of your bosal string, leave enough to tie a little slip knot in there (Figure 19).

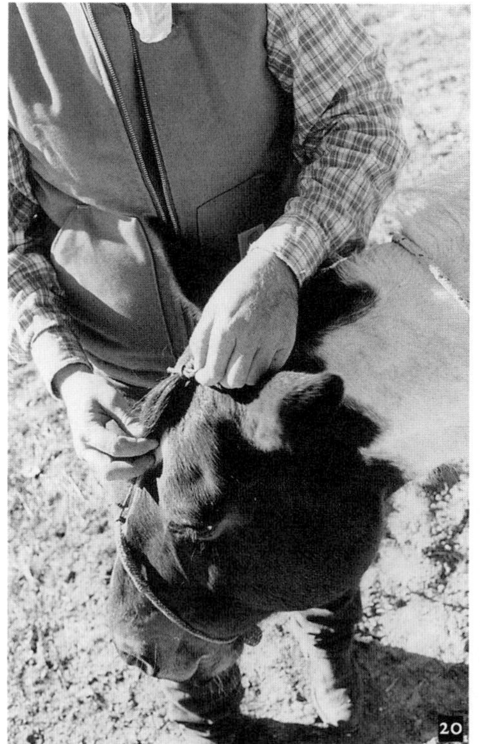

Diamond Lu Collection series

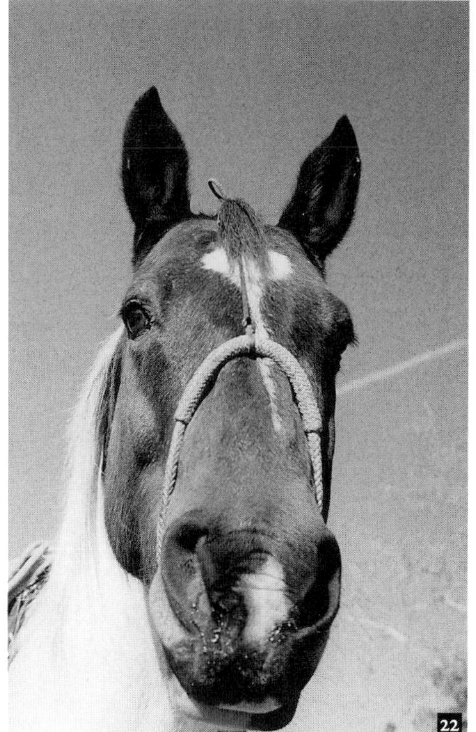

Make sure that your wrapping job isn't down so low on the forelock that the hair gets thinned out too much (Figures 20 and 21). When it's that way, it's apt to slip right off. When the bosal is tied on right, there's no pressure on the horse and there's no hair being pulled on (Figure 22). This set up should last all day.

Bridling

From here, why you'd go ahead with your bridling and these pictures show the steps for that (Figures 23-26, below and continued on the next page). Beaut knows what's expected of her and that makes it real handy when a fella's liable to need a little extra time doing something.

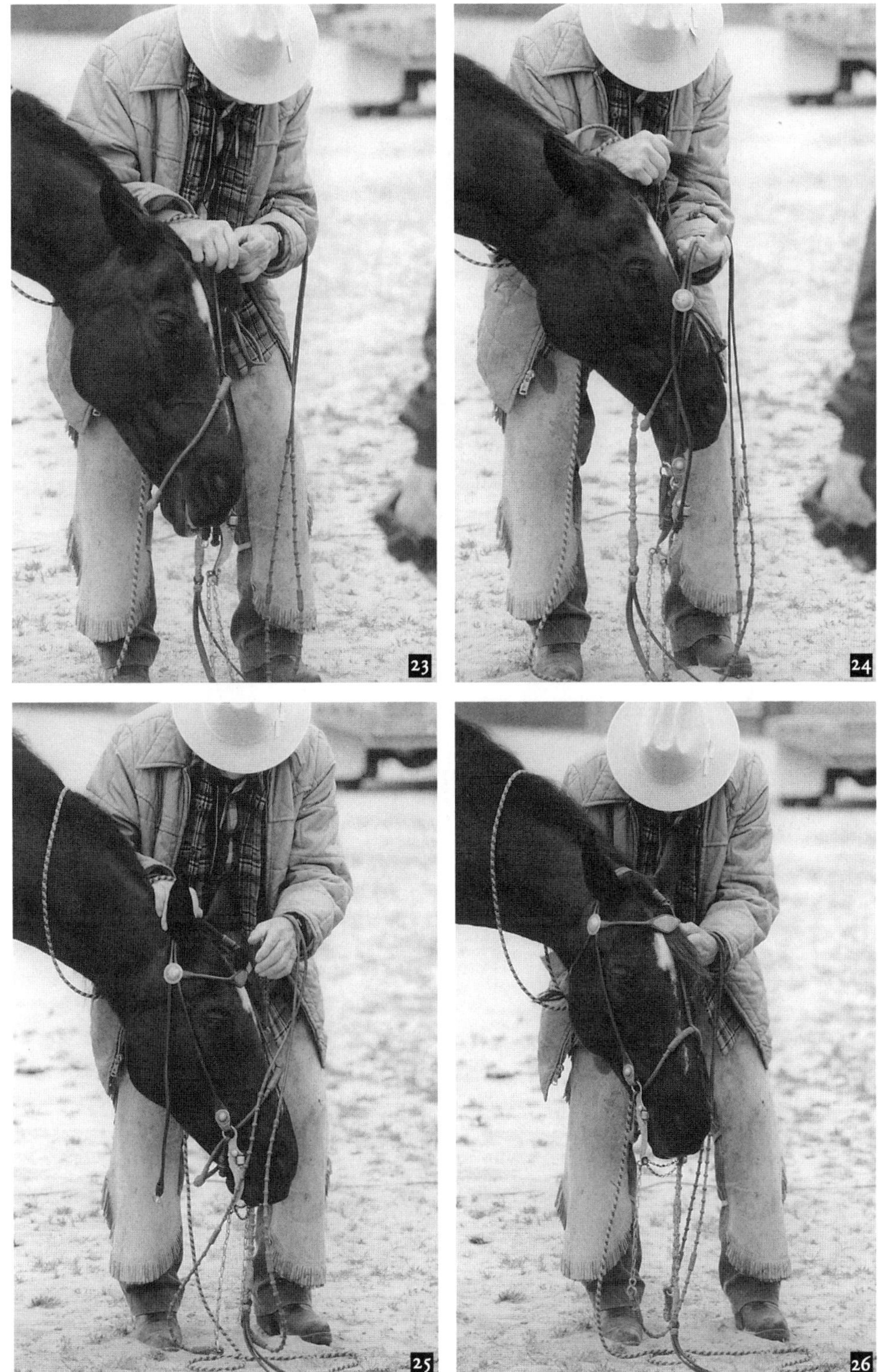

Patricia Weedman series

Richard Field Levine

Bill on Beaut at the Holman Ranch, January 19, 1996. Bill and Joe Wolter were putting on a ranch roping clinic that day — Bill's 90th birthday.

Chapter 8:
SOME QUESTIONS AND BILL'S ANSWERS

One of the nicest things that can happen at clinics is that people can ask questions. This chapter shows my answers to some questions people asked at the clinics I did in Carmel Valley, and Pebble Beach, California. Leslie Desmond did the arranging and helped out some at those clinics in 1996 and 1997. I think the most beneficial thing she did there was let people ride her horses so they could understand what it's like to ride a horse that's been taught to handle through feel. It's not always easy for a person to let others ride their personal horses, but I'll say it's the best way for other people to learn about feel. And, if it's done in moderation, it really doesn't hurt those horses any, not if the person who laid that foundation is right there to supervise things.

Questions About This Approach

Why does this approach work?

Horses have a lot more intelligence and emotions than most people would suppose. They enjoy being comfortable, and it's their natural curiosity and searching frame of mind that causes them to feel for meaning in what a person does. Like I spoke about earlier in this book, horses are real sensitive and feel is all they have to go on. When a person and a horse learn to feel of each other, why then, it's going to work out better for the horse, and the person, too.

Why is this approach not widely known and available?

It seems that this approach we're talking about isn't better known because some people can get by without it. And others are just trying to get by without it because they haven't seen anyone work this way with a horse. People get the urge to pull on those horses because they don't know what else to do. One thing's for sure, most people are handling horses the best they know how. But if they aren't using feel, I'll just say it's not a very good way. That's because the horse and the person can do a whole lot better than that.

It isn't that people are dumb or don't want to do better. No, when they have the opportunity to see someone operate a horse this other way, then I'd say most people can understand that there's a difference just by watching it. This feel we're talking about is something a lot of people can just sense by watching a demonstration. It's what gets a lot of people started. What they really get from watching is a start on understanding how good it can be for the horse, and for them, too. After people see a horse handled or ridden with feel, I'm in hopes that they can get some good supervision. Another thing that's really helpful is when people get an opportunity to learn how it feels to ride and handle a horse that's been started this way. When this can happen, it's the very best way for them to learn. Generally speaking, an amazing change can take place in a person's attitude about horses after they've had an opportunity to handle or ride a horse that's been prepared this way.

How is this book you're writing now going to help me learn this approach?

I'll say it's going to give you a good opportunity to learn to get a better feel of your horse. There's so much that can't be put in words about this. But, I'm in hopes that my book will give you a little thought about what would is taking place, so you can learn to get with the horse in a way that you maybe haven't ever done before.

If there is one main thing that people can do to learn this, what would you say that is?

I'd say it takes time to learn about feel. It takes even more time to learn how to operate with feel, and a good horseman knows this. Those aren't the same thing. One (the concept of feel) is just ideas that have no experience behind them, and the other is the experience you get from doing something successfully. That's the part that becomes your knowledge. There's a lot of value in the independence a person gains from this. After that, your better judgment comes in about how to progress up the line from there on your own, using the new experiences you've added onto your foundation. And where you'd be thinking or speaking about the progress of your learning, it's no different for a horse. It works the same way for him.

This approach has to be taught going real slow from the start, *and staying slow enough to where that slowness has some actual value.* It can be done right or not, even if it's slow. But the chance of a horse remembering what he's supposed to be learning is a lot better when a person isn't trying to rush the results. And if the person's going slow, why he's liable to see when that horse is missing the part he's trying to get across. And if he sees this, it'd likely be due to his ideas being organized in a way that prepares the horse for the future, and the job he'll have for that horse someday. I'd rather think that preparing the horse is the whole point of all that we're doing with them, and not anything else. In most cases, it's the slowness part that I see getting left out. It's a real disadvantage to a horse when this happens. Of course some people are going to realize this, and they'll back-track to try and put something better in there for the horse when they find out that they missed these real important things on the start. Those are the people we're trying to help. If they never heard about these ideas or saw some of these things demonstrated, no one can know that they ought to go this slow, and work with feel. But this approach isn't going to fit everyone, we know that.

Most people just want to go way too fast. People have said that you don't need to start where I'm wanting to start. And maybe they'll keep on saying this, but the way I have in mind, well, it's just a *different* way and there's one thing I know about it, it works.

Let's say, if you take a fella who isn't at the beginning, or even in the middle of the road, but already has quite a bit of experience. Well, when he gets on to this (working through feel) he'll really start to get someplace with his horses. With this working for him, those horses can take him right up the line. I don't think there's any question about that. Of course, that'd be only if he wants them to. But, using feel this way, a horse can sure take a fella where he's wanting to go, all right.

It's a big problem for those horses when the person handling and riding them doesn't know that feel even exists in thought. This feel part is the foundation, and I don't think there's any question about this being important. It isn't much different, maybe, than how you'd want to go about building a house. If you miss out on that foundation, the farther up you go, the more trouble you'll be in. And that's the way it is with the horse. That's why so many people think they have such a big problem with their horse, when really it's the horse that has the problem understanding what those people want him to do, because they haven't built in that foundation for him.

Are there any problems that can't be "fixed" with this approach?

This approach will fit any horse or any human being with his horse. It will fit them. It's a question of how long it takes a person to learn how to apply feel.

Anytime you run into something that bothers a horse, why you welcome that. There's an opportunity there for that horse to learn about the basics. When that life comes up in him and he's got a real interest in being away from someplace, why that's a good time to get with the feel of the horse so he can pick up your feel. You wouldn't use any firmness to go against the lightness that comes up in him. No, that's when you'd flow along with what was flowing inside of him, in terms of his energy and the way he's got it tied to his concern for self-preservation.

Let's say you come to a big ditch. You want to take him into it at an angle so the horse can learn to travel through it and then come out the other side, down a little ways. There's no rush in this. When you have a little time to work at anything that's bothering to the horse, why it's very beneficial. There'd be no speaking about punishing a horse if a problem came up for him, not by any means. This is what we're trying to stay entirely away from.

I've been told that the horse understands when I try to make the wrong thing difficult and the right thing easy. Can you explain why you don't use this in your approach?
Making the wrong thing difficult isn't going to be a fitting approach for the horse, because so many people only do that part. They forget about the part of making the right thing easy for the horse. They just get to that making-it-difficult part and then they put the horse up after that. Someplace, maybe, they'd heard that it was all right to make something difficult and that gets to be their way, *all the time*. I've seen quite a lot of this, and it's real pleasing to me when a person can get this part switched around in their mind. To my way of thinking, instead of *making* that horse do anything, *trying to help* the animal is a better way. I'm in hopes that a fella could think of helping the animal, because without help that horse won't know what he's supposed to do, and really, that's what a fella's main job is here. Just helping that horse.

A person could start trying to help the horse to understand the right thing, through feel, even if he hadn't done much experimenting with it before. It might even bring out something a little different in the person, to not try to make things difficult for that horse. I'm sure that helping a horse understand is more fitting to that horse — any horse. It might be more fitting to most people too.

Questions About Feel

Can feel be taught?
Some people say they don't think it can be taught and in a way they're right. Maybe it depends on who's doing the teaching and who's doing the learning. I think feel can be taught. But there's preparation you need first, before you can learn how to feel. There isn't any mystery about that to me. Because it's there, that feel, in the person and in the horse. And with help from someone who's more experienced, why a person can sure learn how to feel of the horse, if they want to. That's an actual fact.

Which is the most important of feel, timing and balance?
For over thirty years I've been wondering about this myself. I've had many opportunities to think it over, and I still haven't been able to find out which of the three you can do without, or which is the most important. I did finally come up with

balance as maybe the one you couldn't leave out because without that, maybe you wouldn't even be able to get up on the horse. And if somehow you did get up there, why without much balance you'd just fall right off when he started moving. I know that happens.

I can't help but think though, that if you are learning how to feel of a horse, your balance will improve. Then your timing could come in there, and it's a lot easier to get the timing if you can feel of the horse. And the timing, well, even when a rider's timing isn't the best a horse can understand it after a while. And he can do all right.

So I've been thinking that the way a person presents a feel to the horse is pretty important, because that way a horse learns to feel of the rider and then the two can go *together*. When the rider and the horse are together, it's got a better feeling to it for them. *And it's real attractive.* You really can't get too far up the line without this good feel working for you, not in a way that's pleasing to the horse anyway.

How do I know if my horse is feeling of me?

It's easy to tell. You'll know by the way that horse is responding, by his looks and everything about his whole appearance. If he doesn't go where you want him to go, or if you see that his feet are moving when you want him to stand still, then he's not feeling of you. When he stops feeling of you, it's liable to be because you're presenting the feel to him in a way that he doesn't understand. If that happens, then you better go along with him.

If you travel with a horse and then allow him to join you, then he can learn to feel of you as you both travel around together, and we might call it traveling the long way around. We'd call it that because the shortcut way might not fit the horse you're working with. It won't fit most of them, anyway. There's really no telling how long it might take to get things straightened out if a fella ran into trouble spots trying to go straight at something above where that horse could understand. Where it concerns a horse, just about anything could happen. But when a person goes along with the horse, that's how a horse will get ready to go along with the person.

Naturally, he'll want you to get with him and do what he thinks he should do, but if he's wanting to take over, that doesn't fit a person very well, and that's the thing I guard against all the time. I give that horse a feel that says, "stay with my feel." It's not a harsh feel. I like to do just as little as I possibly can, and always be thinking ahead to a spot in the future, but not too far away in the future — because on the spur of the moment, I may need a spot where that horse can have the room he needs to maneuver, so he has a better chance to stay with my feel. As soon as he learns to get with your feel, he'll be under your control. If you haven't had an opportunity to learn this, then you'd continue to think you have to make the horse do something, instead of helping him do it. Before that can come through, he has to be reassured that he can find what you want without being forced.

How much feel is OK to use on a horse? Sometimes I think what I'm doing isn't enough, but I'm afraid of being too forceful.

I can tell if he's feeling of me by seeing what he's presenting me with. If he's a horse that doesn't want to stand and needs to go someplace and pushes into me, then he's not feeling of me and I change the way I'm presenting my feel to him. I'd firm up on him some, with whatever I needed to be effective to get a change to come through. And of course that could take all my strength, or just a tiny amount that I could hardly measure. I can do just a little bit there to meet up with him when he pushes into me. And the timing is real important for this. He doesn't enjoy that firmness and this gives him an opportunity to feel of me and make an adjustment. He has that choice. And I'd ease right off the second when he started to pay attention to my feel again and get with me.

Now, there's also a spot in there on some horses where your better judgment will tell you not to firm up, not by any means, because in some cases you just go with a horse like that. You blend in with him until he can pick up your feel and you go together from there. The judgment on that decision takes in quite a lot. I've always said that the more firmness you use, the more experience you ought to have so you'd understand what to do when that horse responds to what you did, which could be most anything. It just depends on the horse and the situation.

But let's say he's really wanting to move and go someplace and you firm up on him. He doesn't enjoy going into that firmness. That's bothering to him. I never want to upset a horse, but sometimes the understanding of how much firmness to present isn't obvious to me until I see a change. The horse, he'll sort out and try, and then when there's a sign that he's found something better, he'll see I'm not using any more firmness than I have to. I'm watching close for any change that will tell me, through feel, that he's beginning to understand. There's so many little things that you do with feel, and with adjusting your feel to get that horse to learn to stay with your feel.

There's something I want to repeat now. The appropriate feel can be anything from the whisper of a touch to doubling a horse with all the strength you have. It just all depends on the situation. There's going to be some times when the feel that's needed might require firmness, but there's no place for being rough when it comes to handling a horse. None at all.

There was a horse that went to laying down a lot and I know a fella who would pick up his tail and kick him under there, just real hard. Well, that horse, I'd say he got the message straight away. Some fellas do it a little different than I do. Some people can't seem to help but being rough, or don't really care to be any different than they are, and maybe this just fits the person because they never thought about being another way. And then there's other people who want to get that rough part of themselves completely out of the picture. And it's good that some people do, because when a person is that rough way, it's difficult for the horse to understand. A horse will try to avoid a person who's mad or upset, regardless if there's understanding that goes along with it or not. If you're getting your feel applied properly, then you don't have to be rough on the horse. You shouldn't want to be anyway.

I know of a stallion that had been bred a little bit before he'd been taught manners of any kind. There was no respect there. He'd rear and paw when you went to lead him out of the corral. You had to be sure you were out of the way or he'd bump right into you. It got so that when a person would ride up to the corral, the horse would make a connection with the person that wasn't too good. If he could, that horse would bite you hard. This fella had a rope there and used quite a bit of firmness to get the horse to respect him. He'd go in there and work him afoot until the horse respected him, until he could feel of that person indirectly, and eventually he led the horse out of the corral with a float in the line. This happened because feel was applied in a way that made sense to the horse. That horse was a lot happier after that.

You shouldn't try to force a change like this because you can't get the desired results, and still fit the horse. Force just doesn't fit a horse. Some people know this. They'd work with a horse like this one until they could understand him inside and out. That's what this fella did. One day he started pulling that horse's tail and led him out the gate backwards, just that way. The horse didn't take off when he got out the gate because that feel was built in there and he was real content just to stay with that man. And he didn't figure on biting after that. This is an example of how to get feel built in, and it's the actual facts of what took place.

Is feel meant to be applied in the same way on a horse that is being restarted as it is supposed to be applied on a green colt?

A horse that hasn't been started with feel, why this horse might have bad habits and you might have to do things a lot different on that horse than you would on a green horse. I'd work on him to get him to feel of me, but there's going to be quite a little variation on how I'd go about this. On the green colt, I'd work with him and teach him to feel of me, too, of course. That's the way I'd start him. But every horse is different, so every application is different. It's whatever fits best according to your knowledge, and you can only work from where you are.

Questions About Float and Lightness

What is "float" in your lead rope or reins?

Float refers to slack, which is quite a bit less tension than it takes to straighten out the rope or reins. You'll plan to maintain some float in your lead rope or reins whenever possible.

Why do you want to have float in the rope or reins?

So that the horse can learn, through feel, to operate with lightness in his whole body, without resistance to pressure presented to him by a handler or rider. To teach a horse to be light to a person's feel, he needs to learn that he can come off pressure on his own. A person's job is to help the horse learn that he can do this. If you can ease off the tension you put into that rope or those reins just as close as possible to the same instant that the horse eases the pressure off himself, then you are building a solid foundation in that horse that will be the basis of his responsiveness to your feel. This will lead to a dependable lightness in your future together.

How do you fix it so there is a float in the rope or reins?

You do as much as you can not to take the float out in the first place, and you do this by going with the feel of the horse, as long as it is safe for the two of you. You let him drift a bit, you ease off the pressure. And as you learn to maneuver his body by following his feel without excess pressure on his head, he will begin to search for a body position that releases pressure on himself, wherever it exists. This is the beginning of his capacity to get with you by following your feel. Some horses are a little too set in bad habits for this to work out on the start, so you'd maybe keep a shorter line and stay closer to that horse until you could get this to work. Supervision from someone who's got experience at this can be a real help, if you can find it.

How can I encourage my children to get a lighter way of using the reins?

The first thing to do is have them hold those reins between the thumb and first finger, and make sure those other fingers aren't closed up tight. Keep them loose on there. If a person closes those fingers up real tight, why then that tightens up all the muscles in their arms and it makes it difficult to get a light feel on those reins.

I've been riding my horse two-handed in the hackamore and he gets heavy in the front and tips his nose to the outside. I tipped his nose and brought my support rein in to straighten him, but instead of getting light and coming off the pressure, he braced and slowed his feet down. What's the appropriate response?

Ease off a bit, to reward for his feet slowing down and start again. Don't go straight forward from a stop. It's best to take a couple of steps back and then place a front foot out to the side and pick up a new direction.

There are several reasons why this can help your horse learn to feel of you. He learns to wait for your direction and support before he goes. And it's a better feeling to the horse to leave a spot pushing off from the hindquarters, instead of pitched way forward with most all the weight on his front end. When you back up that horse and step him over, you use your legs in time with his feet leaving the ground, of course. If you don't use your legs at all, he might step off kind of dull because he isn't getting the feel from the rider he needs to step off lightly.

Questions About "Problem Horses" — Those Are Problems People Have with Their Horses

My trainer says that my horse is pushy and I should get rid of him because he's dangerous. He's a really nice gelding and I like him a lot. What do you think I should do?

It's real natural for the horse to feel like you're in his way when you actually are in his way. So many people think the horse is wrong for feeling this way. He may want to just stand there with his head and neck in a normal position but he can't, because a person's crowding in real close on him there. There's so many people who do this, and they don't know that they're building a really bad message into that horse's way of operating. It's bound to create trouble spots for him in the future.

What's too bad is that it'd be so easy for people to just leave this part out of what they do with a horse, and maybe they will when they find out about this. Even a lot of those people who have themselves listed as trainers aren't onto it. They need to understand that it's just respect for the horse, through feel — and being around him this respectful way — that teaches him to respect you. He learns to understand your feel, and that includes the feel of your space, of course. Or it doesn't, if you're the type of person who encourages a horse to crowd into you by the way you crowd into him. See, so many "problems" with horses just wouldn't show up if more people only understood this one little particle about feel. It's tied to respect that can go both ways.

If a horse hasn't been taught to feel of a person, why then he'd be lacking in respect for people. *So if he's this way, he might decide to jump or buck and play around and kick just because he feels like doing it. When he's got the idea to be doing some of these things, he wouldn't have any idea that it's a wrong thing to do when a person's right there, if he hasn't been taught to feel of that person.*

It's not the horse's job to know about this unless he's been taught, through feel, about respect. No, he wouldn't have any way of knowing you thought he oughtn't be doing those things, *because he is a horse*. It seems strange, maybe, but there's some people who need to be reminded that this is so. Where it concerns horses, there's a real fine line between doing not enough and doing too much. It's all in how it's applied. And that's all in the feel and timing of what you do.

If I am riding in a circle to the left and my horse bulges his shoulder out to the right, do I correct this with my rein or my leg?

You back down a ways and get that foundation built in there, through feel. I think you'd both find this beneficial, since you've got this sort of question. When he's doing this, he isn't feeling of you, he's leaning against you, and the main thing is to understand that you can get it turned around by going back to feeling of the horse on the ground, so he can feel of you. How you go about this has been explained earlier in this book.

I was a good student in school. I've raised a family and I have a job I enjoy. I don't have self-esteem problems and I'm not the "wimpy" sort, but I still can't get my mare to respect me. I've even gotten a few minor injuries from her. I really like her and she likes me. What should I do?

This sort of thing happens to a person who lacks understanding about the horse's main way of communicating, which is through feel. A person who lacks presence, or approaches a horse without a clear idea of what they intend for him to do, sometimes gets pushed right out of the horse's way. They don't have any idea that the run-in with the horse was already shaping up way ahead of time. Someone like this — who comes up to a horse that's young and inexperienced or troubled — is liable to get hurt. If they got stepped on, bitten, kicked, struck at, run into or dragged around on the end of the lead rope, well, this sort of person might not see that it was their approach that caused the horse to do what he did.

This kind of thing is completely avoidable. It is up to each person to decide whether to yield to the horse or teach the horse how to yield to them, though feel. If they don't teach the horse to yield through feel, this tends to result in a person getting hurt in one way or another, sooner or later. So much of the time these same people think the horse opposed them or harmed them on purpose. But this is no part of the horse's idea in the first place. If he'd been approached in a way that he could understand what was expected of him, he would have done what the person wanted. So people need to get going on this, because their safety in the future is real important.

What should I do when I pony my other horse and he tries to bite the horse I am riding?

Before your horse gets ready to bite that horse, he probably pulls his ears back and lets you know he wants to go faster. When he does that, firm up your feel so that he understands that isn't the best way for him to be. When using that firmness, it's a real delicate thing, how much you use and when you use it. It makes a difference. Your better judgment will give you some idea on this, and you'll experiment to see what is best for your horse. When he finds out that you want him to have more respect for you, he'll have it.

What about a horse that kicks with a hind foot when you pick it up?
That's a good question. That'd come under the heading of how you get a horse used to picking up his foot. Some horses will kick if you just put your hand back there on the hind leg above the hock. You'd want to get such a horse used to feeling of your hand. You'd do this by rubbing him and getting him used to that, but you'd go real slow at this, and you wouldn't keep your hand on that leg too long. Go down there a little ways and then take it right off. When he got so he didn't mind you putting your hand on his leg there, then you go down a little farther and do the same thing. Rub him a little and take your hand off before he gets bothered. When he got so he didn't mind you rubbing your hand all the way down his leg and his ankle, then you'd start pulling on his leg a little, right above his ankle, until he got so he'd take the weight off that leg when you put your hand there and pulled on that leg just a bit. Then you'd hold it a little and you'd work it back and forth a little until he got used to your feel there. You'd just keep doing that until he didn't mind your hand being anyplace on his leg, and you could just reach down there and get his foot. It doesn't weigh anything then.

Next thing you'd do, after you could raise his leg up a little, is take hold of his foot and swing his leg back and forth while you hold on there, and then maneuver that foot a little in your hands, left and right and back and forth. Then you can tap on the bottom of his foot, that'd be the sole, and get him used to that. Real easy at first. You'd only want to hold that up a little while and let it down. Don't wait until he takes it away from you. This can get a horse started on the wrong track altogether about his feet being handled. No, it's a real common thing the way some people think they should just hang onto that leg until one party has to give up or give in. That's entirely wrong and doesn't build one thing into a horse that's good. The horse that gets handled this way gets a real solid start on disrespect and resentment, all right.

If he can't tolerate your hand, then you better get a rope on him. But that'd take someone with more experience at handling a rope and a horse than the general run of people. It's a good idea to know that it's possible to get a horse that's bad to kick changed around this way. I'd probably put a rope on his hind foot and make the loop big enough to where it didn't pinch him. Not a slip knot of any kind, but a big enough loop, tied fast. I'd pull on that rope and get that horse used to giving his leg to me. That's where I'd spend some time.

It could take a dozen or so applications until he gets used to having his foot taken off the ground. Don't take it off the ground too long, but do it often. And you wouldn't jerk that foot away from him, or cause the rope to burn him. Take it back and forward and sideways quite a bit. Maybe three or four times a day. One deal like this for 20 minutes is better than none at all, but several shorter sessions are best.

My horse is the kind that overreacts to me. What should I do to help him?

If you give him a feel for a sudden move that he's not been prepared for, or one that's too difficult for him to make, then he'll be confused. Your better judgment will help you there. It comes in to tell you what's appropriate for the horse at the level he understands you. Of course you'll need to gain a little experience to have that better judgment.

You need to have intentions behind the feel you present and some knowledge of just how (and where) that horse is when you present something. When you don't get the right response back from that horse, that's how you're pretty sure he didn't understand what you intended. You'd need to change what you're doing when this happens, and not crowd in on his mental or physical system with more feel than he can make sense out of. We're in hopes that this'd happen less, over time, because this can lead to other problems of communication between you and your horse. And this is really a frustration. Because when it gets to be like this between a person and the horse, a brace can get in there too, which can be seen in the horse wringing his tail or grinding his teeth and many other undesirable actions. Some surprising things can develop, all right.

I have another horse at home and he's lazy. What should I do?

Well, that horse may not be putting enough effort towards whatever it is you're trying to accomplish. Or maybe it's just that his feet are out of position, and that makes it feel like he's not trying. The actual fact is that he's trying all right, he just can't follow your feel because his feet aren't in the right spot to be able to stay with you. Possibly your feel could stand some improvement, too. In a case like that, you weren't feeling of his feet right in the first place. That's how someday your better judgment will tell you whether his feet are out of position, or whether he's slacking off, or whether he simply didn't understand what you wanted him to do. No, those three things are real different and you have to be cautious. If you misjudge any one of those things, then there's a hindrance to the horse in that. You become a hindrance because he needed your support somewhere for something, and he doesn't get it.

I've heard from several people that I have a so-called "problem" horse, but I don't think I do. What do you say about something like that?

It really depends on what the "problem" is as to how you go about it. The first thing to do is see if your horse will lead up real free on that halter rope. You want to be able to have him lead up real free, and also teach him when you're standing there to put his head anyplace it's necessary for it to be. This could be up or down or to either side or anyplace in between, without it weighing hardly anything. You want to move that head around and get it loosened up from side to side, until you can put it about anywhere, but not all the way to the ground. You wouldn't need him to travel like that. He needs to be real loose and flexible at the poll, and you'll want to be real careful not to put your head above his head under any circumstances. If he gets startled and brings his head up real fast, he can catch you under the chin. No, it's real dangerous to put your head there, above his head.

And, you'll want that horse to back up real smooth, without any rigidness or resentment showing up, and this would be going just one step at a time, real slow. At any place in there when you're working, you'd want to be able to just set that foot down and leave it there until you wanted it to move back another step, no matter which foot it was. There's no need to go too fast here on this backing, because it's easy to get the horse confused about it if you do. And you'll get him to step those front feet around there, too. You'll step the forehand around the hindquarters in both directions, and step the hindquarters away from you, leaving the forehand pretty much where it is. No matter what the problem is, to get it fixed up better for the horse, he's going to have to learn how to feel of you first, and this is the best way to go about it because this is what the horse understands.

Now, some horses aren't gentle. You'll have to get where you can get up to them first, before you do these other things just spoken about. But even when he's loose, you're working on his understanding of things through indirect feel. That's the other kind of feel and it's real important to know about it. Indirect feel is what I call it when you don't have anything on him to hold him with, when there's just space between you. He can still feel you anyway, just not through touching his body in any way. It's more the *idea* of it that he gets, and that's because he's picking up your feel from a distance.

There's no reason to hurry any of this because that's what gets the horse bothered and called a "problem" by someone in the first place. It just takes the time it takes. A person should work this part into their understanding of things about a horse and they will, if they want things to work out through feel.

My horse feels just fine like he always feels. Is there anything I should do to get him to be a better horse?

If he feels that way to you, then you shouldn't be having much of a problem. But a horse that leans on you when you're standing there, like he is doing now, why he wouldn't be feeling of you. He'd be taking over. That's what's taking place now.

If somebody hands me a horse to hold for them for a few minutes or so, why the first thing I do is to see if that horse knows how to feel of me. I could be standing there or I could be on the horse. I prefer horseback because I don't maneuver too well on the ground. The first thing I'd do is see if he can follow a feel to maybe step forward, or to the side, or just back him up a little to see how much feel he has to offer me back. Even just shifting that weight back and forwards can give you something to build on.

How can I break my colt to tie?

You teach those colts to lead. When they're good at that, they're ready to tie up. If they pull back, they aren't ready to be tied and they aren't leading as good as you thought they were. A colt isn't liable to pull back if he's been taught to lead the way we're talking about.

What about a horse that won't be caught?

That's a good one to ask because there's plenty of those horses around. It takes a lot of time to learn how to catch a horse that doesn't want to be caught. With those horses, you better have a little corral to put them in that they won't jump out of. You let them run around in there. As long as he's looking over the fence and going fast, he sure isn't thinking about being caught. Get his train of thought changed around. Every time he goes by, toss the end of your rope out there to get him used to you doing that, not to make him go faster, although he might at first. He'll start watching you and probably in 15 or 20 minutes he'll begin to look at you. And maybe this will take place a lot sooner, too. If he stops, walk up and pet him. If the horse leaves when you go up to him, your presentation is probably what caused him to leave, and you'd walk up to him the next time with more things on your mind about how to help him stay, and we'd be in hopes that he'd stay.

He may want to come up to you. It's best to let him and rub him on or under his neck and down a little on the side, and then step back away and let him go on for a little longer. He may want to stick with you and think it's a good place to be. Right there, I'd rub his neck again and then send him off away from me. Those are pretty delicate spots right there, and it's all about how much you do and when you do it. You can really help the horse make a big change in those moments when he's real interested in you, or you can miss the little things and it'll take a real long time after that before he'll be interested in looking you up again.

When it gets so you can send him away and he isn't afraid of you, that's got quite a little meaning to the horse. When he's not worried about you coming after him, he's liable to be in a better frame of mind to feel of you and you can learn better together that way.

You work on both sides of the horse. This is important. Most people go up and bridle or halter and saddle him from the left side. A lot of times the horse gets so he only wants to watch out of one eye, but you can get him over that. Get both eyes good.

What if he's good to approach and send away without a halter in your hand, but then when you have the halter, he leaves?

On some of these horse-catching projects, you need supervision from someone who has quite a little background at this. A lot of people are ready to give advice, but you've got to know what part of it fits you and sometimes none of it will. Some people can get the job done on their own but there aren't many who can really help a person avoid some of the things that can get them into more problems, if the horse is really hard to catch, I'll say that.

If he starts to move around that corral, why to blend in real smooth with that evading sort of horse, you'd want to be pretty smooth. You can tell when he's going to change direction, and you get yourself to that side where he wanted to go. If he starts to the right, then you get over there to that right side, and same way on the left. You'd be over there. We'll assume he's got his butt towards you and he's turning away with his head.

But with some horses you might have to let them run around that corral quite a little bit, and it takes some knowledge to do that, too. So there's quite a little that takes place teaching a horse how to be caught. When you move and how you move and all those little things are so important to a horse. That's where the experimenting comes into things. It all depends on how experienced you are and how much trouble the horse is to catch. It also depends on what sort of place he's in where he doesn't want to be caught.

Some horses will understand what to do with you anticipating their moves and wanting to blend in with them, and they will catch on right away. Others will do quite a little running around until they find out that they can't get away from you, completely, we'll say. So then it's up to the person to do a little something that will attract that horse's attention, and there's an unlimited amount of variations in there. We'll assume that you aren't on a time clock to catch your horse, and haven't any plans to trap the horse to be caught because you're short on time. When you do that, it's a sure thing you'll be doing more of it later on, and that's just what we're trying to stay away from, is pursuing those horses.

It's usually not helpful to the horse if you're too quick in your movements. If he wants to keep going, then you don't try to stop him. Your better judgment will tell you if he's ready to stop. Most horses, if they have the right opportunity, won't want to run over you or get too close to you. Of course, there are exceptions and this is where your own survival comes in. You'll try real hard not to set up a situation where this takes place. If that horse does get in the habit of wanting to come up to you too fast, then you can hit him over the butt with the rope you have, and change other things about the way you handle that horse on the ground to build in respect. If you can lay that rope over his butt at the right time, then there's a lot of meaning to that horse. It tells him there's a better way to do things. And you'll be positioned far enough away that he wouldn't kick you, and if your adjustment was fitting he wouldn't have that thought anyway, because he'd be real busy leaving. A fella won't rush towards the horse or threaten him in any way before he swats him on the butt, and he'd be sure to have a long enough lead rope for this.

If he takes off and runs fast, then you can encourage that to a certain point and pretty soon he'll start to think of a better way. A person can step out in front of him and that will help to slow him down — he needs to slow down before you can catch him anyway. Some horses will run into you, or surprise you in other ways, so wouldn't do this in a way caused an excess of pressure for the horse, or a rise in his instincts of self-preservation. You don't want him to get afraid and turn back to the fence. Getting the horse physically hurt is just one of many things that can go wrong there if he doesn't understand your presentation. It's best to get some help on this from a person who understands how to get feel applied in a way the horse can understand.

Where do you stand when you're leading a horse?

It depends on the situation — whether he's a horse that wants to go way too fast, or one that wants to go way too slow. If he's too fast, then you're liable to be a shade behind or ahead as you work to get him to feel of you. It can take a little while to get the timing right on this so that it's effective for a horse that's too quick about things.

If he's too slow, then you have to teach that horse to lead up real free and that's in the first part of the book (Chapter 4, Part 2). Where you'd stand really all depends on the picture you have in your mind about leading him, and what you have in mind to offer the horse in the way of feel that will keep him the way he is, or change the way he handles on that lead rope.

Should the horse be kept far away on the lead rope to keep a person safe?
Get up close and get him to feel of you and then you'll be able to handle him out on the end of a rope later on, after he can feel of you up close. If he isn't feeling of you up close, he'll be even less able to at a distance, or when you're sitting up there on his back. You need a foundation first.

Is it all right to use a stud chain over the nose?
Then you're making him stop through pain. You aren't teaching a horse to feel of you. You've failed in the helping part of things, and you're trying to make him do it (whatever it is you are wanting him to do) instead. That's not the right attitude.

(The same person had this follow-up question.) But what if when I ride him, he does fine? We win at the shows and he's basically a really great horse.
He'll do better for you over the jumps and in front of the cows, if you get him better on the ground. It seems to you like he's doing all right, but he'd do better with this other feel, rather than responding to the pain imposed by a stud chain. But if you don't know about teaching a horse to learn to feel of you, then the stud chain approach is just a mechanical solution. It won't work as well because there's always pressure involved, and it's applied in a way that it's difficult for the horse to understand. Without a release that is based on his response to your feel, he can't really understand the meaning of the pressure in that chain — except that he knows the pain of it. That chain won't ever bring out the best in a horse. To get a horse switched over from that takes time, and a lot of people don't want to spend time on that.

Will he ever get soft if I continue using a stud chain?
That really takes experience. Getting a horse to be soft with severe equipment, you've got to be an artist. You have to do so little, and do it so light, that it just isn't probable that you'll get it. It's possible. But really, it's a long shot, because if people are using that equipment they've missed a lot, and maybe too much, down at the bottom. That's the part where you learn about feel on the ground with the horse. Right on the start.

What if someone has to get a horse in a trailer and go someplace right away?
They've got the wrong train of thought to start with, if they've left the preparation out of it. There's some horses that you can make do this. It's just like with two people going out here to do a job. If one fella was going to make the other do what he wanted done, and another pair was going toward the job helping one another get that work done, then there'd be a nicer feeling about the job. The result would have

that feeling of teamwork based on some communication, rather than one fella running the show and the other toeing the line.

But it's real natural for people to want to make the horse do something because the horse is bigger and stronger. The ones who take this to an extreme, why they'll treat a horse like he's their slave, and this should never happen. It does in some places though. If they give it any thought at all, those people know that what they're wanting that horse to do isn't the horse's idea in the first place. If it were up to the horse, why he'd be out there with other horses, instead of doing what that person had in mind for him.

But, if the horse is fairly gentle and can fill in, if he hasn't been thumped on and made afraid, then he isn't going to be trying to get away from you and you can probably get him into that trailer and be going someplace right away. I think it's amazing what a horse will do for you if he can only understand what it is you want. If he can feel it and understand it, the chances are good that he'll do it. And if he doesn't understand, then he's lost and he'd do just about anything to get away from you. That's where people get this idea that they have to force the horse, to overpower him and make him do it. Some people just don't know it's possible to help a horse find a way to do what they are wanting done. But, when they force a horse into a trailer before he's prepared, well, surprising things can sure happen that they might wish to avoid.

What do you mean when you say the horse is "lost" or "filling in"?

It's quite challenging to offer the horse a fitting response just when he needs it the most. This'd be when he's upset, or seems to be "lost" or if he's panicked and unable to make it without some support. People might be liable to hand feed him a carrot or offer him grain if he's riled or upset, but what he needs a lot more than handouts is some direction and support that has purpose he can make sense of. When the life is surging up though his body it has to have someplace to go. His feet need to move when he's upset and agitated. He tells you this. Most people want to box the horse in, or tie him up and make him stand still if he's upset, but this goes completely against a horse's nature. And those handouts, especially at a time like this, why they lead to nothing good.

This is the main reason a person wants to build feel into the foundation on their horse, and this is especially true with young or troubled horses. Get that built in early, so when things get upsetting, the horse knows that you know how he feels. It's good if he knows that you know what he needs. And what he needs is to know that you'll have something to suggest for him to do in the way of movement. He needs to know that there's a way to place his feet and position his head low enough so the very act of raising it up in the air and tightening his stomach and back doesn't get him tense and frighten him even more. If that horse knows he can depend on you and the reliable feel of your hand, he will look to you for support when he gets into trouble or becomes unsure. You want your horse to know your mind, and for that to be possible, you have to learn quite a little about his. When you do, he'll be looking you up, and not for handouts either.

If you have a horse, this is pretty much your job anyway. It's this commitment from the human that helps a horse prepare for the future to a point where many of them will do something called "filling in." This is something a horse will do for certain people. Sometimes that person will be the one who prepared the horse to be able to fill in, and other times he'll fill in for someone who's had hardly any experience around horses at all. Filling in can be a real good thing.

Questions About Experience and Judgment

Are good horsemen made, or born?
There's a little of both that takes place there.

What are the choices that the best horse handlers have?
The feel from the horse tells a person what that horse is understanding and not understanding. A good horseman uses his better judgment to make choices, based on the feel he's getting back from a horse. Another way to say this is that his choices are unlimited, but one will be the best.

How do you get that good judgment?
Well, it has to do with experience. That will include a lot of trial and error. You have to experiment to see what works. That's where a student needs support from an instructor. We have to try to get that student to understand the feel they are getting from that horse, and then judge about how much firmness to use to help the horse make a change. The horse may not show any signs of change with the first application, or even the first several times. But if your judgment is practical, why that tells you whether to keep presenting the same thing, or maybe put a little variation in there someplace. That's what it means to learn from the horse, actually.

Why would anyone who's at the top of their field — for example, a winning cutting horse trainer or a grand prix jumper rider — have any use for this approach?
It would certainly give them more control of their horse, and that's what everybody's after.

Can what they call a "finished horse" benefit from this?

There isn't any horse that's living that doesn't need to be exposed a little bit to learn to feel of us. As long as that horse lives, he can learn to feel of a person and to respond to a person's feel.

My horse was trained the "old" way and I learned this way too, mostly on my own. Most of what I learned about works real good, but sometimes I get the feeling that my horse doesn't really trust me the way I'd like him to. What should I do?

Helping the horse feel of a person is what instills his confidence in that person. Using force or fear doesn't lead to anything good. When a horse is brought under control through force (restraining or leverage devices, electric shock or self-tightening gimmicks), it doesn't build anything good into the horse. And it never will. The use of fear builds in resistance too, because it brings out the horse's need for self-preservation, and this is the very thing you need to avoid if the horse is ever going to be trustworthy. In order for him to be trustworthy, that horse needs to be trusting of you. See, it has to start with the human.

Can people overcome old habits?

Some can. And some can't because they just don't want to change. If change isn't natural or easy for a person, they won't get much out of this. They got started the hard way and might stay there. It's not that they don't have feel, they do. They're using it in a way to *make* the horse do something instead of *helping* the horse do it. There's a world of difference between making and helping. But a person who has a strong desire to learn this, why they sure can learn it, all right. They're just going to need to be willing to make some changes.

Are there some people who will just never "get" this?

I don't like to criticize people who have very little to offer a horse. It's kind of a balance you need in there, and it's real important to remember that most people are doing the best they know how, so we wouldn't speak about fault in any case. There's two kinds of criticism. One is constructive criticism, which I think is very valuable, and the other is hurtful or condemning and does not inspire a person to change. I'm really only interested in that first kind, because it all gets down to the individual — the individual horse and the individual person. What happens between so many different horses and people makes it very hard for one set of words to be applied to everybody. But there's a set of words that will fit just about anybody. That's where the adjustable part of instructing comes in, and a good instructor is a real important part of getting onto this.

Even when a person can get real good help, there's two parts to this. You need to want that help a lot, and that help has to be available when you need it. When you're getting started, you need to be around somebody quite a few times who is more experienced than you are. Get as much help and as many ideas as you can from other people, and then use your better judgment as to what part of it fits. You've got to see whether it will work for you or it won't. You have to be the one able to do the editing. There are lots of people out there with plenty of information to offer you all right, but there are not a lot of instructors who can explain it in a way that others can understand. There's a surplus of them who will tell you what to do, and not be able to show you how to do it.

There could be a lot of reasons for this. Maybe they don't get it, or they haven't had an opportunity to be at the same place that the beginner is. Some fellas are just better working with horses than with people, but people ask them for help anyway because they see that these people can get results they admire. One problem that sure comes in there is when the person doing the demonstrating can't get those ideas about how to get a certain thing done across to the people in a way that's *useful* to them. Sometimes a person can get information that turns out to be really not useful at all.

This can happen because that instructor is lacking in some areas. I've also seen where the person who wants to learn is really way off in what they thought they saw, or heard, or understood. But the person right next to them might understand it the way that instructor intended for him to understand it, and that fella, why he's the one who's liable to get it applied straight away. That's because no two people are the same. That's the main reason why it's so beneficial to a person who's starting out to have a chance to handle a horse that's already been taught to operate real smooth, through feel. When this can happen, it reduces those feelings of doubt that come in for a person about how a horse is supposed to feel to them when he's operating that better way.

And then there's instructors out there who are more interested in starting those horses and students working on up the line a ways and bypassing all this part down at the base, where we're talking about. The place we're talking about is quite a bit further below where a lot of people are wanting to work. There's all kinds of reasons a person feels this way, but those reasons don't matter. What matters is that the horse doesn't understand it when they don't start at the beginning.

What advice would you give a new horse owner?

My advice would be to learn to feel of that horse.

What if a horse rears and runs by a new owner in the beginning, and that person experiences fear?

If that happens, then for sure that horse isn't feeling of that person. If he comes around the person that way, why then he's going to be doing some other things that aren't the best. And someone lacking experience with horses might have good reason to fear one, especially after something like this.

A person will want to try to keep from getting hurt, and keep their horse from getting hurt, too. So it's always nice for an inexperienced person to have some supervision on the start, from someone with more experience. When the person who's a new owner learns about feel and can get it applied to a horse, they won't be so likely to feel afraid. Until then, it's natural that they would feel this uncomfortable way.

How does a new owner, or someone just starting with this approach, keep from getting discouraged?

There's no harm in asking that one. If you're learning, why you wouldn't get discouraged. If you aren't learning, then you've got good reason to feel discouraged, and the most likely reason is that you either don't have good instruction or you've got a horse that's too far above or below where you are, and you don't know how to get with him. You know, a person goes to school for eight years just to get out of the eighth grade, and it seems like so many people think they should have things in the horsemanship department figured out in a few sessions. They need to take the time it takes.

If a person is discouraged, I'd ask them what was causing that, but I'd already have an idea that it could be several things because I've seen a lot of this. In most cases, it's either a lack of understanding of what's taking place, or else the person is short on time and likely to always be. Or, they could have a horse that doesn't fit them, or an instructor that isn't fitting them real well. Why any of these things'd be just cause for some discouragement. But, if they're talking to me about this problem, I'd know if it was the horse or the instructor, or it could just be the person isn't capable of understanding what's taking place. And you'd be sure to stop before you said that, because that would get the person even more discouraged than they were, and for sure you don't want that.

Of course, the best way to answer this is to have the horse and the rider right there in front of you, and then there'd be a limit to the speculating a fella'd need to do on this subject.

Chapter 9:

MEANINGS

❖ **ACTUAL FACTS:** This is the main thing we're interested in, the actual facts where horses are concerned. There's a lot that's spoken about all right, but people seem to want something to read. Those horses need the handler or rider to focus on things that can help the horse, *through feel.* And this book is to help people understand how to help those horses through feel so they can understand what's expected of them — which could be most anything. Without the actual facts figuring in there pretty heavy, well, that understanding part isn't going to be in there either. This is why it's my main goal, as an instructor, to explain about the importance of feel to the horse and how a person would go about getting it applied.

If the person doesn't know about feel and how to apply it, the horse would only have fear and guesswork to fall back on. That fear a horse has of some things he doesn't understand is tied right to his self-preservation. Of course, the person would be operating with some fear and guesswork, too, unless they understood the actual facts that the horse needs them to be working with.

On the start, it might take awhile for the person to understand the right feel to use so he could fit a particular horse. But when they figure it out those horses sure understand. That's why there's such a great need for people to learn about feel and how to apply it. That way we can get together with our horses, for the better results.

❖ **ADJUST:** You change something a little bit, if this word is mentioned. But what you'd do would really depend on what came before the adjustment and what came after it. Anything that isn't fitting to the horse would cause a person to think about adjusting what they were doing.

The word "adjustable" is connected real close to this word, and that's the way you want to have the hindquarters on your horse. You'd need to be able to change those hindquarters around through feel, wherever you needed them to be, and in some cases they would need to be real adjustable right on the spur of the moment.

❖ **ANTICIPATION:** When we speak about anticipation, we're talking about the horse being ready to move in response to your feel, but not to the point where he takes over. If he's feeling of you, he's not liable to be overdoing the anticipation.

❖ **APPLY:** There's no limit to the things that don't work, so it's best to talk about the things that do work. Like feel, and how to apply it.

To get good at applying feel, there's always a place for a little experimenting to see if the animal, and we'll say a horse in this case, can follow the feel that you have presented. If he can, then he would be ready to move up the line a little to learn the next thing you needed to teach him. As he progressed up the line, the foundation he was working from would get bigger, and set in place real solid, so it would be there for him to fall back on.

That foundation is real important, because if there's trouble spots showing up in his future, that foundation is in place for him to rely on. And that takes place right at the bottom, on the start of it, when he had no idea of what a person had in mind for him to do. If a person takes enough time to develop the horse's understanding of each thing they wanted him to know about and be able to do, through feel, and if they were consistent in the way that they applied each particle of feel, there would be no need to progress that horse any faster than he could understand — because he would understand. *And any horse will understand it, if he's brought along with this preparation part worked into his mental system right from the start.*

If that person who'd been doing the experimenting was getting feel applied in a way that fit the individual horse, then he's understanding what he's supposed to do maybe more than before and that horse would start to develop some confidence in himself. That's what a person would build on and then, just a little bit at a time, that horse and the person could move up the line together.

When you learn how to feel of an animal, and we're speaking about horses now but this could take in all animals, then you're in a position for that animal to learn how to feel of you. Then, when he does learn how to feel of you, how far you can go on from there just all depends on how knowledgeable you are about feel and how to get it applied in a way that he can understand what you want. We wouldn't say there's a limit to that.

❖ **ARM** *(holding arm)*: This arm supports the leading arm by bringing the holding rein in against the neck, and you'll be sure not to take that rein *across* the neck. I don't like to speak about the hands and what they do. They're there just to hold the reins or the lead rope. Of course how those reins are held is really important, but it's the arms that have the bigger job, I'll say that.

On a horse that has been taught to feel of the rider, even the slightest pressure from the holding arm will stabilize those shoulders and lead to straightness through his body, which is so important in maneuvering the horse through turns and stopping. A horse gets confused when a rider is off balance and uses that holding arm to stay in the saddle, instead of using it to help the horse.

One real important thing that you use the holding rein for is to feel the horse on both sides, and to teach him to feel of you. That way he has a chance of staying right where you want him to be, which is between your legs and reins. He wouldn't be pushing against you with any part of himself. Respect for that holding rein is what you build in there on the ground (through both direct and indirect feel) before you ever get on him. That way he knows what you want him to do when he feels the rein against his neck after you do get up there.

How the holding arm works right along with that leading arm is a real important function, and this will take time to understand. There's been quite a bit written about that earlier in this book.

In this picture, the horse has a good head position and is not pushing against the bit. Things are working pretty smooth here, and the horse has the support he needs to know what he's supposed to do.

Diamond Lu Collection

In this picture, the rider's left arm is the holding arm, and his right arm is the leading arm.

❖ **ARM** *(leading arm)*: This arm has a real important job. It's the arm that takes the horse's head around one way or another. Many people use the term "leading rein," or "direct rein," but really, it's the arm that does the leading. This arm provides the horse with the feel of whichever direction you intend for him to go — and that's if you're on the ground or on his back. It's real important to understand the function of this arm and how it works with the holding arm, because it's connected to the feel and life in your whole body, and where you're wanting that horse to go. Understanding how to use this arm to get feel applied in a way that the horse can understand fits right in with the basics, on the start.

Diamond Lu Collection

These horses are working something out, and it's between them.

❖ **ATTITUDE:** We'll assume a person is speaking about an attitude the horse has that isn't the best. There's always a cause for this and I'd search to find out what it was, through feel. When the horse is first starting out, his attitude is more or less on survival. Self-preservation causes his attitude to be as it is on the start. A poor attitude can show up if the horse isn't properly handled. When it does show up, then it's up to the person to see what caused it.

Generally speaking, if it was left up to the horse, he would be out eating grass on the hill and not any place around where a person is, and that word wouldn't even come up. He might decide to kick or bite another horse out there, but that would be between them.

If he were left alone, why, the horse wouldn't have a bad attitude towards a human.

❖ **BAD HORSE:** It's a good subject to talk about, but you have to figure out what made that horse the way he is. Was it the way that horse was handled or was it self-preservation that made him do things that weren't good for him, or good for the human either? He's really just a confused horse so we wouldn't use that word "bad." There aren't any bad horses, they are just mixed up and it's important to know the difference. Because the horse had the wrong feel presented to him, the person and the horse both missed that right way to feel of each other on the start. This sometimes leads to people using this word about a horse, but it could sure be forgotten about if certain things shaped up.

❖ **BALANCE** *(for the rider)*: There are many variables that affect a person's balance, the main one being at what age and stage of physical development the person was introduced to horses and riding. Generally speaking, the younger a person starts out, the easier it is for them to learn how to balance when they're horseback. This is just an observation that has many exceptions, depending on what the person is capable of doing with the horse. "Natural" riders are usually people who started young and developed their balance on horseback.

❖ **BARN SOUR:** This is what people say about a horse that always wants to go back to the barn. But if the horse has learned to respect you, through feel, there wouldn't be any reason for him to want to go back to the barn.

Generally speaking, a horse that does this has been handled by a rider who's missed most all the preparation at the beginning. They haven't had the opportunity to understand what caused the horse to want to go back to the barn. Because the horse got confused about things away from the barn, he wanted to go back where he might feel all right about some things that happen there. But he can get to where he's comfortable just about anywhere. You have an advantage if you have prepared him to be with you, through feel. That way, that term "barn sour" would never need to be mentioned.

❖ **BASICS:** Developing feel is what you start with, and it comes in there even before some of these other basics. And getting that better feel — that'd be feel that was real effective — *applied to the horse* comes in anytime after the person has first learned to *feel of the horse.* Even when the horse and the person get together through feel, there's always a place for the basics. There's really not a time when a horse is better without them. The timing and feel a person presents to the horse on the ground is always connected to these basics. Way down at the bottom is what the foundation comes from, and that's just basics. Without those, many surprising things can happen.

How a person goes about laying that foundation has a lot of variables to it, because no two people or horses are alike. It's important to have a real good instructor to help that person learn how to feel of the horse, but one might not always be around.

Diamond Lu Collection

This young person is practicing some basic maneuvers with this older horse.

One thing I've heard, and I think it's all right to say it, is that the last thing some people learn about where horses are concerned is the first thing you need to get understood and applied. And that'd be when a fella's referring to the basics, there isn't any question about that.

We want to get the basics introduced early because so many people like to go fast. They want to start those horses too far up the line — way above what those horses or even the people themselves can understand without a foundation. I'd rather a person who was going to ride a horse, or lead one even, had some fitting ideas about feel that a horse could understand to go along with their plan of doing those things. It would sure make a big difference to the horse if they did. It doesn't matter how far up the line you want to go with your horse, there will be problems cropping up if those basics have been left out. And if they had to get left out for too long, well, could be some people might think they would like to spend their time another way. But, we're in hopes that they'll get it sorted out in plenty of time to keep themselves and their horses out of trouble.

❖ **BLENDING IN WITH THE HORSE:** This has to do with getting together with your horse. This is when you have picked up his feel, and he has picked up yours. When it gets to being this way between a person and a horse, he's understanding what you expect him to do.

❖ **BLIND SPOT:** That would be only if he had one eye out, or a bad eye. Then it would be harder for him to see things on the side that didn't have a good eye and — depending on where he is — his self-preservation would cause him to operate a little different to make up for that eye that has the problem. But if a horse has two good eyes, why, there isn't any blind spot because he will move around so he can see something if he wants to. But people speak about it anyway.

Diamond Lu Collection

Bill attaching a leather thong to a bosal. It will be tied to the fore-lock and used under the bridle.

❖ **BOSAL:** Some people call a hackamore a bosal, but what we mean is that thinner rawhide noseband that goes underneath a bridle. A person can put it on there about three or four ways, but the most practical way to have it is with a light piece of leather that's used as a head piece. Some people just use a little piece of rawhide and tie it up to the forelock.

The lead rope a fella'd use to go along with that is about 12 - 14 feet long, and usually about 1/4 or 3/8 inch thick. It's made of nylon, horsehair, cotton or just about anything you want. You can braid them yourself or buy these lead ropes ready-made. Some fellas take one end of that rope and tie it right onto the heel knot of that little bosal. Then they coil it up and tie it onto their saddle with the front saddle strings.

I tie my lead rope in a loop (with a bowline) around the lower part of the horse's neck and then I bring up that loose end and coil it up rather small, so I can tie it onto my saddle. That way, if a fella needs to hand it to someone to lead their horse, why they just slip it up to his throat latch area and re-tie the loop so it's smaller, and then they run the end down through the bosal. That makes a good way to lead a fella's horse for him, or even your own.

Dorrance Collection

Bill visits with Freddie Howard at the Tularcitos Ranch branding in Carmel Valley, California. Early 1960's.

❖ **BRACE / TIGHTNESS:** This comes from confusion about the feel that's presented to the horse, but he can sure learn to operate without being braced or tight. If he's unsure about the meaning of what a person does, he might get ready to do what he thinks he ought to do instead. This is where his self-preservation comes in, and survival is one thing those horses are sure about. The best thing to do is not to allow a brace to get started in the horse in the first place. But if the horse isn't prepared ahead of time for what you're going to need him to understand in the future, it's liable to show up, all right. Probably somebody got in a hurry on the start and missed a spot, and that is likely what gets those things to show up in the horse. Those spots that get missed, why they aren't the best, I'll say that. But, if one's been in there a while, you'll take your time with him so it doesn't get confusing for him when you start to get his thinking changed around. We try not to get in a hurry because it's going to be confusing to the horse when we do. If his confusion isn't taken care of, other things can happen that you don't expect.

❖ **BRINGING UP THE LIFE:** This would mean a person was livening up the horse for a purpose they had in mind. For sure, you need to have a purpose for livening up that horse. The person needs to have a clear understanding of the way that horse's energy is going to be put to work, because once that life comes up from inside that horse, it needs to be directed. *Bringing up the life is a feel that comes from your body right on through to his body.* This could be called one of the basics, because you need to have it built into your foundation real solid.

That life in the horse that comes up, why it can occur anytime you are sitting on him or when you work with him on the ground. *It can also occur when the horse thought you meant for him to bring up that energy by something you did.* The person might not even realize they did anything to cause the horse to respond the way he did. It could be just some extra little unwanted motion they made, but the horse sure noticed it. So the next time you'd try to notice what you did to cause him to respond the way he did. Maybe you'd have to do something a little different the next time — or you wouldn't, if what you'd done worked out for the best. No, if it was something that you did through feel that got that horse to operate that good way for you, why you'd try hard to remember what it was that you did right on the spur of the moment — so you'd be thinking about what to do when you needed that useful response from the horse sometime in the future. That's where your timing and your experimenting would come in, because those two things fit right in with the plan that you'd need to have ready the next time you needed some extra life in the horse. We'll assume you'd be successful in bringing up the life in the horse, and when it showed up, you'd be prepared for it, or you'd try to be anyway.

The main part of this that people need to understand is that the horse already has life. It's just a question of how a person goes about getting it to show up when there's a need for it, and then getting it to work for them. *It's going to fit your horse a lot better if you have a job to do with him when that life becomes available, than if you don't.*

We'll say another word for that (life in the horse) could be his energy. This might show up all of a sudden and be surprising to a person who didn't have much experience. And maybe they would wish to avoid this. But if they had feel built into their way of doing things on the start, that'd cut way down on some of the more surprising things that can happen.

❖ **BUCK:** Any horse can buck, but we'd prefer that they didn't if someone was sitting up there. They're lost and mixed up when they get to doing that. No, if a horse gets to bucking with a person, it's only due to self-preservation and maybe something that's been left out of his education up to that point. It's confusion that causes a horse to buck, because his mental system doesn't understand what he's supposed to do. When this happens, his physical system responds the way he thinks he should, and where bucking is concerned, he's liable to continue this way until his mental system gets switched around and he can realize he's not going to get hurt. Generally speaking, when there's a different feel presented to the horse in his foundation, he'd get onto that and then the bucking and some other unwanted motions wouldn't show up.

Diamond Lu Collection

Diamond Lu Collection

We'd rather these horses didn't buck when someone was sitting up there.

When I really needed this (approach through feel) was in my teens, because those horses sure bucked. In those days, it was really just a question of how you stayed on because there wasn't anybody who said what you did so that they wouldn't buck. It would have been real helpful to hear that.

When feel is presented in a way that a horse can understand it on the start, most horses aren't liable to buck when they're saddled for the first time — or they won't buck too much, I'll say that. But there's always going to be some exceptions to this. The horses in these pictures got to bucking because those saddles don't feel right and they thought it would help to get rid of them. But a horse can get real comfortable with all that gear on him. This takes more time than a lot of people realize.

Some horses really get so they enjoy that part of having people around and the place you're liable to see a lot of these horses is at the rodeo, because bucking is their job. But if you're working a horse with feel, why then he wouldn't ever be thinking about bucking. Of course, something could always happen to upset him, but generally speaking, he would look to the person for support if he'd been handled with feel on the start.

❖ **CADENCE:** (Cadence refers to the timing and placement of the horse's feet in any gait or, put another way, it's the pattern and rhythm of the hoofbeats. This is not a word that Bill uses, but because the word is sometimes misunderstood, we thought these pictures would be helpful.

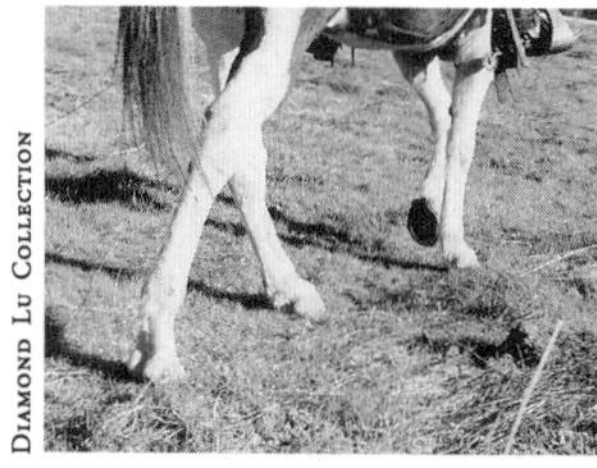

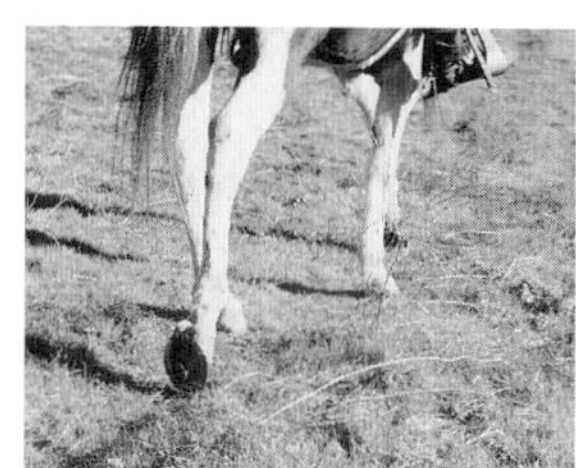

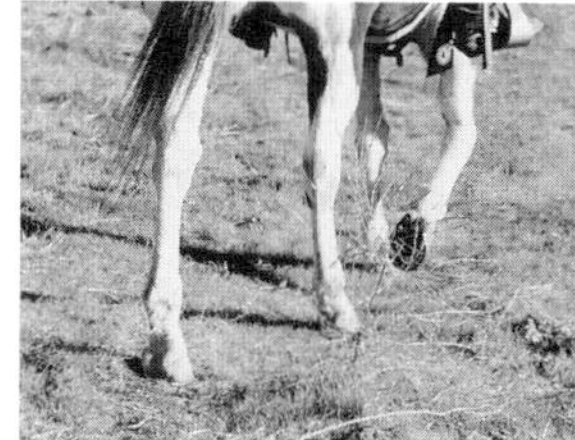

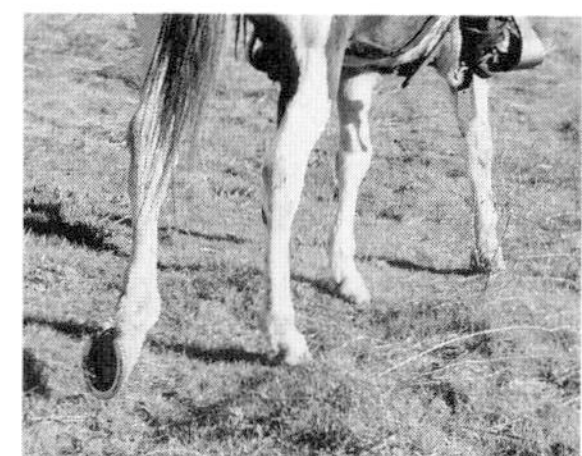

Diamond Lu Collection

These pictures show the footfall at the walk.

Diamond Lu Collection

In each stride of the trot, alternate diagonal pairs of legs support the horse as he goes along. The horse on the left is balanced on his right diagonal pair and the horse on the right is on his left pair.

Diamond Lu Collection

The trotting horse on the left is about to land on his right diagonal. The loping horse behind him is about to land on his right diagonal, too. He's on the left lead, and his leading leg is highest off the ground.

In a single stride of the lope, or canter, the horse's feet land in a different pattern than they do at the trot. As he moves up from the trot to this faster gait, nature has fixed it so he loses one diagonal in exchange for the extra speed and greater reach of the lope stride. He departs in each stride with a hind foot, uses one supporting diagonal for balance in the second beat of the lope, and then lands on a single front foot. There's more written about this in Chapter 5.)

Diamond Lu Collection

These horses are loping on their right leads. The brown horse is on his left hind leg, which is the first beat of the lope stride. The paint horse is on the third beat of the stride, with his right front foot on the ground.

Diamond Lu Collection

In this picture of loping on the right lead, the horse is stepping down on the left diagonal. That's the second beat in the stride.

❖ **CHANGE:** Where horses and that word "change" are concerned, not everything will feel comfortable on the start, because that word "everything" takes in quite a lot. When there's a need for you to make a change, you may try several things, hoping that one will be understandable to the horse. You might be doing quite a little guesswork, but as time goes on you'd probably get it figured out.

After some testing and speculating, there may be one thing you happen to try that fits that horse just right. You'd be sure to change the feel you presented to him as close to when he made that change as you could, and you'd do this by easing off. This way that horse can understand what it is he is supposed to do.

When the change in the horse you're looking for shows up, that good feel that comes to him when you ease off is what matters so much to him. *That's because if you eased off right when that change started to show up, he would remember what you presented before you eased off. And he'd remember the easing off part, too. This is how you teach things to a horse using feel that is properly applied.* Your better timing matching up with your better feel, and the way that you got it applied, is what makes this work.

There are changes that can affect a person, all right, and this will affect a horse because they're real sensitive. It's not always possible to know what causes change in a person's life, even when it's the person's own life. Since the horse can't talk, it's even more difficult to figure out what's bothering him. It takes real careful observation. The changes you observe in the horse are his responses to other things that change, and this process is always taking place — any time you're speaking about horses anyway. We're working towards a spot where change, generally speaking, will not be so bothersome to the horse. When things are understandable to the horse, change won't trouble him.

❖ **CHANGING EYES:** A horse's eyes don't change. It's a horse's body that does the changing. The horse turns his head and shapes up his body so he can see whatever he needs to see. You'd work both sides of your horse so both eyes get used to seeing you, and this way the horse wouldn't think that you belong just on one side. He would get so he could see you anywhere and it wouldn't bother him. So long as the horse is feeling of you, then there isn't a reason for him to be one-sided.

❖ **COLD-BACKED HORSE:** This is just something people say about a horse that has tightness in his back. After they learn how to teach a horse to feel of them, they aren't apt to have a cold-backed horse. It's best not to cinch a horse up tight without moving him around the corral a little bit. Get him to move around the corral (at the walk, trot, and lope and up to the gallop, if there's a lot of room in there), and if he has some tightness in his body, that should loosen him up. If you knew he had some tightness in his back, you'd check him out on this before working him on the ground or getting on him.

❖ **COLLECTION:** This is important to know about and to practice. The feel you build in from the ground is what gives your horse the foundation for true collection. So many people use this word, but the way they go about collecting a horse seems to take away the interest a horse would have in being collected. When you're speaking about collection or lead changes, it's real important to go real slow at those places further back down the line. You'd spend a lot of time on the things that come before collection and that's where a good foundation is built. You need it in there to work from.

Once you have prepared him to be real mellow and flexible at the poll in response to your feel, then you need to have that horse understand *your whole body feel* that causes him to want to liven up *his whole body*.

You'd start this at the walk. If a horse doesn't collect at the walk, it's because he's not been prepared further down to understand how to collect, and you'll need to spend more time there until he can understand what he's supposed to do. You want that horse to respond to the feel of your body when it livens up. He needs to feel of you through those reins, and soften for you as he moves into the walk. He'd tuck his chin down and in, just a little, in response to your feel. When he does he would be liable to leave real smooth from a standstill and never push against that bit. This will take some time to perfect at the walk. Once this is pretty good, he'd be ready to progress to the trot.

Once the trot is real smooth, you'd move to the lope. You'd do this on either lead, too. You'd just present him with the feel for either one and have him pick up either lead. These maneuvers come in way before you'd have any thought of collecting your horse at the gallop and a person will take some time practicing this. A horse that collects up at the gallop is very attractive, even if that horse isn't much for looks.

Gale Nelson

A NICE FEEL IN THE FOUNDATION ON THIS HORSE WAS LAID IN THERE TO START WITH, AND IT'S WHAT MAKES THIS HORSE LOOK THE WAY SHE DOES. IT BRINGS OUT THE NICER APPEARANCE IN THIS HORSE.

❖ **COLTS:** Some people say that about older horses (refer to them as colts), when they're maybe four or five or seven and haven't been handled much, but in this book we're talking about the younger horses that haven't been handled much. And that'd include geldings and fillies.

❖ **COLT STARTING:** It's the "starting" that really deserves our attention. And where that horse is (in his development) determines the way you'd go about starting him. But one thing's for sure, you'll be using feel when you start a colt, or any horse.

Colts that are worked horseback in a group, like those shown in the next picture, can learn a lot about feel from someone who's experienced at applying it. As they move

Diamond Lu Collection

If a fella's had experience starting colts, it's real helpful to drive a group of young horses like this.

around like this, they are getting used to the saddles and are beginning to understand what it feels like to travel in the different gaits. They are responding to the feel of the fella who's driving them around the pasture. They can get an understanding of how to hook on this way, and how to separate between the feel to go left and right, to speed up and slow down and to stop.

❖ **CONFUSION:** Anytime a horse stops feeling of you, he's getting confused and he may appear cranky. So long as he's feeling of you, he's not going to be confused and a lot of undesirable things won't even develop.

In this picture, the horses are confused about what's expected of them. These people are doing their best, and in most cases a person will try to do that. But these people are confused about what's taking place and they aren't sure what to do either.

Diamond Lu Collection

These horses are confused, and so are the people. It's nobody's fault. It just happens.

❖ **CORNERING:** That word takes in so much. A lot of people use this to mean different things. What I mean is just bringing that nose around a little, because that's the start of cornering. Of course, whether you can do that and leave the feet still, just depends on the horse and the ability of the person handling the horse. But you'd like to be able to do that with your horse on the ground and from his back, because when this is in place, he's learned to feel of you.

It's important to get that preparation built in there so when you bring that nose around a little, that horse knows whether or not you want him to move those feet. If you want those feet to stay put, or you don't, he's been prepared through feel to understand the difference. So many maneuvers you might need your horse to be able to do further up the line depend on this part being real clear to the horse. Of course, the person needs to know about this first, and whatever that person needed the horse to do (with his feet) while they were cornering that horse, that's the feel they would present. It's real important for the horse to understand your intent and *the way you present your feel to him is how he finds out what your intent is*. And if you were sitting on him of course you'd be using both reins to get that message across to him. And you'd ease off, of course, when he did anything close to the area of what you wanted him to do, and you'd build on that from there.

There's always so many things taking place at one time that a person needs to be aware of them — because one thing's for sure, that horse is thinking. If you can get that horse to pick up your cornering feel real good, while getting him to travel straight, then he's learned to feel of you. But, of course, that's only one way to corner a horse. There's other things you'd do that figure in there for doubling, and for other jobs that aren't emergencies. *You'd want that horse's hindquarters to be real adjustable, because it's so important to the horse to have it that way. And because it is, it should be real important for the rider, too, I'll put it that way.* No, when you have that cornering built in there, why there isn't any question that your horse has learned to feel of you, and there's a world of difference in that.

Carole Wangenheim

Bill and his mare, Beauty. "She's flexible in the neck and at the poll, and picks up my cornering feel real good here."

❖ **CRANKINESS:** A horse like this is just confused about what he's expected to do. If there's an excess of pressure applied to a horse that is confused, resentment can set in there and when it does, he lets you know about it. If you don't miss some of the important things down the line, crankiness isn't apt to show up.

❖ **CRITICISM:** There's two kinds of criticism. One is constructive and I'd say that means helping. Then there's that other kind and it's destructive and we don't want any part of that. It's not fitting. When criticism is offered in a helpful way it's all right, and when it's used otherwise, it isn't all right. That's why I don't use criticism that way.

❖ **DIAGONALS:** This word refers to two of the horse's legs — one front leg and one hind leg — that are on opposite sides. A left diagonal refers to the left front and right hind leg. A right diagonal means the right front and left hind leg. This is a naturally occurring motion that helps the horse keep better balance in the trot and the back-up. The horse also relies on his diagonals for balance at the walk and the lope, but this isn't so obvious.

❖ **DIRECT & SUPPORT:** These two things go together. If you're using these words, you'd be talking about either your arms, and the meaning you are building into your horse's understanding about those reins, or your legs, and your horse's understanding of their feel on his body. You'd get your whole body involved in feeling of the horse, because when he gets to feeling of you, it's your whole body he needs to rely on so he understands what you need him to do. The actual meanings of these words are what the horse needs you to understand to maneuver him through feel, which you will learn about through some experimenting.

You'd want to be consistent in the way you present yourself to him, and you'll put plenty of variation in there to stay away from patterns. And your lessons, they don't need to be too long.

The horse in this picture is feeling of the person because there is enough direction (from the right arm) and support (from the left arm) for him to understand what's expected. When the horse changes direction, the fella'd switch the rope in his hands and then the function of those arms would be the reverse of what they had been. The arm that was doing the directing would then be supporting the horse, and the arm that was in the supporting position will take over the job of directing the horse back to the left. It's the same idea when you're riding and need to change directions, only then you are holding onto the reins.

Diamond Lu Collection

There is enough direction and support for the horse to understand what's expected of him.

If you are riding along with two hands on the reins and then make a turn to the right, your right arm would be directing your horse to turn in that direction. The motions of your left arm and leg are there to *support* the action of the right arm, as it *directs* the horse on a new line of travel. Depending on what sort of turn to the right you were making, your right leg would be positioned to invite the shoulders or the whole body to move towards the right. It can also be used to help the hindquarters move to the left, if the situation calls for that. It's really no different when you're working on the ground. Your intent determines the function each arm will have at any given moment. If they are in good positions and your timing is clear, then the horse will understand what you want and he will do it.

❖ **DISCIPLINE:** We're trying to help the horse find a better way on his own, not to force anything on him or punish him for being the way he is. Some people think a horse needs discipline. Well, if that means whipping him, then they don't understand that he's just confused about what's expected of him. That whip has no place in horsemanship, not the way the horse needs you to understand it anyway. A horse will start to catch on to what's expected of him when feel is presented to him in a way that has meaning for him, and that's up to the person.

If a person really wants to know about working with a horse in a way that teaches the horse to understand what's expected of him, discipline wouldn't be fitting. Most people want to start way up the line, but without the foundation of feel built in there for him, the horse doesn't have any idea what he's supposed to do. The best thing to do is take enough time on the basics so there wouldn't be a place to use this word "discipline," or a whip.

❖ **DO LESS:** This is what we're hoping people will do a lot more of. When people get onto this good feel of a horse, why then the horse understands it and is making use of it in the work they have for him. These people would be the best ones to show someone else about not doing so much. The horse is capable of doing a lot more than a person sometimes can see that he's able to do for them, and with a good feel in there, why, it doesn't take much. It's amazing what a horse will do *for* you, if he only understands what you want. And it's also quite amazing what he'll do *to* you if he doesn't.

❖ **DOMINATE:** Seems there must be some other words to go along with this word. Because if it's only about this, why there's no place for this idea if you're speaking about horses. A young horse, especially one that gets bothered, will look to the rider for support — through feel. No, this word "dominate" wouldn't fit a horse at all. But that is what some people say about handling one anyway.

❖ **DOUBLING THE HORSE:** This is when you pull him around with one rein to keep him from running into a tree or something. Or, if he got startled and you needed him to put some effort into slowing down, why you'd double him then. Generally speaking, I use this for emergency measures. But for it to be effective when you need it, that preparation (cornering and other basic yielding maneuvers) has to be built into your foundation. I taught all my horses about this and did it in a way that those horses could understand it. You could write a whole lot on this subject, but there's not enough room for it in this book.

❖ **DRAW:** There is no force involved with draw — it's more of an invitation. The draw that we're talking about has to do with first getting the horse's attention, and then waiting for him to take a new direction. You can do this with a direct feel of your halter rope or the reins, or with indirect feel and nothing at all in your hands.

You'd be using feel to draw his attention towards you. When his attention comes that way his head will eventually follow, and if things don't happen to interfere or distract the horse right after that, why then, the rest of his body will follow the general direction of where his mind is focused.

When you're working on the ground with the horse this way — and that's if you're using equipment on him or not — there's things you can do to draw him away from the side of the fence or corral, and it's good to have an idea in your mind of what those things are before you start. This is something that a good instructor can help a person with, because there's room for a lot of mix-up in this part on the start.

And if you're horseback, or working on the ground with your halter rope or rein, why then, I'll say the draw from the feel of that equipment just directs his attention. If the preparation's been taken care of, it directs his body where you'd like for him to go. When you're drawing a horse to change directions on the lead rope or with a rein from his back — say to the left — then when that left foot is coming forward off the ground, you'd just direct that foot out to the side and set it down with your lead rope or your rein. There's no pulling involved in this because you're just getting with the movement of that horse's body and the timing of his feet (as they are) moving. When you do this, that's what gets that horse real used to operating for you with that lightness. You'd all the time try to have a float in your lead rope or your reins when he's picking those feet up and setting them down.

When you draw his nose around with your arm — and a person wouldn't say hand because it's the arm that moves and the hand just holds the rein — well, the timing of it depends on how short you want to make the turn. A horse can step to the side an inch or two, or he can reach clear back and set that leading leg close to the hind foot and really tighten up the turn. How much of the horse's weight needs to be shifted back before he has to do something just all depends on what the person wants, and that could be most anything. But whatever it is will require him to be real responsive to the draw of the leading arm and rein, or the lead rope. When it's this good way, using feel, those feet won't weigh anything in your hand. Just the weight of that lead rope or rein is all.

❖ **DRIFT:** This is what you might have to let the horse do so you can pick up his feel. You let him drift a ways, not real far maybe, but it depends on the horse and the situation just how much actual drifting will be good for him and safe for the person, too. This is real important to know about because if you go along with some horses when they get this idea, they get into a better frame of mind and get real interested in picking up your feel. You'd use this drifting to help shape the horse's understanding of what you wanted and you'd allow for many variables. After you got onto (understood) his feel, why he would get used to the way that was with the two of you going along there, and he would pick up your feel. When he did, that'd be the place where you'd ease off. This easing off lets him know that was the right thing for him to do. You're teaching the horse something that way, because he understands easing off. But you wouldn't let that drifting turn into the horse taking over with ideas of his own that are connected in any way to pushiness. That's out. You don't want that.

There's a fine line in that drifting part where your better judgment comes in. I'd rather head off that pushiness before it ever gets started. No, the drifting that we're speaking about is what you allow him to do if he needs to, or if he's bothered, so he can get comfortable and interested in going along with your feel. Of course, this is more effective if you can work the horse on the ground and build that feel in before you are sitting up there, but a person doesn't always have that opportunity. Someone with more experience, and I'll say quite a bit of it, can start using this same idea to get feel working for him when they're horseback. If there's a job to do, it's real helpful not to wait too long to start building that feel in, so a fella wouldn't need to wait on that, he'd want to build it in there straight away, if he could.

❖ **DRIVE LEG:** This is the leg that a horse pushes off with. Some people speak more about this leg than the horse's other legs because they are inclined to think it's more important than those others. But a horse can push off any leg most anytime, if there's need for it, and this is an actual fact. Whether or not the rider understands this depends on what he's been exposed to in his learning progress, but if he's going to be handling horses through feel, he'll get this sorted out.

The person who understands how important feel is to a horse will likely speak about feel, and not about a drive leg, unless they do it only because other people they are working with are thinking along those lines. These people aren't liable to be relying on feel. In a case like that, it's better to get them off that other way of thinking, because when a person is operating through feel, why he can handle any of the horse's legs and put them anywhere.

It's when a person doesn't know about feel that he can get mixed up on these other subjects, like drive leg. That horse will sure get mixed up, too, and surprising things can happen that a person might rather not experience.

❖ **DRIVING THE HORSE:** It means you teach him to move away from you. That's one definition for it. Then there's also the part of driving the horse that's connected to a job, like going real slow from one corral to another. If you're an inexperienced person, you need to be careful about some of these things on the start, so the horse doesn't get confused about whether you want to catch him or drive him some place. It just all depends on how you approach him and what intent you have, and that takes in quite a lot. It takes time for a person to get these things sorted out. When they do, that horse will understand what the person has in mind if they're using feel when they drive the horse.

❖ **DROPPING A SHOULDER:** When the horse doesn't understand what he's supposed to do in response to the feel of the holding rein, then he's liable to push against it, which is really just a big misunderstanding between the horse and the rider. Pushing against the rein, or any part of the person, is disrespect that the person hasn't taken care of and we'll assume it's because they haven't learned how to correct it. Or, maybe in some cases, they don't know there's a problem. But there's a lot a person can do on the ground before they ever get on the horse so this problem isn't liable to show up. If he's feeling of you, there's respect built into that and there's no part of pushiness where a horse respects that person who's handling or riding him through feel. That way they wouldn't need to call that shoulder a problem, or to correct anything.

(Conventional longeing practices that do not make use of feel actually encourage a horse to lean on the inside shoulder and lower the ribcage towards the inside of the circle. When this happens, there's also a tendency for him to pull against the longe line as he travels. The lack of an understandable feel in the longe line causes him to tip his nose, head and neck away from the person in the center, and elevate the outside hip —all of which gives him the appearance of "dropping a shoulder.")

Most people aren't going to see what there is to see in this picture, at first. There's quite a lot taking place here that will give the horse some ideas he shouldn't have. This horse is prepared to rely on pressure to travel in a circle around the person in the middle. He's been taught how to resist a lot of pressure by leaning into that chain they have across his nose, and this habit will transfer straight over to the rides he's going to have for them. His body isn't soft or rounded in the direction he's going, and his hips are to the outside. It's these things combined that give that horse the education he needs to drop a shoulder while he's traveling in a circle, because he's not being set up to do any different.

Diamond Lu Collection

WHERE A PERSON THINKS THEY NEED A CHAIN TO CONTROL A HORSE, WELL, THEY'VE MISSED IT. YOU CAN'T CONTROL HIS BODY POSITION IN THE WAY WE'RE TALKING ABOUT BY USING A CHAIN, AND IF YOU COULD, YOU WOULDN'T NEED IT ANYWAY.

❖ **DULLNESS:** There's quite a bit of difference between a horse not doing what you want him to do and being dull. A person can think a horse is dull when he's not at all. A horse might resent doing what you're asking him to do, and this will cause him to feel dull, and when a horse starts to take over and do things the way it seems to him like he ought to, that can feel like dullness too.

Let's talk about the actual facts, because then it will be easier for people to understand what's taking place when the horse isn't doing what the person wants. And we won't have to use words like "dull" when we're on the subject of horses.

What's taking place is that the person's getting the wrong message to the horse, or that horse wouldn't feel dull. To help a horse like this, a person would want to know what sort of feel to present to him. They would need to have firmness and life in that feel, and they would have to do a little testing and experimenting to see what amount of firmness was needed. To change things around, why at first the person may need to apply quite a bit of firmness to cause that horse to give the desired response. And when he does, it's liable to show up for only a second or two. What a person does after that, why that's the place where his better judgment comes in.

How long this firmness is needed is difficult to say — except to say a person has to notice where the horse tries to understand. *When you see a change, and when the response is in the neighborhood of what you're looking for, right then is when you'd ease off a little on the pressure, wherever it's being applied.* You ease off right then because when there's a change, that means he's feeling of you. From there, you'd build onto that as you move up the line, little by little, but only as much as that horse could understand. Not more than that. And your observations here, for this part, are real important because some important things are real easy to miss. If your timing and feel fit the horse, then as his understanding expands he'd have more confidence, and you'd do less and less of whatever you're doing to get those better results. The lessons on this wouldn't need to be long.

Emily Kitching

THE PERSON ON THIS HORSE IS PRESENTING A FEEL FOR THAT HORSE TO SOFTEN AND GET FLEXIBLE IN THE POLL. THE SLACK IS TAKEN MOST OF THE WAY OUT OF THE REINS, BUT THAT HORSE NEEDS SOME TIME TO FIGURE OUT WHAT'S EXPECTED OF HIM.

The person has quite a responsibility to the horse, and the main one is that they need to have an idea what response they want from the horse before they start presenting their feel to him. The idea of what a person wants to have happen has to be in place in their mind first. If that isn't there, why the horse can't be expected to understand what they mean when they present their feel to him. Or, he shouldn't be expected to, I'll put it that way. And that's true no matter if they think he's dull, or whether he actually is or isn't dull.

❖ **EASING OFF** *(enough)*: This is what we're hoping to do when it's needed. We're speaking about our reins and legs, or anywhere that we're touching a horse, or about how we present ourselves to him. It could be a lot or a little, it all depends, and it will take quite a bit of experience to build up that judgment so a person has the feel of how much is enough or not enough, or too much. It's never going to be the same because no two horses or people are the same. And a person will remember that there isn't any right or wrong connected to it, it's just something desirable.

Emily Kitching

WHEN HE TUCKS HIS CHIN DOWN AND IN, THE REINS ARE OFFERED BACK UP THE NECK A LITTLE TO EASE OFF. THAT RELEASE TELLS THE HORSE, THROUGH FEEL, THAT HE DID THE RIGHT THING.

❖ **EASING OFF** *(not enough)*: When the person misses the opportunity to ease off, it's just the learning part of things and this is going to happen. Of course, the problem for the horse when people miss this, which they're going to on the start, is that he doesn't have any way of knowing that what he did was right when he did what he was supposed to do. Because you got on the wrong track — and you could call it that — you missed it with your feel and timing. So, it may require quite a little more experimenting on your part before the change that you want to have in that horse shows up again. And you'd wait for that change the same as you did on the start. There's no right or wrong way, but where a person has a plan that isn't flexible, why they're liable to get disappointed and think that horse has done them wrong. But it's not that way.

If you've missed that opportunity to ease off, you'd remember that those better results you'd be hoping for could show up again a lot sooner if you weren't liable to be upset because of what the horse did after you'd missed his understanding of your feel. Or for any reason. You'd need to keep him in that searching frame of mind for the better results, and a person being upset doesn't help that horse keep that searching frame of mind. That better frame of mind is real beneficial to his mental system and his physical system, too. The horse needs a person to know that there's a real close connection between those systems, that's for sure.

❖ **EASING OFF** *(partial release)*: This means ease off the pressure, wherever it exists. A complete release is all right too, but a person is liable to overdo that and lose the connection with the horse. During the learning process, what fits most horses better than a complete release is to ease off to a point to where you still have a connection. There may be a time when the horse gets up against the bit, and then you can hold your firmness steady for a few seconds to give the horse an opportunity to decide what to do. If that horse is feeling of you, he will start to lighten up to match your feel, and at that point you can ease off a little, and it will be enough of a release for him to slow his feet and remain light in your hand.

On the start, some horses might need more of a release because they maybe don't have confidence in your arm movements, or in your way of handling them. Or maybe a horse has the wrong idea about people because he got off to the wrong start. So you might have to experiment and decide when to release and when to use firmness — either less or more of both — after you see how much of your meaning carries over to him. You will know this from his response. Then, right after that, you'd need to give him the feel of what to expect next because that's what he's wanting to know about. People can get mixed up on this part if they've never had an opportunity to get some help understanding the horse and what he's liable to do when he doesn't understand what's expected of him. Which, I'll say, could be most anything.

❖ **EASING OFF** *(too much)*: This is when you lose the connection that you have established with the horse through the rein or lead rope. The same is also true when the horse is loose and you have no direct hold of him because, depending on what you do, there's a good connection you can have there even with nothing on him. Your better judgment will tell you how much to ease off in certain situations, and this should improve as you experiment. If you ease off too much, it causes the horse to be confused. When that happens, the horse will take over and start making decisions on his own and these are apt to be not what you want. This is how you see where easing off less would have been the better choice. And next time, you'd try that.

❖ **EQUIPMENT:** Anything we're talking about in this book can be done with a halter or snaffle bit on the start. When the horse gets used to that, then it's easy for him to learn about some other equipment a fella might want to ride him in, and we'd speak about this in the future.

❖ **EXCESS OF LIFE IN THE HORSE:** This could also be called an excess of energy. Maybe he was born with that, but it might be there for other reasons.

This excess of life can be real useful to the horse if it's used by someone who knows how to use it. If someone's around who can demonstrate how to teach this sort of horse to slow down and stay with their feel, it's real helpful. That way, a person can watch how that more lively kind of horse will respond when that real effective feel is applied in there. There isn't any question about whether or not a horse will slow down and get with someone who knows how to use that excess of life in him — he will. But not a lot of people have a good feel to offer a horse like this, or the better timing to go along with it. But many people will be pleased to learn that this life can actually be used to teach him to *stay* with a person. I'm speaking now about staying with the person mentally. When the horse can do that, then he isn't liable to get confused when a person wants him to slow his feet down, or stand still until there's a need for him to move again. There's been some more writing done on this in the section about teaching your horse to stand.

In a case where he's mixed up about keeping his feet still when you're on him, he's also liable to get mixed up about the pressure he feels on those reins. A person who has a horse like this could benefit from learning how to use this excess of life in a way that fits the horse.

No, when a horse that's this way gets off to a start that isn't the best, people sometimes say things about that horse that they shouldn't. That causes another problem for the horse. But these problems can be avoided because people are smarter than horses and we're in hopes that they'll find out that this other way of handling horses can be real helpful.

Roger Sjolstad

THIS PERSON IS SHIFTING THE HORSE'S WEIGHT BACK USING HER HAND ON THE BRIDGE OF THE NOSE, AND THE UNDERSTANDING IS STARTING TO COME THROUGH. THERE'S BEEN NO SHOVING INVOLVED.

❖ **EXPERIMENTING:** There's always an opportunity to do a little experimenting to see if the horse understands what you're presenting. If he does, then when he's real comfortable with something, that's when you'd move up the line. It's the horse's understanding of these small experiments that prepares him for the future.

The change that horse feels from you, after the change you got from him, is a real important part of how he can understand if he got together with your idea or not. When he can understand something that you intend for him to understand through feel, there's progress occurring in that foundation.

On horses that are real mixed up, they sometimes don't respond well to the feel of a halter or a snaffle bit at first, and a person may have to do different things to get their meaning across to the horse so they can transfer that meaning to the way they operate the equipment later on.

Roger Sjolstad

In your experimenting, it's up to your better judgment to know whether a horse is going to be bothered enough to kick you. You'd not try this experiment on a horse you thought might kick at you.

Another reason experimenting has a place in here is that if you stay on the same old spot for too long without progress, then it's liable to cause the horse to start to develop ideas of his own that aren't the best. If the horse doesn't understand the things you do through feel, then anything that's presented to him up the line will include quite a lot of guesswork and self-preservation maneuvers on his part. And there's better ways to go about things, I'll say that.

It can be real helpful to teach horses that are troubled about getting out of a trailer to step back from a feel on their tail. That limits the amount of confusion they might have built up about the meaning in a halter rope where trailering is concerned. That feel can be introduced after the feel to move the feet is clear, and the horse can operate real smooth when there's a need for him to step back.

❖ **FEAR** *(the horse's)*: I don't think a horse has any conception of what might happen to him other than in the instant that it's happening. But he has fear. He was born with that. So he does whatever he thinks is the best way to survive. Most people call this self-preservation.

❖ **FEAR** *(the person's)*: Someone lacking experience with horses might have good reason to fear one. Those people with fear need someone to help them understand the reasons that they're afraid. They need help from another person to get it changed around, so it's always nice if there's someone with more experience who can supervise. I think most people with some fear operating in them would feel better about that anyway.

❖ **FEEL** *(direct)*: This is the way you touch a horse and ask him to maneuver directly, through the halter and rope, the bridle reins, or by touching him any place on his body. All of this is direct feel.

❖ **FEEL** *(following a feel)*: This part of the foundation is deserving of quite a bit of time. All the ideas and exercises presented in this book are going to work out best for the horse and the person when they are applied from the ground on the start. Before handling any horse, you'd make sure to have the opportunity to observe him and form some ideas about his general makeup. Many people skip over this part. If you have a disrespectful or confused horse, the first thing to teach him is to respect you through feel. To get this done, you can't say how much or how little firmness it might take, because each horse has a different history, and no two have the same sensitivity. Of course, depending on your own experience with horses and how many different horses you have been around, your better judgment will tell you how the horse is, or what he'll respond to. The more experience you get, the better your judgment is likely to be in the future.

❖ **FEEL** *(for the horse)*: Now that'd be your feelings towards the horse, or about him. This is something altogether different than what we're talking about in this book, which is about feeling *of* the horse. People are apt to get these confused on the start. If you think that the horse isn't doing what you want him to do just to be ornery, and then you want to punish the horse for this, why then you haven't got the right feelings or attitude toward the horse.

Lori Kline

THESE HORSES ARE FOLLOWING A FEEL.

❖ **FEEL** *(generally speaking)*: There's nothing a horse will respond to much better than a good feel from the person handling him, which works because it's natural to him right on the start. No, when that feel a person presents isn't clear to the person — which it won't be if they're using those mechanics or any type of restraint rig, then it's not going to be clear to the horse either.

A horse is ready for learning mostly because of his naturally curious side, and if people only knew he was this way, things would go smoother than most people can imagine. Anytime you're working with an animal, all that animal really has to go on is the feel of the person who's around him, or actually handling him. Some people use far less feel than others, but the whole idea of this is to prepare the horse for the future, so he knows what's expected of him. Our main goal here is to bring out the best in the horse. That way, if the subject of the talk concerned horses, that's the part that would be mentioned.

Diamond Lu Collection

THIS PERSON HAS A GOOD FEELING FOR THE HORSE.

❖ **FEEL** *(indirect)*: This is the way you and the horse feel of each other when he's loose and there's no physical connection between you. He already knows this way of going about things from what's inside of him because this is what horses use to communicate with each other a lot of the time.

You can motivate the horse to maneuver — *without touching his body* — in a corral, stall, or most any place that the horse is aware of you and free to move his feet. When you're talking about applying indirect feel this way, it's the timing of things you do that makes all the difference in the world. So many times in our work with a horse there's an opportunity to combine direct and indirect feel, and they go together real good if a person has prepared the horse a little ahead of time.

Kim Murphy

We ought not try to do the job one horse can do for another, but there's a lot to learn about horses if we observe them in most any situation we can, when we have time. Before you learn how to use the horse's communication system in a way that he can make sense of, a person needs to do a lot figuring on the way things in that horse's world look to him. (This is really about one's point of view. We accept that human communication in different cultures is based on *different assumptions* about the results that certain words, gestures or physical interactions are expected to produce. It's not a surprise, then, that similar dynamics apply when you work with a horse.)

The mare in this picture is feeling of her foal, and the foal will learn to feel of the mother through that. That foal learns to follow the mare and come over near her when the mare wants it to, after it gets used to the feel of that mare staying up with her. Those foals are born with the instinct to stand up, get milk and run. Hooking on is the part that gets learned about through feel. They come set up for that, and it's the reason why it works the same way for people who want a horse to pick up their feel — they first need to get with the feel of that horse. In terms of feel and the actual facts of what's taking place, it's not really any different than the picture shows here.

DIAMOND LU COLLECTION

THIS MARE IS FEELING OF HER FOAL AND GOES RIGHT ALONG WITH IT. THIS IS ONE WAY THE FOAL LEARNS TO FEEL OF THE MARE.

❖ **FEEL** *(mellow)*: That's when the horse isn't pushing on you at all. His head takes a normal position and it isn't coming up. He's gentle and has a soft expression when he's this way. This is the way you like to have him in case you had to go do a job with him. When you're riding or doing anything on the ground where he might need to be handy, *you want him to be real mellow.*

❖ **FEEL** *(of the horse)*: This is the main thing a horse needs a person to know about. And we're speaking of connecting with the horse's mind, because his body doesn't really handle the thinking part of the horse. Because this feel part is understandable to the horse's mental system, a person doesn't need to spend a lot of time thinking about just working with that horse's body. His body will maneuver in response to his mind, but it's up to the person to help the horse connect his body with his mental system, and there's a real fine line there. It's up to the person to have a clear picture in his mind of how he wants that horse to operate *before* he presents a feel for that horse to respond to, or the horse is liable to not maneuver in the way the person wants him to. Having this in mind whenever you're around a horse, or holding onto him, is what shapes the future for him in the best way possible.

Even some people who use quite a bit of feel in their work with the horse — and there are a good many who use it real well — may not know how important it is that feel is presented to the horse as clearly as possible. A fella could keep people pretty busy just holding a clinic to explain and demonstrate how you learn to feel of a horse.

❖ **FEEL, TIMING and BALANCE:** Sometimes it's best to talk about feel, timing and balance separately, and to learn how to apply each thing separately on the start. But when you go to apply these three things a little later on in your training, then you see that each one of these things supports the other. They are interconnected and all three are real important. You really can't get along without all three. If one is missing, there's sure to be a poor effect on the other two. The main one you need to have in there when you ride is balance. Without that you'd fall off your horse just as soon as you got up on him.

❖ **FILLING IN:** This is something the horse can do for a person who isn't very far along in their understanding of how to present their feel to a horse. When the horse can't understand what they mean for him to do, that horse would be inclined to fill in with his own way of doing things.

Sometimes what takes place between a horse and a person is not the best, not by any means. But a person might not get hurt if he's got horses around there that fill in for him. Some horses will do this a lot better than others, and this is on account of many variables. Generally speaking, a horse that'll do this has an easy-going disposition and he tries to get along under most any circumstances.

A horse might fill in for a person if someone had built feel into that horse's mental system on the start. If he hasn't been too confused or scared on the start, and if that horse has learned to feel of a person from someone with some experience in fitting a horse — and I'm speaking now about how that person presents things in a way that was understandable to the horse through feel — then, I'll say in most cases, things are liable to work out all right between that horse and a person, even a beginner. No, if someone who was experienced at this had prepared the horse with a foundation that enabled him to feel of a person, why that horse would have an idea about the way some other people might need him to feel *of them.* I'm speaking now about the people without the best timing, and that's even if they had no feel to offer that horse at all. We'd call this part filling in. That's what the horse would be doing for that person with no feel, or with feel that had very little value to it, I'll put it that way.

DIAMOND LU COLLECTION

THERE'S QUITE A LOT TAKING PLACE IN THIS PICTURE, AND IT'S ON ACCOUNT OF THIS OLDER HORSE HAVING ENOUGH EXPERIENCE TO FILL IN FOR THESE PEOPLE WHO ARE LEARNING TO FEEL OF THE HORSE.

The horse in the top picture has learned enough about what's expected of him that these young people can experiment with moving his body around while the rider is counting the steps and learning how to stay balanced without grabbing onto the reins to stay on.

There's a lot more people that have very little to offer the horse involved with horses than you might think, especially today. That's why there's a need for something to be in print that can help a person understand what that horse needs them to know about getting along with him, in a way that brings out the best in him. It could be the person will find it beneficial too. But that's something they won't know about until they've had a chance to experiment long and hard offering a good feel to the horse, which will happen after they learn to get with his feel.

Diamond Lu Collection

❖ **FIRMNESS:** That firmness can be from the very least amount possible up to your full strength, just depending on what the horse is doing and what the circumstances are at the time. You'd be real sure (in the use of firmness) to be watching for the first opportunity that the horse presented you with to ease off. We're in hopes that people wouldn't use it for any reasons except to see how little of it would be needed after that firmness had been applied in there, and I'll say just as soon as possible. That's real beneficial to the horse when they're thinking this way.

The person in this picture is firming up because the horse isn't responding to the feel to lead up real free. She's maybe not sure what to do, so there's some resistance in there. After a few tries at this, she'll pick up his feel and start to move her feet before the slack comes out of the rope. When a fella firms up, there'd be no jerking or yanking on that rope. A firm pull takes place after a few little pulls aren't working for you. It's real important that a firm pull does not come right after slack has been put in that line, because that can cause the horse to think he did wrong, for something he really just didn't understand.

Diamond Lu Collection

You'll need to do some testing on this with each horse because the feel is different from one to another. When he responds to that firmness, why you'd ease off after that.

❖ **FITTING:** That's when the horse or the person understand each other. When something that's done by a person has this understandable meaning to the horse, it's fitting.

Diamond Lu Collection

You can really put a horse at ease around you if he's needing any scratching done for him — and you know about it.

Sometimes it just fits a horse to scratch them under the belly. Flies can get under there and make a sore spot, and a lot of times a horse will be glad you're on hand for the job. It feels good to them. If you didn't do it, they'd have to go find something to scratch themselves on, and in a lot of places, there's just no good place for that.

❖ **FIX IT UP AND WAIT:** I'd rather not use these words for beginners. There's a lot of judgment to this that comes in here. I'd rather talk about how to help the horse to understand what you want him to do through feel.

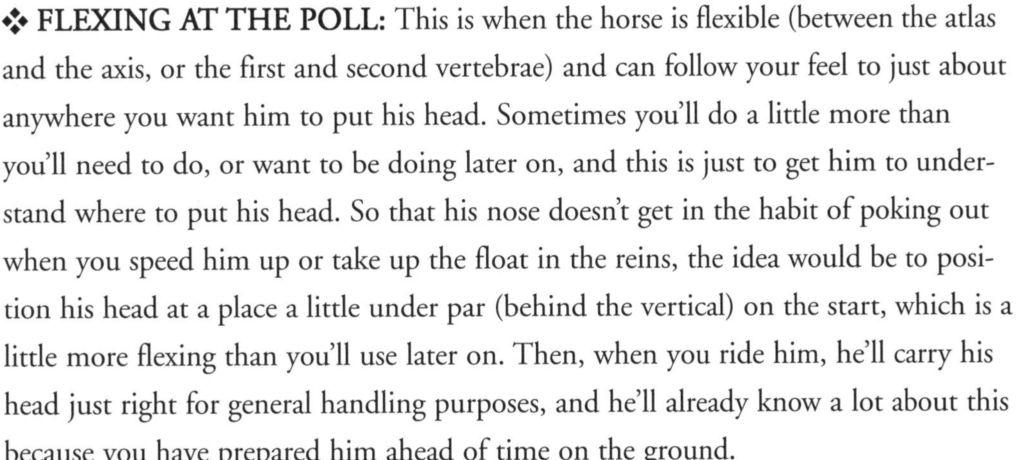

❖ **FLEXING AT THE POLL:** This is when the horse is flexible (between the atlas and the axis, or the first and second vertebrae) and can follow your feel to just about anywhere you want him to put his head. Sometimes you'll do a little more than you'll need to do, or want to be doing later on, and this is just to get him to understand where to put his head. So that his nose doesn't get in the habit of poking out when you speed him up or take up the float in the reins, the idea would be to position his head at a place a little under par (behind the vertical) on the start, which is a little more flexing than you'll use later on. Then, when you ride him, he'll carry his head just right for general handling purposes, and he'll already know a lot about this because you have prepared him ahead of time on the ground.

It's best to teach him this from the ground, before you ever think about getting on him, so he'll have an idea what you mean by the feel you present to him when you finally do get up there. And of course the flexible poll goes right along with all the other parts of the horse being flexible. All those parts are interconnected. It's not the best to find out that your horse isn't flexible where you need him to be after you are on him and trying to do a job.

Diamond Lu Collection

This boy is reaching up the left rein with his leading arm to present the horse with a feel for lateral flexion at the poll. The horse needs a little time to pick up his feel and tip his head to the left.

When a horse has learned to feel of a person, why it doesn't take much at all for them to understand what to do when you start to take the slack out of the lead rope or the rein. In the pictures on the next page, you can see it doesn't weigh any more than just the weight of taking up the slack in the rope to get a nice, light response. The horse can tuck her chin down and in a little, which is the vertical flexion we'd like to have built into our horses for the future. In the last picture, the horse has a little vertical and lateral flexion working together, because that's the feel that was presented to her.

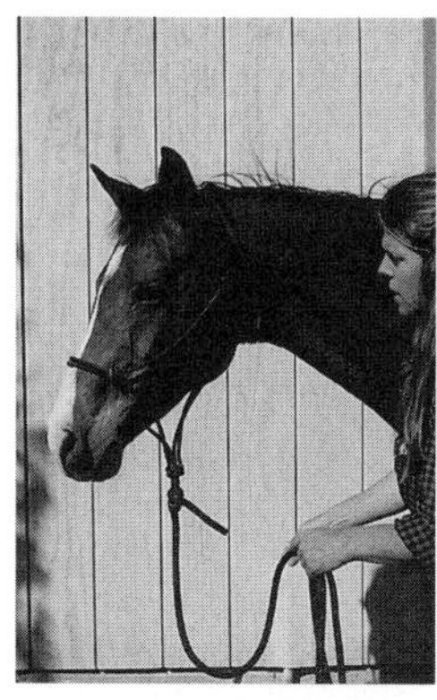

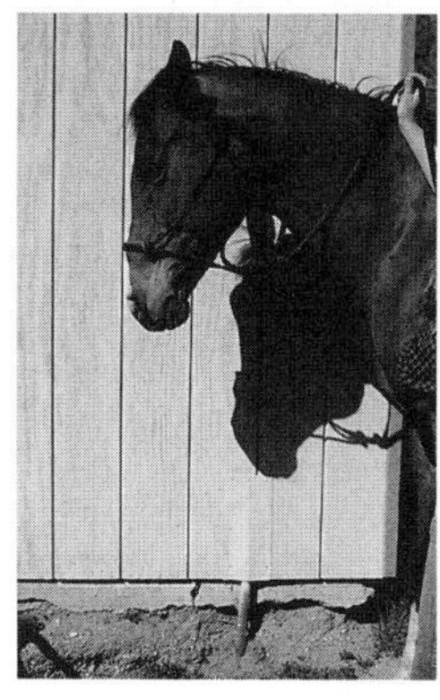

Diamond Lu Collection

The thing about feel that's so valuable is that the horse does whatever you present, if they've learned how to feel of you on the start. This will be real useful for the rider to have built in for maneuvers they're liable to need up the line a ways.

❖ **FLEXION OF THE LOWER JAW:** We might think of this as being a real flexible or pliable or mobile lower jaw. A horse that lacks this has other rigid places throughout his body, which can really affect his ability to get with a person. This rigidness also shows up when he's moving around on his own and will become quite obvious as you move him around on the halter rope. A person who was going to be sitting on a horse like this might have better luck, where it concerns safety, if that horse was better prepared to operate through feel.

There's a close connection between the lower jaw and the poll, and this is easy to observe because a relaxed horse will occasionally work his mouth while he's flexed at the poll vertically, and flexed left or right, and at any of those places in between. It's real important for a horse to be able to do this, and when he does, some people say he's letting down. It's real desirable to have a horse this way. But just because a horse has a flexible lower jaw, doesn't mean he understands how to flex his poll when the rider presents him with the feel for that maneuver. He can't do that unless the feel he's expected to understand from the movements of a person's arms has already been taught to him.

❖ **FLOAT IN THE LEAD ROPE OR REINS:** When you speak about float in your lead rope, you are referring to the slack in that rope, which is quite a bit less tension than it takes to straighten the rope out. You'll plan to maintain some float in your lead rope whenever possible, so the horse can learn to operate with lightness in his whole body — without any resistance. This will carry over to your mounted work later on.

The girl in the top left picture on the next page is sending the horse around her in a circle to the left at the walk. The horse is following her feel to do this with float in the rope, and his head takes a normal position, which is real important because it shows that he is understanding what he's expected to do. Even when you change directions, and speed up a little bit, as you see in the next picture, you'd want to keep some float in your rope.

Whatever that horse is able to understand about moving his body and placing his feet — in response to the feel you present to him through your reins when there's a float in them — will be due to that good foundation laid in down at the bottom. *It wouldn't be something a person could expect that horse to understand without that foundation.* A good foundation in the basics and some preparation on the ground is what makes a person sure that the horse knows what's expected of him when the rider needs him to do a job with a float in those reins.

This is what you like to have when you're riding. Not a tight rein at all. You wouldn't need to get anywhere near using a tight rein on a horse that was operating through feel.

This girl is paying attention to the placement of this horse's feet, and not confusing the horse in any way.

She is also doing a nice job to keep this horse's attention and to keep his body bent in the direction that he's going, but she'd do better with a shorter rope. The reason being, surprising things can happen with a long rope if you aren't very experienced.

There's plenty of life available in this horse and he has a nice expression. The rider is relaxed and has good posture. Her horse is feeling of her and they are going somewhere together at the walk.

Learning how to keep your balance at the trot and leave a float in those reins takes practice. It helps to have someone lead the horse when you haven't had a lot of experience.

When you have more experience at this, your ability to stay balanced on the horse and ride with a float in the reins, like you see in these two pictures, will give a young horse some encouragement and confidence to move out as he gets used to carrying a rider at the trot and the lope. Sometimes when the life comes up in a horse, a rider has a tendency to pull back, and this is liable to bother an inexperienced horse.

People will say that there isn't any contact when you have the reins like we're talking about, but there is, and this is real obvious to the horse because you have put on his bridle and saddle and you're sitting up there, so there's plenty of contact taking

Rhonda Smith Briano

This person has a float in the reins at the lope.

place, all right. It's just that a lot of people have another idea about things, and the horse isn't prepared to understand them if they aren't using feel to get their message across.

❖ **GREEN:** Inexperienced is what this word means. There's no color in this, it's just something people say.

❖ **HACKAMORE:** If you want to ride your horse in a hackamore, why you'd teach him about that the same way you'd teach him about handling for you through feel in a snaffle bit. The hackamore could be made of leather or rawhide, and it would have a headpiece to go with it so it stays in place on the horse's head. Some of the ones they're using now are made out of leather, and they're real nice.

❖ **HEAD ON UPSIDE DOWN:** Generally speaking, this is a badly-appearing horse. This horse would have spent a lot of his time being ridden by people who lack riding experience. This sort of riding teaches the horse to brace against the halter or to push against the bit because the person who prepares a horse to travel this unattractive way is inclined to hold on to the reins to keep their balance in the saddle. It's not a real useful way to have a horse if you have a job for him to do.

If you present a feel to the horse that he can understand, this gets taken care of way down at the bottom, right on the ground. But if you already have this problem, you can teach the horse to not go about things this way by giving him an opportunity to feel of you. This can take place at any time in a horse's life, because if he's traveling this way, then he'll always be looking for something better than what he's got for communication purposes.

The best thing is not to get his head like this in the first place, then there's no need for this description of a horse.

❖ **HEAVY ON THE FOREHAND:** Whatever a rider presents is the way that horse is going to be. And that could be heavy on the forehand, or not. When a horse has learned to feel of you, there won't be any need to speak about that horse being heavy on the forehand. People think words like this are about that horse, but really it's not that way. It's words that describe the way a person has operated the horse is all, and it's hard to get very much done with a horse that travels around like this. But this is the way a lot of people have their horses because they haven't had an opportunity to learn a better way to have those horses operate.

A horse that travels this way needs to learn that there's another way to place his weight when he's carrying a person on his back. And of course the person needs to learn about this first. When the horse has learned how to feel of you, and the feel you present means for him to shift his weight back to the hind end, then he will. It doesn't matter whether he's stopped or going forward or backward — when he gets that feel to shape his body up that way, why, he will. That horse will get light, and stay that way, as long as the rider can stay livened up and always be ready to give the horse a place to go. The location of the horse's body weight shouldn't affect his lightness, and it won't for a person who knows how to get feel applied in a way that the horse understands. How fast this takes place just all depends on the experience a person has and, maybe, on if they can get some good help to see how this looks when it's applied by someone who understands the things a horse needs them to understand.

❖ **HELPING THE HORSE:** That's our main goal and through feel is how you go about this. Whatever you're trying to do is to help him. If a person approaches a horse with other ideas that do not include helping that horse, well, to my way of thinking, there's room for improvement in that. There's a place in the attitude they have about the way a horse's mind works that will make it more difficult for them to develop the better results we're talking about here in this book, I'll put it that way. No, I'm in hopes that getting these ideas getting down in print can help them learn how to help those horses, all right. Because this is my main plan.

❖ **HEPPED UP:** A horse that's this way is liable to be excited, and of course it's natural for a horse to be that way in some circumstances. But where that horse is hepped up due to self-preservation and guesswork, there could be unwanted motions that show up with that excess of energy. A person would want to get that part changed around through feel. That excess of energy is something a person can use to build respect in there, but that idea takes in quite a lot and where there's a need for more experience, that's where you're experimenting would fit in.

If he's hepped up and still feeling of a person, that'd be because he had a good foundation built in there on the start, and also because the person handling that horse was presenting a feel that he understood. A person who really understood how to use this excess of energy in a horse through feel, could arrange things so that horse could do most any job that person needed him to do, but there's not many in that group. Most people would get better results after they've taught that horse how to stand still through feel. And this job could take quite a little time.

❖ **HINDQUARTERS:** The position of those hindquarters is right at the top of the list of things that you need to all the time be thinking about. It's the hindquarters that the horse depends on to maneuver his whole body the way he needs to, whether he's moving around on his own or if there's a rider sitting on his back. It doesn't matter what you're doing with that horse, those hindquarters need to be real agile and adjustable, through feel. It's those hindquarters and the way you can get them operating through feel, that determines so many other things that are important to the horse and to the rider, too, of course.

If there's a rider up there, what that person is able to do with the front end of that horse mostly depends on how the hind feet are operating—and that would be up to the person. *Those hind feet will need to be placed and re-placed to get that front end freed up to go where it needs to go. This takes time and shouldn't be rushed.* But, there's all kinds of people in this world, and some of them are in a rush. And they go about things in a different way, there isn't any question about that.

There's some people who think operating those hindquarters, and even the whole horse, is about mechanics. There's no feel built in to that approach. When that's what they're thinking about, and that's the way they're using it, that's exactly why it doesn't work. It doesn't work for the horse anyway, and that's what we're interested in. No, the horse doesn't understand anything about mechanics. When people use mechanics, generally speaking, they use force to go along with that, and this combination is what really mixes a horse up so bad. *The way it should be done is the way it fits the horse, and that's a different feel entirely from those mechanics, because the only feel that horse can be sure of, well, it comes right out of you. The horse knows the difference right away. That's because the horse can usually understand what a person intends.*

What we're talking about here has not got much to do with anybody's equipment. No, it's more how you go about thinking and moving around that horse through feel when you're on the ground, and influencing what he does with his hindquarters and his whole body through feel when you're on his back. This is how he knows what you want and expect of him, and it gives the horse a chance to feel of you while you're working with him. This is the way a person can set things up for the horse to bring out the best in him. That's the reason this is going into print. Some people aren't going to care too much about this and they'll try and get by another way, but one thing's for sure, their horses understand this way we're talking about.

Maybe some day those people that favor the mechanics — some of them anyway — might want to know about using feel to operate their horses in a way that gets better results. Once they get an opportunity to see some other people using this, they're liable to recognize its value to the horse and to them. Even if they don't have time for it now, I'm in hopes they'll be thinking about using feel with their horses sometime in the future.

❖ **HOLDING HIS BREATH:** If the horse isn't sick he won't stop breathing long enough to stop living, but other things can happen when a horse holds his breath.

He will do this if he's not sure of something, and that's true whether a person is around there or not. And if there's a person holding onto that lead rope or sitting up there on him, that's just the time you want to get him real sure about something, because a lot of things can happen that would surprise you when a horse stops breathing. You don't want too much time to go by before he starts to breathe again. He might have to go someplace to get things to flowing inside of him again, and you'd better be ready to go right along with him when he does.

❖ **HOOKING ON:** This is the horse's willingness to come towards you, but I'd rather that this coming-towards-you part would be in response to a correct feel, and not because you have a treat for him or because he's taking over. And when I say "feel," I'm speaking about a feel that fits that particular horse. We don't want to get this confused with a horse being pushy, or taking over. No, those kinds of horses aren't working with feel and in situations like that, the people aren't either. But, some people are liable to speak about a pushy horse and think, maybe, that he's hooking on. There's a whole lot of mix-up when that's what they're thinking about. There's a world of difference in those two ideas.

If you're working him loose and he doesn't respond by coming in your direction when you want him to, you might liven up his body and send him on (drive him). Get those feet moving. You can just send him away, and when he slows down, you'll have another opportunity to feel of him (and to blend in if you need to) and then draw him towards you.

After a couple of tries, the horse in these pictures could pick up the feel of this person because they'd had experience blending in with the horse before. When you're

DIAMOND LU COLLECTION

IT ISN'T IN THIS HORSE'S MIND TO GET CAUGHT WHEN THIS PERSON WANTS TO PUT A HALTER ON HIM, SO THIS FELLA'S HELPING THE HORSE TO THINK MORE ABOUT LEAVING. HE'S FEELING OF THE HORSE, AND GIVING HIM MORE TIME TO GET READY TO BE CAUGHT.

DIAMOND LU COLLECTION

IT'S HELPFUL TO HAVE A HORSE THAT UNDERSTANDS THE FEEL TO LEAVE, BECAUSE THAT FEEL WORKS REAL WELL TOGETHER WITH THE FEEL TO COME TOWARDS A PERSON. THERE NEEDS TO BE A BALANCE IN THERE BETWEEN THOSE TWO THINGS.

this way, it's a lot easier to draw him off the rail and keep his attention, because that means he's feeling of you then. You'll need to keep his attention to lower his head so you can put a halter on him, and you're in hopes that he'll be in a willing and calm frame of mind about doing other things that you need him to do. If he isn't, then you'd be sure to get him that way before you rode him. That'd be what you'd do in the area of safety, and for other people and livestock to be safe around there too.

A lot of the value to be gained from hooking on a horse can be lost if the person can't drive or send the horse away. If the horse is allowed to get in (or to continue) the habit of crowding into your space and bumping into you at the walk, or when you're standing together, then that better feel isn't figuring too heavy in his foundation.

Respect from the horse is also lacking in a situation like this because the basics are missing. A horse might do any number of other unsafe things around you, or to you, because he doesn't have a clear idea that he shouldn't. Those horses can be taught manners through feel. *This isn't the same thing as allowing him to make a mistake and then punishing him for it. That approach will not teach him manners.* No, punishing a horse when he doesn't understand what you want him to do is a real direct route to a whole list of other problems that are based on his confusion. This is caused by a misunderstanding of the feel you present, and when that horse has no knowledge of your intentions or desires. Some people say that the horse knows what the person wants "but he just won't do it." When he understands what you want him to do, through feel, he will do it. I haven't seen any exceptions to this yet.

It takes time to get this part working for you and it helps if the place you have to work the horse isn't too big or small. The best size depends on the particular horse and the ability of the person handling that horse. A lot of things might surprise a person about this (the concept of hooking on and its application), but after a person has learned to feel of a horse, the horse will feel of them and a lot of those surprises won't show up — not as much, we'll say. And of course this depends on the horse and so many other little particles that go into it. A good instructor can really help a person to get this working for them on the start, and I'll say it's a good idea to have one when you're learning about this part because it's just so easy for the horse and the person to get mixed up on this.

❖ **HORSEMANSHIP:** That'd be the way you're handling your horse, and that could be most any way, but the kind we're talking about is *true horsemanship through feel.* Another way to speak about this is to say that there's good horsemanship and poor horsemanship. And we'll stick with the better kind.

❖ **IMPROVEMENT:** I think there's always room for improvement, regardless of what you're doing. If there isn't room for improvement it isn't very interesting, whatever it is. Not to me anyway.

❖ **INSTRUCTOR:** This person needs to be able to answer any question that's asked in a way that the person asking the question can understand the answer. That takes an unlimited amount of knowledge. You need to understand horses and people to be able to do this in a way that's fitting to the public.

It's also the responsibility of the student and the audiences at clinics to ask questions so they aren't apt to go away confused about what they saw, or about what they thought they understood in what they saw. There's an unlimited amount of things with their horse that need to be understood.

The instructor, and we'll say a good instructor because we really aren't talking about the other kind, really wants to help a person so that when they get home they'll have some idea of how to get these things that we're talking about applied through feel. But this takes time and the process shouldn't be rushed. A good instructor will set it up so there's no reason to feel insecure about anything that you're attempting to learn. One more thing that this instructor will do is leave a student feeling like there's plenty of hope there for them in their effort to learn. The way criticism is handled between people has a big effect on learning, and I'd say there's just one kind that'd do a person any good — and that's constructive criticism. I wouldn't say anyone was dumb or unteachable because there's something for everybody to learn. And the good instructor knows there isn't any dumb question.

I believe all the questions an instructor hears about a horse can be answered through an explanation of feel, and of course it's a big help to demonstrate some things. The best help sometimes comes from a horse that the instructor has already worked with using feel, and this way the person learning can feel it themselves. The ideas we're presenting have different meaning to a person after that.

❖ **JUDGMENT:** If we're speaking about the better judgment, those words take in quite a lot. It's tied right to a person's experience and the judgment they were using before, and maybe that wasn't the best.

❖ **KNOWLEDGE:** What concerns us is the knowledge that the horse and the person have, and this is based on past experience, I'd say. The experiences they're going to have in the future will give them some new knowledge, and they'll work that into the plan they're liable to have ready for whatever happens anytime after that. People need to know that the horse has a real important ability. That horse came equipped to decide if the person is helping him to maneuver his body in a way that's fitting to him, or not. This comes from his own deeper knowledge and he knows if they are helping him or not. A person might want to do more if only he knew that those horses know this.

We're in hopes that when people have the opportunity to see other people's horses operating for them through feel, they'll realize that those horses are putting these beneficial experiences into that mental system in a way that's useful — and that'd be because knowledge that's based on feel is this way. It's real beneficial to the person, too, and, of course, people are more intelligent than horses in every way.

❖ **LAST STRAW:** This means beyond the limit, and we're hoping to stay far away from that place.

❖ **LEADING UP REAL FREE:** It's important to have a horse so he leads up real free, and this isn't any part of dragging a horse along behind you. What we're talking about is real different from the feel that teaches a horse to resist a person, and there's quite a lot written about this subject up near the front of the book.

If the horse isn't feeling of you, why then he isn't going to be responsive, and that means he won't be leading up real free for you either. When he's taught to lead up real free, his feet get livened up and he's looking for a place to go, before the slack comes out of that rope.

The horse in this picture is heading out on a long line, but she has a good feel of the float in that rope. Generally speaking, this would be too long a rope because if something startled the horse, there might be too much slack to get the horse under control. But it's valuable because the horse is learning to feel of the float in that rope. The person has to have a good feel to offer the horse, too.

Richard Field Levine

Most people who look at a picture like this wouldn't give any thought as to what was taking place between the two of them.

Because he should be following a feel in the first place, there won't be any misunderstanding between the horse and the person about the horse taking over with ideas of his own. There's a fine line in there where someone who hasn't had a lot of experience in this will be thinking, maybe, that because the horse follows them when they move their feet, that he can follow the feel on that lead rope to lead up real free. This isn't the same thing at all, and it's real important to the horse that the person knows the difference. It's real important to the person, too, especially if they are planning to ride that horse.

The young horse in this picture has been taught how to lead up real free. It's the way that foundation was laid in there that leaves this colt with an understanding of how not to crowd a person.

Diamond Lu Collection

There's no crowding or stepping on anybody if the horse has been taught to feel of a person on the start.

Even if you aren't walking ahead of him, a horse that understands this difference will move his feet as the slack comes out of the rope. This could be if you needed him to give you a response that had no resistance in it, and you were at his shoulder, or had him standing out at the end of a long lead rope, or at the end of your reins while you were doing something you needed room to do.

The fella and the horse in this other picture have the same idea about going in the same direction at the same time. That horse has learned to feel of the person without any crowding or taking over involved, and they're blending in together. There isn't disrespect in the way this horse appears here, but you'd find out more about him when you had a halter on him and you wanted him to lead up real free. Maybe he would, but maybe he'd have another idea about what to do when he felt that pressure come in there from the halter.

Diamond Lu Collection

Of course, because feel and respect go right together, respect would be part of the way a horse approached you when he is leading up real free. I mean, there'd be no need for concern about a horse that led up real free bumping into you or running around because the rope had a float in it. No, that horse would already be feeling of you, so those disrespectful actions wouldn't need to be discussed.

The ability to lead up real free is also the response you'd want to have built in if you needed your horse to liven right up as he was moving right past you, or to change directions on the end of your reins, or lead rope, *right on the spur of the moment.* There could be many reasons a fella'd need a horse to be able to do this, if he had a real job for him. It could be almost any maneuver that you wanted, and for any reason that a willing response from the horse was desirable. And if it was a willing response in the first place, why there would be not any need to be thinking about that word "speed," or any of those faster motions. When he can respond this way to you on the ground with your halter rope, the chances are better that he'll be able to understand how you intend him to adjust the movement and placement of

Kim Murphy

A colt that's taught to lead up real free on the ground is inclined to handle the same way when a fella's horseback, and this can be real handy if you have to go a fair distance with a colt.

his feet when you're on him, before the slack ever came all the way out of your reins.

But, a lot of people don't know about this better feel because they haven't been exposed to it by handling a horse that leads up real free before. So they need to get onto that before they can teach a better feel to the horse and get him responding in this better way. What makes it better is that there's no resistance in it, because a horse that operates through feel doesn't weigh any more in your hand than that lead rope does. No, it's just sitting there, real light in your hand.

And if this important part is left out, then anything you're doing further up the line will have parts of that resistance in there, and that isn't going to blend in too good with most jobs that a person would have for their horse. And it sure won't feel that good when you're sitting up there either.

❖ **LEADS and LEAD CHANGES:** Certain jobs the horse has call for him to be on a certain lead, so he can balance better. He doesn't stay on the same lead for everything he does, and sometimes he can be on two leads at once. But, unless there's a problem with how the horse maneuvers, or he doesn't understand your feel, then whichever front foot is in the lead, is the name of the lead that your horse is on.

Depending on what job he's doing, the horse could be on a lead that isn't the best. What makes it that way is just if it's wrong for the job he has right then, or the ground you happen to be on causes him to need a different way to balance at the lope. One thing's for sure, when a fella's loping his horse, he has to set things up in a way that allows the horse to shape up those feet, all right.

❖ **LEARNING:** If we're speaking about learning to handle and ride horses, three main ingredients are needed:

- A person needs to have a real strong desire to learn this,
- They need plenty of time to practice, and
- There's a real important place in there for a good instructor. There's also a need for checking back in with the instructor. About every three or four days is ideal, but a lot of people don't have that opportunity.

Years ago I knew a fella who had a real retaining memory. He could see something he was interested in just once or twice and he'd remember how it looked. It wasn't long before he was doing exactly what he saw another fella doing. Most people aren't that way, so they are going to have to experiment.

Any time there's a place for something to be more convenient for a person and the job they have, why I'm liable to be right on the job, just working to find out more about it. Like today, I came out way ahead on a little experiment to see about how a fella could button a shirt using a pair of needle nose pliers. The sleeve had just wore out and after I sewed it up the cuff got tight and sort of out of shape with my sewing job. And that got the buttoning part of things slowed way down. I spent ten minutes on it, and that's a great waste of time, especially when it's morning and you want to get going. But I gained quite a bit of knowledge on it because I found out that it works best to use a pair of tweezers instead, and I got that button on its side and just dragged it through the hole. So, I came out way ahead on the learning part of things today just by experimenting. It's no different when you're working with a horse.

❖ **LEG FEEL:** There should be meaning for the horse when he feels your leg liven up or move in any way when you're riding. This is important for the horse to understand, because this sensitivity isn't anything a horse ought to be confused about. A person would have to do a little experimenting with their timing and the firmness they needed to apply, and they'd be ready to switch things around right away if any tightness started to show up in that horse's body that was causing him to overdo the anticipation and not be responsive to those reins.

But on the start, you'd need to get him sure about the meaning you had in mind when you used your legs, so you wouldn't want to use those reins much, which would confuse him. He'll need to understand the message you're intending to give him with the position of your legs and how they come in against him with some life.

One thing's for sure, you'd want him to be real sensitive to your leg feel and your reins before you'd present him with the idea to collect up at the gallop. This takes time and shouldn't be rushed.

For a lot of people it's a new idea (using the legs to liven up and direct the horse this way), so maybe they'll need to ride a horse that is sensitive to the leg and then they'd know better how to teach this to another horse that didn't have this sensitivity. Of course it always helps to have a good instructor who can demonstrate this, and they should be able to talk things over when questions come up for a person who was trying to learn about this.

❖ **LET HIM FIND IT:** That means that you're giving the horse the opportunity (and whatever amount of time it takes) to learn to pick up your feel and be responsive to it. This involves his natural curiosity, which connects to the searching part of things. It's way over at the other end of forcing the horse to do something and, of course, we're going to stay far away from that.

❖ **LET THE AIR OUT:** This is part of taking a deep breath. The horse will do this when he's relaxing, and sometimes he'll do this when he understands what you want.

❖ **LETTING DOWN:** Relaxing is what that means. It's just what people call it.

Diamond Lu Collection

❖ **LIGHTNESS:** This goes back to feel and the horse's state of mind about how you present that feel. When you are sitting up there and the horse is light, that means your mind and your body are in agreement with his mind and his body about what to do and when to do it. There's a flow that you can actually see between a person and a horse when they are in agreement this way, and that is based on feel, and of course that flow is also connected right to the part you can't see.

When you're speaking about lightness, there's no force in that and there's no making anything happen. Lightness is already in the horse. That's what true lightness is. It's just a question of if the person can leave it in there and get it to work for him, instead of setting that horse up to work against him, because the horse's self preservation is tied right to that lightness.

Lori Klein

This saddle horse has plenty of life and lightness available, but she's not pushing against the bit because she's feeling of the rider.

(This part stumps a lot of people. It might help to think about what happens to a person's body when someone tries to make them do something that they don't understand or want to do, or when a person feels threatened by another person in any way. The person's physical state reflects their mental state under these circumstances, just as it does, in a nicer way, when someone is at ease. When someone feels comfortable in surroundings they like, or with people they feel good around, they are apt to relax and that can bring on a feeling of lightness or spontaneity in that individual. This shows up in the human body just the same as it does with a horse, because people are born with lightness in them, too. It gets taken out, or left in, just about the same as it does with a horse. *It just depends on what's happened up to that point, and how the individual was set up in the beginning to handle whatever took place.*)

❖ **LINE OF SIGHT:** This'd be when you're looking at an object out there in front of you a ways, and then riding the horse towards that object. You'd better be able to get him to go straight towards whatever you're looking at. You'll want a real clear picture in your mind of that object and the straight line you'd ride on to get to it. That's a real important factor, picking out an object and being able to ride there. On the start, that horse weaves all around. But after he gets with your feel, why that horse gets so he'll go straight towards that object, and that's what we want. He's feeling of you when he can do that, and it's part of that foundation you can't afford to leave out if you want that horse to be useful to ride for a job you'd have in the future.

❖ **LIVENING UP THE HORSE:** This is something a lot of people wonder about and the reason is because the idea is new to them. It's new to some horses, too. If a horse hasn't been around people who brought the life he has inside of him right up to the surface, some people might call a horse like that a dull one, even if he wasn't. A person with a slower sort of horse has to liven up their own body first before the horse will get the message to liven up. So long as they feel all right, there isn't any question that the person and the horse can liven up, because they're both alive. And it's this part of livening up that we're talking about.

How you go about this is a little different with each horse, and how it's applied by different people will have some variations, but mainly we want that horse to be responsive to your leg feel. And we're talking about the message that the horse understands from your legs when we say those words "leg feel."

When your leg feel livens up, your whole body livens up, and then that horse learns to liven up his whole body right along with yours. He'll look more alert and be more prepared to respond to you when he learns to liven up when you do. Most of the time, the horse needs the opportunity to learn this from a person on the ground first, but this will be presented in another way — you'll use your whole body to get the livening up message across to him and then, later on, it will take less for him to understand what you mean from the ground, and from his back.

Because that livening up feel that a person builds into the horse's foundation will carry over to the riding you'll do, you can progress up the line from there. Some people just liven up their horse when they ride, but you don't always know when you'll need to rely on his strength and agility to get into a safer situation. It's best if you can prepare the horse to be reliable, no matter where you are, and you'd always hope to be able to keep his life up in the turns.

❖ **LONGEING:** This is one way some people warm a horse up, but how you go about this is very important. What most people call longeing isn't what I mean when I have a horse on a halter rope maneuvering around me through feel. It seems like longeing would come under the heading of a pattern. And if it's a pattern, it's liable to be done without feel, which takes us further away from our goal of getting together with our horses. I like to avoid patterns as much as possible when I'm working with a horse and focus instead on lots of little maneuvers that keep his interest.

If you're using feel, then all that's needed to direct the life in the horse is a halter and rope or the snaffle bit, properly fitted to the horse. No extra equipment is necessary because we wouldn't rely on equipment in the first place. What needs to be reliable for the horse is the feel that we're presenting to him so that he can understand what we want him to do. For any longeing to be a valuable experience for the horse, it needs to be done with feel. If a horse anticipates that a stop will be presented to him when you're riding along there, or if he can't gallop out of a circle on the spur of the moment, there's maybe been a pattern put into that longeing. This can sure get in the way of the work we want to be doing through feel.

(When a person longes a horse repeatedly without feel, the horse can learn to carry himself on the end of the longe line in ways that make handling and riding him somewhat difficult. A horse that has been longed this way learns how to lean into turns with his shoulder and look away from the direction of travel. It's not uncommon for a horse that's been handled this way to swing the hindquarters to either side of a turn, lower his ribcage, speed up and push against the halter or snaffle bit, and/or buck. He will not be relieved of these annoying habits until he's handled with feel. These are habits that seem to get more ingrained when a horse is longed without feel. Conventional disciplinary methods and mechanical restraints might address the symptoms temporarily, but do not fix the problem.)

If you're working with feel, why you'd longe a horse that way too, and these undesirable traits wouldn't be as likely to show up in your horse as he moved around you on the longe line, or when you rode him. If you're operating your horse through feel, maybe you wouldn't get the urge to longe him at all.

❖ **LOOSE CONNECTION:** That loose connection is generally too loose if it's spoken about. This happens when the attention of the person drifts away from the horse. It doesn't matter if they are on him or not, there's no delay between when this happens and when the horse knows your attention is someplace else. It's better when this doesn't happen. It's up to the person to keep that horse's attention, and to do this they need to know where their own is. It should be right with that horse if they're handling him, or sitting up there on his back.

When the connection is too loose, the horse is going to start relying on some combination of his self-preservation and guesswork because the better feel won't be there for him to rely on. When this goes on, especially in a more active or intelligent horse, he can get things going pretty much the way he thinks they ought to be going, and his plan and way of going won't fit some people. So it's best to keep a good connection with the horse through feel, because that's really all the horse has to go on.

❖ **MAKE IT HIS IDEA:** Say instead, "help it to become his idea through feel." No talking about "make" the horse do anything. *That's out.*

❖ **MAKE THE WRONG THING DIFFICULT:** You're wanting to *help* that horse. When a horse gets confused, it's real difficult for him to understand what's expected of him. Especially where our main goal here is to learn to feel of the horse so that the horse can learn to feel of us, any part of making things difficult for the horse is going to interfere with his mental and physical systems. This doesn't fit any horse because it's real bothering to him. And where it's unhelpful to the horse's learning process, it's unhelpful to the person who wants to help that horse.

It's easy for the horse to get mixed up so it takes, I'll say, uncommon good judgment on the part of the person to help a horse understand what he's supposed to do when that person wants to make things difficult for the horse. And where there's any part of making an animal do something, the person comes up against the self-preservation part in that horse, which in some cases is well-developed. The horse's confusion is tied right to that (self-preservation), which is what we're trying to stay away from.

❖ **MASTER HORSEMAN:** When I talk about a master horseman, it would be one who could avoid getting a horse confused. Then there's the other fella, if he got in a storm, why he'd go with the horse and when it was over they'd both still be in business and ready for the future. But, I'd rather see the one who had a horse that never had to get near that big storm. And there's sure a way to do that, which is through feel. This takes a lot of time, and everything else that goes along with it. A lot of people don't have the time that it takes and this limits the number of master horsemen that are ever going to be. And, I'll say master horsepeople, too, because that word takes in all the people interested in horses.

❖ **MEANING:** We want the horse to understand the meaning in our feel. This is our main goal. He needs to have a good foundation for anything that comes up in the future — and that's for anything that he's expected to do. Horsemanship through feel is true horsemanship *for the horse* and that's because, when a person uses feel, it's as close to the actual facts that the horse understands as we can get. Horses can understand intent, and it's difficult sometimes for people to understand this. There's meaning for him in other things that people can present to him, all right. But if they aren't using feel to get the message across, it isn't what we're interested in, because it isn't fitting to the horse.

Diamond Lu Collection

The horse on the left is trying to bite the other horse in a friendly way. That's why the horse on the right is leaning into him, instead of leaving.

Diamond Lu Collection

The horse on the left in this picture wants to bite this other horse on the back. There is plenty of meaning in his presentation and the horse on the right understands what his intentions are. That's why he's trying to get out of the way.

Roger Sjolstad

This girl is waiting for any try to show up. She'll ease off when it does.

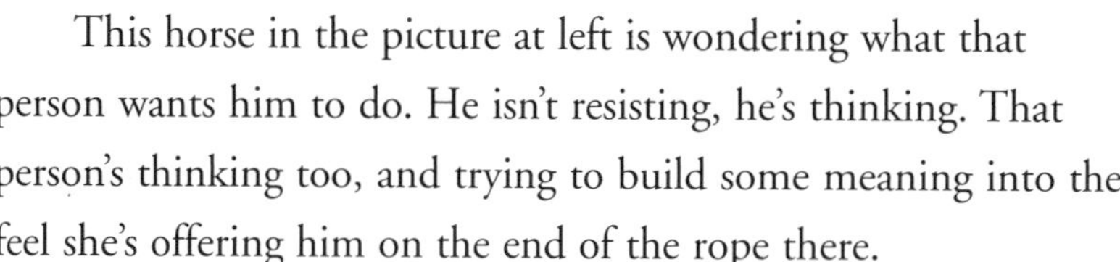

This horse in the picture at left is wondering what that person wants him to do. He isn't resisting, he's thinking. That person's thinking too, and trying to build some meaning into the feel she's offering him on the end of the rope there.

❖ **MECATE:** That'd be Spanish for the rope on your hackamore. Generally speaking, this is what people call it.

Some people prefer to braid their own mecates, and some places you can't get those real nice mecates made of mane hair — so it's good to know how to do some of these things on your own. I made a lot of my own gear for the ranch, and it was real satisfying to do things that way. That way you knew what you were getting, and if you'd made it in the first place, why you sure had an idea what to do with it if it got tore up somehow, and that's where some fellas are at a disadvantage.

Diamond Lu Collection

This boy's just starting to braid a mecate for his snaffle bit.

❖ **MISSING A SPOT:** There's a place that's been overlooked in the horse's education. The rider has been lax in preparing the horse for the future. When a person gets a horse to be this way, there doesn't need to be any discussion about fault, because they did the best with that horse that they knew how.

When you're talking about missing a spot, that could mean there's a lot of little things that have been overlooked, and one main thing it's liable to be is feel. In those spots where the horse is mixed up or lost, one thing's for sure, the meaning in a person's feel hasn't got through to the horse in a way that he can understand what to do. A person wouldn't necessarily know about this until it showed up, and that would be when he asked the horse to do something the horse wasn't prepared to do. If the person had an opportunity to see something done another way, through feel, and had it explained in a way he could understand, then chances are, he'd be trying some of these things out. He'd improve the way he applied it to the horse and his horse would improve. And we'll say if he started using feel in a way that fit the horse, he'd improve in the way he handled any horse after that time. This is where the education part of things takes place, and there's quite a little experimenting that goes into this.

Diamond Lu Collection

This horse hasn't any idea what's expected of him, and because feel hasn't been laid in there at the bottom, he's taking over with ideas of his own.

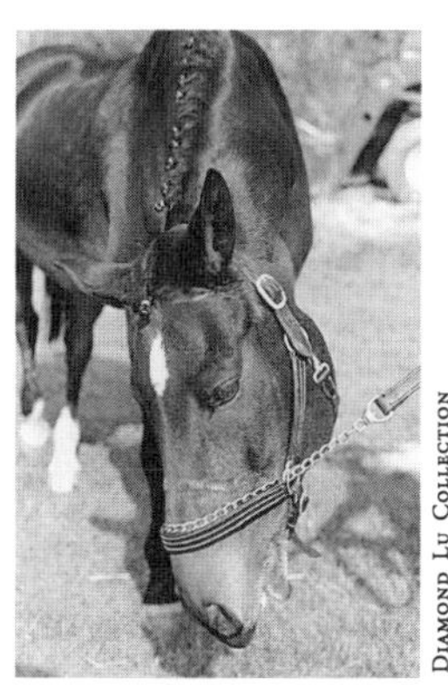
Diamond Lu Collection

It's the same with this horse, except he's in a calmer frame of mind. If he got excited, he'd take on another appearance right away. The person on the end of that lead chain might experience something he wasn't expecting.

❖ **MOVING INTO PRESSURE:** A horse that moves into pressure doesn't feel of a person and is taking over the situation with his own ideas. Maybe he doesn't slow his feet or change direction in response to firmness on the reins, or he crowds you in a stall, or steps into you when you lead him. These situations aren't the best to get in with any horse, but if a person doesn't have experience, this can shape up to where it gets to be a habit for the person and the horse. That needs to get changed around through feel, and soon, or that person is liable to get hurt.

❖ **NATURAL HORSEMANSHIP:** When people think of natural horsemanship that could mean a lot of things. It isn't natural for a horse to be around people, and it's not natural for a person to be sitting on him either. When we use these words, we speak about what's natural for the horse to do within his own boundaries.

Diamond Lu Collection

Diamond Lu Collection

The horses in these pictures are doing some things that horses do when they're getting along real well together on their own. Horses kept in stalls are not as fortunate as these horses.

DIAMOND LU COLLECTION

HORSES THAT HAVE A LOT OF ROOM TO MOVE AROUND ON THEIR OWN SEEM TO ENJOY LIFE.

❖ **OBSERVATION:** This is what a person needs to get good at where horses are concerned. Of course, a fella's *all the time* going to be improving on this if that better foundation is going to get laid in there for the horse and him to rely on in the future. No, it's so many little particles of feel that a person needs to be aware of, and a lot of those an observing person can see.

❖ **OFFER THE HORSE THE BEST DEAL POSSIBLE:** On the start, I'd rather a person was thinking about offering a better feel to the horse, because feel is all that horse has to go on. This other (offering the best deal possible) is what you're able to offer a horse after you've experimented long and hard with offering a good deal. And you'll wait on that.

❖ **OFFER THE HORSE A GOOD DEAL:** That good deal in there — that takes in so much, so I'd rather not use the term "good deal." Might be, after a person was real familiar with other things, in a conversation sometime I'd be willing to discuss it. But, right now, until you've learned how to feel of the horse — and by that I mean to present a *good feel* to him — that's out.

❖ **ON THE FIGHT:** Generally speaking, it's the result of confusion and an excess of pressure from a person that causes a horse to get on the fight. This is his right. That's only his self-preservation when he's this way, which is natural because it's already inside the horse when he's born. We'd rather the horse didn't need to use that side of himself when he's around people, and this'd be due to the human figuring he'd rather get another response from the horse in the first place.

But a horse won't get on the fight with a person unless that person has really missed how to present that good feel on the start. A lot of people bring out that horse's self-preservation and then fight back because they don't know how to help him learn, through feel, to respond to them with respect.

You've missed a lot that's real valuable if you talk about having a fight with the horse. It's a sure sign that there's a need to present another sort of feel to him. *That's entirely wrong when the human gets to fighting the horse.* It's real beneficial for them to get progress on learning to feel of the horse, so they can teach that horse to feel of them. Or maybe they could do something else altogether.

❖ **ON THE START:** This is where a person starts, before you work on up the line on advanced maneuvers.

❖ **OVEREXPOSING THE HORSE:** When he's this way (overexposed), the foundation in that horse isn't solid enough for him to understand what you expect him to do, and the feel you get from the horse tells you that.

Maybe you're asking that horse for something he isn't quite ready for. This would be the time to start over. Then, when you got up to that same point where the horse wasn't able to understand you before, that trouble spot might not even be there. If the foundation you build in is the way he needs it to be, it won't be there.

❖ **PATTERNS:** When people get to working with a horse and they don't have any special job for him to do, they're likely to get into a pattern and keep doing the same thing over and over. This is boring and the horse sort of loses interest. Good instructors who could help you avoid this are few and far between, but if you're working on your own, you'd want to work a lot of variables into the time you spend with your horse.

If you're in a fenced arena, one thing to not do is ride along just following that fence. Keep the horse about ten feet out away from the fence. The reason being, you will be able to feel of both sides of your horse better, and he'll be able to feel of you better too. Some people use the fence as a kind of crutch and may not even realize that they do until they find out that they can't get their horse to travel straight unless they're alongside a fence some place. Don't get into a pattern and repeat the same thing over and over again *because the horse will stay more responsive to your feel if there's variety worked into the things you do with him.* The main problem with patterns is that the horse gets so he can't follow a feel outside that pattern, and we want him to be ready to do any number of different things, through feel.

If a person hasn't got much experience with horses, a horse that's mainly been ridden in patterns is liable to be familiar with taking over and doing things the way he thinks he ought to. Because I want that horse to just follow my feel, and feel is all I want him to follow, I don't work my horse in patterns that are set up for him. There's some who might read this last part and think we're going against what was said before about trying to be consistent when you present things to your horse, and this is understandable. No, that feel you present so the horse learns how to follow a feel is real important. You don't want the horse to get an idea that he should be making any moves towards something he thinks is correct if it means that he avoids your feel to do it, because that's the horse taking over — and he's liable to do that if he's just rehearsing those patterns.

❖ **PERFECT** *(horse or ride)*: When the subject is horses, this is something people think is important to have a conversation about sometimes. We're trying to present just the actual facts in this book. If they had feel working for them, that word "perfect" wouldn't ever need to be mentioned.

❖ **PICKING UP THE FLOAT** *(through feel)***:** This just means that a person gathers up their lead rope or reins to take up a little slack. Before you took the float all the way out of the rope or the reins, you'd want that horse to respond to you in some way that suited you, *and you'd have that idea, and a picture of it in mind ahead of time.* But you wouldn't just pick up the float with no thought or reason connected to it.

If he was just standing still, there wouldn't be any reason to get short and take the float out. There might be a reason to get short all right, but you'd leave that float in there unless you wanted him to do something with those feet — which could be many things. *Any idea* to have him moving his feet would come ahead of the feel you give the horse for that maneuver, and if you do this the same way every time, the horse will learn that he can separate *that* meaning from the meaning you have for him when you pick up the float in your lead rope or your reins. Generally speaking, we'd try not to be confused about a short rein being a tight rein, and we'd try to keep that horse real clear in his understanding of what we wanted him to do when our feel on those reins or lead rope changed. This is a real important part of the knowledge he needs to have, and this will come from his searching and experience, just like it does for the person. That's why the person needs to learn about this first. After that float is picked up, there's no place at all for pulling on the horse's head or on his mouth, or ever jerking on him either. You could give a real firm pull — but never a jerk. This firm pull would be for some reason separate from just taking up the float. Taking up the float can be just part of going along.

❖ **PREDATOR / PREY:** Well, that's something people like to talk about. Maybe it helps them to understand some things about their horses that they didn't know before. To my way of thinking, it's a lot more valuable to spend time learning how to feel of your horse, and to teach that horse to learn to feel of you, because there's sometimes a big gap there between what a person wants the horse to do and what the horse has in mind.

(The horse is a prey animal and his self-preservation instincts are connected to his place in the food chain.)

❖ **PREPARATION:** This is about the person thinking ahead. They need to have in mind the preparing part of things, so they can get that horse ready for the future. A person needs to try as much as possible to make use of any opportunity that shows up to get that horse ready for the future. That horse needs your help to maneuver the best way he can, and you never do let that preparation idea get too far away when you're handling a horse. Because it takes quite a little experience to prepare a horse the way he needs to be ready for the future, you'd learn to feel of a horse on the start. If a fella doesn't know how to feel of the horse, and he's just trying to teach the horse to feel of him, well, then he's lost in all this anyway.

We'll assume you've already learned how to feel of your horse before you start to prepare him to feel of you. These aren't the same by any means, and the order that things get presented to the horse is real important — especially when you're speaking about a horse that's young or troubled about things. There's no part of hurrying when you're working on this preparation part, because a mix-up is liable to develop.

❖ **PRESENCE:** That takes in so much about a person, that word. That'd be just any way that a person was around a horse, and what that horse was feeling that the person might be expecting of him. It wouldn't always be that the horse understood it, he might not — but he'd think he did and he'd do whatever he thought was the best thing to do right then. If the person had another idea, why they'd try to change the way they were around that horse. Another way to say this is that a person would need to be adjustable and be a little different way around that horse to bring out something a little different inside him. Some people are better at this than others.

DIAMOND LU COLLECTION

THE HORSE ON THE RIGHT WANTS THE PAINT COLT TO GO EAT SOMEPLACE ELSE, AND IS LETTING HIM KNOW IT.

If they made that change in how they were touching the horse's body or just being a certain way around him, things would shape up different for both of them after that. It takes quite a little time to get to where you can blend in with most horses. I wouldn't say all horses, because there isn't anyone who can do that — I hardly think a person would be able to fit them all — but a fella could get so he could get along with most of them.

❖ **PRESENTATION:** No two people or horses are the same, so to get feel applied in a way that the horse can understand it, there could be quite a little variation in your presentation. The main thing we're wanting the horse to understand about this is our intent, and whether he can understand what's expected just all depends on how the foundation has been laid in there for him. Not everybody can get an idea across to the horse without that horse taking over with a presentation of his own, and that wouldn't fit some people. It's the experimenting part of things that'd show a person if their presentation was fitting to a horse, or not.

DIAMOND LU COLLECTION

THIS HORSE HAS A REAL MELLOW APPEARANCE. HE'S A GOOD HORSE FOR THESE BOYS TO PRACTICE ON WHILE THEY LEARN THE BASICS.

In this picture, the boy on the left is helping the younger boy with some experiments on his presentation of feel to this horse. He's learning how to apply feel, and they're talking over some little adjustments that younger boy could try that would bring out the change he's trying to get in the horse, through feel.

Generally speaking, if the horse isn't doing what you think he ought to be doing, it's time to adjust your presentation so your horse can understand you through feel. How your judgment figures into your presentation of things is what that horse's future depends on. *It's your responsibility to the horse to make sure he understands what's expected of him through feel.* When he does, then he's liable to be comfortable. That's what we're interested in and that's why your presentation is real important to the horse. One thing's for sure, if it were up to the horse he wouldn't be any place around where a human had a job for him to do, and that'd include being shut up inside any place. There isn't any doubt about that.

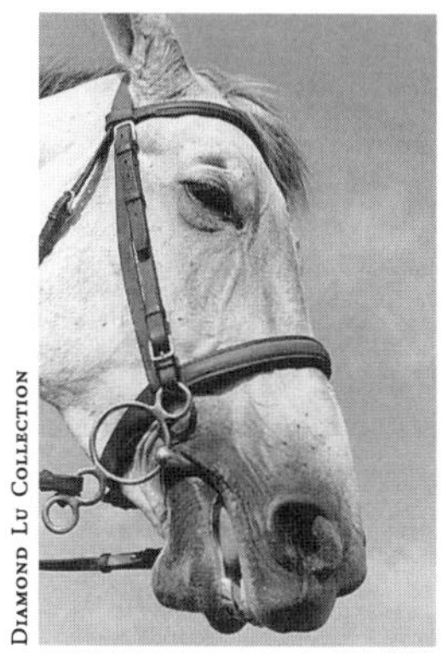

Diamond Lu Collection

Some resistance is liable to show up in a horse that has this appearance. He doesn't know what to do with that excess of pressure from the snaffle bit adjustment.

❖ **PRESSURE:** This is what we're trying to get away from, so we might not mention it. Maybe you could say "excess of pressure" because that's what any of it is where it concerns the horse. What we're in hopes of is that people will want to learn about feel, and how to apply it in a way that a horse can understand it, and that word "pressure" has no part in that. Firmness with your better judgement has a place in some cases, and it all depends on many variables as to how you'd go about applying that firmness.

In this picture, the pressure on that horse's mouth could be there for a lot of reasons, but one thing's for sure, the horse could do a lot more with a lot less of it, if the basics had been laid into a good foundation for him, using feel.

❖ **PULLING BACK:** A horse that does this hasn't been taught to lead up properly. Since this has been left out on the start, he doesn't understand what's expected of him when a person ties him to something. When a horse gets in the habit of that, why that takes in a lot of territory to get him over that. It's real difficult for people to get a horse over that habit because it takes an uncommon amount of knowledge and understanding. No, it's best not to get a horse started on that.

❖ **PUSHINESS:** When that pushiness shows up, that person is missing something real important and, for his part, the horse is overdoing the anticipation. He isn't feeling of the person anymore when he does that. It's up to the person to build feel into the horse, or to get it built back in there if he's stopped feeling of them for any reason. You rebuild feel by going back down the line a ways. Then work on some things that aren't problems down below where the problem shows up, because that's where the horse can understand what he's expected to do through feel.

When the horse is apt to overdo the anticipation he gets pushy and sometimes the person's idea of making him stand comes in. That is going to be just about the time when the horse will start to feel sure that he can't stick around there anymore.

That's when a lot more pushiness is liable to show up. I'd rather use words like *help him stand*, not make him stand, and that pushiness won't be in there as long that way. If you get on to the feel we're talking about in this book, it's possible that this pushiness may not show up, even if the horse is liable to be the excited kind who operates with an excess of energy.

That pushy sort of horse needs a person to think about blending in with him, or letting him drift, or helping him to go. Just any way you can get with the feel of that horse when he leaves, is all. A person ought to leave a place for some experimenting in part of this, too, that's for sure. If you can blend in with the horse for better results, it's best for him when you can find that place. When you go together from there, why that word "pushy" wouldn't have to be mentioned again.

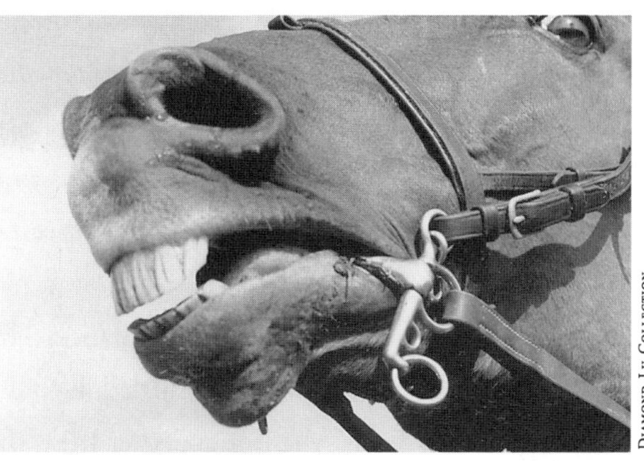

Diamond Lu Collection

It could be the horse got scared of something and the rider lost the feel of him for a little while, or it's a sorry hand on those reins. If you wanted to be sure, you'd have to see what happened before and after this picture.

❖ **PUSHING AGAINST THE BIT:** The horse isn't feeling of you when he does this. That will continue until his thinking can get switched around by working with him on the ground, through feel. This should carry over to your mounted work. I'll say "should" because if the horse picks up a person's feel in a way he can understand it, there's no need for him to push against a bit. There's some people who speak about the horse running through a bit. This doesn't happen unless the bit's broken, and you'd replace that one.

❖ **QUESTIONS:** I don't feel any question is unanswerable, and I want people to feel free to ask any question that comes into their minds about handling or riding their horses. There are no dumb questions and one good way to learn about something is to ask someone who's got more experience. Life is too short to learn what there is to know about horses just working all on your own. I believe that there's a way to answer any question through an explanation of feel. That's because when you're speaking about a horse it all gets back to feel, and how you get feel applied is real important for the horse. Helping a person to understand this is my main plan.

Patricia Weedman

Bill answers questions from spectators at one of the clinics put on by Pebble Beach Equestrian Center, in Pebble Beach, California.

❖ **RELEASE OF PRESSURE** *(full)*: That would be when there wasn't anyone around to bother him. When you do have hold of him on the lead rope or the reins, a full release means you'd let him go, and you wouldn't want to do that until that equipment had been taken off.

❖ **RESISTANCE:** This shows up when the horse doesn't understand what's expected of him. There's always a cause for a horse to start resisting the human, whether it's just a lack of understanding on the part of the rider, or overexposure to a feel that the horse doesn't understand. If the horse is resisting you, it means he's not feeling of you. It's up to the person to offer a feel to the horse in a way that the horse can understand what's intended, whatever it is. When he starts resisting, *this is how the horse tells you that something isn't fitting in there just right for him* and he's giving you another real good opportunity to move to a place of greater understanding. He needs to be better prepared to operate without the resistance. That's your main job.

If your horse is resisting you, you'd drop back, and this means you need to back up a ways to a spot (a place in his understanding) that is below where you are experiencing the resistance. That's where you go to work with the horse on something, just give him a little job to do — like stepping forward or back — and you'll work on up the line together from there. Going back and re-working that foundation is what builds understanding in the horse. You wouldn't move on without that.

There isn't any place for those words "resistance-free," because if resistance isn't there, then we wouldn't speak about it at all. And when he got to operating real smooth for you, you wouldn't ever need to say resistance-free because resistance can show up again anytime for any reason. You could say he understands your feel, maybe that's better, or he's mellow to handle, or light, there's other words better than that "resistance-free" word because the actual fact is that resistance will come in there and that word will lose its meaning when something changes and causes that horse to lose your feel.

There are some things you can't write about, but all I know is when something is presented in a way the horse can understand, he will take care of it. That's for sure. And through feel is how a person goes about this, because it works.

❖ **RESPECT:** I think that word has a lot of meaning, because respect and feel go right together. It's real useful and important to use this word in a way that people can understand it. When the horse has respect for you, he isn't pushing into you. He's doing what you want him to do, within reason. Most horses don't have respect on the start. Maybe you want that horse to do something that he isn't quite ready for. When he doesn't understand the feel that's presented to him, he's not ready. Horses want to stay away from you when they're like that, and of course they want you to stay away from them.

You can use a horse's natural fear of you — I'm talking now about a wilder sort of horse — to develop a response to you that has some respect in it. But, you'd want to get that fear part switched over to feel pretty quick because a person can easily get hurt if they put too much pressure on a horse that feels this scared way around a person. I've always said that the more pressure a person puts on a horse, the more experience they need to have, because they might get back from that horse quite a bit more than they know what to do with. When this happens too much, people say things about that horse that they shouldn't. But these people, they just don't know.

Respect, and how to get that applied in all that you do with your horse, is the most important thing to start learning about — and that takes in quite a lot when you speak about that word "all." When they are this way (respectful), they're also learning to feel of you at the same time. When there isn't respect, you haven't got much to go on, so you'd need to start getting with the feel of that horse — in most cases that's the way you'd go about it, I'll put it that way. Most horses will learn to respect you, given the opportunity, and there's a lot of opportunities to teach this to a horse. I want people to know there's no disrespect going along with true feel — not the way we're speaking about feel anyway.

If you are leading a horse around that doesn't have much respect for you, nibbling at the halter rope or pushing into you, that horse's disrespect for you needs to be taken care of. There are people who think that's cute. If they do, why they're going to be putting up with a lot that they won't want to put up with, and then they'll end up thinking the horse is trying to do them wrong. There isn't any place for that word "cute" where a disrespectful horse is concerned, and we don't need any part of a miserable feel. One that's this way needs to get taken care of in the very near future. *It's the person's responsibility to change the feel they present to that horse. It's real important for a person to understand that whatever kind of feel is in that horse, that's tied right to the foundation, however it got there, and that's all that horse has to rely on right now, and in the future.*

Well, let's take the other kind of horse, one that's more or less gentle and not really scared of you, but maybe he'd just as soon not have you around. But since you are going to be around there, he better understand what you mean when you offer him that feel to lead up real free, which isn't natural to them — not on the start anyway.

It's any unwanted motions that lead to disrespect that we're trying to stay far away from, and it's your observations and timing that gets these things headed off before they turn into something undesirable.

❖ **RESPONSIVENESS:** The only responsiveness we're interested in speaking about is the response we get from the horse to our feel. That's where the understanding part of things comes in for the horse. The horse can respond in his own way for many reasons — like fear, or resentment, or maybe the most common one is going to be confusion. It's up to the person to know about those different reactions in the horse and to know what they are from. Then it's up to the person to change what's presented to the horse so he only responds to what you want him to respond to. That would be a response through his understanding, and you'd like him to be in a willing and calm frame of mind. This is what fits a horse and that fitting response is what would let a person know they were on the right track.

Whenever you're with the horse, you'd need to pay close attention to where that horse's attention is focused, and you'd also be thinking about the sort of feel you present to him and *what it actually means to him*. He'll let you know, and if you're an observing person you'd make some adjustments if there was a need to, and the horse's response would let you know about that. That's what you're all the time looking to build on, just those little particles of information that you observe about the horse, and what you can sense, which is what you start to do when you're learning to pick up that feel he has. When you have his attention and you're aware of this, it is his feel coming back towards you. That's not something that just happens *sometimes*, it's *always* happening and it's real important to the horse that the person knows about this, because the horse does. That's what's inside of him for general communication purposes, so a person can tell what the horse understands about whatever is presented to him. Or what he maybe doesn't (understand), and that's when you'd get thinking about the little changes you could make in there to present something that did fit him.

One thing's for sure, it's all the time changing, and this is the part that is so difficult for some people. Others don't seem to mind as much. Generally speaking, there are some real adaptable people with a talent for feel of horses, and these are the people who really understand a lot of them. Some others don't have the time to do as much with horses. This other (kind of person) is satisfied with a horse that has learned to fill in for them. This might be most people. But, we're hoping to get a lot of them switched over in their thinking because horses are going to be around here in the future. It seems that way now.

❖ **RESTRAINT RIGS:** It's real unfortunate that when things aren't working out too smooth for a person with the horse — any horse — some items are brought out to control the horse's body through force. This is what we're trying to stay away from. Those restraint rigs and the ideas that come in there about that other way of doing things (using force) don't fit a horse, not to my way of thinking anyway.

There's a lot less meaning in the feel of those rigs than some people think there is. This restraint approach is really just more pressure applied to the horse with another word attached to it. The horse has no idea why a person uses these rigs, even if a person thinks he does. What the horse needs is less pressure. What he needs from that person is feel that has meaning in it that he can understand.

See, because that horse is so sensitive, he's really geared in his makeup to understand things down at the bottom, below where most people want to start. He's even sensitive to the ideas and the littlest motions coming from a person, and he's wondering about what they might want him to respond to, in most cases, but a lot of people don't know this.

If you're speaking about horses and wanting to get along with them, then there's no place for that word "force," or for things that are made so a person can force a horse to be a certain way, or do something that he's not prepared to understand through feel. *There isn't any need to tie him up with things to force him to stay in a certain position — not on the ground or riding. This is because if he understands you, he will do it. And we'll assume that what a person wants him to understand is within his physical capacity, and within reason.*

The horse has no reason to understand anything that restricts his movement and binds him up physically in the first place. This isn't natural for the horse. Because of this, he's liable to give that rider a response that proves he doesn't understand what he's supposed to do when these mechanics are rigged up to control him. In most cases the horse will do this, and in most cases this doesn't please the rider.

But, where a person has no idea about feel, they will try to make the horse do what they want, through force. Because that horse is a lot bigger and stronger than most any person, it's understandable that they'd think they might need some rig like that. Especially where they've seen another person use one of these rigs, and it could be any rig, but we won't speak about those. People wouldn't have any idea about this other way that we're interested in (horsemanship through feel). But we're in hopes they'll want to learn about it.

One thing's for sure, when you've got a rig like that on him for suppling purposes, there's thinking that needs to get switched around. There isn't any part of that word "supple" in the horse's response to a rig like this. No, they can sure force his body into some shape, but he isn't liable to be feeling of the person because, generally speaking, that horse would have some resistance to that rig they had on him. If supple was what a person needed that horse to be, why supple is natural for the horse anyway.

A horse can experience a lot of unnatural things with people around and this is something we'd really like to leave out. When you can get feel working for you, why you wouldn't need any sort of restraint rig.

❖ **ROOTING THE NOSE:** A horse that does this pushes his nose out by shoving his head towards the ground or up in the air when someone has hold of the lead rope or the bridle reins. He does this because of the way an inexperienced person has handled him. That person didn't know about the good feel a horse needs, so the horse went on to develop some habits of his own. This habit's one of those undesirable things that a person can put in the horse that has to be corrected if the horse is ever going to advance up the line, so you'd want to get that feel changed around pretty quick if you could.

It's good to spend time on things that work. When a person gets to thinking things through, they will probably remember to present a better feel and get that applied back down below the spot where that horse had his nose poked out, or poked up. Once they do get back below the trouble spot and get things to working real smooth without any resistance coming in there, that habit's not apt to show up in the future. Another way to say this is that when the person rebuilds feel into the horse, rooting that nose out will just stop. They will be on to that good feel before this happens, and they'll proceed up the line a little at a time, right from there. And that nose won't poke out. Some are going to restrain the horse to try to fix this problem because they haven't seen this better way, or because it fits them to do those things. There's all kinds of people in this world, and there's all sorts of rigs people use for this that are supposed to prevent a horse from poking his nose straight out or up into the air. The actual fact is that he's liable to operate worse instead of better with a restraint rig on him. Then, they'll want to fix some other problems that could show up with some other sort of restraint system. *They've missed the whole point of the horse when they do this.*

The actual facts about these things from the horse's point of view are that if his nose is poking up and out, then he doesn't understand what's expected, not even before the extra equipment gets put on him to hold his head or his body in a certain way. He has no good idea about any part of it after it's on there either, except that he's under more pressure than he was before. In most cases, the people applying these rigs on a horse are using guesswork. They put those on like they do because they saw it done that way. There isn't any good idea about it coming from a horse, and that's the main reason I discount the practice. As long as people aren't working through feel, they're lost and so is the horse. That horse is lost because he's looking to the person for support — which means helping that horse, not applying more pressure to him. When this happens, the horse is left wondering . . . *what's really going on?*

❖ **ROUNDPEN:** It's just a round corral that you can work your horse in. It could be 30 or 40 feet across or bigger, and most of them nowadays are made out of metal panels. It's helpful to have one, but to get the feel we're talking about working for you and your horse, you don't have to have a roundpen. It can be done other ways. That's because we're talking about using feel, not about equipment or corrals. But there's some things that can help a person, even if it's not real necessary to have them.

❖ **RUBBER-NECKED HORSE:** When you hear this term it usually refers to a sensitive horse with a real flexible neck. The part missing from this horse's lessons is the placement of his feet in response to the feel of your legs on his body. You have to teach these kinds of horses to be real sensitive to your leg so you can do more (be more effective with your legs, and do less with your hands). *You can do this by presenting your whole body feel to get them to turn their body by moving their feet.* We've done some writing on this before. This type of horse has also missed the connection between the feel of the bit in his mouth and his feet on the ground, and the rider has too, or that person's leg feel would have more meaning to the horse when he was standing still or traveling.

One thing that's really good about this kind of horse is that he's not pushing against the bit. To keep his head and his body in a safe position when you ride him, you'd want to go back to your work on the ground. Get him to understand how to yield his body and step around real slow, left and right, and back and forward in response to the feel of your halter when you're on the ground next to him, or even a little distance from him on your lead rope. Then you'll build in his responsiveness to your body while you're sitting up there doing those same maneuvers, real slow. You wouldn't go any faster than he could operate correctly from that feel of your legs and body, and you'd want him not to lose the good feel in that new connection you laid in there for him. That will take care of the rubber-neck problem and there won't be a need to mention it again.

❖ **RUNNING THROUGH THE BIT OR HACKAMORE:** There isn't any such thing as that. It's just a saying that got started by someone who didn't really know what happened and needed to put some new words in there. That's what people say when they mean that horse wasn't feeling of them and was pushing against whatever they had on him. There isn't any place for those words "running through," in my way of thinking. But if it's an actual fact of what happened, there'd be meaning in that.

❖ **SEARCHING:** If something is presented to the horse right, his natural way of searching is what will help him find it. Generally speaking, it's a release that he's looking for, and this could be called a release from pressure. Searching is how he finds that release, and if a person knew about feel and had some timing in there to go along with their feel, then the horse would begin to understand what was expected of him every time he found that release. A person does some of this (searching) too. But maybe that's more in the experimenting part of things when you're speaking about a person doing this.

❖ **SEAT** *(a good one)*: This kind starts with getting balanced on your horse without depending on the reins.

A rider who looks forward to a specific spot, whether it's ten feet or a few hundred yards away, has a better chance of maintaining correct body position. This'd be where the legs are relaxed and the body is more or less lined up, starting with the shoulder on the top and coming right down through the imaginary line a person can think about between the shoulder and the hip and the lower part of the calf and heel. Someone with a natural seat has the good fortune to sit with good posture. This means that they have a natural sense of balance and the ability to look ahead at an object out in front of them while they keep (directing and supporting) that horse between their legs, and between the reins, too.

❖ **SEAT** *(a poor one)***:** This is the other sort of seat and, generally speaking, the person who is unfortunate to have this way of riding is either rigid or sloppy. And the worst part about this is that he has heavy, unsteady hands on the reins, which causes poor handling of the horse's mouth and this connects right to poor balance. All of this is very confusing to the horse. The person's unable to direct and support the horse in turns and transitions, there isn't any question about that, and it doesn't take very long for people who ride this way to earn their horse's disrespect.

A good seat can be developed from a poor seat, but you'd rather get balanced on the horse with good posture at the beginning, because this is so important to the horse. With a seat like this one it's difficult — and I'll even say almost impossible — to present a feel that the horse can understand. So getting this changed around is top priority for the person who is serious about the future where horses are concerned.

❖ **SELF-PRESERVATION:** That's the horse trying to protect himself because he doesn't know for sure what's going to happen to him. He's fighting to save himself and that's the natural thing for a horse to do, to fight back if he's unsure and can't run.

Diamond Lu Collection

This is a natural response to see in a horse when he's unsure about something. You'd get him sure about many things before you'd ride him.

The young horse in this picture isn't sure what to do and it's a basic instinct to be on the defensive and think about self-preservation, until he knows he's not going to get hurt. He didn't get hurt and was soon saddled.

Some acts of self-preservation include some things that aren't the best for a person without much experience to be around. The actual facts of what's taking place are that the horse thinks something is going to hurt him, so he'll fight back to keep from getting hurt. We want to get along with the horse in a way that allows that self-preservation part to stay in there, all right. Many surprising things can happen when that self-preservation shows up in the horse, and a person might wish it didn't. I'd rather a person went about things in a way so the horse would have some confidence built into himself and understand that he could look to the person for support. And that horse will, if a person's taken the time to lay a good foundation in there for him.

❖ **SENDING THE HORSE:** That's been talked over in the part about driving the horse.

❖ **SHIFTING THE WEIGHT BACK:** This is what you do when you don't want that weight up front. When the weight is forward too much for what you need the horse to do, it can trip him up, or slow him down — either way he gets confused. In a maneuver where you needed him to be ready to liven up and keep those front legs available to go in any direction, you'd lay a good foundation in there on the start, through feel.

It's the same whether you're sitting up there or working on the ground. You'd shift his weight back before you'd set his front foot over to one side or another. This is a basic maneuver that you'd build in on the ground, and then it's not liable to be any problem for the horse when you're sitting up there. He's liable to stay light and available to you then, and that way he can really get with you.

Diamond Lu Collection

THIS COLT IS FEELING OF THE RIDER AND IS SHIFTING HIS WEIGHT BACK TO GET THE LEFT FRONT LEG LIGHTENED UP A LITTLE, SO IT CAN RESPOND TO THE RIDER'S REINS AND LEG FEEL TO TAKE A STEP TO THE LEFT.

❖ **SLINGING THE HEAD:** A horse that slings his head hasn't learned to feel of the person handling him, and it's likely the handler hasn't got much feel to offer the horse either, or the problem wouldn't be there to start with. The main cause of head slinging can be traced to excessive pressure on the mouth or the halter rope. Where a handler has a harsh feel on the mouth, making sudden jerky pulls and then putting some slack in the rein or lead between those pulls — this is what encourages the horse to set his own agenda about what to do with his head. When this is allowed to go on he'll expand his plan to those feet and what they might need to do, so it's best to head this off. This isn't uncommon where horses and people are operating together without feel built into their foundation.

If a person doesn't get turned around in their thinking in time, they're apt to outfit a head-slinger with some rig that creates an excess of pressure across the bridge of his nose for general handling purposes. And the horse, he'll push against this with disrespect as soon as he feels the pressure of a pull. The harder he's pulled on, the more pressure he'll exert in response to that pulling, until the relationship falls apart all the way. And those feet, why the horse has no good idea about what to do with them in connection with a feel like that. There aren't many situations that a horse and a person can get into that are as unattractive as this.

Straightening out a horse who's been taught to operate this way should come *before there's any thought about riding him*, because when you're sitting up there on a horse that slings his head around, real surprising things can happen that aren't desirable. Once that horse has learned how to feel of you, this problem isn't one that'd need to be spoken about again. The reason being, it will not exist.

❖ SLOBBER STRAPS: The slobber straps are the leather pieces folded over the rings of the snaffle bit. The reason they exist goes way back in time when people had to make their own hair ropes and maybe they didn't last as long when they got wet from the horse drinking water and also from rubbing against that metal bit all the time. It turns out that they are a big help in making the contact between the rider's feel and that mouth lighter and more effective, too, but that could have been known about all along by the knowledgeable horsemen who experimented and came up with the idea.

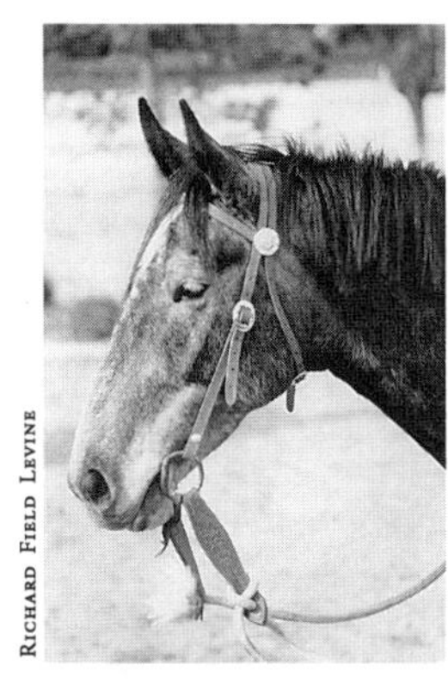

Richard Field Levine

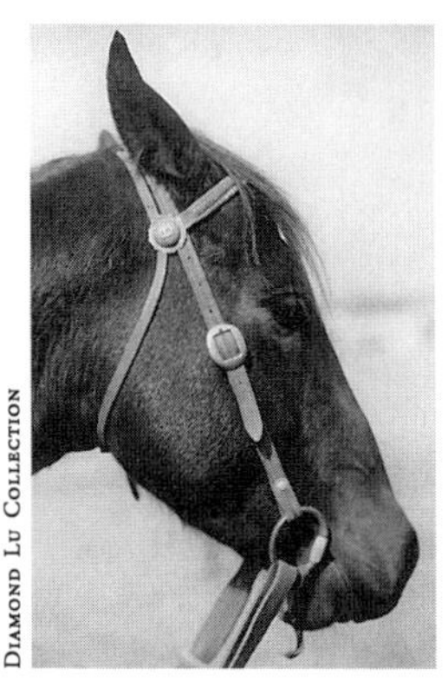

Diamond Lu Collection

Slobber straps don't have to be carved leather or fancy in any way. Real plain is what I like.

❖ SLOW: Getting feel applied is a slow process when you're starting to learn about it, so this is why you need to go slow. It's quite an amazing thing to see that more progress can be made with a horse that isn't rushed than one who gets hurried past the basics. Eventually, if a horse that is rushed is going to be able to work up the line very far in his abilities, then somebody will need to take the time to rebuild that foundation.

Everyone is inclined to go too fast. In my younger years I went too fast myself, and I missed some real important things by going along that faster way. You might have to slow down your feel to help him.

You don't pressure the horse to go fast, because you'd rather he went slow so he can retain what he's learning. It could be because these faster horses sometimes got some help from a person getting that way. So, you'll slow him down, and you might need to slow down your feel a little to get him that way. It's more difficult for the horse to get his feet placed properly when he's operating this faster way. And it's more difficult for him (to be) this way especially when you're working to teach him backwards maneuvers, and turns that make use of vertical flexion and some other flexions of the poll. Any job you have to do will get done a lot easier if the feel you've built in that horse is based on slow, accurate work on the start. That way, there's something built in real solid for the horse and the person to rely on.

❖ SORRY HAND: Any time you're talking about the hand, why that's a real important part of riding, all right. If a person has learned to present a good feel to that horse, they've done it through a good position of the arms. The hands depend on the movement in your arms, because of where they are on your body. When I use the word "hands," it's only as an aid to hold the reins, but what really brings the life into that horse are a person's legs.

You'd use that life that comes up in the horse so you could maneuver him with your arms because, the actual fact is, it's those arms that are operating the reins. Then you'd direct him with your arms, *and these are what can give some important support to the horse in his understanding about what the rest of your body is telling him to do.*

That sorry hand isn't operating with feel properly, and isn't going to get the horse to respond well, so it shouldn't be holding those reins in the first place. If the feel was proper, then there'd be no use for that term "sorry hand" anyway.

❖ **SPEED:** When you're talking about a word to leave out of a conversation about horses and teaching feel, why this word "speed" would be the one. I'd rather speak about that word "slow," and the ideas a horse can get good at understanding by a person being that way — *and by this I mean real slow.*

Diamond Lu Collection

The horse in this picture is stepping over behind from left to right. There's a float in the line and he's just stepping out of the way, because he understands what's expected.

See, the old timers learned something about the value of keeping their horses moving slow from working with those real sensitive wild cattle. Working that way the cattle wouldn't be liable to move off so soon. But if you were in a gallop, there was a lot more motion around there and that would start the cattle moving early. In some cases, that got to be real unhandy, and those fellas had to spend a lot more time than they'd thought they would *doing some real slow work* just to get them gathered back up again to where they were before they got riled up and moved out. And this was due, of course, to the motions in those faster horses in the first place.

There's such a variation in what takes place, but if you can figure out how to make use of speed where horses are concerned then, generally speaking, slow is better. And cattle, why a person who thinks they ought to be running around has missed quite a bit on the start about cattle, that's for sure. And maybe they missed it about horses, too.

❖ **STEP OUT OF THE WAY:** This has to do with the word "yield" and, generally speaking, it's what you'd like the horse to do if you needed to be where he was standing.

Diamond Lu Collection

Here the horse is stepping over from right to left. He's doing this through feel, and filling in just a little for these young girls.

❖ **STEPPING OVER BEHIND:** This is when a horse crosses one hind foot in front of the other. If he stepped back, we wouldn't say stepping over, we'd say stepping back. There's an important difference for the horse in that, and it's something the rider ought to be aware of. To start with, the hind feet need to maneuver real free whenever there's a need for them to be that way, which could be for any reason that could show up most anytime. But the first place the rider needs to learn about the feel of this step would be on the ground, because this is just an exercise to get the feel of where those feet are, so you can get that horse feeling of you. And you'd be sure to do this from both sides of the horse. This is real important to build in before you ever get on the horse. Later on, why this will carry over to your mounted work.

❖ **SUBMISSIVE:** If you want him to submit, OK. But you'd set that up so he could understand your meaning, through the feel that you applied in there — either with the lead rope or the reins. *There's no place for the idea of dominating a horse, not by any means.* The horse wouldn't understand how to respond to this except through self-preservation. But we don't want that horse to feel he has to rely on that part of himself when we are anywhere near him. If he learns to operate that way (out of self-preservation) when we have hold of his lead rope or reins, it means he doesn't have the confidence in us that he should have, and there's fear of the human in the horse that shouldn't be there No, if he's scared and submitting, then it's a sure sign that we've missed something down below where that trouble showed up, and back down below is the place we'd need to go to rebuild that foundation.

❖ **SUPERVISION:** This comes from a person with a real knowledge of how to supervise, and is a big help to anyone trying to learn something difficult. It's not exactly the same as an instructor, but that difference isn't so important to speak about. Without good supervision it's going to be a lot more difficult to learn.

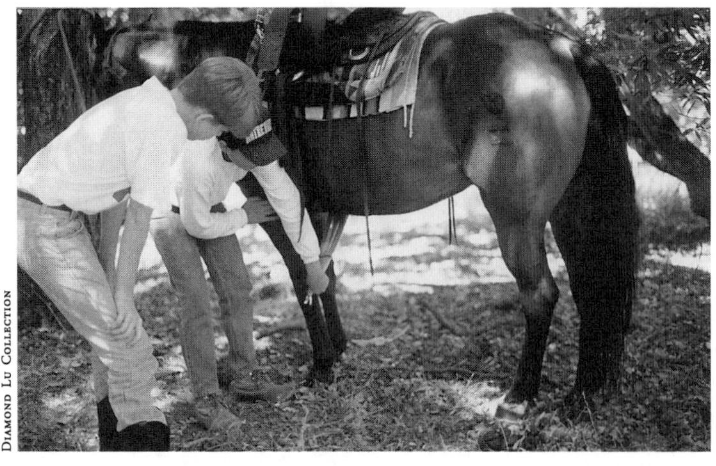

Diamond Lu Collection

Going slow and learning about things a little at a time makes it a lot easier to remember those things that are so important to the horse — and to the safety of the person.

Learning how to handle horses through feel can take place even if you aren't grown, and I'll say it's sometimes easier to learn this slow way when you are in your younger years. And where a person lacks experience on the start, why safety needs to figure in there pretty heavy. You want some experienced help, and that'd be experience in the area of learning how to feel of a horse, and teaching that horse to feel of you. Without that, some supervision might not be the best help there is, I'll say that.

❖ **SUPPLING A HORSE:** You'll get him real flexible in the poll and the neck to both sides, and then you'll need him to flex at the poll, and (to flex) vertically after that. You could have a halter or a snaffle bit on him, either one. If he's supple, then he's feeling of you. If he's allowed enough space to move real free, and mingle around with other horses and eat off the ground, just like he would on his own, then he's supple enough to start on almost anything else, because he already knows how to move. *It's natural for him.* And where he has other horses to be with, then it's pretty certain that a lot of movement and actions will take place.

Horses that aren't supple have had help from the human getting that way. Stiff movement just isn't natural for the horse and there aren't liable to be any man-made things that are going to improve on the way a horse will keep himself supple — if he has that opportunity.

❖ **TAKING THE HORSE'S HEAD AROUND:** People do this to get the horse used to following the feel of rein pressure. This is part of the preparation that you build in ahead of time, before you ride him. Generally speaking, it's what you want to do before you double the horse, and doubling is something the horse needs to be good at. A fella'd build this on the start in case he needed to stop an inexperienced horse on the spur of the moment. The horse could be running, or not running, when you double him. Whatever he's doing, it is going to be a lot easier if you can take his head around on both sides and rub his head while his feet are still. Of course, if the horse was traveling with his head around, why you'd leave out the part about rubbing his head, because there's plenty of other things a person would be planning to do or thinking about during that time.

❖ **TAKING THE SLACK OUT OF THE LINE:** That's pretty much the same as picking up the float, just using some other words. To the horse, it should feel the same.

❖ **TAKING OVER:** If we overdo it, he'll take over. If we don't do enough, he'll take over. That's the thing about taking over — we need to adjust whatever it is we're presenting to the horse so that he can get that understanding part of things working for him. If it fits the horse, he won't take over, and so that's the person's main job — learning how to present what they expect that horse to do in a way he can understand it. The horse doesn't take over unless he stops feeling of you. When that happens, the connection is lost and he gets mixed up. He doesn't know what else to do, so he takes over.

DIAMOND LU COLLECTION

THIS HORSE ISN'T FEELING OF THE YOUNG PERSON HERE SO HE'S BUMPING INTO HIM AND STEPPING ON HIM. THIS IS CALLED "TAKING OVER" AND IS SURE SOMETHING WE'RE TRYING TO AVOID.

It could be that a person has missed a spot in the foundation. Taking over that's (become) a habit for the horse, why we'd call that pushiness and there's no part of a good feel where that comes in. One thing's for sure, if that's in there, you'd better get it changed around before you'd ride a horse that was that way, because many things could surprise you with a horse that had this habit. I'd rather a person prepared the horse for the future in a way they could avoid some of these mix-ups.

Horses that learn to take over like the one in this picture have missed learning how to feel of a person on the start, and it takes a person with experience presenting a better feel to offer the horse to get switched around. But there could be times when a person would be operating a horse that has a good connection through feel built in to the foundation, and that horse just gets startled. In a situation like that, why the self-preservation part of the horse is causing him to take over and lose that connection. It's his right to respond this way. In a case like this, it's our hope that a person would have those basics in there to where that horse is looking to the person for support, instead of taking over with ideas of his own (that are) connected to self-preservation. This takes time.

Most times, I'll say on better-broke horses, it doesn't take much to get that horse to feel of you again after he's been startled.

❖ **TALKING THINGS OVER:** There's value in that. It's important to figure out what might be the most fitting of the things there are to do. This also gives people a chance to have their ideas out and work a little more on their understanding of things. No, there should be a lot of value in this for everyone involved, I'll say that. When I'm helping people, I like to have them ask questions, because then I get a little better idea of what's in their frame of mind. That way, I have a chance to answer that person in a way they can understand.

Richard Field Levine

❖ **THROWING THE REINS AWAY:** Some people are in the habit of doing something with their hands that isn't holding on to those reins, and they're liable to have their leg hooked over that horn at the same time — maybe they're just talking to people. Those horses they're sitting on appear to be just lazy and standing around. People who do this have missed what feel is right on the start, and probably so has the horse. And he just might not be lazy.

A person wouldn't want an excess amount of float in those reins because the horse relies on those reins to know what you want him to do with his weight and his feet. What people who sit and visit with their friends this way don't know is that those horses could liven up on the spur of the moment for any reason. You'd want to have enough of a connection with your reins and legs to direct those feet when they liven up, however they happen to liven up. Of course, when that happens, you'll always be having in mind to look for a place where that horse can go. You'd direct him to a place because if he needs to go on the spur of the moment, why there's an opportunity to begin presenting feel to that horse that will have meaning for him.

You'll always be looking for a useful spot to show that horse where he can go when the life comes up in him that sudden way, and this part is real important, no matter how far along the horse or the rider is. We're in hopes that a person who might like to sit this unuseful way on a horse will have different ideas in the future.

❖ **TIMING:** Feel and timing work together. One without the other isn't very beneficial. And, of course, balance figures in there a lot. Those three things — timing, feel and balance — they are all real important parts of good horsemanship. But, if you're already feeling of the horse, you've already got some timing to go along with that feel. With this in place, the horse will learn how to operate in the way you're hoping he will.

The main thing about timing is those feet. It's real important to know where they are. If that rider or person handling the horse knows two things — *when those feet are coming up off the ground and when they're headed back down to the ground* — then they are in a position to direct that horse far better than someone who never thought about it.

If a person wouldn't know or feel the difference in those two things, and if the person hasn't gotten this geared pretty straight in their mind, well, I'm in hopes they'd find out — in the best way possible, of course — that it ought to get right up to the top of their thinking.

❖ **TRAINING:** You know, a lot of people who are starting out with a horse have an idea that they have to pay a trainer and everything will work out, just because they've paid to have the horse trained. What is sometimes easy for a person to miss is that if they are in it for five minutes or in it for five years, or whether they have a trainer or they don't, *the horse is going to go to where that person is, regardless of who they paid or how much it cost them.*

It takes the riders longer to learn what to do than it does for that horse to learn what to do. It isn't that the rider knows less than the horse, because the rider or the handler knows far more than the horse does. They're just more intelligent in every way, but they may be the ones who mess that horse up the worst. This happens when they *think* they know what to do. But without some help from someone with more experience at handling a horse through feel, why those people haven't really had the opportunity to learn the more important things that a horse needs for them to know — which is feel and how you go about getting feel applied in a way that the horse can understand.

What's difficult to understand on the start, I'll say especially for some people who might not have spent much of their life around horses, is that the horse is going to learn something from the person who is around him. Whatever that person does — even the littlest things a person wouldn't think the horse would learn, he will, because he feels what is taking place in the whole situation around there —

and feel is all the horse has to go on. It's the natural setup he was born with, so he's going to be aware of most things anywhere around there.

That's the actual facts and if a person is listed as a trainer or they aren't, why the horse doesn't care about that. It could be that they (who are listed horse trainers) might get by with what they're teaching that horse and, of course, the horse and that person who owns him might get by too. But we don't want to just get by. Surprising things can happen with that approach — and those things might not be the best.

❖ **TRUE HORSEMANSHIP:** That's when the horse understands through feel what he's expected to do. The horse understands true horsemanship because it's the truth. And that's the truth.

❖ **TUCK:** This is what the horse does when he yields to the pressure on his mouth or on his nose. This happens when he tucks his chin down and in toward his chest. He softens, and he becomes light in your hand. *A horse can learn to carry this posture if the rider doesn't take up the slack on those reins when he does this.* It feels good to the rider, and it doesn't weigh anything in your hand at all when he does this, just the weight of those reins. It feels good to the horse too.

Lori Klein

If all four feet are working properly, and stepping around real free where the rider needs for them to be, *that tuck isn't necessary.* But it can improve the general appearance of a horse, especially where that horse isn't much for looks.

If the feet weren't operating correctly through feel, it would be necessary to have that tuck in there, because you'd need to have a start on feel anyway, and that would be one place you'd need it — because you'd want him real flexible at the poll and in his neck. This is where we don't want any mix-up in the person's understanding. They'd be sure to understand that *the horse's head position isn't the same as having control of those feet the way you need them to be when the horse is feeling of you and can understand what you expect him to do.*

A horse is liable to tuck his chin down and in naturally on his own. He's going to do this sometimes when he is hepped up about meeting new horses, or when he's turning to face something he's unsure of after he's been startled. A horse will sometimes do this for a reason that a person might not have any idea about. When he's in this lively frame of mind and body, he is gathered and prepared for any sudden change of direction and bursts of speed which gives the horse a lighter kind of step, and this is real attractive.

❖ **TUCK** *(too much)*: This is one thing you don't want to build into a horse. This is a common problem, and it usually comes from a person's hands hanging on the horse's mouth. His chin comes too close to his body when too much tuck is in there and because it's liable to develop into a habit for him, I'd rather see a person get this headed off early.

When a horse reaches this position, he's given up on the prospect of finding release from the rider. At one time, that horse with too much tuck had willingness to follow that person's feel to that point (the right amount of tuck). But, when the person didn't give that horse any release, why I'll say they overdid it. The horse would just give up after too much of that poor feel, and under par (behind the vertical) is the way he'd start to travel now. This is liable to be accompanied by a wrong bend in the neck, just a little ways back from the poll, which is a real unnatural way for the horse to be.

Another thing about too much tuck on a horse is that it's a sign the horse doesn't understand the leg feel a person presents. And this is because the person doesn't apply it in a way the horse can understand it.

In a horse that carries himself with too much tuck, a lot of things have been missed in his development. The real important thing to understand is that too much tuck is liable to cut way down on the effectiveness of what a person can get done when he's riding a horse that travels this way. No, if a fella had his horse going this way and needed him for a job, he'd need to get this changed around all right. You'd sure have to present your leg feel to him in a different way and get the ideas in his mind switched around about what a float in those reins was supposed to mean to him. Of course the person first needs to understand these things, and how they work together to help a horse operate with a better feel. This will help on appearance too, in some cases.

You will usually discover some general disrespect and pushiness on the ground in a horse that arranges his head and neck this way. This was also missed by the rider who maintains a horse in this posture. *But, if the person takes the time to get some of these things working on the ground, then they'll be preparing for a future that won't include any of these things.* Once it gets changed around, everyone involved with a horse like this will be better off.

Other problems that show up along with this might include an over-weighted forehand and unresponsive sides, which was spoken about earlier as the horse not understanding the feel presented by the rider's legs. And there's also the tendency for a horse that carries himself this way to run on when the rider prefers to stop. Not having control of the feet through feel does not lead to anything a person will find desirable, especially if they're sitting up there on him.

Under these circumstances, a person might drop back a little and get this horse farther along in his basic understanding of feel, and you'd practice this on the ground, to start, and then progress up to some mounted work. The person has to have this understanding first, before they can teach the horse how to understand their feel. If a horse had this way of carrying himself (with too much tuck), it would be real helpful to a person to have an instructor that was experienced at using feel to show them how this is done.

❖ **UNDER PAR:** This means the horse is carrying his head with his chin tucked down and in so the bridge of his nose is behind the (imaginary) vertical line. A fella needs to have this built in for the future, when it's needed, which isn't liable to be very often. It's a tool, and when you'd use it, all depends.

❖ **WALK OUT:** That means the horse is interested in going some place. He's starting to look for someplace to go and you're helping him go in the direction that is best suited for you. This is a better way to travel than a real slow walk because it's more interesting to the horse and the rider, too. If the horse has already learned to feel of the rider, as we spoke about before, then when the rider's leg feel and his whole body liven up, the horse's feet should liven up.

❖ **WHOA:** Some people say that to stop their horse. But I don't use that word. I ride my horse with feel, not sound.

❖ **WITHIN REASON:** This'd come under the heading of the things those horses can understand. I'd say that takes in whatever that horse can understand that can go along with his physical system. If the person presents his ideas to the horse through feel, why then he's doing it this way (within reason) because that horse is set up to understand that.

❖ **WORDS:** This is my first experience putting a book together and I've tried to avoid as many unnecessary words as possible. We've had to back up and change a lot of words around to try and get them placed better. We're avoiding any part of fiction in this book because we're interested in the actual facts. We're in hopes that the words we've picked out will help people get a better understanding of these ideas about horses. A fella might think about mentioning only words that he feels are truthful. And in this book we've tried to use only words that are that way. These words are chosen because of the truth about horses, or as close to the truth about the actual facts of horses as we knew how to get. There's a lot of room for talking about the words a fella might use, but we have to draw the line someplace and get this book out.

❖ **WORKING THE MOUTH AND LICKING THE LIPS:** A horse will do this if he's relaxed and comfortable. You won't see this happen much on a horse that's troubled or upset. One thing's for sure, you don't want to have a tight noseband on a horse, not on any horse. A horse needs all the encouragement that he can get to stay relaxed and work his mouth when he's being ridden.

He'll stay a lot more relaxed and focused on the job you have for him if he can work those jaws. There's no part of a tight or nervous horse that will help you get a job get done any better, no matter what it is that needs to be done. Restraining his mouth movements and forcing those lips closed is a good way to get both those things to happen (tightness or nervousness), and other things a person wouldn't want to have happen can sure get started from there.

Diamond Lu Collection

When a horse works his mouth he sometimes yawns. This is natural and doesn't necessarily mean the horse is tired. A tight noseband prevents the horse from doing this, which is why I don't use one.

❖ **WORKING ON UP THE LINE:** This is what most people do with their horses instead of starting down at the bottom. When you work up there without building in that foundation, then you're working above the level of things that a horse can understand. When you've missed the opportunity to build meaning into the feel you present to the horse on the start, you'll need to get that taken care of.

A lot of people don't feel there's any advantage to them in working on the basics. But you don't ever want to get too far away from the basics, because that's how the horse knows what you want. No matter how far up the line you're asking him to do something, it all boils down to: Did he understand you on the start? Because if he didn't, a lot will show up to reveal how really confused he is when you need him to do something up the line. And so many surprising things can happen when a horse is this way. When the horse gets real mixed up is about the time a person's self-preservation starts to show up. But in order for his horse to become reliable that person needs to switch around his *understanding about the value of that preparation* the horse needs down at the bottom. And when he does, why that value is liable to start to figure in there for him real heavy.

❖ **YIELD:** If he's feeling of you, why you shouldn't ever need to push on a horse to move him. Horses feel of each other, and it works about the same way.

That horse can understand meaning in your body motions when you're sitting up there, and he can understand what you expect of him from the way you take a step when you're on the ground. That word "yield" has to do with you stepping

Diamond Lu Collection

Diamond Lu Collection

This paint colt was looking for a place to get some feed. The black horse didn't want to share any part of his feed and he used indirect feel that carried some meaning to get this horse to yield away from him.

towards the horse or letting him know by the motions of your body that he should move, and him stepping out of the way — as long as that's what you intend. If he's not feeling of you, he's not likely to yield when you need him to, and it's a sure sign that the basics have been glossed over on the start. That's a good time to get started working on some things that were missed back down a little ways.

Diamond Lu Collection

It's not much different here with this saddled colt and the fella with the flag. He's teaching this colt how to yield.

HAVE YOU GOT THE MAKINGS . . .

"I'm just getting a loop built here . . ."

You say you ride, but can you rope
And can you read a brand?
Pardner, have you got the makings
Of a top cowhand?

You have the boots, you bought the saddle,
But how are you alone with cattle?
Are you savvy, are you mean?
And were you ever really green?

You have a horse, but does he know
How to free right up and go?
Did you take the time to get him right?
Does he handle for you smooth and light?

You spent the time, but did you learn
To keep the life up through a turn?
Is there a place on him for you to sit
Where your saddle and his soul just fit?

What's it take to read that steer
And will your rope reach him from here?
You ride your horse, past dark you say,
Do you feel his feet most all the way?

Joe Wolter and Bill (on left) at Wolter's ranch, 1996.

Photos in this section from Diamond Lu Collection.

Before he jumped did you really know
That he was shaping up to go?
Will you count the cattle that you see?
Do you read the weather on that old tree?
Does the full moon raise a song in your heart?
Can you ride all day without shakin' apart?

Is your horse too tired to trot another mile?
Do you know when to stop and let him rest awhile?
Did you air out his back and jerk your saddle down?
Is your mind on the job, or does it drift to girls in town?

Can you take it? Will you make it?
Or, are you just passing time?
Will you still be roping cattle
When you're crowding 99?

Bill and Beaut holding a calf, 1998.

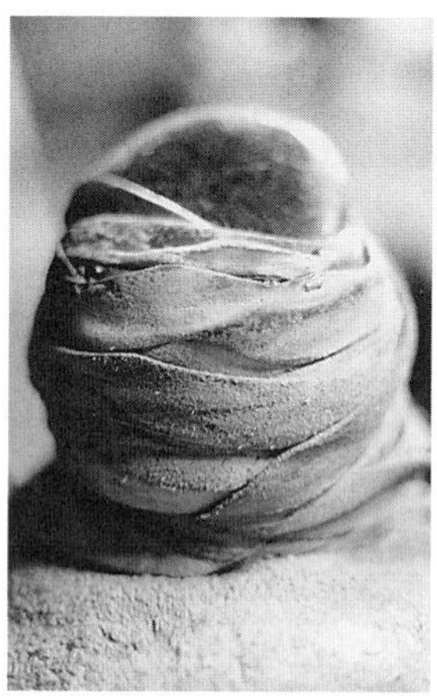

"I haven't any idea how many times I've rewrapped my horn. I just put another wrap right over the top, before it gets worn through is all. Of course, the bigger the horn, the less dallies you have to take."

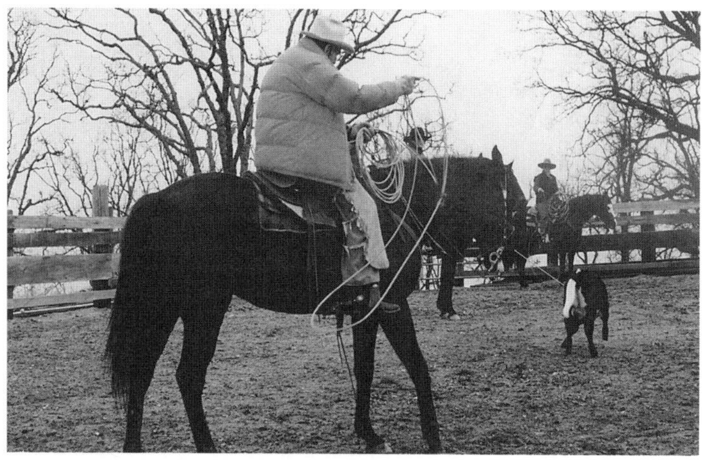

"I'm just getting Beaut into position." Still roping at 92.

LAPTOP BUCKAROO

It's a strange and changing world
But the horse still thinks the same
And there's still a cowboy's job to do
Out on the open range

There's a sick cow yonder and a fence to mend
He wonders if she's near the end
Swing, pitch, dally and tie her fast
'Cuz that next step could be her last
He thinks she'll make 'er, he's saved a few,
He's a genuine buckaroo

The cell phone rings in his medicine bag
The Dow has changed his broker calls to say
Should I buy, sell, trade — and how are you today?

It looks like rain and we need it bad
Feed's about gone and we need more men
To see us through until we ship again,
Said the hard workin' buckaroo

The Pony Express is a thing long gone
Got my laptop, e-mail and dial tone
I reach my girl on the cellular phone
But the horse still thinks the same

There's still a cook wagon and the cattle boss
There's a bedroll, badger hole and spotted horse
I got calves to pull and prayers to say
If we get that rain then we won't need hay,
Said the long ridin' buckaroo

It's a changing world and the pace is fast
But slow is better when you're working cattle
And the horse still thinks the same

But hang on, hello, on the second ring
It's stocks and bonds and that blue chip thing
Check my C-drive, cinch knot and piggin' string
Tin cup, coffee up and ride all day
A man still has to draw his pay,
Said the laptop buckaroo

There's rap songs, welfare and foreign cars
And small town action at the local bars
There's scraps of rawhide on the bunkhouse floor
He's got MTV on Channel 4
There's a new breed of fella out on the range
But the horse he rides still thinks the same

He's a hard-workin', long-ridin', genuine laptop buckaroo.

Dave Dorrance gets ready to tack on a shoe. Top of the mountain, Dorrance Ranch, Salinas, California.

LORD, LET ME BE A COWBOY TODAY

Got my Chevy truck, can of Cope and dog named Blue
'Cuz life didn't change when I met you
Raised the kids and private school hulla-balloo
Passed another 20 years before I knew what to do

I kept the job, climbed the ladder, started drinking, nothing mattered
You left with him, I had a fit, you said there's no way out of it
I had it all, or so it seemed, but I lived in someone else's dream

Who am I, do I know, do I care anyway?
Oh, Lord, let me be a cowboy today

With a shucks and a shuffle and a yee' haw pard
Got a ropin' dummy in my backyard
Got my sixty-foot rope and how-to video
Got a set of spurs that jingle and make the horse go
Got my heel shot, hip shot and ocean wave
Got my chew can, houlihan and I don't shave

Ain't a day goes by that I don't wonder why
I can't find country with enough blue sky
Got my mortgage, alimony and a college degree
I just came to my senses, but I'm almost 63

Who am I, do I know, do I care anyway?
Oh, Lord, let me be a cowboy today

Got my truck and my dog and two years to go
Then I'll get out the map and head down the road
Like the guys back when, who followed the sun
Sittin' on a horse with just a rope and loaded gun

Got a Carhart jacket and a baseball cap
Got my lip full of chew and my western rap
Got new stained Levi's and the boots don't fit
Got an old busted saddle and a rusted bit
For the wall in the den where I sit all night
In the armchair dreamin' of the great gunfights

So it's camp coffee, flank shot and do-si-do
Don't know about you but I really have to go
Got the dually runnin' with the radio on
It's the Nashville thing, and it's soon long gone

Who am I, do I know, do I care anyway?
Oh, Lord, just let me be a cowboy today!

I'LL TROT FOR YOU

Don't grab those reins
Don't whip my back
Keep your spurs to yourself
You'll get more for that

To turn my head just look that way
I'll trot for you the rest of the day
And I'll still be going when the sun comes up,
I'll trot for you, so you can fill your cup

I'll trot for you 'til your work is done
If you want more, just ask, I'll run
I'll swim the rivers, I'll get us there, and
I'll pull your wagon to the county fair

I'll trot for you, you know by now
To the bear, to the moose, to the biggest cow
I'll trot for you through snow and sleet
I'll keep on going, you can save your feet
I'll trot to the top of that hill right there
I'll trot for you, *just tell me where*

Remember the day in the four-up hitch,
When the coal black mare just kicked and pitched?
I had the wheel and she was ahead
When you said "Whoa," she went instead

She was hot and nervous and travelin' tight
Those traces pinched and she started to fight
With the sun beating down and the bugs so bad
Still, she gave every bit she had

But she was mixed up so, with pain and fear
She could only think to run from here
Oh, surely, you'd cut her a better deal
And reach her worried heart, through feel

I let her know every way I could
That the folks I'd met were all pretty good
But she'd jump away at the sight of a hand
With her head in the corner she'd go and stand

I wanted to show her a better way and
I stood with her while she ate her hay
We heard your voice and looked around
Then she saw your saddle layin' on the ground

When she broke a sweat it was plain to tell
That a man and a saddle meant living hell
She paced that fence all through the night
Come the feed wagon and the new day's light
She was still real bothered, not feelin' right

So I shared my hay, and nuzzled her
She smelled of sage, and wind and conifer
It would be a long day with her troubled so
Where she didn't know how to free up and go

But I'll trot for you, 'cuz you're my best friend
I'll trot for you 'til the long day's end
And I'll go right on 'til my feet give out
It won't matter if I'm old and slow
I'll trot for you, because I love you so

And that mare would too, if she just knew how
It's not hard to tell that she's searching now
She wants things right . . . it's plain to see
She's got one last chance and that'd be me

When the world ain't safe and the mind ain't free
That's a real bad place for a horse to be
It might work out and it just might not
But one thing's sure, there's a better spot

The folks she'd known, they weren't long gone
And they'd given her whippin's, just plenty strong
But they'd no idea that it wasn't right
To put a good horse like her on the fight

But the horsey folks come, and soon they go
When they're done packin' kids to fairs and horsey shows
They sure want us gentle, and they want us fit and clean
With thick manes, long tails, and minds serene

In no time at all, they're grown and they go,
The backyard horse gets old, you know
So the ads are placed and comes the check
New owner, halter, and what the heck

They don't really know a better way to do
Than the last folks who tried, and they quit too
They always tried to ride their best
They'd enter in shows like all the rest
To see whose horse could do this or that
And they'd want to win, of course, right off the bat

It takes all kinds but there's some that's born
For a horse, reata and saddle horn
This ranch has seen one or two of these
And I thank God my work is between your knees

Now if only the coal black mare could be
Right along side in your string with me
When she didn't make the wagon, they gave her to Hank
And he, possessing neither skill nor rank
Was a town sorta fella and a real green dude
And I knew he'd handle her pretty crude
She held her breath and then closed her eyes
There was nothing to do but hope she'd try

I know she'll make 'er, if she just gets a chance
To spend a little time with us here on the ranch
But where saddle horses come and go so often
They show up lame, half-starved and coughin'

And the boss, he's busy, and no one here
Really knows a horse or has any idea
So it's the pick of the draw, could be her or me
Fills a spot on the cattle truck leavin' at three

If I have my way, she'll trot for you
Right by my side, she'll trot for you
Her feet will glide over hill and dale
Over rocks, through water, on hard-packed trail

Let her stretch her neck out, long and low
Let her drop her head for a look at the road
On an uphill climb when the flies are thick
You won't need a spur, no quirt or stick
With a rookie on board and the footing bad
She'll dig right in and give her all to the lad

If I guess it right . . .
She'll trot for you to the very last
She'll trot for you to forget her past.
That mare and me, we'll trot for you
We'll take you there
You can count on us just anywhere
We'll trot for you and be glad to go
We're here for you . . . *because we know you know.*

INDEX

M

N

O

P

Q

R

S

T